Psychology

FOR AS-LEVEL

third edition

Mike Cardwell
Liz Clark
Claire Meldrum

An imprint of
HarperCollins*Publishers*

Published by HarperCollins*Publishers* Limited
77-85 Fulham Palace Road
Hammersmith
London W6 8JB

www.CollinsEducation.com
Online support for schools and colleges

Psychology for A Level first published 1996
First AS edition published 2000
This edition first published 2003

Reprint 10 9 8 7 6 5 4 3 2 1

ISBN 0 00 715363 5

British Cataloguing in Publication Data.
A cataloguing record for this publication is available from the
British Library.

Commissioned by Thomas Allain-Chapman
Project managed by Hugh Hillyard-Parker
Editorial support by Sarah Clarke
Edited by Rosamund Connelly, Carol Schaessens
Cover design/internal design template by Blue Pig Design, Essex
Typesetting by Hugh Hillyard-Parker
Permissions by Rebecca Green
Picture Research by Thelma Gilbert
Cartoons by Mike Parsons, Barking Dog Art, Gloucestershire
Index compiled by Christine Boylan
Photo treatment by Pip Blakemore, Design Study, Norfolk
Production by Hilary Quantrill
Printed and bound by Imago, Thailand

You might also like to visit: www.fireandwater.com
The book lover's website

Acknowledgements

Writing is a solitary and all-absorbing task that can put a strain
on even the strongest relationships. It is with smug satisfaction,
therefore, that Mike Cardwell acknowledges his enormous debt
to his ever-patient wife Denise. She provides the secure
emotional base that allows him the luxury of long hours spent
staring at a computer screen and 'doing' psychology.

Liz Clark would like to thank Charley for his continued support
and patience through both the planned and unplanned periods of
disruption to home life during this major editing project. Also, to
family near and far for always being there to provide those all-
important words of calm and encouragement when deadlines
loom and threaten to take over one's entire life. Finally, for a
niece who has recently completed her AS- and A-level studies
using our book – there's nothing like some robust and focused
feedback from a lively group of psychology students to trigger
some significant improvements to this latest edition!

Claire Meldrum would like to thank Stuart who, as always,
continues to provide support and understanding. My thanks also
to the students at Notre Dame High School in Norwich who have
helped me keep sight of those for whom this book is intended.

The editors would also like to thank the staff at HarperCollins,
particularly Thomas Allain-Chapman whose quiet, focused
approach facilitated the entire process and always provided
exactly the right balance between carrot and stick, ensuring that
the various strands kept moving in the right direction!

Finally, we are hugely grateful once again to Hugh Hillyard-Parker,
responsible for the book's editorial production. Hugh continues to
live up to his reputation for achieving the impossible and for
always remaining calm when everyone around him seems to be
panicking. His constructive suggestions and encouraging words
never fail to produce the desired outcome. We are indebted to
both Thomas and Hugh.

Mike Cardwell, Liz Clark and Claire Meldrum
March 2003

Contents >> Psychology for AS-Level

Mike Cardwell, BSc, PGCE, MEd, is Senior Lecturer in Psychology at Bath Spa University College, where he teaches courses in social psychology, and a Senior Examiner for a major examination board. Mike's other publications include *The Complete A–Z Psychology Handbook* (Hodder & Stoughton) and *The Complete A–Z Psychology Coursework Handbook* (with Hugh Coolican). Mike is also an Editor of the journal *Psychology Review* and a regular contributor to student conferences. Although psychology takes up most of his time, he still avidly follows the fortunes of his home-town football teams, Premier League Liverpool and Marine of the Unibond League.

Although a psychologist at heart and also by training, and someone who is passionate about learning and good teaching, *Liz Clark* has worked in nurse education for the past 15 years. She is currently Head of Distance Learning at the Royal College of Nursing (RCN), where she is responsible for developing and delivering five distance-learning degree programmes for qualified nurses, in addition to developing bite-sized chunks of learning on the RCN Learning Zone to support members' personal and professional development. The experience of creating effective and highly accessible learning resources that can be studied with the minimum of teacher support contributed to the original ideas and vision behind the first edition of this book. The publisher and editors believe that AS-level students deserve texts that intrigue, challenge and support, and above all that kindle their curiosity to find out more.

Claire Meldrum, MA, MSc, PGCE, teaches part-time at Notre Dame High School, Norwich. She has over 20 years of experience teaching psychology on A-level, degree, and 'Access to Higher Education' courses. She has also been an A-level psychology examiner and has written *Instant Revision AS Psychology* (2002) and been a co-author on *Do Brilliantly AS Psychology* (2001). Claire also acts as a consultant for the National Extension College and, when time and weather allow, she enjoys gardening, the theatre and cinema.

Graham Davies, BA, MSc, PGCE, is a lecturer at Eastbourne College of Arts and Technology and, from 1997 to 2000, was Principal Examiner for the AQA AS-/A-level psychology module on Perspectives and Research Methods. He was previously the Principal Moderator for A-level psychology coursework and remains one of the team of Regional Coursework Advisers. He has written various journal articles and has been a speaker and workshop leader at a number of psychology conferences. He is an Honorary Life Member and former Chair of the Association for the Teaching of Psychology, for whom he edited the journal *Teaching Psychology* for some years. A keen mountain climber, he also thoroughly enjoys watching the rise of AFC Wimbledon in the light of Wimbledon Football Club's move to Milton Keynes.

Cara Flanagan is a senior examiner for a major awarding body and a freelance academic author, having written extensively for psychology A-level. Her books include the Letts' *A-level Revision Guides* and *Psychology AS: The Complete Companion* written with Mike Cardwell. She contributes regularly to *Psychology Review* and speaks at many student conferences and teacher courses.

Simon Green, BSc, PhD, is Head of the School of Psychology at Birkbeck College, University of London. He was the Chief Examiner for AQA Psychology between 1983 and 1986, and remains a Principal Examiner today for Unit 2. He is the author of *Principles of Biopsychology* and a contributor to several other psychology books. Simon has also written articles for a number of journals, including the *Psychology Review*. His main interest is finding better ways of managing stress.

Paul Humphreys is Senior Lecturer in Psychology at University College Worcester. His teaching and research interests include social relationships, sexualities, psychology and the media, and (ab)normality. He has been Chief Examiner for psychology at every pre-undergraduate level (O-level 1983–88; AS-level 1989–91; A-level 1992–97) and is now Principal Examiner for the new A2 examination. Paul is the author of several books and, in 1997, was conferred Honorary Life Membership of the Association for the Teaching of Psychology for his services to psychology. Paul has Chartered Psychologist status with the British Psychological Society and is a Full Member of the Division of Teachers and Researchers in Psychology.

Pamela Prentice, BA, MedCPsychol, AFBPsS, is Programme Manager for Humanities, including psychology, at Filton College, Bristol. She teaches A-level psychology and counselling up to HND level, and is an experienced AQA A-level examiner and OCN Moderator. She served five years on the committee for the ATP and two years on the BPS committee for the Division for Teachers and Researchers in Psychology. Her background, prior to teaching, was as a Counselling Psychologist with the NHS. She has written a number of articles for *Psychology Review*.

Jane Willson is Director of Studies for the A-level programme at City College, Norwich. She has many years' teaching experience in schools and FE colleges, and currently teaches psychology at A-level and at degree level. She is a team leader for the AQA psychology A-level and is a member of the ATP. She has written several other publications for A-level students and has also co-authored a book based on a research project about children's interaction with screen-based technology.

WHAT IS PSYCHOLOGY?

<< Psychology, like all other sciences, can be misapplied. But, rightly used, psychology can make an immense contribution to human happiness .>> (Rex and Margaret Knight 1959, p. 264)

Psychology is the scientific study of behaviour and mental processes (the mind), and psychologists are interested in every aspect of behaviour and every type of mental process.

You may have come across the comment that "psychology is just common sense". Be assured, it is much more than that! Of course, sometimes psychology reinforces what people call 'common sense' or 'gut feelings' (intuitions). For example, most people believe that children who are raised in warm, loving families are best placed to be warm and loving parents in their turn. Psychologists carrying out research in this area have confirmed this 'common sense' view. However, psychological research sometimes produces results that are not what you would expect. That is, the findings are what are called 'counterintuitive'. Who, for example, would have predicted that during a memory experiment, 65 per cent of participants would obey a stranger who asked them to give electric shocks of 450 volts to a mild-mannered man who had earlier complained of heart trouble? Certainly, none of the people (including psychologists) whom the researcher, Stanley Milgram, asked before he carried out his research! Common sense predicted that the vast majority of people would refuse to give anything but the mildest shocks, but common sense was wrong. Milgram's research is discussed in detail in Unit 5, on pp. 171–5.

The important point to remember is that psychology bases its claims on research evidence, not guesses or mere anecdotes. Of course, the quality of the evidence offered by psychologists varies and one of the things you will be better able to do by the end of your AS course is evaluate (judge) just how convincing the evidence being offered is.

Note, also, that so-called common sense may be neither sensible nor consistent. Common sense proverbs often contradict each other. If "many hands make light work", why also may "too many cooks spoil the broth"? If common sense says "absence makes the heart grow fonder", how do we reconcile this with "out of sight out of mind"?

THE GOALS OF PSYCHOLOGY

Sometimes myths masquerade as common sense and one important goal of psychology is to clarify what is myth and what is reality. Take the common sense adage "spare the rod and spoil the child". Psychological research has played a significant role in demolishing the myth that only by using regular punishments could parents raise well-behaved children or teachers instil diligence in their pupils. Owing to the research of psychologists such as Skinner (Unit 4, p. 134), we know that rewarding desirable behaviour is more important for learning than punishing what is undesirable.

In order to distinguish myth from reality and to understand human behaviour better, psychology sets out to describe, explain, predict, and (where appropriate) change or control behaviour.

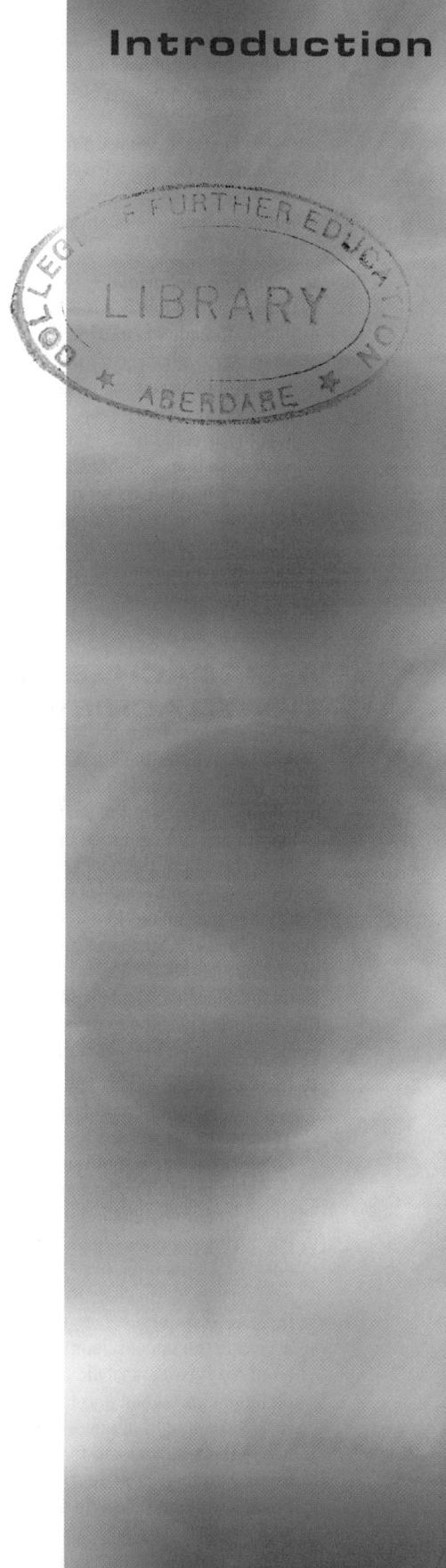

Describing behaviour – The first step to understanding behaviour is to describe it accurately. For example, if we wish to find out whether boys are more physically aggressive than girls, we must first describe exactly what we mean by 'physical aggression'. Once we have a precise definition, we can begin to observe whether there is any difference in levels of physical aggression between boys and girls.

■ *Explaining behaviour* – The next step in understanding behaviour is to explain why it occurs, that is, to understand what causes it. Psychologists often start with a theory (hypothesis) about an observed behaviour and then test to see if there is evidence to support their theory. For example, our hypothesis could be: "Boys are more physically aggressive than girls because boys are rewarded more often than girls for physically aggressive behaviour." To test this, we might carry out an observation study in a school to see if boys do indeed receive more reinforcement than girls for their aggressive acts.

■ *Predicting behaviour* – After describing and explaining a behaviour, psychologists will often try to predict when that behaviour is likely to occur. For example, we know that lacking a sense of control is associated with so-called stress symptoms such as migraine and gastric ulcers. We might predict, therefore, that people whose work is monotonous, repetitive and regulated by others will be more likely to have high rates of absenteeism than people whose job allows them some freedom to organize their work. Unit 3 looks in more detail at causes of stress.

■ *Changing/controlling behaviour* – Under certain circumstances it may be desirable to modify behaviour. Take, for example, the case of someone who suffers from a life-threatening eating disorder, such as anorexia nervosa. Although some treatments for this condition are controversial, there are therapists who work with anorexic people to help them overcome their disorder and adopt healthier eating behaviours. See Unit 4 for more information on eating disorders.

APPROACHES IN PSYCHOLOGY: HOW PSYCHOLOGISTS TRY TO ACHIEVE THEIR GOALS

People have always been interested in how the mind works and what causes behaviour. The roots of modern psychology go back to the ancient Greek philosophers of the 4th and 5th centuries BC. However, it was only towards the end of the nineteenth century that psychology became established as a branch of knowledge (discipline) in its own right when Wilhelm Wundt (1832–1920) began the first experimental psychology laboratory in the University of Leipzig in Germany. Since then, many different approaches (perspectives) have been developed in psychology. Some of the most important current approaches are:

■ *Psychoanalysis* – This approach developed from the work of Sigmund Freud (1856–1939). The term 'psychoanalysis' relates to both the theory that much of our behaviour is motivated by unconscious thoughts, and to the therapy that Freud developed for treating neurotic conditions. In the course of treating psychiatric patients, Freud became convinced that adult problems often have their origins in early experiences, particularly those that occur during the first five years of a person's life. To help people gain access to the unconscious mind, Freud developed a number of psychoanalytic techniques, including dream interpretation and free association. By these means, he sought to uncover unconscious conflicts, help people understand their causes and come to terms with their problems. You will read all about Freud's work and ideas in Unit 4 (see pp. 130–3).

■ *Behaviourism* – Behaviourism dates from 1913 when John Watson (1878–1958) stated that psychologists should concentrate on observable behaviour instead of mental processes. However, its roots stretch back to the Russian physiologist, Ivan Pavlov (1849–1936), famous for his work in conditioning animals (see Unit 4, p. 133). Behaviourism had a profound effect on psychology for about 50 years and some of its basic ideas remain important in contemporary psychology. For example, one important legacy from the behaviourist approach is the scientific concept of an 'operational definition', a precise statement of how a concept (such as aggression – see above) is measured. You will learn more about the importance of operational definitions when you come to Unit 7 (p. 225).

■ *Social learning theory* – In the 1960s social learning theorists such as Bandura demonstrated that sometimes learning was possible without the need for reinforcement (being rewarded for a behaviour). All that was needed was the chance to observe the behaviour of others. This observational learning was called imitation or modelling.

■ *The cognitive approach* – Cognitive psychology concentrates on the mental processes that people use to acquire, store, retrieve and use the knowledge they have about the world. This approach arose as a reaction against the narrow view taken by behaviourists, which concentrated solely on observable behaviour and neglected complex activities like perceiving, remembering and planning. In Unit 1, you will come across the cognitive approach in the study of human memory.

- **The physiological (biological) approach** – Physiological psychologists believe that to describe and explain human behaviour and experience we need to look closely at human biology. For example, how do different areas of the brain contribute to behaviours? In Unit 3, you can read about the physiological response to stress, while Unit 4 discusses the biochemical explanations for eating disorders.

- **The evolutionary approach** – The evolutionary approach also emphasizes the importance of biological factors. Its starting point is Darwin's theory of evolution: that processes of natural selection have shaped human behaviour and experience. According to evolutionary psychology, individuals should act to maximize their own and their relatives' chances of reproducing (called 'inclusive fitness'). While this approach has become popular in recent years, there are many who criticize it, pointing out that social and cultural factors influence behaviour and shape it in a way that has nothing to do with natural selection. You will learn more about the evolutionary approach if you go on to study psychology at A2-level.

USING THE BOOK

This book aims to provide a detailed coverage of all aspects of the AS psychology course offered by the Assessment and Qualifications Alliance (AQA), Specification A.

Since the first edition of *Psychology for AS-Level* in 2000 there have been some modifications to the AS-level specification. This new edition matches the revised specification and introduces a number of new features, as well as a full-colour design with many new pictures and illustrations.

As before, the contributing authors are all teachers and/or examiners of psychology, and so have a clear understanding of the needs of students. Our aim is to make the study of psychology at AS-level informative and fun, and to prepare you thoroughly for the examinations that you will take at the end of this part of your course.

Key features

- A *Preview* at the start of each unit and a *Unit summary* at the end to enable you to check quickly the topics covered.

- *Getting you thinking...* at the start of each topic provides a way in to new topics, designed to help you engage with new ideas before getting to grips more closely with the technical issues or terms involved.

- *Key terms* that you may need to define are listed and boxed at the start of each topic. These should prove extremely useful when you are preparing for your examination.

- *Activities*, within each topic, are designed to help you test your knowledge, apply psychological findings, carry out practical exercises and discuss ethical implications.

- *Key studies* are clearly laid out in the form that will help you tackle those AQA questions that ask you to describe aims, procedures, findings, conclusions and criticisms of research. Many of the key studies feature an AO2 check 'magnifying glass' which is designed to help you consider how to evaluate criticisms of studies when answering AO1+AO2 questions.

- Frequent *diagrams*, *tables* and *pictures* help make the psychological material even more accessible.

- A *Check your understanding* feature at the end of each topic will help you review what you have just read and help you pinpoint any areas of the topic you need to revisit.

- *Expert interviews* – A number of distinguished psychologists have provided us with their own views about some of the important areas within AS-level psychology. Who better to comment on the effects of stress on the immune system, for example, than the leading researcher in the field, Professor Janice Kiecolt-Glaser? These interviews are specifically aimed at helping you deal with the demands of the 18-mark questions in your AS psychology exam.

- For certain topics, *An eye on the exam* provides an examiner's commentary on key issues when answering questions in this area.

- At the end of each topic, we have included a *Revision summary* that is focused on the exact requirements of examination questions appropriate to that topic area.

- Unit 8, *Preparing for the AS examination*, has been expanded to include focused advice on answering the different styles of exam questions, together with a full sample exam paper with answers and examiner comments.

AQA (A) AS specification and examination

This book is designed specifically for the AQA, AS-level psychology course (Specification A) and the contents of the book correspond very closely to the specification. Before you use this book as part of your study programme, we recommend that you look closely at the specification and information about the examinations provided by AQA. You can obtain this either direct from

AQA or by downloading it from their website (details at the bottom of the page). We shall provide only a brief outline here.

The AS-level specification is designed to be midway between the skills required for GCSE and the full A-level (A2), and to take account of the target age (17+) of the majority of students who will be taking this exam. The AQA (A) AS-level course is organized into three modules, which mysteriously change their name to units when it comes to assessment. Thus, you will be taught a module on Cognitive and Developmental Psychology, but examined on a unit of the same topics – simple really!

You will learn about the five core areas of psychology and about research methods. Each of these core areas is represented by a topic that will give you a good introduction to that area of psychology. The five core areas and their related topics are as follows:

- *Cognitive Psychology* – Human memory
- *Developmental Psychology* – Attachments in development
- *Physiological Psychology* – Stress
- *Individual Differences* – Abnormality
- *Social Psychology* – Social influence.

Each area also contains a 'critical issue', which represents either a key application of an area (e.g. eyewitness testimony in memory) or something that has special relevance to a particular topic area (e.g. ethical issues in social influence). The specific issues surrounding the assessment of these topics and critical issues are covered in Unit 8, but it is worth emphasizing a few points here.

- The five core areas above, together with Research Methods, are grouped together in three assessment units, each of which is worth one-third of the total marks:

  Unit 1 – Cognitive and Developmental Psychology

  Unit 2 – Physiological Psychology and Individual Differences

  Unit 3 – Social Psychology and Research Methods.

- All areas of this specification are compulsory – this means that you must cover everything in this book. The specification entries are very carefully worded and questions will tend to reflect that wording. We have endeavoured to use the same wording as the specification, wherever possible, to make it easier for you to track your route through each topic. When questions are set, the question-setter will attempt to sample (eventually) all areas of the specification. Therefore, it is unwise to leave out any areas, even small ones, simply because they do not appeal to you.

- There is some choice of questions in the examination, but there will not necessarily be a question on everything that appears in the AQA

specification. There will, of course, be two questions on every area (i.e. Cognitive, Developmental, Physiological, and so on), so a good proportion of the specification will be covered in every examination.

- The examination will test your knowledge and understanding (known as 'Assessment Objective 1' or simply AO1), and your analysis and evaluation (known as AO2) skills, together with your ability to design, conduct and report (in the Research Methods section, and known as AO3). As we stress in Unit 8, AO2 questions are really quite different from AO1 questions and require you to engage with the subject material in the topic areas. We have attempted to show you how you might address each of these skills in the Revision summaries at the end of each unit. Although these Revision summaries are comprehensive accounts of what is required in each area, they should not take the place of the subject specification that is published by AQA.

- Several entries on the AQA specification are preceded by the words 'including' or 'e.g.'. Although the word 'including' indicates prescribed material on which questions may be asked, the use of 'e.g.' is merely illustrative of appropriate subject material. We have covered all prescribed material in this book, and have endeavoured, wherever appropriate, to cover all the examples mentioned in the specification as well.

Do, please, let us know, care of the Publisher, what you think of the book. Feedback from readers is enormously helpful and we shall pay close attention to it when we come to write the next edition of *Psychology for AS-Level*.

Mike Cardwell, Liz Clark, Claire Meldrum

AQA address

AQA
**Stag Hill House
Guildford
GU2 5XJ**
www.aqa.org.uk

Introduction

Psychology

FOR AS-LEVEL

UNIT 1

HUMAN Memory

PREVIEW

After you have read this unit, you should be able to:

>> discuss research into the nature and structure of memory

>> explain the differences between short-term and long-term memory

>> understand the processes of encoding, capacity and duration

>> explain different models of memory, including the multi-store, the working memory and the levels of processing models, and discuss research into these models

>> explain why people forget from both short-term and long-term memory

>> discuss research into emotional factors that affect forgetting, including flashbulb memories and repression

>> discuss research into eyewitness testimony.

INTRODUCTION

Memory is studied within the branch of psychology known as cognitive psychology. This research field focuses on the mental processes humans use to acquire, store, retrieve and apply their knowledge about the world. Cognitive psychologists have investigated a wide range of topics including perception, attention, imagery, language, problem-solving, reasoning and decision-making. In this unit, we look at memory, central to *all* cognitive processes because we use it whenever we need to maintain information over time.

In the first topic in the unit, we will look at the structure of memory and the way that it is divided into short-term and long-term stores. We will also discuss some important models of memory, i.e. explanations of how memory works.

As we know from experience, our memories can sometimes let us down, and cognitive psychologists have also been interested in the mechanisms involved in forgetting. In Topic 2, we will look at the reasons why people sometimes fail to retrieve information.

Psychologists are increasingly turning their attention to more everyday aspects of memory. In the final topic in this unit, we will look at one such practical application, namely research into eyewitness testimony.

Jane
Willson

On the right is a description of the case of Clive Wearing – a man with a particularly profound case of amnesia (based on Baddeley 1997).

Imagine for a moment what would happen if you woke up one morning to find that you had completely lost your memory. To help you think about this, try to answer the following questions:

1 What do you normally do in a day that you would no longer be able to do because of your memory loss? Consider, for example, when you need to know your name, your age and where you live. Write a list of up to ten things.

2 What would you be unable to do if you could not recognize your friends or members of your family?

3 What experiences would you miss if you could not remember TV programmes or articles in newspapers?

4 If you were unable to recall what you were thinking about just moments ago, how would you plan your day?

After contracting a viral infection called encephalitis, Clive Wearing, a highly talented musician and broadcaster, was left with extensive brain damage, causing major memory disruption. He is still able to talk, read and write, and can still sight-read music and play quite complex piano pieces. In all other respects, however, his memory is dramatically impaired. For example, he has no recollection of his wedding, pictured below.

KEY TERMS

Memory: the mental processes involved in registering, storing and retrieving information.

Capacity: the amount of information that can be stored in memory at any particular time.

Duration: the length of time that information can be kept in memory.

Encoding: changing sensory input into a form or code to be processed by the memory system.

Short-term memory (STM): a limited capacity system for storing information for short periods.

Long-term memory (LTM): an unlimited capacity system for storing information for long periods.

Multi-store model of memory: an explanation of memory as a flow of information through a series of stages in a fixed sequence. The best-known model of this type was proposed by Atkinson and Shiffrin.

Working memory: a model of memory formulated by Baddeley and Hitch to replace the concept of short-term memory. It proposes a multi-component, flexible system concerned with active processing and storage of short-term information.

Levels of processing: a theory of memory put forward by Craik and Lockhart, that the amount of information retained in LTM depends on how deeply it is processed during learning.

As your answers to the questions in 'Getting you thinking...' will have highlighted, you would be virtually helpless without your memory. In fact, we take memory so much for granted that it can be hard to imagine the impact of its loss on our daily lives.

Psychologists have learned a great deal from the study of people such as Clive Wearing who suffer from loss of memory (amnesia) after brain damage. More details of the effects of amnesia on Clive's life are described in the panel below.

Clive Wearing's case demonstrates that memory is crucial to our wellbeing and everyday functioning. It also demonstrates the enormous complexity of human memory. The fact that Clive continues to be able to talk, walk, play music, read and write in spite of huge impairments in his memory for personal history and general knowledge suggests that memory is not a unitary system.

Even more disturbing is Clive Wearing's apparent inability to lay down new memories. Clive is convinced that he has only just woken up and keeps a diary in which he records this obsessive thought. There are pages of closely written text, in which he gives the date and time followed by the statement, "I have just regained consciousness" or "I'm conscious for the first time". Whenever his wife visits, he greets her effusively as if he has not seen her for ages. If she leaves the room for a couple of minutes, the emotional greeting is repeated and this can happen time and time again.

ACTIVITY

Why can't Clive Wearing remember?

Clive Wearing's case raises a number of questions for cognitive psychologists. This activity will help you to explore some of them.

Why is Clive unable to recall a visit from his wife just two minutes earlier? One possible explanation is that her visit never actually registered in his brain and so no memory trace is laid down. Try to think of two other explanations. You may find it helpful at this point to read the definition of 'memory' (see Key terms on p. 3).

An answer to this question is proposed at the end of the unit (see p. 38)

Clive Wearing's 'living hell'

Clive Wearing's memory for past events in his life is hazy although he can recall certain key highlights with prompting. His visual memory is impaired: for example, he is unable to recognize pictures of his old Cambridge college, where he had spent four years of his life and which he had visited many times in subsequent years. His general knowledge is also reduced and he has no idea who wrote the play *Romeo and Juliet.* Nor can he recall anything about the sixteenth-century composer Orlando Lassus, in spite of having written a book about him.

Years after the onset of the illness that caused Clive's memory loss, he is still trapped in an eternal present – he cannot use the past to anticipate the future. He is unable to enjoy books or television because he cannot follow the thread, and he does not read newspapers because he has no context within which to embed the news stories. He cannot go out alone because he immediately becomes lost and is unable to tell anyone who finds him where he is going or where he has come from. Clive himself has described his situation as "Hell on earth. It's like being dead".

Clive Wearing can play the music of Orlando Lassus, but cannot recall any details of the composer's life, despite having been an authority on him.

THE NATURE AND STRUCTURE OF MEMORY

Several theories of memory are based on the assumption that there are three kinds of memory:

- sensory memory
- short-term memory
- long-term memory.

We shall consider each of these in turn, but note that this distinction is no longer accepted by all memory researchers. It is most associated with structural models such as the one proposed by Atkinson and Shiffrin (1968), discussed on p. 13.

Sensory memory

Sensory memory is a storage system that holds information in a relatively unprocessed form for fractions of a second after the physical stimulus is no longer available. Baddeley (1988) suggested that one function of this kind of storage is to allow information from successive eye-fixations to last for a long enough time to be integrated and so to give continuity to our visual environment. For example, if you watch a film, your conscious experience is of a continuous visual scene in which all of the action appears to be moving

smoothly. In fact, the film is actually being presented as a rapid series of frozen images interspersed by fleeting moments of darkness. In order to make sense of it, your sensory store has to hold the information from one frame of film until the next is presented. Such everyday examples seem to suggest that we are capable of storing visual images for very brief periods. It is assumed that we have separate sensory stores for all the senses, but it is the visual sensory store (iconic memory) which has attracted most research.

Memory researchers, however, have focused their interest more on short-term and long-term memory.

SHORT-TERM MEMORY

Short-term memory (STM) is a system for storing information for brief periods of time. Some researchers (e.g. Atkinson and Shiffrin 1968) see STM simply as a temporary storage depot for incoming information, whereas others (e.g. Baddeley 1986) prefer to use the term 'working memory' to indicate its dynamic, flexible aspects. We shall return to this difference of opinion when we consider various models of memory later in this topic. For the moment, we will look at specific aspects related to the nature of STM:

- capacity
- duration
- encoding.

The capacity of short-term memory

Please try the next activity before you read any further.

You probably found problem **1** extremely easy and that problem **2** was also possible. Problem **3**, however, is much more of a challenge: it will have stretched the limits of your STM by requiring you to carry too much information at once. It can feel quite frustrating as you struggle to hold on to relevant bits of information while manipulating others.

This exercise indicates that STM has a limited capacity, that is, we can only hold a small number of items at any one time. One way of assessing how much your STM can hold – its capacity – is by finding out how many digits you can repeat in correct order immediately after hearing them. This is known as your immediate digit span. This technique, which has frequently been used in psychological studies of memory, usually involves reading out a list of random digits and requiring the participant to repeat them back in the correct order. The sequences usually begin with about three digits and steadily increase in length until it becomes impossible to recall them in serial order. Over a number of trials, the sequence length at which the participant is correct 50 per cent of the time is defined as their digit span. Most people have a digit span of "seven, plus or minus two" (Miller 1956). This has been called Miller's magic number seven. Miller claimed that this finding holds good for lists of digits, letters, words or larger chunks of information.

According to Miller, 'chunking' occurs when we combine individual letters or numbers into a larger meaningful unit. For example, the digits 9, 3, 7, 1 would represent four separate items to most people, but would form a single chunk for you if they happened to be your bank PIN number.

Factors affecting capacity

- *Influence of long-term memory* – There are some difficulties in using immediate digit span as a measure of STM capacity. One problem is that it is difficult to exclude the influence of long-term memory. For example, Bower and Winzenz (1969) found that digit strings that are repeated within a series of immediate memory span trials become progressively easier for participants to recall. This indicates that information stored in LTM is helping to increase STM capacity temporarily.

- *Reading aloud* – If participants read the digits aloud before attempting to recall them, performance is better than when they simply read them subvocally to themselves.

- *Rhythmic grouping* – Performance also improves if the numbers are grouped together rhythmically. This is probably why we tend to divide up telephone numbers into rhythmic groups rather than reciting the whole string of numbers in a monotone.

KEY STUDY >> CAPACITY OF STM

study of immediate memory span by Baddeley *et al.* (1975)

Aim >>

To see whether people could remember more short words than long words in a serial recall test, and so to demonstrate that pronunciation time, rather than the number of items to be recalled, determines the capacity of short-term memory.

Procedures >>

- The reading speed of the participants was measured.
- Participants were then presented with sets of five words on a screen.
- The words were taken from one of two sets: a set of one-syllable words (e.g. *harm, wit, sum*) or a set of polysyllabic words (e.g. *opportunity, aluminium, university*)
- Participants were asked to write down the five words in serial order immediately after presentation. They recalled several lists of both short and long words.

Findings >>

- Participants could recall considerably more short words than long words.
- They were able to recall as many words as they were able to articulate in about 2 seconds.
- There was a strong positive correlation between reading speed and memory span.

Conclusions >>

- Immediate memory span represents the number of items of whatever length that can be articulated in approximately 2 seconds.

Criticisms >>

- It might simply be that short words are easier to recall than long words because they are more familiar to us.
- This was a laboratory experiment using lists of unconnected words and did not reflect everyday use of STM.

AO2 check

Baddeley and colleagues responded to this criticism in later versions of the study and showed clearly the importance of pronunciation time over familiarity.

- Miller was not able to account for the findings of research which showed that immediate span depends on the nature of the stimulus, i.e. the kinds of words and the language in which they are spoken. This study can explain such findings.

■ *Pronunciation time* – Some more recent researchers have found that pronunciation time may be a more important indicator of STM capacity than Miller's digit span. Schweickert and Boruff (1986) tested immediate memory span for a number of different types of stimulus, such as letters, colours, shapes and nonsense words. They found that people consistently remembered as many items as they were able to pronounce in approximately 1.5 to 2 seconds. Naveh-Benjamin and Ayres (1986) have tested immediate memory span for speakers of various world languages. They found, for example, that the digit span for native English speakers is considerably greater than for Arabic speakers. The only explanation for this finding is that Arabic numbers take longer to pronounce than English numbers. These results confirmed earlier findings in a classic experiment by Baddeley *et al.* (1975) (see key study, *Capacity of STM,* on p. 6).

The duration of short-term memory

However capacity is measured, it seems clear that STM is only able to hold a few items at any one time. It is also the case that, by its very nature, STM has a brief duration. STM is a temporary store and anything we need to remember for longer needs to be transferred to LTM. The first attempts to measure the duration of STM used an experimental method known as the Brown-Peterson technique. The key study, *Duration of STM,* below, explains how Peterson and Peterson used the technique in this experiment.

Factors affecting duration

■ *Rehearsal* – The key point about findings based on the Brown-Peterson technique is that items disappear from STM only when rehearsal is prevented. New items can only take their place if existing items move on – either to LTM or because

KEY STUDY >> DURATION OF STM

study of duration by Peterson and Peterson (1959)

Aim >>

To test how long STM lasts when rehearsal is prevented.

Procedures >>

■ Participants (Ps) were briefly shown a consonant trigram (i.e. three letters such as CPW or NGV).

■ Participants were asked to count backwards in threes from a specified number to stop them thinking about the letters.

■ After intervals of 3, 6, 9, 12, 15 or 18 seconds, participants were asked to recall the original trigram.

■ The procedure was repeated several times using different trigrams.

Findings >>

■ Participants were able to recall 80 per cent of trigrams after a 3-second interval.

■ Progressively fewer trigrams were recalled as the time intervals lengthened.

■ After 18 seconds, fewer than 10 per cent of the trigrams were recalled correctly.

Conclusions >>

■ If rehearsal is prevented, information vanishes rapidly from STM.

■ Therefore, decay is the mechanism for forgetting in short-term memory.

Criticisms >>

■ Trigrams are rather artificial things to remember and may not reflect everyday memory.

■ It is possible, however, that interference from the counting task (not merely decay) caused the poor recall.

A02 check

Note that the experimental method used in this study allows us to see the (causal) effect of time passing (independent variable) on recall (dependent variable).

they are forgotten. If we want to remember something for a short period of time, we tend to repeat it to ourselves, as for example when we look up a number in the phone book and need to hold it in our memory for long enough to dial it accurately. This repetition serves as a method of continually re-inserting the information into STM and thereby strengthening the memory. Without rehearsal, the duration of STM is very brief.

■ *Deliberate intention to recall* – Sebrechts *et al.* (1989) briefly presented participants with lists of three common English nouns and then gave them an unexpected, serial recall test. Correct recall of the items fell to 1 per cent after only 4 seconds. Studies such as these demonstrate that information can vanish from STM in a matter of a few seconds if people are not making a conscious effort to retain it.

■ *Amount of information to be retained* – Murdock (1961) presented participants with either a single three-letter word such as *cat* or three unrelated words such as *hat, pen, lid*. He then followed the same procedure as in the Brown-Peterson technique. The forgetting curve for the three unrelated words was the same as for the consonant trigrams in the Peterson and Peterson study. However, the single, three-letter word (which could be processed as one chunk) was remarkably resistant to forgetting and accurate recall level was still at 90 per cent after 18 seconds. This shows that, as in Miller's digit span, the important factor is the number of chunks to be remembered rather than the number of individual items, i.e. letters.

Encoding in short-term memory

A further question about the nature of STM concerns coding. When information arrives at the sensory registration stage, it is still in its raw form or original 'modality'. For example, information presented visually is still in the visual modality. Psychologists have been interested in the question of what happens to such information when it reaches the STM. Does it stay in its original modality or is it recoded in some way?

There are various ways in which we can encode stimulus inputs. Imagine looking at the word 'glove'. This could be stored as a visual representation so that you form a visual image of either the printed word itself or a pictorial image of an actual glove. You could form an acoustic representation by saying the written word aloud or under your breath – this has the effect of converting the written word into a verbal or speech code. Alternatively, you could form a semantic representation, which depends on your knowledge about the meaning of the word. You might, for example, think about circumstances in which you need to wear gloves or a specific pair of gloves that you own.

It is not possible simply to ask people what codes they are using because memory processes are often unconscious. Much of the evidence about coding comes from studies into so-called substitution errors. These occur when people confuse one item for another. If, for example, they confuse letters, which *sound* alike, it indicates that acoustic coding is being used. If, however, letters that *look* similar are confused, it indicates that visual coding is being used. (See key study, *Encoding in short-term memory*.)

Factors affecting encoding

■ *The sound of words* – Conrad's study suggests that short-term memory relies heavily on acoustic coding. Other researchers thought that the type of stimulus to be remembered might affect the way it is encoded. Baddeley (1966), for example, wondered whether Conrad's results were dependent on using consonants as his stimulus material. After all, they

A stimulus input can be encoded visually as a word or picture (left), acoustically (middle) or semantically (right). Can you work out how you process stimuli?

AS Cognitive Psychology

study of acoustic confusion by Conrad (1964)

Aim >>

To find out whether people use acoustic coding in STM, even when information is presented visually.

Procedures >>

- Participants were shown a random sequence of six consonants projected in rapid succession onto a screen.
- Strings of consonants were either acoustically similar (e.g. P, C, V, T, B, D) or acoustically dissimilar (e.g. L, Z, F, X, H, W).
- Participants were asked to write down the letters in the same order as they appeared.
- Letters were presented too rapidly for the participants to keep up, so they had to rely on memory.
- Conrad carefully noted the errors made by participants.

Findings >>

- The majority of the errors involved the substitution of a similar-sounding letter (e.g. B for D, or S for X).
- Participants found that it was more difficult to recall strings of acoustically similar letters in the correct order than acoustically dissimilar letters, even though they were presented visually.

Conclusions >>

- Items are stored in STM in some form of acoustic code.
- Even if consonants are presented visually, they are recoded into acoustic form in order to be stored in STM.

AO2 check

Other studies have shown that acoustic coding is not exclusively used in STM. When steps are taken to prevent acoustic coding, visual coding may be substituted (see the study by Brandimonte *et al.* (1992) on the next page).

tend to be more similar in sound than in any other characteristic, such as visual form or meaning. Baddeley set about testing this idea by presenting participants with words rather than consonants and comparing the effect of acoustic similarity with similarity of meaning (semantic similarity). He presented participants with sequences of five short words that were acoustically similar (e.g. *man, mad, mat, map, can, cat, cap*). He noted how well they were recalled compared with a sequence of short, acoustically dissimilar words (e.g. *pen, day, few, sup, cow, pit, bar, hot*) and a sequence of short, semantically similar words (e.g. *big, large, wide, high, great, tall, long, broad*). Baddeley found that words with similar sounds were much harder to recall than words which did not sound alike. Similarity of meaning had only a very slight detrimental effect on performance. Baddeley's study in fact supported Conrad and he, too, concluded that short-term memory relies more on the sound of words than on their meaning. Interestingly, he found that the effects of sound similarity disappeared when he tested participants' long-term learning (see key study, *Encoding in STM and LTM*, on p. 12). This suggests that a major factor affecting encoding is whether the items are being stored in STM or LTM.

ACTIVITY

Conrad on acoustic confusion

Reread the description of the study of acoustic confusion that Conrad undertook in 1964 (see key study, above). Then answer the following questions:

1 What type of research did Conrad use to study encoding in short-term memory?

2 Does this type of research allow Conrad to conclude that there is a causal relationship between the nature of the stimuli and accuracy of participants' recall?

3 Note down one important criticism of this study that limits the usefulness of the findings.

Answers are given on p. 38.

- *Other ways of encoding* – It seems likely that acoustic coding is the preferred method of encoding in STM, but there are several studies that show that other modes of representation are also possible (see the panel on p. 10).

Visual coding in short-term memory (Brandimonte *et al.* 1992)

An interesting study by Brandimonte *et al.* (1992) demonstrates not only that visual coding can be used in STM, but that, under certain circumstances, it is a superior method. Participants were presented with six line drawings of familiar objects, such as the one shown in Fig. 1.1, and were asked to memorize them in order.

Participants were then asked to form a mental image of each one in turn and to subtract a specified part of the drawing as shown. They were then asked to name the resulting image; for example, the left-hand picture is a wrapped sweet, but it becomes a fish when the right-hand section of the image is removed. Participants were able to name on average 2.7 of the six items.

Another group of participants was given the same tasks to do except that they were prevented from articulating during the learning stage. While they were being shown the original pictures, they were

asked to repeat the meaningless chant "la-la-la-...". This prevented them from converting the pictorial image into a verbal code, as they would have done under normal circumstances. They were actually more successful when it came to identifying the subtracted image and were able to name 3.8 items correctly. Because they were using visual coding, they found it easier to subtract a part from the visual image than the first set of participants who had coded the original stimulus in verbal form.

This study shows that the nature of the task may affect the type of coding used. If prevented from using acoustic coding, visual coding may be substituted. There is also some evidence that items in STM can be coded in terms of their meaning, so it seems reasonable to conclude that acoustic coding is generally the preferred, rather than the exclusive, method of representation.

Line drawing

Subtracted part

Remaining part

Figure 1.1 »
Sample of the line drawings used by Brandimonte and colleagues

LONG-TERM MEMORY

Long-term memory (LTM) holds a vast quantity of information, which can be stored for long periods of time. The information kept here is diverse and wide-ranging, and includes all of our personal memories, our general knowledge and our beliefs about the world. It also includes plans for the future and is where all our knowledge about skills and expertise is deposited. LTM is not a passive store of information, but a dynamic system that constantly revises and modifies stored knowledge in the light of new information. LTM is a much larger, more complex memory system than STM, from which it differs in terms of such factors as capacity, duration and simple encoding. It seems likely that LTM is not a single store, but a number of different systems with slightly different functions.

Capacity of long-term memory

It is not possible to quantify the exact capacity of LTM, but most psychologists would agree that there is no upper limit – we are always capable of more learning. The huge capacity of LTM requires a highly organized structure, otherwise items would be difficult to retrieve. Many researchers have suggested that LTM is divided into a number of different memory systems. This would

explain why Clive Wearing (the case study described on pp. 3–4) can remember some things from his LTM but not others.

Duration of long-term memory

The duration of the memory trace in LTM is considerably longer than in STM and can last almost a whole lifetime. Bahrick suggested the term 'permastore' to refer to memory held for a very long time (see key study, *Duration of long-term memory*, on the next page).

Factors that affect duration of LTM

■ *Childhood amnesia* – Try to jot down some of your earliest memories. You may have some quite vivid memories, but it is unlikely that you can accurately remember many events from before your third birthday. If you can, it is probably because you have been told about these events by your family or have seen them recorded in photos. The most likely explanation for this so-called childhood amnesia is that very young children are incapable of laying down well-organized and integrated memories, and so these are not available for later recall.

study by Bahrick *et al.* (1975)

Aim >>

To establish the existence of very long-term memory (VLTM), and to see whether there was any difference between recognition and recall.

Procedures >>

- Investigators tracked down the graduates from a particular high school in America over a 50-year period.
- 392 graduates were shown photographs from their high-school yearbook.
- For each photo, participants were given a group of names and asked to select the name that matched the person in the photo (recognition group).
- Another group of participants was simply asked to name the people in the photos without being given a list of possible names (recall group).

Findings >>

- In the name-matching condition, participants were 90 per cent correct even 14 years after graduation.
- After 25 years, these participants were 80 per cent accurate; after 34 years, 75 per cent accurate and, even after 47 years, 60 per cent accurate.
- The second group who had to identify the photos without any name cues were not quite as successful. They were 60 per cent accurate after seven years, but the level of accuracy had dropped to less than 20 per cent after 47 years.

Conclusions >>

- People can remember certain types of information for almost a lifetime.
- The accuracy of very long-term memory is better when measured by recognition tests than by recall tests.

Criticisms >>

- Unlike many memory experiments, this study used meaningful stimulus material (high-school yearbooks) and tested people for memories from their own lives.
- It is unclear whether the drop-off in accuracy after 47 years reflects the limits of duration or a more general decline in memory with age.

study by Baddeley (1966)

Aim >>

To explore the effects of acoustic and semantic coding in STM and LTM.

Procedures >>

■ In the STM study, participants were asked, immediately after presentation, to recall, in serial order, a list of five words taken from a pool of words in the following categories:
  – acoustically similar words (e.g. *man, mad, map*)
  – acoustically dissimilar words (e.g. *pen, day, few*)
  – semantically similar words (e.g. *great, big, large*)
  – semantically dissimilar words (e.g. *hot, old, late*).
■ In the LTM study, each list of words was extended to ten and recall was tested after an interval of 20 minutes.

Findings >>

■ Words with similar sounds were much harder to recall using STM than words with dissimilar sounds.
■ Similarity of meaning had only a very slight detrimental effect on STM.
■ When participants were recalling from LTM, recall was much worse for semantically similar words than for semantically dissimilar words.
■ Recall from LTM was the same for acoustically similar and acoustically dissimilar words.

Conclusions >>

■ STM relies heavily on acoustic coding.
■ LTM primarily makes use of semantic coding.

Criticisms >>

■ The use of the experimental method allows a causal link to be drawn between type of coding used in STM and LTM and the accuracy of recall.
■ The conclusions of this study may not reflect the complexity of encoding. Evidence from other studies shows that, in certain circumstances, both STM and LTM can use other forms of coding.

■ *How duration is measured* – Another factor that seems to be important in measuring the duration of LTM is the method used to tap into memory. As you can see from Bahrick's study, people are much better at remembering information from long ago if they are tested by recognition, rather than by free recall.

■ *Thorough learning* – It also seems that people are more likely to hold material in permastore if they learned it very well in the first place and if they continued to learn about related material in the interval. Bahrick and Hall (1991) tested long-term memory for algebra and geometry. They found that people who had only taken maths up to high-school level showed a steady decline in the accuracy of their recall over the years, whereas students who had taken a higher maths course at college showed remarkably high levels of accuracy as much as 55 years later.

Encoding in long-term memory

As far as coding is concerned, there is some evidence that the meaning of the stimulus is often the main factor here. In other words, semantic coding is important (see key study, *Encoding in STM and LTM*, above).

Factors affecting encoding in LTM

It is clear from our own experience that material can be represented in other ways as well. Our ability to recognize sounds such as police sirens and telephones ringing shows that we can store material in an acoustic form. We can also easily bring to mind pictorial images of people or places, which suggests some visual coding in LTM. It seems that the type of stimulus material can affect the way we encode in LTM.

MODELS OF MEMORY

The multi-store model of memory

A number of memory theorists have proposed that the memory system is divided into three stores as outlined in the previous section. Atkinson and Shiffrin (1968) proposed a typical model of this type. Their model arose from the information-processing approach where memory is characterized as a flow of information through a system. The system is divided into a set of stages and information passes through each stage in a fixed sequence. There are capacity and duration limitations at each stage, and transfer between stages may require recoding. Models based on information processing are represented in the form of flow charts, such as the one illustrated in Fig. 1.2.

Atkinson and Shiffrin proposed that external stimuli from the environment first enter sensory memory where they can be registered for very brief periods of time before decaying or being passed on to the short-term store. STM contains only the small amount of information that is actually in active use at any one time. Information is encoded at this stage in terms of its sounds. Atkinson and Shiffrin believed that memory traces in STM are fragile and can be lost within about 30 seconds unless they are repeated (rehearsed). Material that is rehearsed is passed on to the long-term store where it can remain for a lifetime, although loss is possible from this store through decay or interference. Coding in LTM is assumed to be in terms of meaning, i.e. semantic.

In addition to describing the structural features of the memory system, Atkinson and Shiffrin also proposed various control processes, which are strategies used by individuals to manipulate the information flowing through the system. One of the most important of these is rehearsal that allows information to be recycled within STM and passed on into LTM.

In evaluating the multi-store model of memory, the key points are as follows:

- The multi-store model has stimulated considerable research, but it is too simplistic to explain the whole memory system.

- A crucial aspect of the multi-store model is that it distinguishes between short-term and long-term stores, which suggests that LTM and STM operate differently in terms of capacity, duration and encoding. Evidence in support of the distinction between STM and LTM comes from case studies of people with brain damage that gives rise to memory impairment (see panel below).

The distinction between LTM and STM

Milner (1966) reported on a young man referred to as H.M., who was left with severe memory impairment after brain surgery. He was able to talk normally and to recall accurately events and people from his life before surgery, and his immediate digit span was within normal limits. He was, however, unable to retain any new information and could not lay down new memories in LTM. When told of the death of his favourite uncle, he reacted with considerable distress. Later, he frequently asked about his uncle and, on each occasion, reacted again with the level of grief appropriate to hearing the news for the first time. Cases such as these and that of Clive Wearing (see p. 3) lend support to the multi-store model by pointing to a clear distinction between LTM and STM.

Figure 1.2 >> *Summary of the Atkinson and Shiffrin (1968) model of memory*

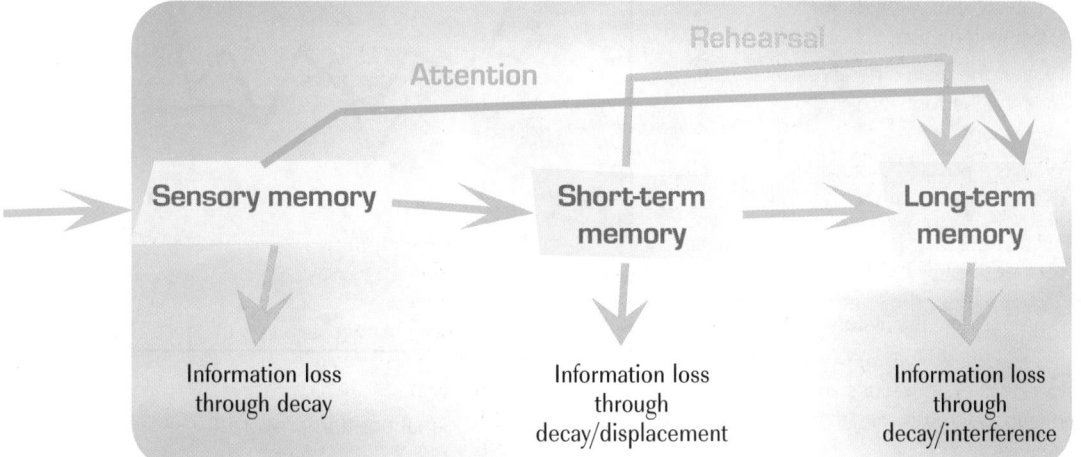

There are, however, problems with the model of Atkinson and Shiffrin. The model is too simple and inflexible, and fails to take account of factors such as the strategies people employ to remember things. It also places emphasis on the *amount* of information that can be processed rather than its nature. Some things are simply easier to remember than others, perhaps because they are more interesting, more distinctive, funnier, etc. The multi-store model cannot account for this.

It is also criticized for focusing on the structure of the memory system at the expense of adequately explaining the processes involved. For example, visual stimuli registering in sensory memory must be changed to an acoustic code for access to STM. In order to translate the pattern of the letter 'M' into the sound 'em', the individual needs to access knowledge about letter shapes and sounds that is stored in LTM. This means that information from LTM must flow backwards through the system to the recoding stage prior to STM. This suggests that the flow of information through the system is interactive rather than strictly sequential as Atkinson and Shiffrin suggested.

The suggestion that rote rehearsal is the only means of transfer from STM into LTM has also been criticized. This criticism will be considered in more detail in the discussion of alternative models of memory, such as the levels of processing approach on p. 16.

Similarly, another model – the working memory model of Baddeley and Hitch (1974) – casts doubt on the assumption of Atkinson and Shiffrin that STM is a unitary store with a severely limited capacity.

ACTIVITY

Evidence for separate stores

Look back at the section under the heading 'The multi-store model of memory', and note that in the multi-store model of memory, short-term memory and long-term memory are viewed as two separate, distinct stores.

Glanzer and Cunitz (1966) conducted the following experiment to see if they could find evidence for these separate stores. Participants were presented with a list of words one at a time. They were asked to recall the words and could do so in any order (this is known as *free recall*).

- Half of the participants recalled the words immediately after they had memorized them (the *immediate recall* condition).

- The other half of the participants counted backwards for 30 seconds before they recalled the words (the *recall after distraction* condition).

The results are shown in the graph on the right.

Now answer the following questions:

1 In the immediate recall condition, which words were remembered best?

2 Why do you think this happens?

3 In the recall after distraction condition, which words are remembered best?

4 What is the main difference in the recall performance of the two groups?

5 What is a possible explanation of the difference in the way that the two groups performed?

6 Do these results provide evidence that supports or challenges the multi-store model of memory?

Answers to these questions are given on p. 38

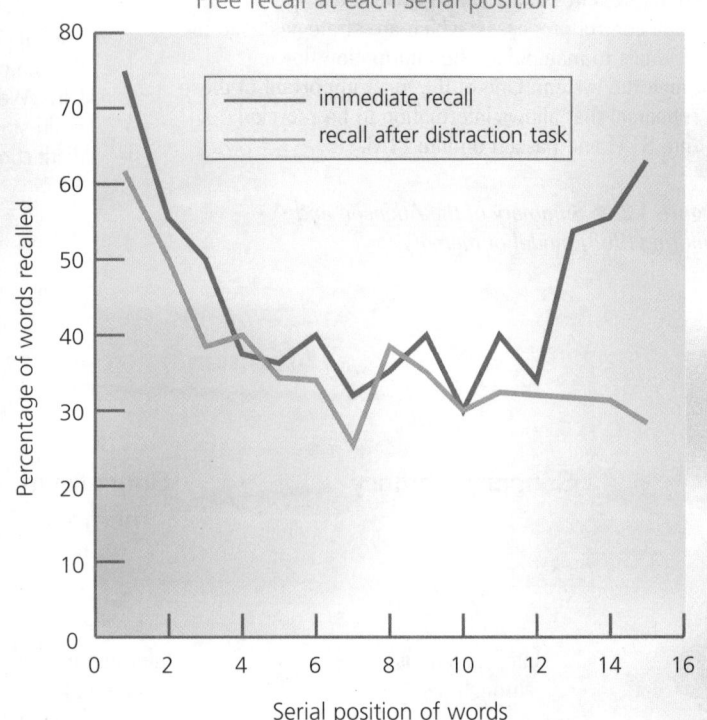

Free recall at each serial position

immediate recall
recall after distraction task

Percentage of words recalled
Serial position of words

The working memory model

One of the criticisms of the multi-store model is that it is too simplistic and assumes that STM and LTM act as unitary stores. It seems much more likely that both memory systems are divided into separate components that have different functions. The first people to explore the notion of a multi-component short-term store were Baddeley and Hitch (1974). They conducted a dual-task study in which participants were given digit strings to rehearse while, at the same time, carrying out verbal reasoning tasks similar to those in the activity on the right. Try the activity now.

Imagine trying to do these reasoning tasks and simultaneously rehearsing a string of digits – you probably think that this would be very difficult if not impossible. However, the participants in the study were able to recall six-digit strings and perform accurately on the reasoning task. This finding is not compatible with Atkinson and Shiffrin's view of a short-term store that can hold only a small amount of information. Instead, it suggests that STM, or working memory as Baddeley and Hitch prefer to call it, consists of several different components that can work independently of one another and so handle more than one task at a time.

Baddeley and Hitch concluded on the basis of this and other studies that STM is a flexible and complex system that consists of a central control mechanism assisted by a number of slave systems. The model has been modified slightly in the light of experimental studies and is shown in simple form in Fig. 1.3.

ACTIVITY

Verbal reasoning task

Read the following list of ten short statements and decide for each one, as quickly and as accurately as you can, whether it is true or false.

1	B is followed by A	BA
2	A does not follow B	BA
3	A is not preceded by B	BA
4	A is not followed by B	BA
5	B follows A	AB
6	B is preceded by A	BA
7	A does not precede B	BA
8	B is not preceded by A	BA
9	B is followed by A	AB
10	A follows B	AB

Baddeley (1997) suggested that you can get a good idea about how working memory operates by carrying out the task in the Activity on p. 16. Try it for yourself.

Figure 1.3 >> *The working memory model*
Source: Cohen et al. *(1993)*

Central executive

The central executive is the most important component in the model and is responsible for monitoring and coordinating the operation of the slave systems. It is flexible in that it can process information from any modality and also has some storage capacity, although this is very limited. It seems to play a major role in attention, planning and in synthesizing information, not only from the slave systems but also from LTM.

Phonological loop

The phonological loop stores a limited number of sounds for brief periods and can be thought of as an inner ear. It is thought to consist of two components. One component is the phonological store (inner ear) that allows acoustically coded items to be stored for a brief period. The other component is the articulatory control system (the inner voice) that allows subvocal repetition of the items stored in the phonological store.

Visuo-spatial scratchpad

The visuo-spatial scratchpad stores visual and spatial information and can be thought of as an inner eye. Like the phonological loop, it has limited capacity, but the limits of the two systems are independent. In other words, it is possible, for example, to rehearse a set of digits in the phonological loop while simultaneously making decisions about the spatial layout of a set of letters in the visuo-spatial scratchpad.

How working memory operates

Work out how many windows there are in your home. When you have finished, make a note of how you did it and then discuss your answer a friend or fellow student. Did you use similar strategies?

If you are like most people, you will have formed a mental image of your home and counted the windows either by imagining the outside of the house or by walking through the house room by room. The image will be set up and manipulated in your visuo-spatial scratchpad and the tally of windows will be held in the phonological loop as you count them subvocally. The whole operation will be supervised by the central executive, which will allocate the tasks and recognize when the final total has been reached.

In evaluating the working memory model, the key points are as follows:

- The working memory model appears to have a number of advantages over the concept of STM as outlined in the multi-store model. It effectively accounts for our ability to store information briefly, while at the same time actively processing the material.

- There is a considerable body of empirical research that seems to support the existence of the phonological loop slave system. For example, Baddeley *et al.* (1975) conducted a series of studies that investigated the word-length effect (see key study on p. 6). If participants were prevented from rehearsing the words subvocally by repeating an irrelevant sound such as "la-la-la..." (articulatory suppression), the word-length effect disappeared (i.e. short words were recalled no better than long words). It is assumed that the articulatory suppression task fills the phonological loop and, therefore, takes away the advantage of rehearsal. Since *some* words could be recalled, it is likely that the central executive takes over the recall task.

- The visuo-spatial store has not been investigated in the same depth as the phonological store, but there is experimental evidence that supports its existence. For example, Baddeley *et al.* (1973) gave participants a simple tracking task that involved holding a pointer in contact with a moving spot of light. At the same time, participants were asked to perform an imagery task. Participants were required to imagine the block capital letter 'F' and then, starting at the bottom left hand corner, were to classify each angle as a 'yes' if it included the bottom or top line of the letter and as a 'no' if it did not.

Participants found it very difficult to track the spot of light and accurately classify the angles in the letter imagery task. However, they were perfectly capable of carrying out the tracking task in conjunction with a verbal task. This suggests that the tracking and letter imagery tasks were competing for the limited resources of the visuo-spatial scratchpad, whereas the tracking task and the verbal task were making use of the separate components of the visuo-spatial scratchpad and the phonological loop respectively.

- The working memory model has proved influential and is still being developed and expanded. The main weakness, however, is that the component we know least about (the central executive) is the most important. It has a limited capacity, but no one has been able to quantify it experimentally. Richardson (1984) argues that there are problems in specifying the precise functioning of the central executive. He believes that the terminology is vague and can be used to explain any kind of results. In other words, it can give rise to a circular argument. For example, if we give participants an articulatory suppression task and this affects performance, we assume the phonological loop is normally utilized in the task, but if performance is not affected, we assume the central executive is normally utilized in the task, rather than the phonological loop. Hence, it is difficult to falsify the model.

Levels of processing

The working memory model has been much more effective than the multi-store model in explaining the active nature of short-term memory processing. However, it does not consider the effects of differential processing on long-term retention of information. An important approach which looked specifically at this aspect was put forward by Craik and Lockhart (1972). They rejected the idea of separate memory structures put forward by Atkinson and Shiffrin, believing instead that stimulus inputs go through a variety of processing operations. According to them, processing varies in terms of depth.

- *Shallow processing* – the first stages of processing are shallow and involve recognizing the stimulus in terms of its physical appearance, e.g. the shape of the letters a word is written in.

- *Deep processing* – the deepest level of processing involves coding the input in terms of its meaning.

- Rehearsing material simply by rote repetition is called *maintenance rehearsal* and is regarded as shallow processing. It is distinguished from *elaborative rehearsal*, in which links are made to semantic associations.

The assumption of the model is that shallow processing will give rise to weak, short-term retention, whereas deep processing will ensure strong, lasting retention. This central assumption has been tested in numerous studies, such as Hyde and Jenkins' study (1973) (see the panel on the right).

An evaluation of the levels of processing approach brings out the following points:

- The levels of processing approach was influential when it was first formulated and researchers in the field welcomed its emphasis on mental processes rather than on rigid structures.

- However, it soon became clear that the model was descriptive rather than explanatory. A major problem is circularity, i.e. there is no independent definition of depth. The model predicts that deep processing will lead to better retention – researchers then conclude that, because retention is better after certain orienting tasks, they must, by definition, involve deep processing. In the Hyde and Jenkins study, for example, the orienting task that gave rise to the lowest level of recall was the sentence frame task. Hyde and Jenkins assumed that the poor recall reflected shallow processing and yet, on the face of it, judgements about sentence frames would appear to require semantic analysis and, thus, deep processing.

- Other researchers have questioned the idea that depth of processing alone is responsible for retention. For example, Tyler et al. (1979) gave participants two sets of anagrams to solve. Some were easy (such as *doctro*), and others were more difficult (such as *ocdrto*). In a subsequent, unexpected recall task, participants remembered more of the difficult than the easy anagrams despite processing levels being the same. Tyler and colleagues suggested that retention was influenced by the amount of processing *effort* rather than depth. Craik and Lockhart (1986) have since suggested that other factors such as elaboration and distinctiveness are also important in determining the rate of retention and this idea has been supported by research. For example, Hunt and Elliott (1980) found that people recalled words with distinctive sequences of tall and short letter sequences better than words with less distinctive arrangements of letters.

Hyde and Jenkins' study (1973)

Hyde and Jenkins presented lists of 24 words auditorily and asked different groups of participants to perform one of the following so-called orienting tasks:

- rating the words for pleasantness
- estimating the frequency with which each word is used in the English language
- detecting the occurrence of the letters 'e' and 'g' in any of the words
- deciding the part of speech appropriate to each word (e.g. noun, adjective)
- deciding whether the words fitted into a particular sentence frame.

Half the participants were told in advance that they would be expected to recall the words (intentional learning group) and the other half were not (incidental learning group). In addition, there was a control group which was required simply to learn the words without doing any of the orienting tasks. After testing all the participants for recall of the original word list, Hyde and Jenkins found that there were minimal differences in the number of items correctly recalled between the intentional learning groups and the incidental learning groups.

This finding is predicted by Craik and Lockhart because they believe that retention is simply a by-product of processing and so intention to learn is unnecessary for learning to occur. In addition, it was found that recall was significantly better for words which had been analysed semantically (i.e. rated for pleasantness or for frequency) than words which had been rated more superficially (i.e. detecting 'e' and 'g'). This is also in line with the theory because semantic analysis is assumed to be a deeper level of processing than structural analysis.

ACTIVITY

Expert interview

1 What two problems does Phil Beaman identify concerning the multi-store model of memory as an adequate explanation of human memory?

2 Why does he think that the working memory model offers a better explanation?

3 Why does remembering where you heard a voice or recalling touch pose problems for the working memory model?

Working *memory*

Dr Philip Beaman is a Lecturer in Psychology at the University of Reading. His PhD research undertaken at Cardiff University on the effects of noise on human cognitive performance was followed by a postdoctoral research fellowship at the Medical Research Council's Cognitive Development Unit, University College London. His current research interests are auditory attention and memory, particularly the distracting effects of unwanted noise, short-term or 'working' memory, and the effects of memory limitations on problem-solving and reasoning.

Q What was wrong with the multi-store model as a representation of human memory?

A In the model, any information not passed on to long-term memory is lost within about 30 seconds. Information can be held in short-term memory (or passed on to long-term memory) only by repeating it to yourself (rehearsal). However, in many studies of individuals with brain-damage, a patient may have obvious difficulty with short-term recall but no real problems when their longer-term memory is tested. You have also probably learned information 'all in one go', without repeating it to yourself. If all information had to be encoded first in short-term memory and could only be passed on to long-term memory by rehearsal, none of this should be possible.

Philip Beaman

Q In what way does working memory offer a better account of memory?

A Working memory acknowledges the complexity of memory and suggests that memory is used for something rather than existing just as an object of study for psychologists. Working memory aims to provide an explanation for the type of memory consulted on a daily basis to support everyday tasks, for example carrying out the sort of simple verbal reasoning and comprehension necessary to follow complicated conversations and arguments, keeping track of the locations of objects in a room without needing to continually look for them, and so on.

Q Are there any problems with the current view of working memory?

A Maintaining that such-and-such a subsystem of working memory model is involved in a particular task isn't, by itself, much of an explanation. This is a particular problem with the central executive component. Suggesting that a particular activity (e.g. planning) is 'governed by' the central executive is not very helpful without a clearer idea of how the central executive works. The visuo-spatial sketchpad and phonological loop are much better worked-out components of working memory, but it is still not clear how information from these systems might be coordinated, or what happens to information that could be coded in both systems (e.g. the spatial location of a voice) or neither (e.g. the memory of a touch).

AS Cognitive Psychology

✓ CHECK YOUR UNDERSTANDING

Check your understanding of the nature and structure of memory by answering these questions. Try to do this from memory at first. You can check your answers by looking back through Topic 1.

1 What do you understand by the following terms:
   (a) short-term memory (b) long-term memory?

2 List three differences between STM and LTM.

3 According to Miller, how does 'chunking' increase the capacity of STM?

4 Identify two factors that affect the duration of STM.

5 Outline the procedures and findings of the Peterson and Peterson study of duration in STM.

6 What is the preferred method of encoding in (a) STM (b) LTM?

7 Outline the findings of the study by Bahrick *et al.* (1975) into very long-term memory. Identify one criticism of this study.

8 Outline the main features of the working memory model.

9 Outline findings of research investigating the levels of processing model.

10 To what extent does the multi-store model explain how memory works?

REVISION SUMMARY

Having covered this topic you should be able to:

✓ define 'short-term memory', 'long-term memory', 'capacity', 'duration' and 'encoding'

✓ explain the differences between STM and LTM

✓ discuss research into aspects of STM and LTM

✓ describe the multi-store model and evaluate research that has investigated this model

✓ describe working memory and evaluate research that has investigated this model

✓ describe levels of processing and evaluate research that has investigated this approach

✓ describe the aims, procedures, findings, conclusions and criticisms for a key study in duration in STM, duration in LTM, capacity in STM, encoding in STM and encoding in LTM.

Working either on your own or in a small group, write down three lists:

1 some examples of the types of things that you regularly forget, such as people's names or where you put something important, such as your keys, purse or wallet)

2 the main reasons why you forget these things

3 techniques you have used to try to improve your memory – which ones have been the most successful and which the least successful?

FORGETTING IN SHORT-TERM MEMORY

To understand how the memory system works, it is important to look at some of the reasons why we lose information – in other words, how we forget. The way we forget seems to differ depending on whether the information is in STM or LTM.

Displacement in STM

We have already considered the view that the capacity of STM is limited to approximately seven chunks of information (see Miller's magic number seven, p. 5). If this were the case, a possible mechanism for forgetting from STM could be displacement. In other words, material currently circulating in STM which has been insufficiently processed to pass on to LTM, will be pushed out or displaced by new, incoming information.

Waugh and Norman (1965) investigated this idea using the serial probe technique. They presented a set of

digits followed by the repetition of one of those digits (the probe). Participants then have to recall the digit that followed the probe in the original list. Waugh and Norman found that recall was good if the probe came towards the end of the 16-digit list, but poor for items at the beginning of the list. This is consistent with the notion of displacement because digits at the end of the list would still be available in STM whereas digits at the beginning of the list would seem to have been displaced by the ones that came later.

Displacement may not be the only explanation. Shallice (1967) found that a faster rate of presentation of the digits produced better recall, which suggests that time may be an important factor in forgetting. With the faster presentation rate, earlier digits had less time to disappear from memory. In practice, it has been difficult to isolate the effects of displacement from decay.

Decay in STM

According to decay theory, information is forgotten because of the passage of time rather than because of the displacement of the memory trace. It is thought that some kind of structural change occurs in the brain when a memory is laid down. Hebb (1949) believed that, as a result of excitation of the nerve cells, a brief memory trace is laid down. At this stage of the process, which corresponds to STM, the trace is very fragile and likely to be disrupted. With repeated neural activity (e.g. brought about by rehearsal), a permanent structural change comes about and the memory is transferred to LTM where it is no longer likely to decay.

Studies based on the Brown-Peterson technique discussed on p. 7 seem to provide support for the decay theory of forgetting in STM. You will recall that forgetting of consonant trigrams was rapid when rehearsal was prevented. This finding was initially interpreted as evidence that the memory trace for the trigram becomes increasingly faded and decayed as time elapses. However, it is notable that participants generally have little trouble recalling the trigrams on the first couple of trials. Problems seem to set in only as the number of trials increases, suggesting that earlier trigrams may be interfering with later ones. Try the activity below before you read any further.

You probably found that the first triplet of words was accurately recalled, but that it was harder to recall the subsequent triplets. However, you should have noticed that recall improved again when you got to column 5 (*dog, goat, pig*). This seems to be because items from a *new* category give you the opportunity to start afresh and avoid confusion with earlier items. This kind of evidence suggests that forgetting can be explained in terms of interference rather than decay.

It is difficult to test decay theory without introducing confounding factors such as interference, but Reitman (1974) proposed a technique which she hoped would be as pure a measure as possible. Participants were given a task that intervened between learning and recall, which not only prevented rehearsal but also offered no opportunity for interfering with learning. She showed participants lists of five words for two seconds and then, for a further 15 seconds, asked them to listen out for a faint tone presented over earphones. She reasoned that this tone detection task would require effort and attention, but not involve any new learning. Under these conditions, recall of the five words declined by about 24 per cent over the 15-second period. She concluded that this decline in performance could be explained by decay. However, it is of course impossible to guarantee that no new information entered STM during the 15-second delay.

STM is clearly a fragile store from which information can be easily and quickly lost. The precise mechanism of forgetting is unclear, but it seems likely that interference, displacement and decay all have a role to play.

ACTIVITY

Interference or decay?

Cover up the lists of words below with a piece of paper and uncover them, from left to right, as you work through the exercise. Under each list of words is a number. Looking away from the lists, count backwards in threes from this number for 10 seconds and then, without looking back, try to write down the three words in the list. Carry on until you have completed all eight lists. When you have finished, write down how many words you recorded correctly for each list.

banana	apple	cherry	apricot	dog	cat	sheep	daisy
peach	grape	lemon	melon	goat	cow	horse	rose
plum	orange	pear	lime	pig	fox	mouse	tulip
327	519	128	385	729	610	486	923

Unit 1 // Human memory

21

FORGETTING IN LONG-TERM MEMORY

Decay in LTM

We have already seen that memories transferred to the long-term store are relatively stable and long lasting. It is, however, only too obvious from our own experience that we often fail to remember things. Trace decay was discussed above as a method of forgetting in STM, but some psychologists have also argued that material can be lost from LTM in the form of decay through disuse. The idea here is that knowledge or skills that have not been used for a long time will eventually fade away. However, skills that require motor memory, such as riding a bicycle or swimming, do not seem to be forgotten, even after long periods without practice. This lack of forgetting does not, however, seem to be true of all skills.

McKenna and Glendon (1985) studied 215 shop and office workers who had volunteered to learn the skills of cardiac resuscitation. Various measures of performance were tested over a three-month to three-year period after completion of training. Performance dropped sharply on all measures after only three months and declined to extremely low levels after three years. Baddeley (1999) suggests that riding a bike involves a continuous skill where each action provides the cue for the next action. Such skills appear to require little maintenance to be retained. Skills such as resuscitation, however, are much more complex and require accurate knowledge as well as motor skill. According to Baddeley, these need frequent refreshing if they are to be maintained.

There is evidence to suggest that certain verbal memories are remarkably resistant to long-term decay. Bahrick and Phelps (1987), in a long-term study of American college graduates, found that they showed rapid forgetting of Spanish vocabulary over the first three or four years after graduation, but then showed remarkably little further decline over the following 30 to 50 years.

All these findings suggest that, even where time plays a part in forgetting, it cannot be the only factor. It seems likely that we forget because other, similar memories get in the way.

Interference in LTM

There are problems in separating out the effects of time and interference, but Baddeley and Hitch (1977) conducted a study in which they attempted to avoid these difficulties.

Baddeley and Hitch asked rugby players to recall the names of teams they had played against during the previous season. Because of illness, other commitments, etc., some of the players had been unable to play in all the fixtures. This meant that, for some players 'two games back' meant two weeks ago, whereas for others 'two games back' meant four or five weeks ago. In other words, over the same period of time, some players had taken part in more games than others. This allowed Baddeley and Hitch to find out whether forgetting depended on elapsed time or the number of intervening games. The findings clearly showed that the mere passage of time was not the factor that determined how well team names could be recalled. The critical factor was the number of games played during that time period. In other words, forgetting appeared to be due to interference rather than trace decay.

If interference is the major cause of forgetting in LTM, it should be the case that people will remember things over time provided no interfering material intervenes. It is clearly difficult to create a situation where human participants are isolated after learning with no opportunity for any intervening new learning. Instead, researchers have turned their attention to looking at the effects of different types of interfering material on recall. McGeoch and MacDonald (1931) conducted a classic study into interference (see right).

McGeoch and MacDonald's study of interference (1931)

McGeoch and MacDonald asked participants to learn and relearn lists of adjectives and then compared their performance on recall tests after delays during which they carried out unrelated tasks.

Findings:

- Forgetting was least when participants simply had to rest during the interval between learning and recall.
- Forgetting rates increased when participants were required to learn unrelated material, such as nonsense syllables in the interval.
- Rates were even higher when other adjectives were learned in the interval. Rates were at their highest when the adjectives to be learned were similar in meaning to the original list.

Conclusion:

This study demonstrates that forgetting increases as a function of the similarity of the interfering material.

Types of interference

A distinction has been made between two types of interference:

- *Retroactive interference* – when new information interferes with old information. For example, if you move house and change telephone number, you will soon find that the new number supersedes the old.
- *Proactive interference* – when an old memory trace disrupts new information. You may, for example, suddenly find yourself dialling your old number even though you have not used it for months.

Retroactive interference was widely studied up until the 1960s, but has attracted less attention since then. Such studies typically made use of the technique of paired-associates in which a word is associated with one word on list A (e.g. *apple – fish*) and with a completely different word on list B (e.g. *apple – shoe*). Participants are required to learn list A and then to learn list B. When given the stimulus *apple* and asked to recall its paired associate from list A, participants frequently suffer from retroactive interference – in other words, they recall the paired associate from list B.

Proactive interference was studied by Underwood (1957). He noted that students who had learned a list of nonsense syllables showed a greater rate of forgetting when tested after 24 hours than would be expected. Given that these students had not been required to learn any more nonsense syllables in the intervening period, Underwood decided that retroactive interference was not causing the forgetting. Instead, he realized that this group of students had taken part in a number of his earlier memory experiments and so concluded that the interference causing their forgetting was proactive. He confirmed this suspicion by gathering data about the number of previous studies completed by the students and found that, the more lists of nonsense syllables they had learned earlier, the more likely they were to forget a new list over a 24-hour period.

There seems to be little doubt that interference between memory traces can cause forgetting. Recall can be impaired both from prior learning (proactive interference) and from later learning (retroactive interference) and, in both cases, the greater the similarity of the interfering material, the greater the interference. However, much of the evidence for interference theory has come from artificial laboratory experiments which have little relevance to everyday situations. There is also experimental evidence that demonstrates that interference cannot be a complete explanation of forgetting (see panel below).

Tulving's study of free recall (1966)

Tulving gave lists of words to participants and then tested their free recall. One group was given one presentation of the words followed by a single recall test. These participants were then re-presented with the list and tested again. A second group was given the list of words and then tested on three separate occasions without any further presentation of the list. A striking finding was that participants in this group recalled, on average, about 50 per cent of the words on each of the three tests, but that the words differed on each trial. Tulving concluded that all the words were still available in memory but not always readily accessible. This finding is difficult to reconcile with interference theory. How could a word that had been lost through interference on trial 1 suddenly become available again on trial 3? Studies such as these made psychologists think that forgetting can occur as a result of problems at the retrieval stage.

Retrieval failure in LTM

According to retrieval failure theory, forgetting occurs because the correct retrieval cues are not available. We are all familiar with the feeling that we know something, but just cannot bring it to mind – the name of an actor in an old film on TV, for example.

Brown (1991) has reviewed 25 years of research into the so-called 'tip-of-the-tongue' phenomenon, and reported that people can generally correctly recall the first letter of the target name or word between 50 and 70 per cent of the time. They also seem to be fairly accurate at identifying the correct number of syllables in the word.

Tulving has conducted much of the research into retrieval cues. For example, Tulving and Osler (1968) presented participants with lists of words, each of which was paired with a weakly associated cue word, e.g. *city – dirty*. Participants were then tested either for free recall (i.e. required to recall the first word of the pair without any prompt) or were cued with the associated word, e.g. given the word *dirty*. Cued recall consistently produced better performance than free recall. To counteract the argument that any semantically associated word might have elicited the target, Tulving and Osler gave some participants weak, semantic associates that had not been the original cue words, e.g. *busy*. Such cues did not facilitate recall and so Tulving and Osler (1968, p. 593) reached the following conclusion: "Specific retrieval cues facilitate recall if, and only if, the information about them is stored at the same time as the information about the membership of the word in a given list."

While Tulving has continued to stress the importance of cues at the memory encoding stage, he later (1983) acknowledged that cues not present at the time of learning can be helpful under certain circumstances.

Context-dependent retrieval

While it is clearly important how we encode material at the time of learning, psychologists have also been interested in the effects of the learning environment on recall (see the panel describing Smith's study). Smith's findings obviously have practical applications and raise

the question of whether students will perform better in exams if they are tested in their original lecture rooms.

In general, it has been found that environmental differences need to be substantial before any significant difference in recall performance can be demonstrated. It has also been shown that simply imagining the original environmental setting can be helpful.

State-dependent retrieval

There is some evidence that the internal environment (i.e. physiological state or mood) might also affect retrieval. Goodwin *et al.* (1969) found that heavy drinkers who learn things in a drunken state are more likely to recall them in a similar state. Eich (1980) has shown this effect with a range of other drugs, including marijuana.

Although there is less conclusive evidence that mood affects retrieval, a review of research studies into mood dependence (Ucros 1989) found a moderately strong relationship between mood at the learning and retrieval stage. She also found that mood-dependence was more likely if the stimulus material was about real life rather than artificially constructed material, and that adults were more likely to demonstrate mood dependence than children.

THE ROLE OF EMOTIONAL FACTORS IN FORGETTING

Psychologists have often ignored the role of emotion in human cognitive processes, but it seems likely that the way we feel has an impact on the way we remember things. There is some evidence that memory is better for material that fits a person's current mood. For example, depressed people tend to recall more unhappy memories than non-depressed people do. Clark and Teasdale (1982) investigated people whose depression fluctuated through the 24-hour cycle and found that they were consistently less likely to recall happy memories during their sad phases than during their relatively neutral phases.

Flashbulb memories

One particular type of memory that seems to be influenced by emotion has been called a flashbulb memory. This is a particularly vivid, detailed and long-lasting memory of the circumstances surrounding a momentous event. The event is usually highly significant and emotional, and is often somewhat unexpected. It can be personal or something that provokes worldwide interest, such as the assassination of President Kennedy in 1963 or the death of Princess Diana in 1997. According to Brown and Kulik (1977),

September 11th – a flashbulb memory?

1 What time of day was it and where were you when you first heard about the terrorist attacks on the World Trade Center in New York on 11 September 2001?

2 Who told you the news?

3 What were you doing at the time?

4 Who else was with you at the time?

5 How did you react and how did you feel when you heard the news?

6 If others were with you at the time, how did they react?

7 Did you pay particular attention to the news bulletins as the details of the series of terrorist attacks in the United States on the morning of September 11th unfolded?

8 For many people, the recollection of hearing about the terrorist attacks on September 11th can be described as a 'flash bulb memory', because it is a vivid, relatively permanent record of the circumstances in which they heard the news. Can you think of any other incident(s) about which you have an equally vivid memory?

Ask an older person this same question and note down their answer.

who first described this type of memory, the event must be surprising and have real consequences for the person's life. They believed that such an emotional event triggers a neural mechanism that causes the details to be imprinted on the memory. They believed that this is a special type of memory because of the detail and accuracy with which the event is remembered and the fact that the structural form of the memory is always so similar. They found that six kinds of information were most likely to be recalled about the moment when the news of the event was first heard. People remember:

- where they were
- what they were doing
- the person who gave them the news
- what they felt about it
- what others felt about it
- what happened in the immediate aftermath.

Research on flashbulb memories

Conway *et al.* (1994) found that 86 per cent of British undergraduate students had vivid and accurate memories of the unexpected resignation of Margaret Thatcher as prime minister in 1990, even after 11 months. This compared with only 29 per cent of non-British students. Conway claimed that this event met the criteria for a flashbulb memory for British people: somewhat unexpected, highly significant and arousing deep emotions.

Not all psychologists agree that flashbulb memories are special (see key study, *Flashbulb memory*). Neisser (1982), for example, believes that the enduring nature of such memories results from frequent rehearsal and reworking after the event, rather than from neural activity at the time. As far as the uniformity of the memories is concerned, Neisser believes that this is caused simply by our using the common conventions of storytelling. In other words, when we recount important events, we do so by using conventional storytelling techniques. Neisser also argued that flashbulb memories are subject to the same types of inaccuracy and forgetting as any other memories. It is difficult to check the accuracy of so-called flashbulb memories.

A flashbulb memory ...

Where were you and what were you doing when you found out that Princess Diana had died after her car crashed in a Paris subway?

KEY STUDY >> FLASHBULB MEMORY

a study by McCloskey *et al.* (1988)

Aim >>

To test the accuracy of flashbulb memory.

Procedures >>

- People were interviewed a few days after the explosion of the American space shuttle *Challenger* in 1986 about their memories surrounding the event.
- The same people were interviewed again after nine months.

Findings >>

- There were inaccuracies in the memories.
- There were discrepancies between what was recalled shortly after the accident and what was remembered nine months later.

Conclusions >>

- So-called flashbulb memories are subject to the same types of inaccuracy and forgetting as other memories.
- Therefore, so-called flashbulb memories are not special memories but are products of ordinary memory mechanisms.

Criticisms >>

- This was not an artificial, laboratory study. People were asked to recall a real event that they had witnessed on TV or heard about through the media.
- Conway and colleagues reject the idea that flashbulb memories are simply stronger versions of ordinary memories. They have claimed that the Challenger accident did not meet the criteria for flashbulb memories.

For example, Neisser was sure that he had been listening to a baseball match on the radio when he heard about the Japanese bombing of Pearl Harbor (during World War II). However, when he checked this, he discovered, much to his surprise, that this was impossible as the bombing happened outside the baseball season.

Weaver (1993) found that American college students had no more vivid memories about the decision of the US president George Bush to bomb Iraq in 1991 than they had of a trivial event, such as meeting a friend.

Conway (1995) has criticized such studies by pointing out that such an event (i.e. the bombing of Iraq) did not meet the criteria for a flashbulb memory. He believes that it was neither unexpected nor likely to have immediate consequences for the students concerned.

As you can see, the evidence is mixed and it is still unclear whether flashbulb memories represent a particular type of memory, or whether they are substantially similar to most memories for events.

Repression

According to Freud (1915), repression (or motivated forgetting) is an unconscious process, which ensures that threatening, or anxiety-provoking memories are kept from conscious awareness. Freud formulated his ideas on repression in the course of treating patients with neurotic disorders and he gave examples in his case studies. It has proved more difficult to demonstrate the existence of repression in the laboratory although a number of attempts have been made (see Key study, *Emotional factors in forgetting*).

KEY STUDY >> EMOTIONAL FACTORS IN FORGETTING

a study of repression by Levinger and Clark (1961)

Aim >>

To investigate the retrieval of associations to words that were emotionally charged, compared with the retrieval of associations to neutral words.

Procedures >>

- The time taken to produce associations was recorded.
- Immediately after the word associations had been generated, the participants were given the original cue words and were asked to recall their associated words.

Findings >>

- Participants took longer to provide free associations to the negatively charged words compared with the neutral words.
- Compared with the neutral words, the negatively charged words produced higher galvanic skin responses (GSR) in the participants.
- Participants found it more difficult to recall their associations for the negatively charged words compared with the neutral words.

Conclusions >>

- Repression led to the emotionally negatively charged words being more difficult to recall. This may have arisen from the arousal these words produced (as shown by the GSR data).
- Results, therefore, support Freud's theory that repression (of anxiety-provoking responses) causes forgetting.

Criticisms >>

- More recent evidence challenges these findings. Bradley and Baddeley (1990) ran a similar experiment using 32 student participants and found that when words were recalled after 28 days, the emotional associations were better recalled than the neutral associations. This does not support the repression hypothesis since emotional words actually became more memorable over time.
- Holmes (1990) has reviewed a number of studies of repression and forgetting, and concludes that there is no convincing experimental support for repression causing forgetting.

Although laboratory studies have not produced clear-cut support for the repression hypothesis, there is some evidence that real-life experiences of pain are forgotten more easily than those associated with pleasure.

Memory for pain

Robinson et al. (1980), in a study on the effectiveness of three different types of painkillers, asked women to rate the pain they had experienced during childbirth. They rated the pain at the time of the birth, after 24 hours, after five days and, again, after three months. Although the levels of pain experienced varied depending on the type of analgesic used, all three groups of women demonstrated that the memory of the pain faded considerably over time.

However, it could be argued that the pain of childbirth is not typical. Hunter et al. (1979), for example, found no decline in pain ratings over time when patients were asked to assess painful procedures such as sampling spinal fluid.

Recovered memories

Recently, research interest has focused on repressed memories associated with child sexual abuse. This is a controversial area because memories of abuse

'recovered' in psychotherapy can lead to great distress and, in some cases, to prosecutions years after the alleged events. The controversy revolves around the issue of whether these recovered memories are genuine. The main problem with establishing the validity of the claims is that there is usually no independent, objective, corroborative evidence. There is sadly no doubt that cases of child abuse do occur and it may well be that memories of abuse are repressed. Williams (1992), for example, found that 38 per cent of a group of African-American women who were known to have suffered abuse some years before, had repressed memories of the abuse. However, it also seems clear that some of these so-called repressed memories are false memories.

Loftus (1997) has conducted an extensive review of studies. These indicated that even psychologically healthy individuals can be made to alter their memory for events on the basis of false suggestions. As Baddeley (1999, p. 143) has written about reports of recovered memories:

>> It is important to exercise great caution in interpreting such reports, particularly when they become part of a legal process which is likely to be costly both financially and emotionally to patients and their families. >>

✓ CHECK YOUR UNDERSTANDING

Check your understanding of the nature and structure of forgetting by answering these questions. Try to do this from memory at first. You can check your answers by looking back through Topic 2.

1 What do you understand by the term 'forgetting'?

2 Outline two ways of forgetting from STM.

3 Explain how the serial probe technique used by Waugh and Norman supported the idea of displacement in STM.

4 Outline the findings of Reitman's study of decay in STM. Explain how she tried to rule out the effects of interference in her study.

5 What is the difference between retroactive and proactive interference?

6 Give two criticisms of interference theory as an explanation of forgetting in LTM.

7 Outline the findings of research into retrieval failure.

8 Explain what is meant by the term 'flashbulb memory'.

9 Explain why Conway criticized previous research into flashbulb memories.

10 To what extent does the theory of repression explain forgetting from LTM.

or, in this case, an eye on the clock!

One of the most important skills in answering examination questions *effectively* is to get your time management right. You can apply a simple formula when answering a typical AS question.

30 marks = 30 minutes

Simple? Well, almost. The problem is that this same 30 minutes includes many other things that have to be accomplished within the same time period. For example, you have to *choose* which question you are going to attempt, *plan* your response, and do anything else you have to do along the way (*including* taking a breather between questions).

The first two parts of each question constitute the AO1 component (see pp. 247–8). These are worth 6 marks each, and should take you about 5 minutes each to answer. The 'tricky' part of each question is the (c) part, as this inevitably has a number of different things that have to be dealt with in the time available. A typical part (c) for this area of the specification is as follows:

<< Give a brief account of, and evaluate attempts to explain forgetting in long-term memory. >>

[18 marks]

- 18 marks = 18 minutes, but you will need to *choose* carefully and *plan* your answer before embarking on your response to the question above. That effectively gives you about 15 minutes writing time for this part of the question, or about 300 words.

- There is a split in the marks awarded for all part (c) questions. AO1 (the descriptive part of the question) is worth **6 marks**, and AO2 (the evaluative component) is worth **12 marks**.

- '*Give a brief account of ....*' indicates the AO1 component and requires a brief précis of at least *two* explanations of forgetting in long-term memory. Given the ratio of AO1 to AO2 is one-third to two-thirds, that's **5 minutes** on the AO1 content or about $2\frac{1}{2}$ minutes (or 50 words) on each of the two explanations – such as retrieval failure (see p. 24) and interference (see p. 22).

- As the AO2 or *evaluation* component of this question should be two-thirds of the time available, that allows you **5 minutes** (or 100 words) to evaluate retrieval failure and **5 minutes** to evaluate interference.

There are many advantages in good time management of AS psychology questions. Time spent planning and arranging your response in advance means that you organize everything in such a way as to maximize your marks, and – let's face it – tackling small tasks (such as a 50-word description or 100-word evaluation) is far less intimidating than a 300-word 'mini-essay'.

REVISION SUMMARY

Having covered this topic, you should be able to:

✓ define 'forgetting', 'displacement', 'decay', 'interference', 'retrieval failure', 'flashbulb memory' and 'repression'

✓ explain the processes of decay and displacement from STM

✓ explain the processes of interference and retrieval failure in LTM

✓ describe and evaluate research that has been carried out into the role of emotional factors in forgetting

✓ describe the aims, procedures, findings, conclusions and criticisms for a key study in the areas of flashbulb memories and emotional factors in forgetting (repression).

GETTING YOU THINKING...

Without looking anything up, try to do the following three tasks.

1 Draw a picture of a 10p coin.

2 Write down the name of the person shown on the back of a new £5 note. Write down the words written at the top of the front of a note of any denomination (i.e. £5, £10, £20 or £50).

3 List the three main colours on the front cover of this textbook. Draw a picture or write a brief description of the front cover of this textbook.

You may be surprised how difficult it is to remember exactly what a 10p coin looks like without having one in front of you. If you compare your drawing with a real coin, you will probably find a number of inaccuracies. In everyday life, you do not need to remember every detail, as long as you are able to recognize coins so that you can use them appropriately. Similarly, you may not have remembered that Elizabeth Fry is shown on the back of a £5 note or that the words "Bank of England – I promise to pay the bearer on demand the sum of 5 pounds" are written on the front. And even though you use this textbook regularly, you may not be able to recall either the colour or the detail of the front cover. In other words, there are many areas of everyday memory where we don't need exact recall. However, in certain instances, such as taking exams or giving testimony about a crime, accuracy is vitally important.

In 1978, Neisser wrote a paper called *Memory: what are the important questions?* He criticized contemporary psychologists for concentrating almost exclusively on theoretical concepts and ignoring practical issues about memory. One exception to this was the work of Bartlett (1932) described below, but his ideas had little influence at the time. Since Neisser's challenge there has been a growing interest in practical, applied aspects of memory. One particular area of interest is eyewitness testimony.

KEY TERMS

Eyewitness testimony: an area of memory research that investigates the accuracy of memory following an accident, crime or other significant event, and the types of errors that are commonly made in such situations.

Reconstructive memory: a term usually associated with Bartlett which refers to a memory distorted by the individual's prior knowledge and expectations

Inaccurate eyewitness testimony can have very serious consequences leading to wrongful convictions and, in some cases in the US, to the death penalty (Loftus and Ketcham 1991). For example, Rattner (1988) reviewed 205 cases of wrongful arrest and found that, in 52 per cent of cases, this was due to mistaken eyewitness testimony. Psychologists have been interested in investigating some of the reasons why eyewitness testimony can be unreliable, and some of the ways that accuracy might be improved.

RECONSTRUCTIVE MEMORY

One possible reason why people recall events inaccurately is that memory is distorted or reconstructed by the individual's prior knowledge and expectations. Bartlett (1932) carried out the pioneering work on reconstructive memory. He argued that we do not record memories passively, as we would if we were taking a photo. He believed that we need to make what he called 'effort after meaning' in order to make more sense of the event. So, instead of storing an exact replica of the initial stimulus, we weave it with elements of our existing knowledge and experience to form a reconstructed memory (see Key study, *Reconstructive memory*).

Bartlett carried out a number of other studies to investigate how people recall things such as stories, pictures and faces. For example, he presented line drawings, such as those in Fig. 1.4, and then asked his participants to draw them from memory.

Although not asked to do so, participants spontaneously gave a label to the drawing; for example, they variously named the second picture 'pickaxe', 'turf-cutter', 'shovel', and their subsequent reproduction reflected this label, so that the final drawing was a distortion of the original.

Figure 1.4 >> *Figures used by Bartlett to study memory for drawings*
Source: Bartlett (1932)

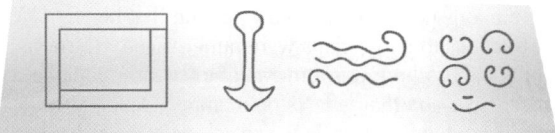

KEY STUDY >> RECONSTRUCTIVE MEMORY

a study by Bartlett (1932)

Aim >>
To investigate the effects of unfamiliarity on the recall of a folk story.

Procedures >>
- English participants heard an unfamiliar North American folk tale called 'The War of the Ghosts'. The story contained words and ideas that would not have appeared in a conventional Western story.
- After 20 hours, participants were asked to recall as much of the story as possible.
- Hereafter, participants were asked to retell the story many more times.

Findings >>
- The recalled story was distorted in a number of ways. Participants retold the story using language and narrative techniques that were influenced by their own cultural and literary background. Specifically, Bartlett found the following differences: rationalizations, omissions, changes in the order, alterations in importance and distortions of emotions.
- Distortions became even more pronounced over time, so that it increasingly resembled an ordinary English story.

Conclusions >>
- Memory for the folk tale continued being reconstructed over time and became less like the original story.
- The reconstruction made the story more coherent and so more easily remembered by the participants.

Criticisms >>
- This was an important study that drew attention to the way our schemas influence how we store memories.
- The study has been criticized for being poorly designed and controlled. For example, Gauld and Stephenson (1967), in semi-replications of Bartlett's story studies, found that errors were significantly reduced where participants were given explicit instructions that highlighted the importance of accurate recall.

SCHEMAS

According to Bartlett, we store memories in terms of our past experience or schemas. Schemas are knowledge packages which are built up through experience of the world and which can aid the interpretation of new information. Imagine, for example, that you are going for a meal in a restaurant. Through past experience, you will already be familiar with the kinds of things you would expect to see in a restaurant (for example, tables, chairs, waiters, menus, other customers) – in other words, you will have a restaurant schema.

Bartlett's ideas were regarded as rather vague and his studies were seen to lack experimental rigour by his contemporaries. It is certainly true that his experiments were poorly designed in some ways and that his instructions to participants were rather vague. However, in the 1970s, there was a revival of interest in the idea of schemas and their effects on memory. Cohen (1993) has suggested five ways in which schemas might lead to reconstructive memory.

1 We tend to ignore aspects of a scene that do not fit the currently activated schema.

2 We can store the central features of an event without having to store the exact details (e.g. the gist of a conversation rather than the exact words).

3 We can make sense of what we have seen by 'filling in' missing information (e.g. we see someone running and a bus pulling away from a bus stop, and assume that the person was running for the bus).

4 We distort memories for events to fit in with prior expectations (e.g. we might 'remember' that a bank robber wore a stocking mask, whereas he had actually worn a cap).

5 We may use schemas to provide the basis for a correct guess (e.g. if we cannot recall exactly what we had for breakfast last Tuesday, our schema for weekday breakfast supplies 'cereal' and this has a good chance of being correct).

This means that schemas are usually useful to us because they make our experiences more predictable and use our attentional resources efficiently. However, research has shown that schemas may also lead to distortions in memory.

Research findings on schemas

Brewer and Treyens (1981) investigated the effects of schemas on visual memory by asking their 30 participants, one at a time, to wait in a room for 35 seconds. The room was designed to look like an office and contained 61 objects. Some objects were compatible with an office schema, such as a desk, calendar and typewriter (this was 1981!), but a few items were included which were incompatible, such as a skull, a brick and a pair of pliers. In a subsequent, unexpected recall test, participants were most likely to recall typical office items, i.e. items with high schema expectancy. They were less successful at recalling the incompatible items such as the brick, but eight participants recalled the really bizarre item – the skull. Most of the errors in recall were substitutions, i.e. participants tended to recall falsely the presence of objects such as books, pens and a telephone, which would have high schema expectancy but which were not actually present on this occasion. Other errors involved wrong placement of items, e.g. a note pad was 'remembered' as being on the desk (where it might be in an office schema) instead of being on the seat of a chair (as it was in reality). These findings suggest that participants were using schemas to ensure rapid encoding of the visual information available to them during their 35-second wait. At the retrieval stage, recall was influenced by the schema so that typical items were recalled, even if they were not actually present. The Brewer and Treyens experiment showed that people can sometimes falsely remember objects that did not exist. List's shoplifting scenarios (see below) give another example of how schemas influence what is recalled.

List's shoplifting scenarios (1986)

List asked people to rate various events in terms of their probability in a shop-lifting scenario. She then compiled a video showing eight different shoplifting acts, each of which incorporated some of the events rated as high probability and some rated as low probability. She showed this video to a new set of people and, one week later, tested their recall. She found that they were more likely to recall high- rather than low-probability events and that, if they made inclusion errors of events that had not actually occurred in the video, they were more likely to be high-probability events.

Evaluation of Bartlett's research

■ Bartlett has been criticized for his choice of material in his studies of reconstructive memory. He used folk tales that he assumed would be less meaningful to people of other cultures, but he had no objective measure of meaningfulness.

■ Later studies have provided support for some of Bartlett's ideas by using more rigorous methods. Bransford and Johnson (1972), for example, constructed some prose passages that would be difficult to understand in the absence of context. They then compared recall performance between a group of participants who had been supplied with contextual information and a group who had not received this additional information. You can try one of their studies for yourself in the activity (right).

■ You probably found the task in the activity quite difficult because the passage was hard to understand – in other words, you lacked an appropriate schema and so could not relate the passage to stored information. However, if you now turn to p. 38 and look at Fig. 1.5, then read the passage again, it will probably make sense. Bransford and Johnson found that recall was significantly better for the group given the picture than for the group that simply read the passage.

■ There seems little doubt that we do use stored knowledge and past experience to make sense of new information, and that memories for events can be distorted (reconstructed) because of this. This

ACTIVITY

Activity (based on Bransford and Johnson 1972)

Read the following passage through once at normal reading speed. Then cover it up and write down as many points from the passage as you can remember.

<< If the balloons popped, the sound wouldn't be able to carry since then everything would be too far away from the correct floor. A closed window would also prevent the sound from carrying, since most buildings tend to be well insulated. Since the whole operation depends on the steady flow of electricity, a break in the middle of the wire would also cause problems. Of course, the fellow could shout but the human voice is not loud enough to carry that far. An additional problem is that the string could break on the instrument. Then there would be no accompaniment to the message. It is clear that the best situation would involve less distance. Then there would be fewer potential problems. With face-to-face contact, the least number of things could go wrong. >>

may well account for some instances of inaccurate eyewitness testimony. However, schema theories have been criticized on several counts (Cohen 1993). The main problems are that a schema is rather a vague concept and schema theory offers no explanation as to how the schemas are acquired in the first place.

LOFTUS' RESEARCH INTO EYEWITNESS TESTIMONY

Jurors place considerable importance on the evidence provided by eyewitnesses. Baddeley (1997) has reported that 74 per cent of suspects were convicted in 300 cases where eyewitness identification was the only evidence against them. However, numerous research studies have identified several problems with eyewitness testimony. One of the leading researchers in this field is Elizabeth Loftus.

Misleading post-event information

We have already seen that schemas (i.e. prior knowledge) can affect the way we remember events. Elizabeth Loftus has been primarily interested in the effects on memory of information provided *after* the event. She and her colleagues have carried out many studies that show that memory for events can be changed or supplemented by later information. They used the experimental method which has the advantage of the controlled environment of the laboratory, but which uses stimulus material that mimics real-life situations. In a typical experiment, participants are first shown a film or series of slides depicting an event such as a car accident. In the interval between viewing the slides and being tested for recall, participants are

provided with information which either conflicts or is consistent with the original witnessed event.

For example, Loftus (1975) showed 150 participants a film depicting a car accident. After the showing, participants were divided into two groups and each group was asked ten questions about what they had seen.

■ Group 1 was asked questions which were entirely consistent with the original film, e.g. "How fast was the white sports car going when it passed the 'Stop' sign?"

■ Group 2 was given the same questions with the exception of one – "How fast was the white sports car going when it passed the barn when travelling along the country road?" This question was misleading because there was no barn in the film.

After one week, the participants were all asked a further ten questions and, for both groups, the final question was: "Did you see a barn?" Loftus found the following:

- Only 2.7 per cent of the participants in Group 1 gave the incorrect answer "Yes".

- On the other hand, 17.3 per cent of those in Group 2 (i.e. those given the misleading question) answered "Yes".

Loftus concluded that for those in Group 2, the non-existent barn had been added to the original memory representation of the event at the question stage so that it was now recalled as being part of the original event (see key study, *Eyewitness testimony*, opposite, for another example).

Other factors that affect eyewitness testimony

- *Leading questions* – Loftus and Palmer (1974) showed participants a film of a car accident and then asked them: "How fast were the cars going when they hit each other?" All participants were asked the same type of question except that the word 'hit' was variously replaced with 'smashed', 'collided', 'bumped', or 'contacted'. It was found that the word used affected speed estimation – 'smashed' produced the highest estimate (40.8 miles per hour) and 'contacted' produced the lowest estimate. A week later, when people were asked if they had seen any broken glass, those in the 'smashed' group were consistently more likely to answer 'Yes' (wrongly).

In a similar study, in which film footage of a car accident was shown, participants were asked either "Did you see *a* broken headlight?" or "Did you see *the* broken headlight?" People who had seen a version of the film in which there really was a broken headlight were equally likely to answer 'Yes' to either of the questions. However, people who had seen a version with no broken headlight were more than twice as likely to recall one when asked about 'the' rather than 'a' broken headlight.

- *Anxiety of the witness* – Loftus (1979) reported a study where participants were exposed to one of two situations:

1 They overheard a low-key discussion in a laboratory about an equipment failure. A person then emerged from the laboratory holding a pen and with grease on his hands.

2 They overheard a heated and hostile exchange between people in the laboratory. After the sound of breaking glass and crashing chairs, a man emerged from the laboratory holding a paper knife covered in blood.

Participants were then given 50 photos and asked to identify the person who had come out of the laboratory.

1 Those who had witnessed the man holding the pen accurately identified the person 49 per cent of the time, whereas

2 Those who had witnessed the man with the bloodstained letter-opener were successful only 33 per cent of the time.

This finding has come to be known as the 'weapon focus', whereby the witness concentrates on the weapon (in this case, the bloodstained paper knife) and this distracts attention from the appearance of the perpetrator. Loftus concluded that the fear or anxiety induced by the sight of a weapon narrows the focus of attention and gives rise to very accurate recall of the central details of the scene, but diminishes accurate recall of peripheral details.

- *Consequences* – Findings from laboratory studies have not always been supported by evidence from real life. It is possible that participants in experiments are less accurate than genuine witnesses because they know inaccuracies will not lead to serious consequences. Foster *et al.* (1994) tested this possibility in a study where participants were shown a video of a bank robbery and subsequently asked to identify the robber in an identity parade. One group of participants were led to believe that the robbery was a real event and that their responses would influence the trial, while the second group assumed that it was a simulation. Identification of the robber was more accurate for the first group, suggesting that the consequence of identifying someone is an important factor for witnesses.

How would you approach the task of choosing a suspect from an identity parade if you knew your choice could make all the difference in getting someone convicted?

a study of the effects of misleading information on accurate recall
by Loftus *et al.* (1978)

Aim >>

To see whether participants would recall an event inaccurately if they were fed misleading questions.

Procedures >>

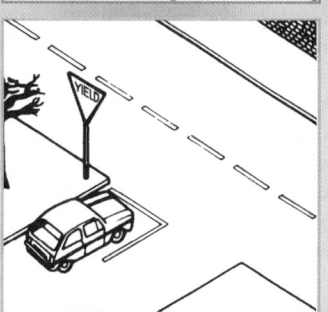

- Participants were divided into two groups.
- Both groups were shown a set of slides depicting events leading up to a car accident.
- The sets of slides were identical except for one slide: for one group, this slide depicted a red car stopping at a junction with a 'Yield' (Give Way) sign; the other group saw the same car stopping at a junction with a 'Stop' sign.
- After the slide presentation, both groups were given a set of 20 questions. For half the participants in each group, this set included the question "Did another car pass the red one while it was stopped at the 'Stop' sign?", while for the other half, the critical question was "Did another car pass the red one while it was stopped at the 'Yield' sign?" (i.e. half the participants received a misleading question and half received a question that was consistent with what they had actually seen).
- After 20 minutes, the participants were given 15 pairs of slides to look at and had to pick from each pair the slide that had been included in the original set (a recognition test). The critical pair consisted of one slide showing the car stopped at the 'Yield' sign and the other slide showing the car stopped at the 'Stop' sign.

Findings >>

- 75 per cent of participants who had received consistent questions picked the correct slide, as opposed to 41 per cent who had been given the misleading question.
- When the recognition test was delayed for a week, accuracy in the misled group fell to 20 per cent.

Conclusions >>

- Loftus and her colleagues concluded that the misleading question had served to delete the correct information from memory and replace it with false information.
- The effect of misleading questions becomes more pronounced over time.

Criticisms >>

- The conclusions of this study have been supported by other studies. For example, Loftus and Loftus (1980) found that accuracy in the misled group did not increase even when they were offered money for picking the correct slide.
- Although the results of this study are significant, it is important to note that by no means everyone in the misled group was inaccurate in the recognition task.
- Participants were simply shown static slides. We cannot conclude that memory would be affected by misleading questions in a real-life situation.

Method of testing witnesses – Loftus often used forced-choice tests (e.g. picking one of two slides), but this may give a false picture. Koriat and Goldsmith (1996) have shown that witness accuracy can be dramatically increased if tests do not rely on forced-choice format and if witnesses are allowed to give no answer if they feel unsure. It also seems to be the case that witnesses are able to produce far more accurate memories for events if they are given the appropriate cues. The Cognitive Interview technique, for example (see p. 37) seems to elicit memories that are more accurate and richer in details than other types of questioning.

So far we have looked at factors that seem to increase witness fallibility, but under some circumstances, recall seems less susceptible to error.

■ *Witnessing real-life events* – For example, Christianson and Hubinette (1993) questioned 110 witnesses who had, between them, witnessed a total of 22 genuine, as opposed to staged, bank robberies. Some of these witnesses had been onlookers who happened to be in the banks at the time, whereas others were bank employees who had been directly threatened in the robberies. Victims were more accurate in their recall and remembered more details about what the robbers wore, their behaviour and the weapon used, than people who had been bystanders. This superior recall continued to be evident, even after a 15-month interval. Christianson and Hubinette concluded that people are good at remembering highly stressful events if they occur in real life rather than in the artificial surroundings of the laboratory.

■ *Blatantly incorrect misinformation* – People are generally not misled by information if it is blatantly incorrect. Loftus (1979) showed participants a set of slides that depicted the theft of a large, red purse from a handbag. In an immediate recall test, 98 per cent of the participants correctly remembered the colour of the purse. They were then asked to read

ACTIVITY

Assessing Christianson and Hubinette's research

1 What do you think is the main strength of the study that Christianson and Hubinette undertook in 1993?

2 Why is it sometimes important for researchers such as Christianson and Hubinette to study recall after a long period of time (e.g. after a 15-month interval), rather than just gather data over short periods of time, as tends to be the case in much laboratory-based memory research?

an account of the incident allegedly written by a professor of psychology (this was designed to lend weight to the accuracy of the account). One of these accounts contained errors relating to unimportant items in the slide sequence, e.g. the wrong colour was given for items that were not central to the action. The other account contained, in addition to these minor errors, the more glaring statement that the purse was brown. In a second recall test, all but two of the participants resisted this blatantly wrong information and again correctly recalled that the purse was red. This suggests that memory for information that is particularly noticeable and salient at the time is less subject to distortion than memory for peripheral details. In other words, people can ignore new information under certain circumstances and so maintain their original memory representation intact.

What happens to the original memory?

Loftus believes that, in the light of misleading information, the original memory is deleted and replaced by the new, false memory. Other researchers have disputed this and claim that the original memory trace is still available, even though it has been obscured by new information. Bekerian and Bowers (1983) replicated the study by Loftus *et al.* (1978) in which a car is shown stopping at either a 'Stop' or a 'Yield' sign (see key study, *Eyewitness testimony*, on p. 35). In the recognition phase of the study, the participants were presented with the pairs of slides in chronological order, i.e. the order in which they were first shown (unlike the Loftus study where presentation was random). Under these circumstances, recall of the misled participants was almost exactly as accurate as of the control group. Bekerian and Bowers concluded that the original memory representation had not been lost for these participants. Looking at the slides in the correct sequence provided enough cues to reactivate the original memory in spite of the post-event misleading information. However, other researchers have failed to replicate this result, so it remains unclear whether the original memory trace is destroyed or obscured.

Evaluation of Loftus' research

■ Loftus and her colleagues have made an important contribution to our understanding of the fallibility of eyewitness testimony. It seems clear from her research that memory for events can be fundamentally altered in the light of misleading post-event information. This has important implications for the way in which the police question witnesses and also in the courts.

■ However, her studies have been criticized for artificiality. In real life, events that might have to be recalled later in a court of law, often take place unexpectedly and in an atmosphere of tension. It is difficult to reproduce such conditions in the laboratory for various practical and ethical reasons, and it is quite possible that eyewitnesses remember real events rather differently from staged events (e.g. see Christianson and Hubinette above).

■ She has also been criticized for her method of testing recall. People are much more accurate if they are asked questions in a logical order and if they are not forced to answer if unsure. The success of the Cognitive Interview technique has demonstrated that the type of questioning has a huge effect on witness accuracy (see below).

Accounts from eyewitnesses are often fallible and incomplete

THE COGNITIVE INTERVIEW

In view of the finding that accounts from eyewitnesses are often fallible and incomplete, psychologists have attempted to develop memory retrieval techniques aimed at eliciting more accurate information. One example is the Cognitive Interview Schedule that was developed by Geiselman *et al.* (1985) and designed to be used by police investigators. The interview technique is based on four instructions:

■ *To recreate the context of the original incident* – This does not involve revisiting the scene of the crime, but trying to recall an image of the setting including details such as the weather, the lighting, distinctive smells, any people nearby and what you were feeling at the time.

■ *To report every detail* – You are required to report back any information about the event you can remember, even if it does not seem to you to have a bearing on the crime.

■ *To recall the event in different orders* – You are encouraged to describe the event in reverse order, or to start with an aspect of the scene which seems most memorable and work backwards or forwards from that point.

■ *To change perspectives* – You are asked to *try* to describe the incident from the perspective of other people who were present at the time.

Geiselman and colleagues tested the effectiveness of the Cognitive Interview Schedule by comparing it with standard police interviewing techniques. They showed police training videos of violent crimes to a group of 89 students. About 48 hours later, the students were interviewed individually by American law enforcement officers (detectives, CIA investigators and private investigators). The interviewers had either been trained in standard police interviewing techniques or in the new Cognitive Interview Schedule. Each interview was taped and analysed for accuracy of recall. Results were recorded as:

■ the number of correct items recalled

■ the number of errors – this category was subdivided into incorrect items (number of items incorrectly recalled, e.g. the assailant was wearing a brown coat instead of a black one) and confabulated items (number of items described, but not actually shown on the video).

As you can see, people recalled considerably more items in the Cognitive than in the Standard interview, although error rates were very similar. The interviewees in this study were undergraduate students who watched videotapes and so the study could be criticized for artificiality. However, Fisher *et al.* (1989) later trained a group of detectives in Florida in the use of the Cognitive Interview and then assessed their performance when interviewing genuine witnesses to crimes. When their performance was compared to pretraining levels, it was found that the information gain was as much as 47 per cent.

There have since been a number of studies that have investigated the effectiveness of the Cognitive Interview Schedule. Bekerian and Dennett (1993) have reviewed 27 such studies and found in all cases that the Cognitive Interview approach has provided more accurate information than other interview procedures.

Average number of items recalled in Cognitive and Standard Interviews

	Cognitive	Standard
>> Correct items	41.15	29.4
>> Incorrect items	7.3	6.1
>> Confabulated items	0.7	0.4

Source: Based on Geiselman (1988)

Expert interview

Use the information provided by Elizabeth Loftus in the interview on the next page to outline:

1 why our memories are not always reliable

2 which factors are likely to improve the accuracy of eyewitness testimony.

WEBSITES

www.faculty.washington.edu/eloftus
To find out more about the work of Elizabeth Loftus.

www.faculty.washington.edu/chudler.stm0.html
For an interactive test on short-term memory.

ANSWERS TO ACTIVITIES

Activity, p. 4

Another possible explanation for Clive Wearing's inability to remember is that the memory trace is laid down, but fades away very quickly.

The third possibility is that the memory trace is laid down, but cannot be retrieved. The answer is not clear, but it is important to recognize that a normally functioning memory system must be capable of:

- registering information
- storing information over time
- retrieving information when required.

Activity, p. 9

1 Conrad used the experimental method to study encoding in STM.

2 A well-designed experiment allows a researcher to draw conclusions about the cause-and-effect relationship between the independent variable and the dependent variable. Conrad concluded that the nature of the stimuli (i.e. whether or not they sounded similar) affected the accuracy of participants' recall.

3 A laboratory study using artificial stimuli does not necessarily reflect everyday memory, so this study may be criticized for lacking ecological validity.

Activity, p. 14

1 The first and last words on the list are remembered best.

2 Where there are too many words for them all to be remembered, the primacy effect results in the first words being recalled and the recency effect results in the last words being recalled. According to Glanzer and Cunitz, the primacy effect occurs because words remembered from the beginning of the list have already been stored in LTM, while the words at the end of the list are still in STM and so are also easily recalled. The words in the middle of the list are displaced from STM memory but have not yet had a chance to be stored in LTM.

3 Words at the beginning of the list.

4 There is no recency effect for the 'distraction' group (but note that both groups show the primacy effect).

5 By introducing a distraction task before the participants recall the words, Glanzer and Cunitz show that information in STM is easily disrupted while information in LTM is not affected. Therefore, they claim, STM and LTM are two separate stores.

6 As interpreted by Glanzer and Cunitz, these results support the multi-store model. However, other researchers have suggested that recency effects can be explained differently. For example, Crowder (1993) proposed that recency effects occur because the most recent items are simply the most distinctive, not because they are held in a separate STM store.

Activity, p. 33

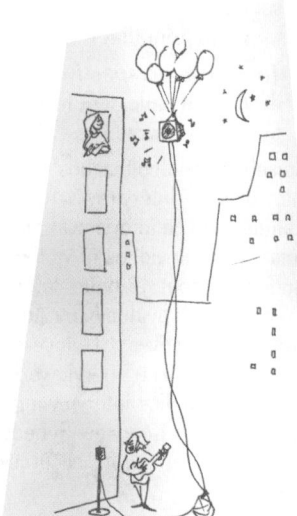

Figure 1.5 >>
Visual source for activity on p. 33

Eyewitness *testimony*

Elizabeth Loftus is Distinguished Professor of Psychology at University of California, Irvine. Professor Loftus's research has focused on human memory, eyewitness testimony and courtroom procedure. She has served as an expert witness or consultant in hundreds of cases, including the trial of former White House adviser, Oliver North, the trial of police officers accused in the Rodney King beating case, and the Michael Jackson case. Professor Loftus is the author of 20 books and over 250 scientific articles. Her fourth book, Eyewitness Testimony, *won a National Media Award from the American Psychology Foundation.*

Q **Eyewitness testimony is sometimes referred to as the 'most damning' of all evidence. It is based on memory, which is not a foolproof system. Why isn't it?**

A Human memory is far from perfect. Forgetfulness is a fact of life. One of the most obvious reasons for poor memory is that the information was never stored in the first place. We look at one part of a crime and fail even to notice other parts or details. But even if we are careful observers and take in a relatively accurate picture of what we have seen, it does not stay intact in memory. Other forces begin to corrode the original experience. With the passage of time, or with the introduction of interfering or contradictory facts, our memories can change, often without our conscious awareness. We can then come to believe in memories for details or events that never happened.

Elizabeth Loftus

Q **If psychological research has shown that eyewitness memory is sometimes unreliable, what are some of the situations where it is particularly unreliable?**

A Eyewitness memory can be mistaken because of things that go wrong at the time of the event itself. For example, poor lighting or extremely high stress or fright. Memory can also be mistaken because of things that go wrong after the event is over. For example, one witness is exposed to the mistaken recollection of another witness, or the witness is questioned in a biased way, or the test of memory is unfair in some way, and leads the witness to say the wrong thing.

Q **Are there some situations where eyewitness memory is likely to be more accurate?**

A Many factors are known to make eyewitness memory unreliable, such as poor lighting, brief exposure to the crime details, and long passage of time between the crime and the witness's memory report. Conversely, the absence of these factors would lead to more accurate eyewitness memory: good lighting, extended exposure to crime details, and a short passage of time between the crime and the memory report.

Other situations that lead to better eyewitness memory include:

- when the witness is close to the crime, rather than viewing from a distance
- when the witness and the criminal suspect are of the same race, rather than a different race
- when the witness is sober, rather than under the influence of alcohol or drugs
- when the witness is interviewed in a neutral manner, rather than in a biased or suggestive manner.

Check your understanding of eyewitness testimony by answering these questions. Try to do this from memory at first. You can check your answers by looking back through Topic 3.

1   What do you understand by the terms 'eyewitness testimony' and 'reconstructive memory'?

2   Why do you think that eyewitness testimony research is important?

3   Outline some of the ways participants changed the details in the 'War of the Ghosts' study.

4   What did Bartlett mean by the term 'schema'? Give three ways in which schemas might produced reconstructive memories, according to Cohen.

5   Explain why people sometimes falsely remember objects and events that did not exist in the original event.

6   Give two criticisms of the study by Loftus et al. (1978) that used the 'Yield' and 'Stop' signs.

7   Briefly outline two factors that affect the accuracy of eyewitness testimony.

8   Explain why the study by Christianson and Hubinette (1993) was different from studies carried out by Loftus.

9   What is meant by the 'Cognitive Interview'? Why do you think that it improves accuracy of recall?

10 To what extent has psychological research supported the idea that eyewitness testimony is largely unreliable?

REVISION SUMMARY

Having covered this topic you should be able to:

✓ define the terms 'eyewitness testimony' and 'reconstructive memory'

✓ describe the aims, procedures, findings, conclusions and criticisms for a key study in the areas of eyewitness testimony and reconstructive memory

✓ describe and evaluate findings from a range of research in the areas of eyewitness testimony and reconstructive memory.

UNIT SUMMARY

Topic 1: Short-term and long-term memory

■ **Short-term** and **long-term memory** (STM and LTM) are two types of memory store.

■ STM and LTM differ in terms of capacity, duration and encoding:
  – **Capacity** of STM is limited, but is infinite in LTM.
  – **Duration** of STM is limited to a few seconds, but can last up to a lifetime in LTM.
  – **Encoding** in STM is primarily acoustic, but is primarily semantic in LTM.

■ The **multi-store model** of memory, first proposed by **Atkinson and Shiffrin** in 1968, distinguishes between STM and LTM. It was the first information-processing model of memory and was very influential. However, it was criticized for being too simplistic and inflexible.

■ **Baddeley and Hitch** (1974) believed that STM operated more like a **working memory** and proposed that it consisted of a flexible and complex system of components under the control of a central executive. This model has been supported in many experimental studies. Its major weakness, however, is the lack of evidence about the precise role and functioning of the central executive.

- In the **levels of processing model**, **Craik and Lockhart** (1972) believed that the crucial factor in laying down new memories is the amount and depth of processing they receive. This model has received experimental support, but is criticized because it is descriptive rather than explanatory.

Topic 2: Forgetting

- We are generally good at retrieving information stored in memory, but we do sometimes forget. There are several **explanations** for **forgetting**.

- Decay and displacement seem to be the main forgetting mechanisms in STM:

  - **Decay** occurs when the memory trace simply fades away over time because of lack of rehearsal.

  - **Displacement** occurs because of the limited capacity of STM – new items can only find a place in STM if existing items are pushed out.

- Retrieval failure and interference account for much of the forgetting from LTM.

  - **Retrieval** failure occurs when the correct cues are unavailable.

  - **Interference** occurs when memory traces are obscured by other memories. In retroactive interference, new information interferes with old, and in proactive interference, old information interferes with new.

- **Cognitive theories** often fail to take account of **emotional factors**, but it seems possible that we forget some things because they are too painful to recall. **Freud** called this kind of forgetting **repression** or **motivated forgetting**, and suggested that we push threatening memories out of our conscious awareness. There is some research evidence to support this view, but it is difficult to demonstrate unconscious processes experimentally.

- **Flashbulb memories** have been a particular area of interest. These are memories associated with important events in our lives which appear to be remembered with enormous clarity and accuracy. However, some psychologists, such as **Neisser**, reject the idea that flashbulb memories are special in any way. They believe that they are subject to the same kinds of distortion and forgetting as other memories for events.

Topic 3: Eyewitness testimony

- One important application of memory research is **eyewitness testimony**. People are often able to recall events accurately and in detail, but eyewitness testimony can be fallible. Given the potentially serious consequences of inaccurate testimony, psychologists have sought to understand why people remember inaccurately and to find ways of improving their recall.

- One important factor is a tendency to distort or reconstruct memories. **Bartlett** introduced the concept of **reconstructive memory** to explain how we store memories in terms of our past knowledge and experience (**schemas**), which influence us when we come to recall the memory. Bartlett's research has been criticized for lack of experimental rigour, but the concept of schemas continues to be important.

- **Elizabeth Loftus**, one of the most influential researchers into eyewitness testimony, has been particularly concerned with the effects of misleading information provided after the event. Her studies, showing that testimony can be distorted by post-event information and by leading questions, have serious implications for the legal system.

Answering exam questions on Human memory

For sample examination questions and answers on Human memory, together with examiner comments on the answers, see pp. 251–2.

Unit 1 // Human memory

41

2 UNIT

ATTACHMENTS IN
Development

PREVIEW

After you have read this unit, you should be able to:

>> describe the development and variety of attachments, including individual and cross-cultural variations

>> explain how such attachments form (e.g. learning theory and Bowlby's theory of attachment)

>> distinguish between and discuss separation, deprivation and privation

>> describe the effects of being separated from one's attachment figure and being deprived of emotional care at this time, and the effects of having formed no attachments at all (privation)

>> discuss the critical issue of day care and how it may affect children's cognitive and social development.

INTRODUCTION

When you become attached to someone, it means you have formed a special bond or relationship with that person, and they with you. Relationships and attachments are important throughout people's lives, but they have a special importance during infancy. In Topic 1, we will look at the sequence of the development of attachments, and at how development varies from one individual to another. We will then consider explanations of *why* an infant becomes attached, and why they become attached to one particular person rather than another. (Psychologists generally use the term 'infant' to refer to children of less than 2 years; the term 'child' is used to refer to anyone between the age of 2 and adolescence.)

If attachments are so important, then this would lead you to expect that a loss of attachments would have negative consequences for an individual. In the second topic, we will consider the short- and long-term effects of separation on development. Furthermore, we will consider the different effects of loss of attachment (deprivation) and lack of attachment (privation).

Does this psychological research have any relevance to 'real life'? It most definitely has. People are very concerned about the effects of separation when parents go out to work and their children are placed in day care. Does this harm the cognitive and social development of their children? The final topic in this unit considers this critical issue.

Cara
Flanagan

GETTING YOU THINKING...

In psychology the term 'attachment' is used to describe a special kind of relationship between two people. Attachments are a special kind of affectional bond. According to Mary Ainsworth (1989), an affectional bond is a "relatively long-enduring tie in which the partner is important as a unique individual ... [and where there] is a

desire to maintain closeness to the partner". Bearing this in mind, do the following activities:

1 Make a list of the people with whom you have an affectional bond.

2 Now select from your list any people with whom your relationship would be better described as an attachment.

3 Make a list of the attachment behaviours that you and the other person use. These are the behaviours that psychologists could use to infer the existence of an attachment.

Now work in a small group to discuss the following:

4 If an attachment is designed to maintain proximity to another person, what attachment behaviours are commonly used by:

 (a) *infants* – to maintain closeness to their parents or to those who care for them?

 (b) *school-aged children* – to maintain closeness to their parents or to those who care for them?

 (c) *adults* – to maintain closeness to their parents or to those who cared for them?

KEY TERMS

Attachment: a strong emotional and reciprocal bond between two people, especially between an infant and its caregiver(s). Attachments serve to maintain proximity between infant and caregiver because each experiences distress when separated. The attachment relationship also serves as a basis for subsequent emotional development.

Secure attachment: the optimal form of attachment, associated with healthy emotional and social development. Securely attached infants feel content to explore a strange environment using their caregiver as a safe base. They show some distress when left by their caregiver, but are relatively easily comforted and show joy at reunion. Securely attached children are more likely to show stranger anxiety than insecurely attached children.

Insecure attachment: a less optimal form of attachment, at least in Western culture. Insecurely attached children show disturbed behaviour during separation and reunion. One type of insecure attachment is called resistance-insecure. Children who are resistant-insecure are distressed on separation and resist reunion with their caregiver. A second type, avoidant-insecure, are indifferent at separation and avoid contact on reunion. Insecurely attached children tend to have less successful relationships with peers, lovers and their own children later in life.

Cross-cultural variation: variations between people of different cultures. A culture is a set of beliefs and customs that bind a group of people together, such as child-rearing practices. These practices may influence the kind of attachments, so that people from different cultural groups have different kinds of attachments with their children. These differences tell us something about the effects of child-rearing practices on attachment.

THE DEVELOPMENT OF ATTACHMENTS

Attachment is a strong emotional tie that develops over time between an infant and their primary caregiver(s) – the person(s) to whom they are most strongly attached. It is a reciprocal tie because each partner is attached to the other. Maurer and Maurer (1989) suggested that attachments "are welded in the heat of interactions". In other words, attachments depend on interaction between two people rather than their simply being together. Maccoby (1980) identified four characteristic effects of this tie:

- seeking proximity, especially at times of stress
- distress on separation
- pleasure when reunited
- general orientation of behaviour towards the primary caregiver.

Schaffer and Emerson (1964) conducted a classic study of the development of attachments in order to investigate the way infant behaviours change over time. Specifically, Schaffer and Emerson wanted to find out how old infants were when they first became attached, who they became attached to and how strong these attachments were. Schaffer and Emerson also wanted to search for any individual differences between infants in their attachment behaviours. They studied 60 infants from a mainly working-class area of Glasgow. The infants were observed every four weeks until they were 1 year old and then again at 18 months. At the start of the investigation, the youngest participant was 5 weeks and the oldest 23 weeks.

Observations were conducted in the children's homes. Schaffer and Emerson used two measures to determine the strength of attachment. One was separation anxiety

– the distress shown by the infant when separated from their main caregiver. This is regarded as a sign of attachment because infants only show such distress when separated from certain people. Schaffer and Emerson asked the mothers about situations where separation protest was shown, and to whom these protests were directed. This meant that they could rate the strength of attachment at each monthly visit. They asked the mothers to consider seven everyday situations, i.e. where the infant was:

1 left alone in a room
2 left with other people
3 left in their pram outside the house
4 left in their pram outside the shops
5 left in their cot at night
6 put down after being held by an adult
7 passed by while sitting in a cot or chair.

The second measure of attachment was stranger anxiety. Very young infants show no anxiety when they are left with a stranger but, at a certain age, this stranger anxiety starts. Schaffer and Emerson regarded this as another sign of the onset of attachment. Schaffer and Emerson measured stranger anxiety by approaching the infant at the start of every visit and noting at what point the infant started to whimper, thus displaying anxiety.

Schaffer and Emerson's findings were as follows.

- *Age of first attachment* – Half of the children showed their first specific attachment (i.e. displayed separation anxiety with respect to one primary caregiver) between 6 and 8 months. Fear of strangers occurred about a month later in all the children.

- *Attachment figures* – Soon after one main attachment was formed, the infants also became attached to other people. By 18 months very few (13 per cent) were attached to only one person. One third of the infants had five or more attachments, such as their father, grandparent or older sibling. In 65 per cent of the children, the first specific attachment was to the mother. In a further 30 per cent the mother was the first joint object of attachment. Fathers were rarely the first sole object of attachment (3 per cent), but 27 per cent of them were the joint first object.

- *Strength of attachment* – This peaked in the first month after attachment behaviour first appeared. However, there were large individual differences. Schaffer and Emerson observed that intensely attached infants had mothers who responded quickly to their demands (high responsiveness) and offered the child the most interaction. Infants who were weakly attached had mothers who failed to interact.

Seeking proximity in times of stress a sign of attachment. Who do you turn to when you are anxious?

- *Time spent with infant* – In 39 per cent of the cases, the person who usually fed, bathed and changed the child was *not* the child's primary attachment object. In other words, many of the mothers were not the individuals who performed these tasks, yet the mother did tend to be the main attachment object.

The three main conclusions are these:

- Specific attachments appear to be formed first around the age of 7 months.
- Multiple attachments develop soon afterwards.
- Attachments seemed to be formed to individuals who were prepared to play, be responsive and interact socially with the child, rather than simply with those who were most often present.

The sequence of development

Schaffer and Emerson's account indicates a sequence of development: infants display separation anxiety first with respect to one primary caregiver, and soon afterwards they show separation anxiety from other caregivers. Stranger anxiety appears to be a developmental stage. Such stage accounts are common in developmental psychology as a means of outlining the *typical* ages when infants and children achieve certain milestones – physical or psychological. Sometimes the word 'phases' is used instead to suggest that there are no clear distinctions between one stage and another.

John Bowlby (1969) proposed a four-phase framework for viewing the changes that take place in attachment behaviour over time. The information in Table 2.1 is based on this account.

An evaluation of Bowlby's phase account

More recent research suggests that some aspects of this phase account are not entirely accurate. Very young infants appear to be far more social than was once thought. They recognize their caregivers at an earlier age and interact far more with other people. For example, Bushnell *et al.* (1989) found that infants who were less than 24 hours old looked longer at their mother than at another woman.

Table 2.1 >> Phases in the development of attachment

Age	Phase	Description
>> 0–2 months	Pre-attachments (indiscriminate social responsiveness)	Infants produce similar responses to all objects, whether they are animate or inanimate. Towards the end of this period, infants are beginning to show a greater preference for social stimuli, such as a smiling face, and to be more content when they are with people.
>> 2–6 months	Attachment-in-the-making (recognition of familiar people)	Infants become more social. They prefer human company and can distinguish between familiar and unfamiliar people. However, they are still relatively easily comforted by anyone and do not yet show anxiety with strangers. The most distinctive feature of this phase is their general sociability (enjoyment of being with people).
>> Around 6 months	Specific attachments (separation protest and stranger anxiety)	Infants begin to show a distinctly different sort of protest when one particular person puts them down (separation protest). Equally, they show especial joy at reunion with that person and are most comforted by this person. They are said to have formed a specific attachment. Around the same time, the infant also begins to display stranger anxiety, an uneasiness with strangers. Soon after the main attachment is formed, the infant also develops a wider circle of attachments depending on how many consistent relationships they have. Nevertheless, according to Bowlby, the primary attachment bond remains special (called monotropy).
>> 2 years onwards	Goal-corrected partnership	Relationships become more two-sided. The infant learns to predict and understand the mother figure's behaviour, which means that the mother's behaviour can be consciously controlled. The mother figure has been doing this all along. In this enduring phase, individuals in a relationship can adjust their behaviour to the others' needs, the beginning of a real partnership adjusted according to each individual's needs.

Source: based on Bowlby (1969)

Camras *et al.* (1991) found that, by about 3 months, infants are beginning to smile more at familiar than unfamiliar people, suggesting that they are relatively discriminating in their social interactions, even at that early age.

As regards the appearance of separation anxiety, there appears to be close agreement, according to a recent review of research evidence by Schaffer (1998). This may be explained in terms of general mental or cognitive development. Around the same age that the first specific attachments form (at about 6 months), there are other aspects of development that are also changing. Perhaps most important is the infant's sense of object permanence – the knowledge that things that are out of sight actually still exist. It was Piaget (1954) who introduced the concept that younger infants lose interest in things that disappear (you can demonstrate this yourself by trying to play the game of peek-a-boo with a very young infant – they are simply not interested). Once infants have acquired a sense of object permanence, they are also aware that when their caregiver leaves the room, the caregiver continues to exist. They continue to watch for the caregiver's return rather than instantly turning their attention to something else.

We should also consider physical development. It is no accident that the time when specific attachments develop in human infants is also the time when they first become mobile.

Interestingly, Ainsworth (1967) reported that Ugandan babies expressed stranger anxiety at the slightly earlier age of 6 months *and* that their motor development was more advanced.

Therefore, we can conclude that there is support for the view that a certain kind of attachment appears around this age of 6 months – the kind of attachment where an infant expresses separation anxiety. However, other evidence is less supportive of the phase theory. Infants are much more social at an earlier age than was once thought and the attachment process begins from the moment of birth, if not before that.

Games such as peek-a-boo only work when infants have acquired a sense of object permanence

VARIETY OF ATTACHMENTS: INDIVIDUAL DIFFERENCES

We will now move from the topic of the development of attachments to the topic of individual differences, i.e. the ways that attachment varies from one individual to another, and from one culture to another.

Secure and insecure attachment

One way to distinguish between individual infants is in terms of the *quality* of the attachment bond between them and their mother figure or primary caregiver. Schaffer and Emerson (see p. 44) found that some infants were more strongly attached to their primary caregiver than others. This was shown by the extent of their anxiety when separated from their caregiver.

Mary Ainsworth, who worked with Bowlby in the 1950s, sought to develop a reliable method of measuring quality of attachment using a procedure called the Strange Situation, which is described in the panel on the right and in the key study on p. 47.

The main reason for having a method of classifying attachment is to be able to measure the effects of attachment on later behaviour – the long-term consequences of early attachment. Bowlby claimed that early attachment is important for healthy psychological development. In order to test this belief we need some

The Strange Situation

What happens in the Strange Situation:

1 Mother and child are introduced to the room.

2 Mother and child are left alone and the child can investigate the toys.

3 A stranger enters the room and talks with the mother. The stranger gradually approaches the infant with a toy.

4 Mother leaves the child alone with the stranger, and the stranger interacts with the child.

5 Mother returns to greet and comfort the child.

6 The child is left on its own.

7 The stranger returns and tries to engage with the child.

8 Mother returns, greets and picks up the child. The stranger leaves inconspicuously.

measuring secure and insecure attachment by Ainsworth & Bell (1970)

Aim >>

To produce a method for assessing quality of attachment by placing an infant in a situation of mild stress (to encourage the infant to seek comfort) and of novelty (to encourage exploration behaviour). Both comfort-seeking and exploration behaviour are indicators of the quality of attachment.

Procedures >>

- About 100 middle-class American infants and their mothers took part in this study.
- A method of controlled observation was developed. This involved observing infants with their mothers during a set of predetermined activities (this is known as the Strange Situation – see the box on p. 46 for a description). All the sessions, except the first one, took three minutes.
- Observers recorded the infants' and mothers' behaviours, especially noting the following:
  - separation anxiety: the unease the infant showed when left by the caregiver
  - the infant's willingness to explore
  - stranger anxiety: the infant's response to the presence of a stranger
  - reunion behaviour: the way the caregiver was greeted on return.

Findings >>

The observational record led Ainsworth and Bell to classify the infants into three broad groups:

- *Type B: Securely attached* (66 per cent) – One group of infants tended to explore the unfamiliar room; they were subdued when their mother left and greeted her positively when she returned. The infants showed moderate avoidance of the stranger, although were friendly when the mother was present. The mothers were described as sensitive.
- *Type A: Avoidant-insecure* (22 per cent) – A second group did not orientate to their mother while investigating the toys and room; they did not seem concerned by her absence and showed little interest in her when she returned. These infants also avoided the stranger, but not as strongly as they avoided the mother on her return. It was observed that these mothers sometimes ignored their infants.
- *Type C: Resistant-insecure* (12 per cent) – A third group showed intense distress, particularly when their mother was absent, but they rejected her when she returned. These infants showed ambivalent behaviour towards the stranger, similar to the pattern of resistance and interest shown to the mother on her return. These mothers appeared to behave ambivalently towards their infants.

Conclusions >>

- This study shows that there are significant individual differences between infants.
- It also shows that most American children are securely attached.
- There appears to be a distinct association between the mothers' behaviour and the infants' attachment type, which suggests that mothers' behaviour may be important in determining attachment type.

Criticisms >>

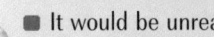

- It would be unreasonable to make generalizations about all infant behaviour on the basis of this sample. The study and its findings are restricted to middle-class American infants, i.e. are culturally biased.
- In another study, Main and Cassidy (1988) identified a further group of children; this classification group is referred to as disorganized (type D). These children show inconsistent behaviour, confusion and indecision. They also tend to freeze or show stereotyped behaviours such as rocking.

AO2 check One of the major concerns with any study is the extent to which it is *valid,* i.e. that the findings of the study are legitimate or real. A study that is based on a particular group of people (in this case, middle-class American infants) can only really tell us about how *this* particular group of people behaves. This is called *population validity*.

Unit 2 // Attachments in development

reliable and valid measure of early attachment. Any form of measurement (such as a ruler) should be reliable or consistent. It should also be valid – it should be measuring something that is real.

In general, studies have found that for a particular child the Strange Situation Classification (SSC) is usually the same at different ages (i.e. it is reliable). For example, a study conducted in Germany found 78 per cent of the children were classified in the same way at the ages of 1 and 6 (Wartner *et al.* 1994). When differences occur, these are often associated with changes in the form of care, such as changes in family structure (Melhuish 1993).

On the other hand, there are studies that challenge the meaning or validity of the SSC. For example, it has been found that infants behave differently depending on whom they are with. For example, they may be classified as having a secure attachment to their mother and an avoidant relationship with their father (Lamb 1977). This suggests that what is being measured is particular attachments rather than a general attachment type. For example, if infants are securely attached to their mother but appear insecurely attached to their father, then what are we to conclude about these infants' attachment type? This leads us to conclude that the Strange Situation only measures particular relationships and not some general characteristic of the child.

Van IJzendoorn *et al.* (1992) discussed this multiple caregiver paradox: the idea that infants have qualitatively different relationships with different caregivers (mother, father and perhaps a professional caregiver). They found that the best predictor of later development was a kind of aggregate of all the child's attachments – by considering a kind of average of all the child's attachments. This suggests the Strange Situation measurement is valid, but that attachment type must be derived from a consideration of more than just one attachment relationship.

One important question about attachment types is whether they are *caused* by the primary caregiver's behaviour or something else. Why are some children securely attached whereas others are not? Ainsworth and Bell supposed that secure attachments were the result of mothers being sensitive to their children's needs. Isabella *et al.* (1989) supported this in a study that found that mothers and infants who tended to be responsive to each other at 1 month were more likely at 12 months to have a secure relationship. Those who had a more one-sided pattern of interaction tended to have insecure relationships. If you recall, Schaffer and Emerson (1964) produced similar findings. Ainsworth *et al.* (1974) called this the caregiver sensitivity hypothesis, that attachment depends on the warm and loving responsiveness of the caregiver.

There is an alternative explanation. Some infants may form secure attachments because they are born more friendly. This is called the temperament hypothesis

(Kagan 1982). Certain innate personality or temperamental characteristics might account for behaviour in the Strange Situation, rather than it being the result of the caregiver's sensitivity. (The term *innate* refers to any behaviour that is inherited.) It may be that some children are innately more vulnerable to stress, so each child will respond differently according to their innate temperament. Research has found, for example, that newborns who showed signs of behavioural instability (e.g. tremors or shaking) were less likely to become securely attached to their mother than were newborns who did not (Belsky and Rovine 1987). Thus, there is a possibility that infant temperament, rather than caregiver sensitivity, contributes to the form of attachment and to later behaviour.

Evaluation of the Strange Situation technique

The importance of the Strange Situation as a research tool is that it enables us to assess whether or not children are securely attached and how attachment type relates to later behaviours. We have already considered some evidence about the reliability and validity of the SSC, including the question of ecological validity (do these findings apply to settings beyond the laboratory?) and population validity (do these findings apply to societies other than middle-class Americans?). In the next section we will consider the validity of the Strange Situation in relation to research conducted in different cultural settings.

Cross-cultural variations in attachment

Most psychological research has been conducted in the USA, which means that most psychological theories are based on this group of people and assume that all other people the world over will be similar. In the last few decades, psychologists have come to recognize that this is a narrow view of human behaviour. To redress the balance, psychologists endeavour to look at studies conducted in different cultural settings to see whether their theories are universal (apply to all people because they concern innate behaviours) or are culture-bound (apply only to the culture in which the research took place because the behaviour is related to cultural practices).

An increasing number of studies have measured attachment behaviours in cultural settings outside middle-class America. Strictly speaking, these are not cross-cultural studies as they do not always explicitly make comparisons between two or more different cultures. However, this comparison is implicit in many of the studies, as is demonstrated by their conclusions about cultural variation. Note that culture is not a group of people, but is the beliefs and customs that a group of people shares, such as its child-rearing practices. A subculture is a group within a society that shares many practices with the dominant culture but also has some special, different characteristics.

Research on secure and insecure attachment

Researchers in many different countries have used the Strange Situation to investigate secure and insecure attachment. The results of 32 such studies undertaken in eight different countries have been summarized (this is called a *meta-analysis*) by Van IJzendoorn and Kroonenberg (1988), as shown in Table 2.2.

Bee (1999) also points out that the most striking finding of the data that Van IJzendoorn and Kroonenberg (1988) bring together is that there is considerable consistency across cultures. She concludes that it is likely that the same caregiver–infant interactions contribute to secure and insecure attachments in all cultures. However, the universal nature of caregiver–infant interactions may be cultural rather than innate. Van IJzendoorn and Kroonenberg observe that the similarity between countries may well be due to the increasing effects of the mass media (i.e. nurture rather than nature).

The finding of consistency across cultures is in direct contrast to the conclusions drawn by Takahashi (below) and others such as Grossmann and Grossmann (1991), who studied German infants and found that these infants were more likely to be classified as insecurely attached. This may be related to the German cultural norm of keeping some interpersonal distance between parents and children. As a result, infants do not engage in proximity-seeking behaviours in the Strange Situation and thus *appear* to be insecurely attached. It may not

Table 2.2 >> Cross-cultural differences in secure and insecure attachment

Country	No. of studies	Percentage of each attachment type (to the nearest whole number)		
		Secure	Avoidant	Resistant
>> West Germany	3	57	35	8
>> Great Britain	1	75	22	3
>> Netherlands	4	67	26	7
>> Sweden	1	74	22	4
>> Israel	2	64	7	29
>> Japan	2	68	5	27
>> China	1	50	25	25
>> United States	18	65	21	14
>> Overall average		65	21	14

Source: Van IJzendoorn and Kroonenberg (1988, pp. 150–1)

be reasonable to make comparisons between different countries/cultures because it appears likely that the Strange Situation may not mean the same thing in different cultures. This means the findings from Van IJzendoorn and Kroonenberg lack validity.

Another limitation of the data presented in Table 2.2 is that, although it tells us how many studies were included from each country, it does not include the number of infants involved in each study. You need, therefore, to be cautious about interpreting these figures because in many cases the sample sizes were fairly small. For example, there were only 36 infants in the single Chinese study.

KEY STUDY >> CROSS-CULTURAL VARIATIONS

study of Japanese children by Takahashi (1990)

Aim >>

To consider whether it is appropriate to use the Strange Situation procedure with Japanese children. The key question is whether the Strange Situation is a valid procedure for cultures other than the original one, i.e. other than American, middle-class, white, home-reared infants and their mothers.

By making comparisons between the American and Japanese group, it may be possible to reveal the cultural assumptions on which the procedure is based.

Procedures >>

- The participants were 60 middle-class Japanese infants, aged 1 year, boys and girls, and their mothers. They were all raised at home.
- The infants and mothers were observed in the Strange Situation (as described on p. 46).

Findings >>

- 68 per cent of the infants were classified as securely attached, almost identical to the original American sample.
- There were no infants classified as avoidant-insecure.
- 32 per cent were classified as resistant-insecure.
- When the observational data were examined in more detail, differences emerged. The Japanese infants were much more disturbed after being left alone. In fact, the 'infant alone' step was stopped for 90 per cent of the participants because the infants were so distressed. If the infants had not become so distressed, many more of them (possibly more than 80 per cent) would have been classified as securely attached (the observation of distress led to an alternative classification).

Conclusions >>

- The findings suggest that there are cross-cultural variations in the way infants respond to separation and being left alone. This difference may be due to the fact that Japanese infants experience much less separation, for example they generally sleep with their parents until over 2 years of age, are carried around on their mothers' backs and bathe with parents. Japanese infants are almost never left alone. This means that, for them, the Strange Situation was more than mildly stressful, and thus the behaviours observed were reactions to extreme stress – not the original aim of the Strange Situation.
- The findings also highlight a second cross-cultural variation – the total lack of avoidant behaviour in this sample. This can also be explained in cultural terms. Japanese children are taught that such behaviour is impolite and they would be actively discouraged from displaying it.
- The final conclusion must be that the Strange Situation does not have the same meaning for the Japanese as it does for American participants and therefore is not a valid form of assessment for that culture.

Criticisms >>

- Research with children, especially with infants, needs to be especially careful in terms of potential psychological harm to participants, which is an important ethical issue.
- Takahashi's study was carried out on a limited sample of only middle-class, home-reared infants (as was the original study by Ainsworth and Bell). It may therefore not be reasonable to generalize these findings to all Japanese people, although the results do demonstrate that there are important cultural or subcultural differences in attachment.

AO2 check

A common means of criticizing any study is to consider ethical issues and guidelines, but you must be clear about *why* any particular study infringes ethical guidelines (considered fully in Unit 5). One of these guidelines is that participants should be protected as far as possible from psychological harm. Takahashi showed sensitivity by stopping those observations where infants became too distressed. However, the study itself was not stopped, even though it became obvious that extreme distress was likely.

When using any kind of psychological assessment, it is important to be cautious about attributing what is measured (in this case the type of attachment) to the individual. There might be something about the test situation that makes some of these infants *appear to be* insecurely attached.

Research on monotropy and multiple attachments

Bowlby (1969) claimed that infants need one special attachment relationship, which is qualitatively different from all others, in order to develop an internal working model and emotional maturity. He used the term monotropy, which literally means 'being raised by one person', to describe this special relationship which is at the top of the hierarchy of all other relationships. The internal working model is a mental model of the world that enables individuals to predict, control and manipulate their environment. Individuals have many such models or schemas (a concept you should be familiar with from your study of cognitive psychology). Some schemas are concerned with the environment or world in general, while others are organismal and tell us about ourselves and our relationship with the world. One such organismal model is concerned with the relationship between oneself and one's primary caregiver, and Bowlby suggested that this model provides a basis for all other relationships.

There is considerable debate about whether this primary bond (monotropy) is universally true. In some cultures, children have equivalent relationships with many caregivers, and still develop into psychologically healthy adults. Thomas (1998) questions whether the tendency to form a single main attachment is actually good for healthy psychological development. It might be more desirable to have a network of attachments to sustain the needs of a growing infant who has a variety of demands for social and emotional interactions. Thomas claims that in Caribbean cultures, multiple

attachments are the rule. Even in Western European culture, infants do form several attachments and these are all beneficial, probably precisely because of their qualitative differences. For example, fathers' style of play is more often physically stimulating and unpredictable, whereas mothers are more likely to hold their infants, soothe them, attend to their needs and read them stories (Parke 1981).

On the other hand, in Schaffer and Emerson's study (1964), it was found that even though infants do form multiple attachments, they appear usually to have one primary attachment. Ainsworth (1967) studied members of the Ganda tribe of Uganda, where the pattern of childcare involved multiple carers, and concluded that the infants nevertheless formed one primary attachment. Tronick *et al.* (1992) studied the Efe (Pygmies from Zaire, Africa) who live in extended family groups. Infants and children are looked after by whoever is closest to hand. They are breastfed by different women, but usually sleep with their own mother. Tronick and colleagues found that by the age of 12 months, the infants still show a preference for their mothers, a single primary attachment.

A study by Fox (1977) looked at life in kibbutzim in Israel, where children spend most of their time with nurses called metapelets, but see their mothers for a few hours a day after work. When the children were placed in the Strange Situation, they protested equally when either mother or metapelet left, but were more comforted by their mothers at reunion. This would again suggest that, despite having multiple carers, the infants still had one special relationship. However, we should note that the metapelets changed fairly frequently. They also had to divide their attention among many children and had less interest in any one individual, which would explain why the children were usually less attached to their metapelet. On the other hand, the children slept communally, which might reduce their maternal attachments.

Studies in Africa found the existence of a single primary attachment even when childcare involved multiple carers

EXPLANATIONS OF ATTACHMENT

Why do infants become attached to one person rather than another? What is the purpose of attachment? We have already considered some answers to these questions. For instance, it appears that a child becomes attached to a sensitive caregiver (Ainsworth's caregiver sensitivity hypothesis). Here, we will focus on two explanations for who and why: learning theory and Bowlby's approach. Learning theory takes the view that attachment is a learned process (nurture), whereas Bowlby argued that attachment is an inherited behaviour (nature). These are examples of the 'nature–nurture' debate.

Learning theory

Learning theory is the view put forward by behaviourists to explain how all behaviour is acquired, using the principles of conditioning:

- *Classical conditioning* – Dogs salivate when they feed. Salivation is an unconditioned response (UR) to an unconditioned stimulus (US), in this case food. The stimulus (US) and response (UR) are innately linked. If a bell is rung every time food appears, the animal comes to associate bell and food so that the bell alone will produce the UR. The bell was a neutral stimulus (NS), but is now a conditioned stimulus (CS) and the salivation is now a conditioned response (CR). Thus the animal has learned a new stimulus–response link.

- *Operant conditioning* – An animal is placed in a cage where food will be delivered if it presses a lever. At first the animal presses the lever accidentally and is rewarded by receiving food. This reward increases the probability that the behaviour (lever pressing) will be repeated. The food or reward is reinforcing. If the lever press results in an electric shock, this will decrease the probability of the response being repeated. The shock acts as a punishment.

Classical conditioning

We can explain attachment in terms of the principles of classical conditioning. An infant is born with reflex responses. The stimulus of food produces a response of pleasure – an unconditioned stimulus and an unconditioned response respectively. The person providing the food (usually the mother) becomes associated with this pleasure and therefore becomes a conditioned stimulus. The food-giver then becomes a source of pleasure in herself, independent of whether or not food is supplied. This, according to learning theory, is the basis of the attachment bond.

Operant conditioning

Dollard and Miller (1950) proposed a further adaptation of the learning theory account of attachment, based in part on operant conditioning, but with the inclusion of a mental state (mental states are usually excluded from behaviourist accounts). Dollard and Miller suggested that the human infant, when hungry, feels uncomfortable and enters a drive state. The drive motivates the baby to find some way to

lessen the discomfort of being hungry. Of course, in early infancy the baby can do little more than howl and it is up to other people to feed it. Being fed satisfies the infant's hunger and makes it feel comfortable again. This results in drive reduction, which is rewarding, and the child learns that food is a reward or primary reinforcer. The person who supplies the food, the mother, is associated with the food and becomes a secondary reinforcer. From then on, the infant seeks to be with this person because she is now a source of reward. The infant has thus become attached.

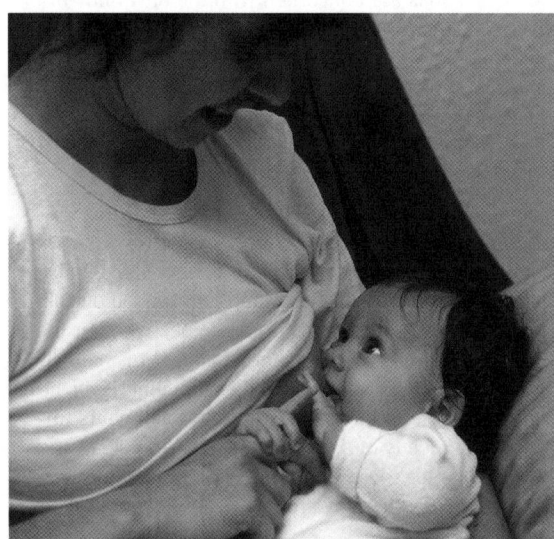

ACTIVITY

Learning theory and attachment

Learning theory predicts that an infant's attachment will be to the person who gives greatest pleasure or drive reduction. Look back to the description of the study that Schaffer and Emerson carried out in 1964 (see p. 44) and also at the classic research undertaken by Harlow and Harlow, investigating the formation of love in infant monkeys, described below on p. 53.

Does the evidence from these studies (a) confirm, or (b) contradict the predictions from learning theory? Explain the reasons for your answer.

The formation of love in infant monkeys (Harlow and Harlow 1962)

Perhaps the most famous study to show that attachment is not based on the supply of food was conducted by Harlow and Harlow on infant monkeys. The infant monkeys were placed in a cage with two wire mesh cylinders, each with a face. One cylinder was bare and provided the baby monkey with milk from a teat, while the other cylinder was covered with towelling (giving contact comfort). If food were the cause of attachment then one would expect the monkeys to cling to the bare cylinder that supplied the milk. In fact, the monkeys spent most of their time on the towelling-covered cylinder and would jump on to this cylinder when frightened, a characteristic of attachment behaviour. They also used the towelling-covered cylinder as a secure base for exploration, another characteristic of attachment behaviour. The study indicated that simply supplying food is not sufficient for the formation of attachment.

However, the towelling-covered 'mother' did not provide sufficient 'love' to enable healthy psychological development. In later life, the monkeys were either indifferent or abusive to other monkeys and had difficulty with mating and parenting. This shows that contact comfort is preferable to food comfort, but not sufficient for healthy development. Presumably, infants need a responsive carer.

In another experiment four young monkeys were raised on their own, without any 'mother'. They spent the first few months huddled together, but gradually developed more independence and finally appeared to have suffered no ill-effects. This suggests that the infant–infant affectional bond can be just as effective as the mother–infant bond.

This work, which would now be considered unethical, was critical in demonstrating that neither feeding nor physical contact could explain attachment and healthy development.

One of the monkeys in the Harlow and Harlow research, shown with the cloth-covered 'mother'

Evaluation of learning theory as an explanation of attachment

Clearly, learning theory predicts that an infant's attachment will be to the person who gives greatest pleasure or drive reduction, probably the person who feeds the infant. Schaffer and Emerson (1964) found that this was not always true. In their study, fewer than half of the infants had a primary attachment to the person who usually fed, bathed and changed them. Another piece of evidence against the role of reinforcement came from the classic research by Harlow and Harlow on the behaviour of rhesus monkeys (see above). This, again, showed that feeding was not the main source of reinforcement and, therefore, not the sole basis for attachment. However, Harlow and Harlow did find that contact comfort was a key source of reinforcement, but this was still not sufficient for healthy development. We should, of course, be cautious about making any generalizations about human behaviour on the basis of research with rhesus monkeys.

Behaviourism is often criticized for being reductionist. This means it 'reduces' the complexities of human behaviour to over-simple ideas such as stimulus, response and reinforcement. It then uses these concepts as building blocks to explain complex human behaviours such as attachment. It may be that these behaviourist concepts are too simple to explain such a complex behaviour as attachment.

Bowlby's theory

John Bowlby (1969) proposed that attachment was important for survival. Infants are physically helpless and need adults to feed, care for and protect them; without such assistance they cannot survive. Therefore, it is likely that infants are born with an innate tendency to form an attachment that serves to increase their chances of survival. Since attachment is a reciprocal process, it is also likely that adults are innately programmed to become attached to their infants – otherwise they would not respond to their infant, and the attachment bond would not develop.

It is also likely that attachment has a long-term benefit in addition to the short-term benefit of ensuring food and safety. In the long term, it may be of fundamental importance for emotional relationships because it provides a template for relationships, as a result of the internal working model discussed earlier (see p. 51). These short- and long-term effects of attachment are similar to the effects of imprinting observed in some non-human animals (see below).

There are three important features of Bowlby's theory:

- Infants and carers are programmed to become attached.
- As attachment is a biological process, it takes place during a critical period of development or not at all.
- Attachment plays a role in later development – monotropy and the continuity hypothesis.

Innate programming

Bowlby suggested that attachment could be understood within the framework of evolutionary principles, that all psychological and physical characteristics are naturally selected. A characteristic is selected because it helps those individuals who possess it to survive and reproduce. This notion of selection is clearly a passive one: no one is doing the selecting – it is selective pressure. The essential principle is that any inherited behaviour that increases an individual's chances of survival and reproduction will be passed on to the next generation and thus continues to reappear in subsequent generations. It has been selected because of its usefulness.

The result is that infants are born programmed to become attached, and adults are also programmed to form this kind of relationship with their infants. Social releasers are necessary to ensure an interaction takes place. These are social behaviours that elicit a caregiving reaction from another, such as smiling, crying, cooing and simply looking appealing. Bowlby suggested that these behaviours are innate in infants (and other animals), and that the responses are innate in caregivers. They are critical in the process of forming attachments.

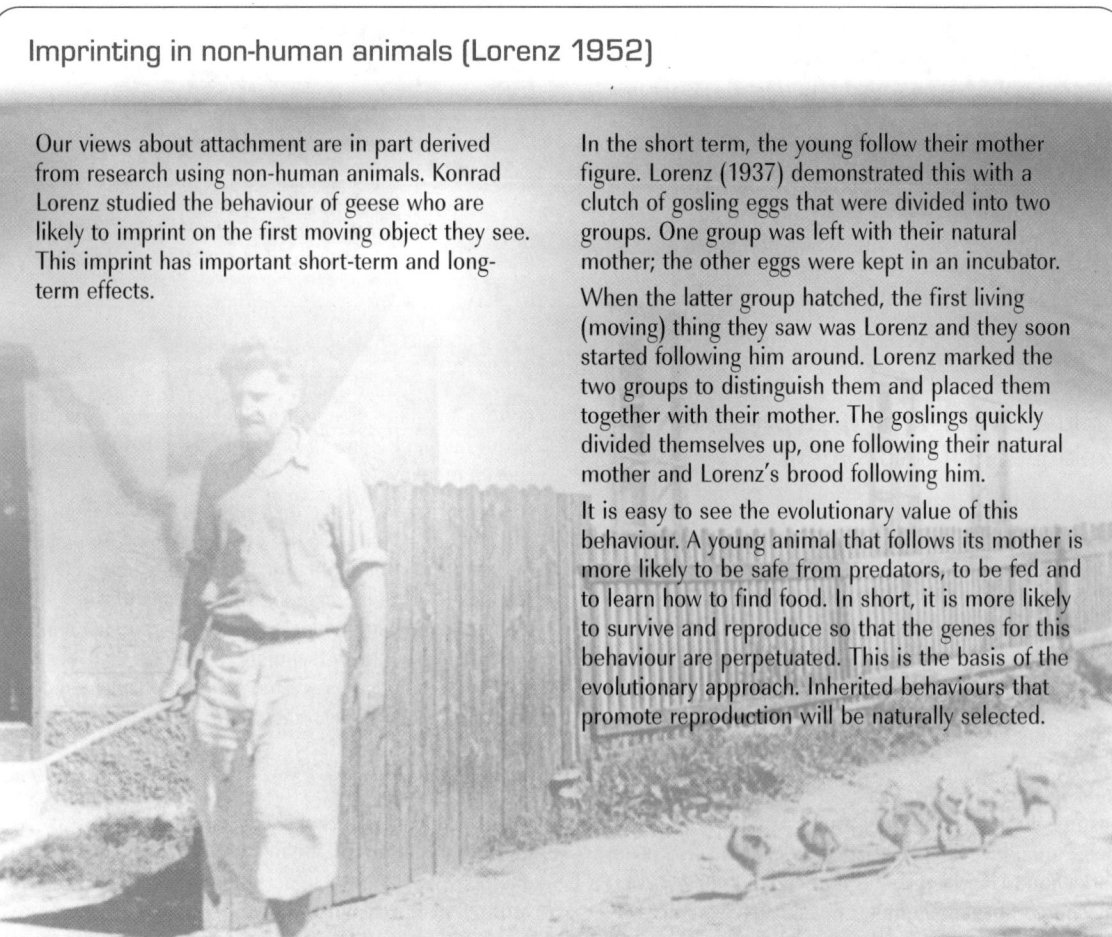

Imprinting in non-human animals (Lorenz 1952)

Our views about attachment are in part derived from research using non-human animals. Konrad Lorenz studied the behaviour of geese who are likely to imprint on the first moving object they see. This imprint has important short-term and long-term effects.

In the short term, the young follow their mother figure. Lorenz (1937) demonstrated this with a clutch of gosling eggs that were divided into two groups. One group was left with their natural mother; the other eggs were kept in an incubator.

When the latter group hatched, the first living (moving) thing they saw was Lorenz and they soon started following him around. Lorenz marked the two groups to distinguish them and placed them together with their mother. The goslings quickly divided themselves up, one following their natural mother and Lorenz's brood following him.

It is easy to see the evolutionary value of this behaviour. A young animal that follows its mother is more likely to be safe from predators, to be fed and to learn how to find food. In short, it is more likely to survive and reproduce so that the genes for this behaviour are perpetuated. This is the basis of the evolutionary approach. Inherited behaviours that promote reproduction will be naturally selected.

Social releasers

A social releaser is any behaviour that encourages a caregiver reaction from another person. Work with one other person to draw up a list of ten social releasers used by infants, children or individuals of any age. For each social releaser on your list, state whether you think that the behaviour is innate (I) or learned (L) and identify what response(s) you think it might elicit from a caregiver.

Do you think that the caregiver's responses to the social releasers are innate or learned? To what extent do you think caregivers differ in their responses to the same social releaser, and why?

A critical period

The concept of a critical period is a feature of biological characteristics. If development does not take place during a set developmental period, then it may not take place at all. For instance, in the development of the human embryo, the arms begin to develop between Day 24 and Day 26. Any interference with development at this critical stage will permanently affect the limbs' development. If attachment is innate and therefore biological, we would expect there to be a critical period for its development. Bowlby suggested that if a child does not form an attachment before the age of $2\frac{1}{2}$ years, then it would not be possible thereafter. We will consider the evidence for this in the section on deprivation and privation.

The continuity hypothesis

The argument behind the continuity hypothesis is that the relationship with one special attachment figure (monotropy) provides an infant with an internal working model of relationships (described on p. 51). Secure children develop a positive working model of themselves, based on their feelings of security derived from having one sensitive, emotionally responsive and supportive primary caregiver (the caregiver sensitivity hypothesis). In contrast, avoidant children are assumed to have a primary caregiver who is rejecting, resulting in their having a working model of themselves as unacceptable and unworthy. Ambivalent children have a primary caregiver who is inconsistent; consequently, the children tend to have a negative self-image and exaggerate their emotional responses as a way to obtain attention. This continuity hypothesis provides one possible explanation of the fact that early patterns of attachment are related to later child characteristics.

Evaluation of Bowlby's theory

There are many studies that support Bowlby's theory, as shown in the summary of Bowlby's theory on p. 56. We will now consider evidence to support the continuity hypothesis. The Minnesota longitudinal study (Sroufe *et al.* 1999) has followed a cohort of children from the age of 12 months to adolescence. The children were rated throughout their childhood by teachers, trained observers and camp counsellors at special events arranged for the children. Those children who were rated as being securely attached in infancy were also later rated as being more popular, having more initiative, and being higher in social competence, self-confidence and self-esteem. In other words, social competence was associated with early attachment style, supporting Bowlby's views of continuity from infancy to adulthood in terms of social development.

McCarthy (1999) also used attachment data from infancy. A group of women were contacted who had been assessed in infancy as insecurely attached. The study recorded their attitudes and experiences of friendships and romantic relationships. Women previously classified as avoidant-insecure were more likely to have romantic problems, while those classified as resistant-insecure were more likely to have problems in friendships.

However, even though there are positive correlations between early experiences and later social experiences, you may remember that there is an alternative explanation to that of the internal working model – namely that some infants may simply be better than others at forming relationships, the temperament hypothesis (see p. 48). Children who are appealing to their parents are also likely to be appealing to other people and this can explain continuities.

A second study that investigated the continuity hypothesis perhaps offers some better support because it involved individual's attitudes. Hazan and Shaver (1987) printed a 'love quiz' in an American newspaper, collecting information from people about (1) their early attachment experiences and (2) their current romantic attitudes and experiences. They found that individuals who were securely attached as infants tended to have happy and lasting love relationships and to believe that love was enduring and about mutual trust. In contrast, insecure types found relationships less easy, were more likely to be divorced and felt that true love was rare. This supports Bowlby's concept of an internal working model because it assesses attitudes that must be generated from an internal working model.

A summary of Bowlby's theory

- Attachment is adaptive and innate: infants are born with a drive to become attached.
- They elicit caregiving through innate social releasers. Adults respond to social releasers.
- Bonds are formed with adults who respond most sensitively – e.g. Ainsworth's caregiver sensitivity hypothesis (see p. 48), and evidence from Harlow and Zimmerman (1959).
- This must occur during a critical period of development.
- Infants form one special relationship: monotropy – evidence from Schaffer and Emerson (1964).

- This leads to an internal working model (a schema) and the continuity hypothesis – evidence from Sroufe et al. (1999 and Hazan and Shaver (1987).

There are also flaws with the theory. For example, it does not explain *why* some children are able to cope with poor attachment experiences while others suffer long-term consequences, as we will see in the next topic on deprivation and privation.

One final point to note is that the evolutionary argument is a post-hoc (after the fact) assumption rather than proven fact. In other words, we are making the judgement by looking backwards and arguing that a specific behaviour must be adaptive because it persists. We cannot *know* this is true, but are assuming it is likely. It could be that the value of the behaviour is simply neutral rather than positive.

Despite the criticisms, Bowlby's theory continues to be the major theory of attachment, to generate a great deal of research (an important positive feature of any theory) and to have an enormous impact on the emotional care of young children.

✓ CHECK YOUR UNDERSTANDING

Check your understanding of the development and variety of attachments by answering these questions. Try to do this from memory at first. You can check your answers by looking back through this first topic.

1 Fill in the blank space: "Attachments depend on _____ between two people."

2 Briefly explain the term 'internal working model' as used by Bowlby with reference to attachments.

3 What exactly is a 'critical period'?

4 What does the term 'imprinting' mean?

5 Why is imprinting so important for a young animal?

6 How many stages did Schaffer and Emerson (1964) identify in the development of attachments?

7 Give two criticisms of Schaffer and Emerson's stage account of developments in attachments.

8 List four characteristics seen in an 'attached' infant.

9 What aspect of cognitive development coincides with a child showing separation anxiety?

10 List the steps in the Strange Situation procedure.

11 What are the three types of attachments that Mary Ainsworth identified?

12 Name the fourth type of attachment that Main and Cassidy identified in 1988 and list two of its features.

13 In which country have most Strange Situation studies been carried out?

14 Why is it difficult to show that a child's early attachment style (as measured by the Strange Situation procedure) affects the nature of their later relationships?

15 Define the term 'monotropy'.

16 Why might it be beneficial for infants to develop more than one attachment?

17 Name one study that supports the claim that infants tend to become primarily attached to one person even though several people may look after them.

18 According to learning theory, what two processes explain the development of attachment? Give one criticism of the learning theory explanation of attachment.

how good is an explanation?

When asked to evaluate an 'explanation' of attachment, you are being asked to do more than simply describe material that may be relevant to this subject area; you are being asked to *show* how this enhances, or even detracts from, the overall value of your chosen explanation. Examination questions always present you with a fairly challenging task in the final part of each question. These AO1 + AO2 questions (part (c) of each question) test your ability to work with the material you have learned in order to consider a particular issue in a more critical light.

In practical terms, these questions always have 6 marks available for descriptive content and 12 marks for analysis and evaluation, so it is important to get the balance right. For example, when asked to 'consider' an explanation of attachment, there is a temptation to spend much of the time available describing it and not enough doing the AO2 bit!

Take the learning theory explanation of attachment as an example. The task of answering an AO1 + AO2 question requires a brief descriptive response followed by a slightly more extended evaluative response – for example: *"Give a brief account of, and evaluate **one** explanation of attachment."*

- *Task 1* – Can you précis this theory in such a way that it illustrates how learning theory has been used to *explain* attachment (rather than just describing learning theory itself). Remember that this part of your response is only worth 6 marks, and so it does need to be brief. On p. 56, we have shown you the main points of Bowlby's explanation of attachment, but can you do the same for the learning theory explanation?

- *Task 2* – Is your evaluation *informed* (i.e. how much is there, and is it *relevant*?) and is it *effective* (i.e. have you done more than *identify* some critical points)? This is not always as easy as it sounds, so it pays to look carefully at the evaluation covered on the preceding pages.

Harlow and Harlow's study (p. 53) clearly casts doubt on the learning theory explanation of attachment, but why? This is where you need to show evidence of engaging with the material in order to construct a convincing critical argument. By adding a few well-chosen words or phrases (shown in bold below), it shows that *you* understand the significance of each piece of information you are using, within the wider context of the question you are answering. For example:

<< **Contrary to the claims made by the learning theory** explanation, it showed that feeding was not the main source of reinforcement and, therefore, not the sole basis for attachment. **However**, Harlow and Harlow did find that contact comfort was a key source of reinforcement, **but this was still not sufficient** for healthy development. We should, of course, be cautious about making any generalizations about human behaviour on the basis of research with rhesus monkeys, **as we cannot assume that the processes of attachment are exactly the same for each species.** >>

The secret of effective performance, then, is to choose your material carefully, make sure you are using it in an evaluative context, and elaborate each point sufficiently to give it impact.

REVISION SUMMARY

Having covered this topic you should be able to:

✓ define 'attachment', 'secure attachment', 'insecure attachment' and 'cross-cultural variations'

✓ describe research findings and conclusions related to the development of attachments

✓ describe phases in the development of attachment

✓ describe and evaluate research into individual differences in attachment, including secure and insecure attachment and cross-cultural variations

✓ describe the aims, procedures, findings, conclusions and criticisms for a key study in the areas of secure and insecure attachment and cross-cultural variations

✓ describe and evaluate two explanations of attachment.

Topic 2 >> Deprivation and privation

1 Read the following experiences of children being separated from people they love. What possible short-term and longer-term effects do you think the separation might have on the individuals concerned:

   (a) a 1-year old going into hospital for a long period, part of it being spent in intensive care?

   (b) 8-year-old twins who go off to boarding school for the first time – their older brother is already at the same school?

   (c) two sisters, aged 12 and 15, who had always lived in Glasgow with their parents, being evacuated during the Second World War to a farm in a rural, English community?

2 Think back to some of your own experiences of being separated from people you love – either when you were younger or more recently. How did the separation make you feel? What things helped you to feel better?

During World War II, thousands of children experienced the shock of separation from loved ones

DEPRIVATION AND SEPARATION

Around the time of the Second World War, a number of psychologists became interested in the negative effects of separation on the emotional development of children, leading eventually to a formal statement of the link between separation and emotional maladjustment – Bowlby's maternal deprivation hypothesis.

KEY TERMS

Deprivation: to have something taken away, such as food or warmth, i.e. a *loss*. In the context of attachment, deprivation refers to the loss of emotional care that results in the breaking of emotional bonds. A child is denied emotional care for a period of time. Bowlby's maternal deprivation hypothesis proposes that emotional deprivation disrupts the attachment process, which may harm emotional and social development.

Separation: to be physically set apart from something – in the context of attachment, to be physically apart from one's caregiver, especially one's mother figure. Separation does not inevitably result in deprivation. Substitute emotional care can be provided to avoid the disruption of emotional bonds.

Privation: a lack of the necessities of life. In the context of attachment, privation refers to a complete lack of emotional care, especially during the first few years of life. Such a lack of emotional care results in no attachments being formed. It has been proposed that this lack of early attachment results in permanent harm to emotional and social development.

Bowlby's maternal deprivation hypothesis

Some 20 years before the publication of his attachment theory, Bowlby proposed the maternal deprivation hypothesis (Bowlby 1953). This hypothesis was the forerunner of the attachment theory (described on pp. 54–6) and was considerably less complex (after all, it was called a hypothesis and not a theory).

The maternal deprivation hypothesis stated the belief that if an infant was unable to develop a "warm, intimate, and continuous relationship with his mother (or permanent mother-substitute)" (Bowlby 1953, p. 13), then the child would have difficulty forming relationships with other people and would be at risk of behavioural disorders.

There are three important things to note:

- The hypothesis focuses on the importance of a continuous relationship between a child and mother. Relationships that are discontinuous (i.e. where there are separations) become unstable and less predictable, which disrupts the development of the relationship.

- Bowlby suggested that the development of this continuous relationship must occur during a critical period. If a child experienced repeated separations before the age of $2\frac{1}{2}$ years, then it would be likely to become emotionally disturbed. Bowlby felt that there was a continuing risk of disturbance up to the age of 5. After that age children are better able to cope with separation.

- Bowlby did not suggest that the relationship had to be with the child's mother. The term 'maternal' was used to describe mothering from a mother 'or any mother-substitute'. He did believe that a child needed to form a relationship with one primary caregiver for healthy emotional development to take place (the concept of monotropy). This is most likely to be a child's mother, but does not have to be.

Note that there is no mention in this hypothesis of evolutionary principles, of adaptiveness, social releasers, internal working models and the continuity hypothesis. It is important to be able to distinguish between Bowlby's attachment theory and his maternal deprivation hypothesis.

The key contribution of this hypothesis was to identify the importance of emotional care in healthy emotional development. In the 1940s, it was a common belief that children simply needed a good standard of physical care and that emotions would look after themselves. Bowlby famously said "mother-love in infancy and childhood is as important for mental health as are vitamins and proteins for physical health" (Bowlby 1953, p. 240).

Research into the effects of deprivation

One source of evidence for Bowlby's maternal deprivation hypothesis was his own research, described in the key study, *The effects of deprivation*, on p. 60.

A number of studies conducted in the 1930s and 40s strongly influenced Bowlby's views and led to the development of his maternal deprivation hypothesis. For example, Spitz and Wolf (1946) studied 100 apparently normal children who became seriously depressed after staying in hospital. The children generally recovered well if the separation lasted less than three months. Longer separations were rarely associated with complete recovery.

Research into separation

There is often an interchangeable use of the words separation and deprivation. Bowlby believed that separation threatened the attachment relationship and led to emotional deprivation. However, research done by James and Joyce Robertson (Robertson and Robertson 1971) showed that separation need not lead to emotional deprivation. A mother and child may be separated but if substitute emotional care is provided, then deprivation may be avoided.

The Robertsons filmed various children under the age of 3 during short separations. One boy, John, spent nine days in a residential nursery. The staff had little time to attend to his personal needs. The film shows him being overwhelmed by the strange environment and, just as Harlows' monkeys clung to the cloth-covered mother when frightened, John clung to a teddy bear.

John progressively became more withdrawn and despairing, and when his mother came to collect him, he struggled to get away. He continued for months to show outbursts of anger towards his mother.

In contrast, several other children were filmed while they were cared for by Joyce Robertson, a foster mother, in her own home. She arranged for the children to visit their mothers in hospital and to bring things from home with them, thus maintaining emotional bonds with home during separation. These children ate and slept well while staying in foster care, and welcomed their parents at the end of their stay.

Did you have a favourite toy or 'cuddly' as a child that gave you comfort when you were anxious?

a study of 44 juvenile thieves by Bowlby (1944)

Aim >>

To test the maternal deprivation hypothesis, that is, to see whether frequent early separations were associated with a risk of behavioural disorders: in particular, a disorder termed 'affectionless psychopathy'. Bowlby used this term to describe individuals who have no sense of shame or guilt; they lack a social conscience. Is it possible that such individuals were more likely to have experienced a disrupted early childhood?

Procedures >>

- The participants in this study were 88 children ranging in age from 5 to 16 who had been referred to the child guidance clinic where Bowlby worked.
- Forty-four of the children had been referred to the clinic because of stealing (the 'thieves'). Bowlby identified 16 of these thieves as affectionless psychopaths (described above).
- The remaining 44 children in the study had not committed any crimes; they were emotionally maladjusted, but did not display antisocial behaviour. None of this control group were diagnosed as affectionless psychopaths.
- Bowlby interviewed the children and their families and was able to build up a record of their early life experiences.

Findings >>

- Bowlby found that a large number (86 per cent) of those thieves diagnosed as affectionless psychopaths had experienced "early and prolonged separations from their mothers".
- Only 17 per cent of the other thieves (the ones who weren't classed as affectionless psychopaths) had experienced such separations.
- Even fewer (4 per cent) of the control group ('non-thieves') had experienced frequent early separations.

Conclusions >>

- These findings suggest a link between early separations and later social and emotional maladjustment.
- In its most severe form, maternal deprivation appears to lead to affectionless psychopathy. In its less severe form it leads to antisocial behaviour (theft).
- These findings support the maternal deprivation hypothesis.

Criticisms >>

- The evidence is correlational, which means that we can only say that deprivation/separation and affectionless psychopathy are linked, not that one *caused* the other.
- The data on separation were collected retrospectively and may not be reliable. Parents may not have accurately recalled separations during infancy. They may have over- or under-estimated the frequency. In addition, how do we know whether these children experienced deprivation (the loss of emotional care) or whether they had good substitute emotional care during their separations?

AO2 check

This issue is a frequent problem in many developmental studies where it is difficult to manipulate an independent variable. Bowlby's study demonstrated a *link* between two variables: frequent early separations and emotional maladjustment. The maternal deprivation hypothesis proposed that the first *causes* the second, but the evidence cannot support this causal conclusion. It could be, for example, that children from unhappy homes are more prone to becoming ill. This leads them to spend more time in hospital and also leads to emotional maladjustment. In this case it would be the unhappy home that is the causal factor, not the separations. This is discussed further on p. 61, under Rutter's criticisms.

It would appear, from the Robertsons' research, that separation need not lead to deprivation as long as:

- separation is minimized
- substitute emotional care is provided.

This conclusion is supported by another early study by Skeels and Dye (1939). They compared the development of one group of orphans raised in a home for women who were mentally retarded (where the women there gave them attention) with a control group who remained in the original institution. After one and a half years, the IQs of the control group fell from an average of 87 to 61 points, whereas the average IQs rose in the group who were transferred to the home from 64 to 92 points. Skeels (1966) assessed the children 20 years later and claimed that the effects were still apparent. This was credited to the emotional care they received from the adults that reduced the emotional deprivation experienced in the institution.

Evaluation of Bowlby's maternal deprivation hypothesis

There are various issues to be considered. First, much of the evidence used to generate and support the maternal deprivation hypothesis came from studies of children in institutions where they were deprived *in many ways*. Therefore, it may not be maternal deprivation, but other forms of deprivation (e.g. physical deprivation) that affected subsequent development.

Second, not all research has found that deprivation leads to maladjustment. Another study by Bowlby *et al.* (1956) found no such ill effects. A group of children with tuberculosis was studied. They were under the age of 4 when they were first hospitalized. The nursing regimes tended to be strict and the care impersonal. Many of the children were visited weekly by their families, but this probably did little to prevent emotional deprivation (John in the Robertsons' study

was also visited regularly by his father). Information was obtained about these children when they were between 7 and 14 years old. Psychologists assessed them and their teachers were also interviewed. When the children who had TB were compared with a control group of children who had not been in hospital, it was found that there were no differences in terms of delinquency or problems in forming social relationships. Therefore, it would appear that deprivation does not inevitably have harmful effects. Bowlby and colleagues suggested that individual differences might be important. For example, children who are securely attached may cope better with deprivation.

Michael Rutter (1981) identified some further problems with the maternal deprivation hypothesis in a classic book entitled *Maternal Deprivation Revisited*. Rutter supported Bowlby's hypothesis in general, but felt refinements were needed. He claimed that:

- Bowlby confused cause and effect with an association (see p. 60). The fact that early separation and later maladjustment are linked does not mean that one caused the other. Rutter suggested that instead, it could be that some families are 'at risk' because of, for example, poor living conditions or unsettled interpersonal relationships. These factors might lead to both early separation and later maladjustment. Rutter (1976) interviewed over 2,000 boys and their families on the Isle of Wight and found that delinquency was most common in cases where boys had experienced separations due to discord in their families. This supports Rutter's hypothesis that it is family discord, rather than separation on its own, that causes delinquency and emotional maladjustment.

- Bowlby did not distinguish between different kinds of deprivation. An infant or child can be deprived of a caregiver's presence, meaning that the child had formed attachment bonds, but these were now disrupted; or the child can suffer from privation,

ACTIVITY

Putting it into practice

Imagine that you are a psychologist and have been invited to advise a unit where sick children are being cared for. The senior management team wants to know what they should do to improve children's experiences while staying in hospital, particularly with regard to their separation from parents.

1 Discuss in a small group what advice, based on sound psychological research, you could offer them.

2 Note down three pieces of advice that you would give and the research on which each recommendation is based.

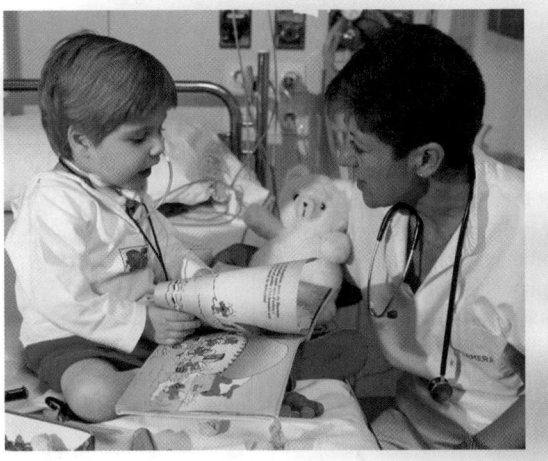

which is the lack of ever having any attachments. It may be privation rather than deprivation that has permanent and irreversible effects.

Before moving on to consider privation as distinct from deprivation, there is one final point to make. Bowlby's maternal deprivation hypothesis was developed in the early 1950s. He later went on to formulate the more positive attachment theory (described on p. 54). This theory focuses on the benefits of attachment rather than the consequences of deprivation. The maternal deprivation hypothesis also had an enormous impact on the way we treat children. For example, it changed the treatment of children in hospitals. In 1950, parents were discouraged from visiting their children because it was thought to cause too much distress to them; today, parents are encouraged to stay overnight when their children are in hospital because it is recognized that this prevents emotional deprivation and promotes quicker recovery through reduced anxiety. (This may be one of the measures you thought of in response to the activity at the bottom of p. 61.)

PRIVATION

Rutter suggested it might make better sense to look at privation (lack of attachments) rather than deprivation (loss of attachments). Bowlby's hypothesis may be refined as the maternal privation hypothesis and again tested to see if it is correct. There are three main lines of evidence regarding privation:

- longitudinal studies of children in institutional care
- case histories of children raised in extreme isolation
- studies of reactive attachment disorder, a category of mental disorder attributed to a lack of early attachments.

Longitudinal studies of children in institutional care

One way to study privation is to consider the effects of institutionalization in situations where infants have never had the opportunity to form any attachments. One early study showed that children living in orphanages did improve dramatically in terms of intellectual development when they were given greater emotional attention (Skeels and Dye 1939, described on p. 61). Barbara Tizard and colleagues conducted a larger-scale study of institutionalized infants over a period of 16 years. This is described in the key study, *The effects of privation*, opposite.

One of the consequences of psychological research into the effects of institutionalization has been to reduce greatly the extent to which children are placed in such care. As a result, it has not been possible to replicate such studies until recently, when a natural opportunity for further study presented itself. In Romania, many children were placed in orphanages from birth and experienced considerable deprivation. Rutter *et al.* (1998) studied 111 Romanian orphans adopted in the UK before the age of 2. On arrival, these children were physically undersized, but by the age of 4 they had caught up spectacularly to age-related milestones. However, age at adoption was negatively correlated with attainment of developmental milestones. In other words, the later the children were adopted, the slower their progress. This suggests that the longer children experience emotional deprivation, the longer it will take for them to recover – but that recovery is possible.

An earlier study by Quinton *et al.* (1985) found the reverse. The researchers followed a group of ex-institutional women (reared in institutions). These women had extreme difficulties when they became parents, for example their children were more frequently in care and the women were less sensitive, less supportive and less warm with their children than a control group of non-institutionalized women who were also observed. However, it may *not* be early privation that explains their lack of parenting abilities. It may be more simply that they had inadequate models for how to parent and this made them less able to cope as mothers. This is supported by further data from Quinton and colleagues, who found that those institutionalized women who had had positive school experiences in childhood and favourable psychosocial circumstances in adulthood functioned as well as the comparison group. This again suggests that continuing poor experiences are associated with poor recovery, but that recovery is possible when a child has improved care during childhood.

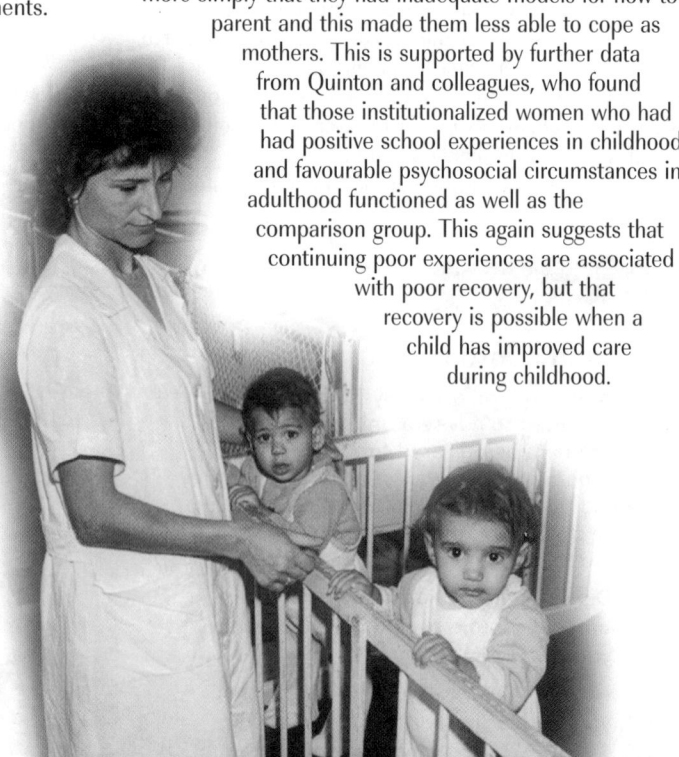

a study of ex-institutional children by Hodges and Tizard (1989)

Aim >>

To investigate the effects of early privation on subsequent social and emotional development, and to test the maternal deprivation (or privation) hypothesis. The study aimed to follow the same children over a long period of time (a longitudinal study) to collect reliable information linking early experiences to later outcomes for the same individuals.

Procedures >>

- This longitudinal study was a natural experiment. The independent variable (attachment experiences) varied naturally. The participants were 65 children who had been placed in an institution when they were less than 4 months old. There was an explicit policy in the institution against caregivers forming attachments with the children. This would suggest that the children experienced early privation.
- By the age of 4, 24 of the institutionalized children had been adopted, 15 had returned to their natural homes, and the rest remained in the institution.
- Assessment at ages 8 and 16 involved interviewing those children who were adopted and those who had returned to their original homes. Their parents, their teachers and their peers were also interviewed. Data were also obtained about a control group of 'normal' peers.

Findings >>

- There were some differences between the adopted and 'restored' children. The adopted children generally had close attachments to their parents and good family relationships, whereas this was much less true for the restored children.
- However, there were similarities in the behaviour of the adopted and restored children *outside* the family. For example, both groups were more likely to seek adult attention and approval than the control children, and both groups were less successful in peer relationships.

Conclusions >>

- There is evidence that does *not* support the maternal deprivation hypothesis. The two ex-institution groups, adopted and restored, differed *within* their family relationships. The restored children often returned to the same difficult circumstances that had precipitated the need for care in the first place, and to parents who may have felt ambivalent about them. In contrast, adopted children went to homes where the parents had very much wanted a child. This shows that recovery is possible given the right circumstances.
- There is evidence that *does* support the maternal deprivation hypothesis. *Outside* the family environment it would appear that early privation did have an effect on subsequent social development. Clarke and Clarke (1979) put forward a transactional model to explain the findings. It may be that the adopted children in Hodges and Tizard's studies got on well within their families because the families made special efforts to love them, whereas they did not experience this outside the home and thus were unable to form relationships as easily or well.

Criticisms >>

- Random allocation of participants to experimental groups is used to ensure that the participant groups in an experiment are equivalent. In Hodges and Tizard's study, there may have been important differences between the two groups – the adopted and the restored group – *besides* the independent variable. It is possible, for example, that the children selected for adoption were the more attractive and socially able children. The children's temperament thus becomes a confounding variable in this study – confounding because it acts as another independent variable. This means that we cannot infer a causal relationship between the effects of early privation on later social and emotional development from this study.
- Attrition is a common problem in longitudinal research. Inevitably, some participants are no longer available or willing to take part in the study as the years pass by. It is possible that a certain kind of individual is more likely to drop out from the study – for example, those who are less highly motivated or, in the case of Hodges and Tizard's study, those who were less well adjusted. This leaves the study with a biased sample. If a study sample is biased, the researchers have to be very careful about what conclusions they can draw and it is not appropriate to generalize the findings.

Unit 2 // Attachments in development

Children raised in extreme isolation

Case histories of children who have been raised in isolated and deprived circumstances demonstrate two things:

● Some children never recover from early privation.

● Other children show remarkable recovery.

Two case histories of isolation are described in the panel on the right. Read these now, before continuing with the text below

Why did Genie fail to recover while the other children seemed to be more resilient? It may be due to the length of time in isolation. Genie was 13, which may be beyond the age of recovery, whereas the others were much younger. It may be because of the actual experiences in isolation. The Czech twins had each other, although Genie's mother claimed to have had a relationship with her daughter (Rymer 1993). It may be related to some unique characteristic of the individual – Genie's father had locked her up because he thought she was retarded. It may be related to subsequent care – the Czech twins were cared for by a pair of loving sisters, whereas there is uncertainty about the quality of the foster care that Genie received because there were continuing wrangles about who should look after her. Also, she was later fostered by a family where she was abused.

These questions highlight some of the problems with the case history approach. The evidence is also retrospective, so we cannot be sure about the actual conditions the children endured; nor is it possible to make generalizations about human behaviour on the basis of individuals who may have unique characteristics. Nevertheless, we might cautiously conclude from these case histories that recovery from privation does seem possible when good emotional care is offered at a sufficiently young age.

Studies of reactive attachment disorder

Some children who experience early disruptions in the attachment process *do* appear *unable* to recover. These are children who are diagnosed with reactive attachment disorder. The symptoms are: lack of ability to give and receive affection, cruelty to others especially pets, abnormalities in eye contact and speech patterns, lying and stealing, lack of long-term friends, and extreme control problems (Parker and Forrest 1993). It is suggested that the cause of the disorder is a lack of primary attachments due to early maternal rejection and separation. For example, one typical case history described a young boy whose mother had not wanted him and offered him for adoption. This was followed by a series of foster homes until he was finally adopted at age 18 months. However, he appeared unable to accept the affection that his adopted parents tried to give him and, as an older child, engaged in lying, stealing, sending death threats and going into wild rages (Flanagan 1996).

Two cases of isolation

● The first case involves Czechoslovakian, male, identical twins whose mother died after giving birth (Koluchová 1976). The children went to a children's home for 11 months, then spent six months with their aunt, and next went to stay with their father and stepmother. The father was of low intelligence and the stepmother was exceptionally cruel. The boys were never allowed out of the house and were kept in either a small, unheated closet or in a cellar. When discovered at 7 years, the children could hardly walk, had acute rickets, were very fearful and their spontaneous speech was very poor. After placement in a hospital and then a foster home, excellent gains were made. The children are now adults and appear well adjusted and cognitively able (Clarke, personal communication).

● Genie, the second case, was found when she was 13 years old (Curtiss 1977). Her history was one of isolation, severe neglect and physical restraint. She was kept strapped to a child's potty in a bare room. Her father punished her if she made any sound. On discovery aged 13, her appearance was of a 6- or 7-year-old child. Curtiss described her as "unsocialized, primitive, and hardly human"; she made virtually no sounds and was hardly able to walk. Genie never achieved good social adjustment or language despite intervention and being placed with a foster family.

Maternal rejection can occur even when the mother remains present, as in the case of primary rejectors (Jones *et al.* 1987). These tend to be middle-class women who have had an unwanted child, a difficult pregnancy, and/or experienced early separation from their infant due to problems at the time of birth. The mothers may well have good relationships with other offspring and are able to offer a good standard of physical care. Rejection starts from the time of birth and the mother–infant relationship never recovers. Gradually, the guilt and lack of empathy that the mother feels turns into anger and later, as the child grows up, a period of stress or naughtiness may result in excessive punishment and abuse.

However, it is possible that the reason for the initial breakdown between caregiver and child was some aspect of the child's temperament, and this has continued to affect other attempts to form relationships.

Maternal *deprivation*

Penelope Leach is a research psychologist specializing in child development. Best known as the author of Your Baby and Child *(Penguin Books 1997) and as a passionate advocate for children and parents, she is a Fellow of the British Psychological Society, and an Honorary Senior Research Fellow in the Leopold Muller Centre of Child and Family Mental Health at the Royal Free and University College Medical School, where she is currently Co-Director of the UK's largest programme of research into the effects of various kinds and combinations of care on children's development in the first five years.*

Q **Is Bowlby's view of the importance of the bond between mother and child justified?**

A Yes, indeed, and his recognition of the nature of that bond – for which he coined the term 'primary attachment' – did the world a great and lasting service. Many earlier observers had noted that infants seek to get close and stay close to their mothers and had assumed that this was entirely in order to assure themselves of food and warmth; a clear case of cupboard love. Bowlby realized that it was not only physical requirements babies sought from their mothers, but also comfort and closeness for their own sake. Babies are born primed to 'attach themselves' to an adult – usually, though not necessarily or invariably the birth mother – because without adult care they cannot survive. But the survival that is at stake is emotional as well as physical. Bowlby came to see the bond between mother and child as the primary love relationship in every individual's life.

Penelope Leach

Q **Are children more vulnerable to absence of that bond or to its disruption?**

A The first. This first love relationship is irreplaceably important. It is through it that babies learn about themselves, other people and the world; experience emotions and learn to cope with them. And it is through this baby-love that they will become capable of more grown-up kinds of love; capable, one far-distant day, of giving children their own the kind of devotion they now need for themselves. Loss of a primary attachment figure is always a tragedy, but as long as babies have had such a relationship with at least one special person who loves them and whom they love, they will be able to make good use of secondary attachments to other special people.

Q **Is there evidence to suggest that deprivation or disruption of attachment has long-term effects?**

A Those orphanage babies used to be described as suffering (and even dying) of 'maternal deprivation', but we now see what they were missing in terms of an active and interactive relationship rather than passive dependency, and we can see that lesser degrees of deprivation matter too. Babies are liable not to develop as fast or as far as their innate drive and their potential for personality allow if:

- they receive adequate physical care but little emotional response (as sometimes happens if a mother is very depressed)

- they are looked after by a succession of caretakers who either never make themselves special to each baby or form a special relationship, which is then broken because they leave. The development of babies who are suddenly separated from parenting-people is always put at risk.

But as long as babies *do* have at least one special person who loves them and whom they love, they can make excellent use of other special people too. A baby's capacity for love is not rationed, any more than an adult's is. The reverse is true. Love creates love.

Expert interview

In the interview on p. 65, research psychologist Penelope Leach gives her views on the importance of the attachment process. For this activity, take the following statements from the interview and find evidence from elsewhere in this unit that gives research support to these views.

<< Loss of a primary attachment figure is always a tragedy, but as long as babies have had such a relationship with at least one special person who loves them and whom they love, they will be able to make good use of secondary attachments to other special people. >>

<< Babies are liable not to develop as fast or as far as their innate drive and their potential for personality allow if they are looked after by a succession of caretakers who either never make themselves special to each baby or form a special relationship, which is then broken because they leave. >>

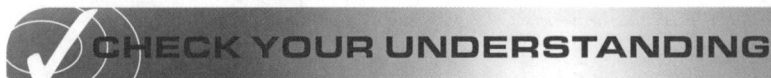

CHECK YOUR UNDERSTANDING

Check your understanding of deprivation and privation by answering these questions. Try to do this from memory at first. You can check your answers by looking back through Topic 2.

1 Define the terms 'deprivation' and 'privation'.

2 What did Bowlby's maternal deprivation (1953) hypothesis predict?

3 List the three most important elements of Bowlby's maternal deprivation hypothesis.

4 What are the three main conclusions from Bowlby's (1944) study of 44 juvenile thieves?

5 Give two criticisms of this study of juvenile thieves.

6 The Robertsons' research suggests that separation need not lead to deprivation. What two elements do they claim are important in avoiding deprivation becoming a consequence of separation?

7 Although Rutter (1981) broadly supported Bowlby's maternal deprivation hypothesis, he did feel that certain refinements were necessary. List the two main refinements that Rutter proposed in his classic book *Maternal Deprivation Revisited* and explain why these refinements are important.

8 Name the researcher who studied the Czech twin boys who were discovered at the age of 7 after years of neglect and abuse.

REVISION SUMMARY

Having covered this topic you should be able to:

✓ define 'deprivation', 'separation' and 'privation', and explain the differences between these terms

✓ describe and evaluate the maternal deprivation hypothesis

✓ describe research findings and conclusions related to the effects of deprivation

✓ describe research findings and conclusions related to the effects of separation

✓ describe research findings and conclusions related to the effects of privation

✓ describe the aims, procedures, findings, conclusions and criticisms for a key study on the effects of deprivation and on the effects of privation

✓ consider the reversibility of early deprivation and/or privation.

Consider the following statement:

<< Day care jeopardizes the development of children. >>

Think carefully about this statement and decide whether or not you agree with it. Make a note of your decision.

If possible, arrange to discuss or debate this statement with a group of other students studying psychology. If you arrange a formal debate, divide the group into two smaller groups, one to prepare arguments in support of the statement, and the other to prepare arguments opposing it.

Present each side of the debate in turn, allowing an opportunity for questions.

At the end of the debate, take a vote to see what support exists for either side of the argument about the effects of day care. Then consider the following questions:

■ Did you change your views as a result of hearing other people's views?

■ How many people (and what percentage) supported the statement before the debate?

■ How many people (and what percentage) supported the statement after the debate?

Day care: a form of care for infants and children, offered by someone other than close family, taking place outside the home. Children spend part or all of the day in care, but return home at night. This is distinct from a residential nursery, where children are looked after for a short spell, such as a week, and sleep there as well. Day care also differs from institutional care, which refers to long-term, 24-hour care.

Cognitive development: the changes that take place throughout one's life with respect to mental abilities, including memory, perception, language and intelligence. Attachment promotes cognitive development because it offers a secure base for exploration and increases opportunities for stimulation. Deprivation may therefore harm cognitive development.

Social development: the changes that take place throughout one's life with respect to social behaviour, such as relationships with friends and family, popularity, ability to negotiate with peers, friendliness and aggressiveness. Attachment promotes social development because it provides an internal working model for conducting relationships. Separation may therefore harm social development.

Some of the research looked at so far in this unit may seem rather dated. This is because psychology has moved on from the issue of how deprivation and privation affect children, to focus on how we can improve situations where children are experiencing separation, deprivation and privation. The care of adopted children is one area of concern; another relevant issue is the effects on children of day care.

We almost take it for granted that local communities should be equipped with good preschool day-care facilities. However, psychologists have not always promoted this idea. One of the major issues raised by Bowlby's (1953) maternal deprivation hypothesis was the potentially detrimental effect of day care. If separations from the child's main caregiver are harmful, especially before the age of 2, then shouldn't we stop mothers (or primary caregivers) going out to work? Although Bowlby did not actually suggest that women should stay at home to look after their children, this was the message taken from his work (Holmes 1993).

Unit 2 // Attachments in development

67

EFFECTS OF DAY CARE ON COGNITIVE DEVELOPMENT

Cognitive development concerns the growth of a child's mental abilities. There are several factors that would lead us to expect that separation (i.e. disruption of attachment bonds) might cause delays in cognitive development:

- *A secure base for exploration* is important for cognitive development. Bowlby's theory of attachment proposed that a key purpose of attachment is the provision of a secure base. Children who are insecure are less able to explore their world confidently and this may hinder their cognitive development. This is supported by research. For example, Hazen and Durrett (1982) found that securely attached young children were more independent explorers of their environment and were also more innovative in their approach to problem-solving.

- *Stimulation* is important for cognitive development. Greenough *et al.* (1987) found that rats reared in an enriched environment had larger brains, neurons with more connections and were smarter than rats reared in an impoverished environment. It is possible that children in day care receive less stimulation. For example, Bryant *et al.* (1980) found that childminders tended to reward quiet behaviour, thereby encouraging passivity and understimulation. On the other hand, day care may provide a more stimulating environment, especially for children from disadvantaged backgrounds.

The negative effects

The research described above provides support for the view that day care has negative effects on cognitive development. This is confirmed by a survey conducted by Russell (1999) of the findings of about 100 studies of day care. Russell concluded that, overall, the effects of day care were negative rather than positive. The studies surveyed were conducted between 1957 and 1995. It is possible that the *quality* of day care has improved considerably in this time; studies that look at poor-quality day care may well find negative effects, as we will see.

However, research continues to indicate a link between poor cognitive development and day care. For example, Ruhm (2000) found that preschool children had lower reading and maths skills if they spent time before the age of 3 in day care.

The positive effects

Not all research has found that day care has negative effects on cognitive development. In fact, some studies have indicated that there are actually *beneficial* effects for cognitive development. Such beneficial effects are found in situations where the quality of care is high. They are also found in situations where enrichment programmes linked to day care are provided for disadvantaged preschool children.

High quality of care

One of the reasons that day care may be detrimental is lack of stimulation, therefore it stands to reason that where day care is stimulating (high quality), it may actually be beneficial. Campbell *et al.* (2001) conducted a 20-year follow-up study of children who had been in day care. They found that those children who attended high-quality day care scored significantly higher on reading and maths tests. A study by Andersson (1992) in Sweden, a country that provides high-quality day care, found that school performance (at age 8 and age 13) was highest in those children who entered day care before the age of 1. School performance was lowest for those who did not have any day care. Such findings suggest that high-quality day care is beneficial.

Studies have found that attending high-quality day care can improve children's later performance at school. How does this tie in with your own experience?

Perhaps the most impressive evidence comes from an ongoing study being conducted in America by the National Institute of Child Health and Human Development. This study has followed over 1,300 children from birth through childhood (the cohort is currently nearing the end of primary school). Reports are published at regular intervals. In 1997, NICHD reported that the higher the quality of child care in the first three years of life, the greater the child's language abilities at 15, 24, and 36 months, and also the better the child's performance on the Bayley Scales of Infant Development (a measure of cognitive development) at age 2, and the more school readiness the child showed at age 3. High-quality care included frequent interactions between carers and children, referring to such things as how often caregivers spoke to children, asked them questions and responded to their vocalizations.

EFFECTS OF DAY CARE ON SOCIAL DEVELOPMENT

Social development concerns the growth of a child's abilities to interact with others and behave in a prosocial manner. There are several factors that might lead us to expect that separation might affect social development:

- Secure attachment is claimed to be of prime importance for emotional and social development. If separation affects the security of a child's attachment by disrupting their continuous relationship with a caregiver, then we would expect to see differences in terms of social and emotional development in those children placed in day care.

- On the other hand, the opportunities for social interaction that occur in day care might promote social development. For example, children in day care are more likely to have to learn negotiation skills.

The negative effects

An early study, Belsky and Rovine (1988) found that children who spent more than 20 hours per week in day care were more insecurely attached (as assessed in the Strange Situation) than home-cared children. This has led many people to conclude that day care is harmful. Recent findings from the NICHD (2001) support this. They found that those children who spent more than 10 hours per week in day care were more aggressive when they reached school age, both at home and in school. Such aggressiveness may be due to insecure attachment.

The lack of negative effects

Clarke-Stewart et al. (1994) investigated the relationship between time spent in day care and quality of attachment in 150 American children. They found that 15-month-old children who experienced high-intensity childcare (30 hours or more a week from age 3 months) were equally distressed when separated from their mothers in the Strange Situation as low-intensity children (less than 10 hours a week). The NICHD study in 1997 showed that infants with extensive day-care experience did not differ from infants without day care in terms of the distress they exhibited during separations from their mothers in the Strange Situation. The findings of these studies suggest that the day-care experience had no negative effects on attachment.

The positive effects

There is evidence to show that children who attend day care are more sociable and popular when they attend school. For example, Clarke-Stewart and colleagues also found that children who had attended day care coped better in social situations in their first year at school and were better able to negotiate with peers.

Enrichment programmes, such as Headstart, have also been assessed in terms of their benefits for social development. Schweinhart et al. (1993) found that children who took part in the High/Scope Perry Preschool Project had lower delinquency rates in adolescence and were less likely to have a criminal record when young adults than a control group who did not take part in the project.

FACTORS WHICH AFFECT THE EXPERIENCE OF DAY CARE

When considering the research findings, we have already noted that the quality of care is important in determining whether or not day care has positive or negative effects. We have also seen that time spent in day care may be significant (NICHD findings on aggression), but that it may not always be a significant factor (Clarke-Stewart and colleagues found no difference). A third factor apart from quality of care and time spent in day care, may be the child's age. In Andersson's study, children in day care before the age of 1 actually did *better* in terms of school achievement.

There are many other factors. One is individual difference. Pennebaker et al. (1981) reported that shy children find the day-care situation quite threatening and are likely to find it a less beneficial experience. Another possible factor is the quality of experiences at home. Securely attached children may respond differently to day care than insecurely attached children. Egeland and Hiester (1995) found an interesting interaction effect. They looked at about 70 children, half of whom entered day care before the age of 1, while the rest remained at home with their mothers. All the children came from impoverished backgrounds. Security of attachment was assessed around the age of 1 and again at 3. Day care appeared to have a negative effect for secure children, but had a positive influence for insecure children. However, we might be able to explain this in terms of the fact that insecurely attached children *needed* compensatory care, and therefore benefited from day care, whereas the securely attached children did not require this extra attention and separation from good-quality care was detrimental.

Such variations as those discussed above make it very difficult to make any definitive statements about day care in general.

SO DOES DAY CARE HARM CHILDREN'S DEVELOPMENT?

There is evidence that day care can have harmful effects. For example, Ruhm produced evidence of lower school performance in children who had been in day care. This may be due to less willingness to explore or to a lack of stimulation. In terms of social development, Belsky and Rovine found that children who spent more time in day care were more insecurely attached, and we have seen previously (see Sroufe and colleagues, p. 55) that insecure children are less popular. The NICHD study found that day care children were more aggressive when older.

There is also evidence that no harm is done. For example, Clarke-Stewart found no evidence of attachment differences between children cared for at home or in day care. Harvey reached a similar conclusion (see the panel below).

There is evidence of day care having beneficial effects on children's development, in terms of sociability and negotiating skills, for example. What is your view about the benefits and drawbacks of day care? Would you choose it for your children?

<< Children are not harmed by working moms >>

<< A study (Harvey 1999) evaluating the development and health of more than 6,000 youngsters suggests that children of women who work outside the home suffer no permanent harm because of their mother's absence.

Harvey's study came to a different conclusion than some earlier studies of the same group of children. The new work examined the children at a later age, 12 years old. This suggests that problems detected in children of working mothers at age 3 and 4 may have gone away by the time the children were 12.

Fundamentally, said Harvey, the study suggests issues exist in raising children that are more important than outside employment of the mother. These include the quality of the parent–child relationship and the quality of the child's day-care arrangement, she said. 'The message should be that being at home during the early years, or being employed during those years, are both good choices,' Harvey said. 'Both can result in healthy, well-developed children.' >>

Source: Adapted from the Beloit Daily News, 1 March 1999

And there is evidence of day care actually having beneficial effects. Andersson found improved school performance from children placed in day care at a very young age. Enrichment programmes have had moderate success for both cognitive and social development. Clarke-Stewart found that day-care children were more sociable and better able to negotiate with peers, and Schweinhart and colleagues found lower delinquency as a result of an enrichment programme.

One important question to ask is why the research findings are so inconsistent? The simple answer is that it is a complex issue – as we have seen there are many factors that influence a child's cognitive and social development, such as different attachment experiences, different kinds of day care and different temperaments. This means one factor (being in day care) is not likely to have consistent effects.

USING RESEARCH FINDINGS TO IMPROVE DAY CARE

Studies of day care tend to focus on the question of whether it is harmful or not. It may be more productive to consider the question: "What factors contribute to good day care?"

Schaffer (1998) suggests that consistency and quality of care are important. The question of consistency, according to Schaffer, is an organizational matter. A day-care centre needs to find some way of ensuring minimal turnover of staff, and to arrange that each child is assigned to one specific individual who is more or less constantly available and feels responsible for that child. It may also be important to establish consistent routines and physical environments.

It is probably more difficult to define quality, although Schaffer suggests that it can be expressed in terms of:

■ the amount of *verbal interaction* between caregiver and child, which should ideally be one to one as far as possible – Tizard (1979) found evidence that, irrespective of social class, the conversations between mother and child were more complex than between nursery teacher and child

■ having *sufficient stimulation*, such as suitable toys, books and other play things

■ giving *sensitive emotional care* – the NICHD study found that about 23 per cent of infant care providers gave 'highly sensitive' infant care, while 50 per cent of them provided only 'moderately sensitive' care, and 20 per cent were 'emotionally detached' from the infants under their care.

One study (Howes *et al.* 1998) considered the value of a programme designed to improve the quality of caregiver interactions. A number of caregivers were involved in in-service training to increase their sensitivity. Six months after training, Howes and colleagues found that the children (aged around 2) became more secure and the caregivers were rated as more sensitive after training. There was a control group of caregivers who received no training. The attachment of the children in their care and their own sensitivity remained unchanged. The results of this study suggest that a modest intervention programme that is directed at improving caregiving practices can improve the attachment security of the children in day care.

ACTIVITY

Reviewing your ideas

Before carrying out this activity, read the interview with Jay Belsky on the next page.

Think back to the statement that you considered at the beginning of Topic 3 that *Day care jeopardizes development*.

Now that you have read about some of the research that has been carried out into the effects of day care, and have heard the views of Jay Belsky, are there any additional conditions that you would wish to highlight when discussing this statement?

In particular, think about:

1 the effects of day care on cognitive development

2 the effects of day care on social development

3 the effects of the quality of the day care on development

4 whether some children are more vulnerable to the effects of day care than others.

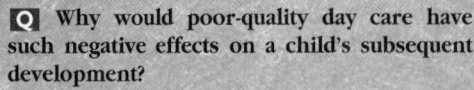

Expert interview >> Jay Belsky on

Effects of *day care*

Jay Belsky is Director of the Institute for the Study of Children, Families and Social Issues and Professor of Psychology at Birkbeck College, University of London. Professor Belsky is an internationally recognized expert in the field of child development and family studies. Amongst other things, he is involved in a multi-million dollar investigation in the USA of the effects of early childcare on children's development to the age of 11. He is also involved a long-standing longitudinal study of 1,000 young adults in New Zealand who have been studied intensively since the age of 3. He served as a consultant to former US Vice-President Gore on the issue of work and families.

Q **Research seems pretty inconclusive about whether day care has any significant effects on children's development. Is this a fair statement?**

A Not really. Evidence indicates that the more time that children spend in day care across their infant, toddler, and preschool years (combined), the more likely they are to behave in aggressive and disobedient ways as 4– to 8-year olds. Starting day care on a full-time basis in the first year may be especially risky in this regard. The evidence also indicates that children who experience better-quality day care tend to benefit, especially in terms of their cognitive and language development, when compared to those who experience poorer-quality care. The degree to which caregivers are attentive, responsive, affectionate, and stimulating defines the extent to which day care is of high or low quality.

Q **Why would poor-quality day care have such negative effects on a child's subsequent development?**

A When children are not caringly attended to and regularly stimulated, they find it difficult to develop the secure and positive sense of self that comes from being loved and attentively cared for, and which fuels so much of development. After all, knowing that one is loved and cared for fosters self-

Jay Belsky

confidence and curiosity, both of which stimulate learning. Poor-quality care also directly undermines intellectual and language development by not providing children with the kind of stimulation they need to learn about the world and how to communicate with others. And if children's language and knowledge are not developed, then it is difficult for them to succeed in school. And failure in school feeds back to further undermine one's sense of self-esteem.

Q **Is there evidence to suggest that some children are especially vulnerable whereas others are more resistant to these effects?**

A There has been repeated indication that boys may be more vulnerable to the adverse effects of poor quality or to too much day care than girls. But such findings do not emerge in relevant studies either all the time or even most of the time, so it is difficult to conclude with certainty that boys are more at risk to the effects of poor day-care experiences. There is also some evidence that infants and young children who are highly negatively emotional may benefit more from exposure to good childrearing and be more adversely affected by poor childrearing than other infants. Although strong conclusions are premature, it is reasonable to treat as a working hypothesis that boys and highly negative infants/toddlers may be more vulnerable to poor day-care experiences than other children.

✓ CHECK YOUR UNDERSTANDING

Check your understanding of the critical issue of day care by answering these questions. Try to do this from memory at first. You can check your answers by looking back through Topic 3.

1 Define 'day care'.

2 Give two reasons that are sometimes given for why day care involving separation from a parent might be thought to delay cognitive development.

3 What conclusions can you draw from Andersson's (1992) study undertaken in Sweden and also from the ongoing study by the National Institute of Child Health and Human Development in the USA?

4 Give two possible reasons why day care involving separation from a parent might be thought to delay social development.

5 Which of the following statements are true and which are false?"

(a) "Opportunities for social interaction such as negotiation skills that occur in day-care situations may serve to promote children's social development."

(b) "All research undertaken to date has found that day care has negative effects on cognitive development."

(c) "Intervention programmes designed to reverse the effects of social disadvantage by providing intensive preschool education through day-care programmes failed to boost cognitive development or tackle the cycle of failure."

(d) "One of the reasons that day care may be detrimental is lack of stimulation; therefore, it stands to reason that where day care is stimulating, it may actually be beneficial."

(e) "Schweinhart and colleagues found that children who took part in the High/Scope Perry Preschool Project had similar delinquency rates in adolescence and were just as likely to have a criminal record when young adults than a control group who did not take part in the project."

6 What five factors may affect the experience of day care?

7 Why do the factors that you listed above in response to Question 6 make it difficult to make any definitive statements about day care?

8 Cite (name) one study that found day care does harm to children's development, one that found no evidence of harm, and one that reported evidence of day care having beneficial effects.

9 List at least four ways in which research findings can be used to improve day care.

10 Explain briefly why the single factor of being in day care or not being in day care has generated inconsistent research findings.

REVISION SUMMARY

Having covered this topic you should be able to:

✓ define 'day care', 'cognitive development' and 'social development'

✓ describe research findings and conclusions related to the effects of day care on cognitive development, including why day care might harm or benefit cognitive development

✓ describe research findings and conclusions related to the effects of day care on social development, including why day care might harm or benefit social development

✓ consider whether day care has harmful effects on the development of children

✓ describe how research can be applied to improving day care.

Unit 2 // Attachments in development

Topic 1: The development and variety of attachments

- **Attachment** is a strong emotional and reciprocal bond between two people, especially between an infant and its caregiver(s).

- Infants become attached to **one person first**, followed soon by **multiple attachments**. Strength of attachment varies between individual infants and appears to be related to responsiveness rather than time spent with a caregiver.

- **Bowlby** proposed **four phases of development**: pre-attachment, attachment in the making, specific attachments and goal-corrected partnership.

- Research into secure/insecure attachment is based on the **Strange Situation** classification.

- **Ainsworth and Bell** found that infants could be classified as **secure** (Type B), **avoidant–insecure** (Type A) or **resistant–insecure** (Type C). Type B was the most common group. A further group (Type D) has been identified.

- Further research shows that the Strange Situation is **reliable**, but may not be **valid**. Classifications vary from attachment figure to attachment figure (multiple caregiver paradox), but this can be resolved by taking an aggregate of attachment relationships.

- The **caregiver sensitivity hypothesis** proposes that sensitivity in caregiver interactions is a key feature of secure attachment. The **temperament hypothesis** suggests infants' innate temperament explains their behaviour in the Strange Situation.

- **Cross-cultural research** tests the validity of the Strange Situation and may indicate which aspects of attachment behaviour are innate and which due to cultural practices.

- **Takahashi** found that Japanese infants were much more distressed when left alone in the Strange Situation, which distorted the classification of the participants. Further research by **Van IJzendoorn and Kroonenberg** found similar rates of secure and insecure attachments in different countries.

- Advantages have been claimed for both **monotropy** and **multiple attachments**. There is evidence that infants do form one primary attachment in many cultures.

- Learning theory suggests that attachments form through **classical conditioning** (associating food with the person doing the feeding) and **operant conditioning** (food is the primary reinforcer, and the person supplying the food is the secondary reinforcer).

- Criticisms come from research by **Schaffer and Emerson** and from **Harlow and Harlow**, indicating that infants are not most attached to the person who feeds them.

- **Social releasers** encourage adult responses, and sensitive responses (caregiver sensitivity hypothesis) lead to the formation of attachments during a critical period. One special relationship (monotropy) leads to the formation of an internal working model and continuity in later relationships (the continuity hypothesis).

- However, correlations do not demonstrate a cause. Further criticisms are drawn from studies of deprivation and privation, and lack of evidence for evolutionary theory.

Topic 2: Deprivation and privation

- **Deprivation** refers to the loss of emotional contact with a primary caregiver.

- The **maternal deprivation hypothesis** states that healthy emotional development depends on having a warm, continuous relationship with a mother (or mother-substitute) before the age of $2\frac{1}{2}$ years.

- **Bowlby** found that young thieves were more likely to have experienced separations than children who were disturbed but not antisocial.

- Further research found that **hospitalized** children could recover if separations were for less than three months (**Spitz and Wolf**).

- **Separation** is a physical disconnection between child and caregiver that may, but need not, result in deprivation. The **Robertsons**, and **Skeels and Dye** demonstrated the benefits of emotional care during periods of separation.

- **Rutter** suggested that negative effects are not due to separations but to other intervening variables, and that privation rather than deprivation may be more important.

- **Privation** refers to the lack of contact with a primary caregiver. Privation is not the opposite of deprivation.

- **Hodges and Tizard** found that the **adopted children** appeared to recover (not supporting the maternal deprivation hypothesis). However, both groups had difficulties outside the home, which does support the maternal deprivation hypothesis.

- Further research into institutional care indicates that recovery is possible (**Rutter and colleagues**) although not all evidence supports this (**Quinton and colleagues**).

- Case histories suggest that recovery is possible if good subsequent care is provided at a young enough age. However, such studies are highly flawed. Studies of **reactive attachment disorder** indicate that sometimes recovery is not possible.

- There is evidence for and against the view that deprivation/privation is irreversible. All studies have problems related to methodology and/or explanations for the findings, which makes the data difficult to interpret.

Topic 3: Critical issue – Day care

- **Day care** is care that takes place outside the home, by someone other than close family, and does not involve overnight care.

- Day care may affect **cognitive development** because disruption of attachment bonds affects the secure base for exploration and reduces opportunities for stimulation.

- Studies indicate a link between poor school performance and preschool day care, e.g. the survey by **Russell**, and studies by **Hazen and Durrett**, **Bryant and colleagues** and **Ruhm**.

- Studies of **high-quality** day care show that day care can have beneficial effects. **Enrichment programmes** such as Headstart have been found to have small but significant long-term effects on the cognitive development of disadvantaged children.

- Day care may affect **social development** because it affects the continuity of the infant–caregiver relationship.

- Some research points to **negative effects**: less security of attachment (**Belsky and Rovine**) and increased aggressiveness (**NICHD study**).

- Some research has found **no negative effects**, e.g. **Clarke-Stewart and colleagues**.

- Some research has found **positive effects** in terms of better social abilities (**Clarke-Stewart and colleagues**) and less delinquency (**Schweinhart and colleagues**).

- Many factors affect a child's experiences of day care, including **time spent** and **quality** of day care, age, **temperamental** differences and **attachment** experiences at home.

- Research can be used to improve day care. Consistency and quality of care are important. Caregivers can receive training to improve quality.

Answering exam questions on Attachments in development

For sample examination questions and answers on Attachments in development, together with examiner comments on the answers, see pp. 253–5.

Unit 2 // Attachments in development

3 UNIT

Stress

PREVIEW

After you have read this unit, you should be able to:

>> explain stress as a bodily response, including the physiological systems underlying the stress-response

>> discuss research into the links between stress and physical illness, and the effects of stress on the immune system

>> discuss research into the sources of stress, such as life changes and workplace stressors

>> understand individual differences in reactions to stress, including factors such as personality, culture and gender

>> discuss methods of managing the negative effects of stress, including the strengths and weaknesses of physical and psychological approaches

>> understand the central role of 'control' in the ways that stress is perceived.

INTRODUCTION

Stress is a common topic of conversation nowadays. For instance, we often hear people say: "I'm feeling really stressed at the moment." Stress is believed to account for high levels of anxiety and depression, for increased vulnerability to colds and flu, and for heart attacks and strokes (damage to the brain's blood supply). Every week in papers and magazines, there are articles on how to cope with the high levels of modern-day stress, while thousands of professional and amateur psychologists make a living out of helping people to manage stress and its consequences.

You will notice that stress is generally referred to in a negative way. Yet, Hans Selye, one of the pioneering researchers into stress, pointed out that stress can also be associated with positive as well as negative experiences. To distinguish between the two, he referred to 'eustress' and 'distress', where eustress is the amount of stress needed for an active, healthy life. However, when levels of stress increase and exceed a person's ability to cope, it becomes potentially harmful; this is distress. The focus of this unit will be on the negative experiences associated with stress that is maladaptive.

In this unit, we shall look at the background to modern stress research, and evaluate the evidence for links between stress, and psychological and physical disorders. We shall see that some common assumptions about the effects of stress are well founded, but that some are not supported by experimental evidence. Topic 1 looks at stress as a bodily response, while in Topic 2 you will explore different sources of stress.

We shall also see how successful methods of coping with stress have to take into account the causes of stress and the physiological mechanisms of the stress-response. Stress management is the focus of Topic 3.

Simon Green

Topic 1 >> Stress as a bodily response

1 Look at the three photos above. Do any of these photos show something that you typically find stressful?

2 List some of the other causes of stress (i.e. stressors) that you experience in your life.

3 Compare your list with the lists of one or two other people in your class. Alternatively, ask one or two of your friends to tell you about their list of stressors. Are there many differences between the stressors identified?

KEY TERMS

Cardiovascular disorder: any disorder of the cardiovascular system, e.g. high blood pressure, coronary heart disease (heart attack) or stroke. (The cardiovascular system consists of the heart and the blood vessels. It is responsible for distributing oxygen and nutrients to the body's organs.)

General Adaptation Syndrome (GAS): a model, described by Hans Selye, of how the body reacts during stressful situations. There are three stages: (a) alarm stage when an arousal response is activated, (b) resistance stage when the body is apparently coping with the stressor, (c) exhaustion stage – if stress continues for too long, it can lead to physical symptoms such as a stomach ulcer or heart attack.

Immune system: the system that protects the body against infection; a network of cells and chemicals that seek out and destroy invading particles.

Stress: can be defined in three ways: (a) as a response or reaction to something in the environment, (b) as a stimulus or stressor, i.e. a feature of the environment that produces a stress-response, (c) as a lack of fit between the perceived demands of the environment and the perceived ability to cope with those demands; this transactional model of stress is the most popular among psychologists.

Stressor: any stimulus in the environment that produces the stress-response, as described by Selye – for example, life events (such as dealing with death and bereavement or the breakdown of a long-term relationship) or events associated with the workplace (such as workload, conflict between home and work, keeping up with changes or lack of career prospects).

MODELS OF STRESS

Before we look at the bodily responses involved in stress, we have to be clear about what we mean by stress. The term, as we use it today, was first used by the American physiologist, Walter Cannon, in 1914. However, it was the experimental work of Hans Selye in the 1930s that really introduced the topic into the scientific and psychological world. After studying the reactions of rats to the stress of repeated daily injections, Selye proposed that in animals and humans, the body responds to a range of psychological and physical stressors with the same pattern of physiological activation. He called this pattern the General Adaptation Syndrome (Selye 1956), and suggested that it could in some circumstances lead to harmful changes in the body. This was the beginning of the modern study of stress.

The transactional model of stress

The transactional model of stress is the most popular approach to studying stress today. This model proposes that stress is a lack of fit between the perceived demands of the environment and the perceived ability to cope with those demands.

Selye had a stimulus view of stress, whereby any stimulus that produced the physical signs of the stress-response was defined as a stressor. The transactional approach argues that the key to defining the degree of stress experienced by an individual lies in their perception of themselves and their world. It defines a state of stress as a mismatch between the demands we perceive the world is making on us and our perceived strategies for coping with those demands, i.e. our coping strategies.

Some people overestimate the demands of exams, and underestimate their preparations. They will be highly stressed, even though, objectively, they should not be and will do extremely well. Others underestimate the

ACTIVITY

The transactional model and your stressors

Look back at the list of stressors you wrote in response to the questions in 'Getting you thinking...' on p. 81. For each stressor you noted, write down how the transactional model of stress would help to explain why it causes you stress.

demands of the examination and overestimate their preparations; they will do badly, but at least they will not be stressed when they fail. The key features are how people perceive and evaluate demands, and coping abilities. The important development, then, compared with Selye's original ideas is the introduction of a central cognitive element. This allows us to emphasize and explain the role of individual differences in how people perceive and react to stressful situations. It also means that we can use cognitive strategies to help people cope with stress, as we shall see later.

Before considering Selye's General Adaptation Syndrome (GAS), however, we need to look at some physiology in order to understand the stress-response.

The body's response to stressors

There are two main ways in which our body responds to stress, and both involve the adrenal gland.

We have two adrenal glands, lying just above the kidneys. Each adrenal gland is made up of two distinct sections – the adrenal cortex and the adrenal medulla. These two sections release different sets of hormones into the bloodstream (see Fig. 3.1) and are controlled by two different pathways.

The transactional model emphasizes the role of individual differences in how people perceive and react to stressful situations. What is stressful to one person may not be so for another person.

The hypothalamic–pituitary–adrenal cortex pathway

This is under the control of the hypothalamus and the pituitary gland. The hypothalamus is a small structure at the base of the brain, while the pituitary lies in the skull cavity just below the hypothalamus (to which it is connected by the infundibulum). The pituitary has been called the master gland of the body because it releases a number of hormones into the bloodstream, which in turn control many vital body functions. One of these hormones is the adrenocorticotrophic hormone (ACTH), which travels to the adrenal cortex and stimulates the release of hormones called corticosteroids into the bloodstream. There are a large number of corticosteroids which have a range of effects on the body and are a vital part of the stress-response. The hypothalamic–pituitary–adrenal cortex pathway (HPAC) is activated when higher brain centres evaluate a situation as stressful and instruct the hypothalamus to stimulate the release of ACTH from the pituitary.

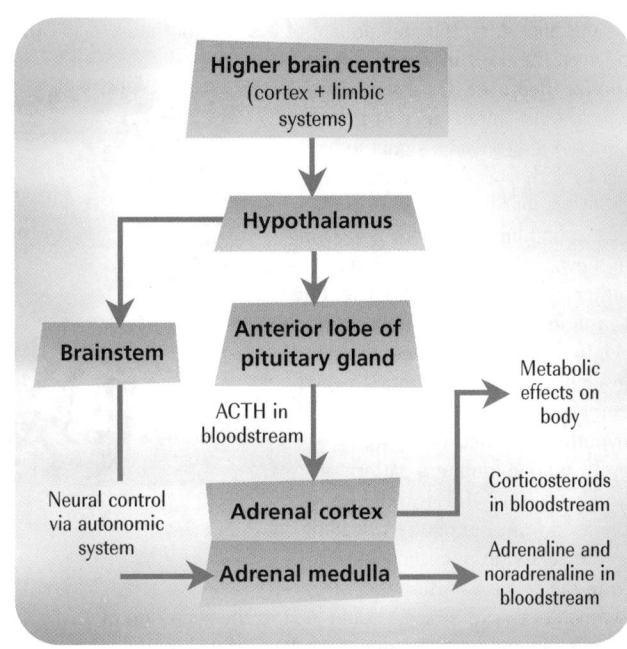

Figure 3.1 >> *Physiology of the stress-response*

The hypothalamic–autonomic nervous system–adrenal medulla pathway

The control of this part of the adrenal gland is very different. The autonomic nervous system (ANS) is a network of nerve pathways running from centres in the lower parts of the brain (the brainstem) out to the organs of the body such as the heart, digestive system, the circulatory (blood) system and various glands, including the adrenal medulla. The ANS centres in the brainstem are in turn controlled by higher brain structures, especially the hypothalamus. The role of the ANS is to maintain the normal functioning of bodily systems in response to demands. When you run, you need more energy and oxygen supplied to the muscles, so our energy reserves (fats and carbohydrates) have to be converted into sugars and fatty acids in the bloodstream, and our heart rate and blood pressure have to increase. All this is carried out by the ANS without our conscious control.

To help it carry out its functions, the ANS has two subdivisions – the sympathetic and the parasympathetic. Each has nerve pathways running to the internal organs of the body.

- When the *sympathetic* subdivision is activated, we see a pattern of bodily arousal: heart rate and blood pressure increase; fats and carbohydrates are mobilized; activity in the digestive tract slows down – this pattern is known as 'sympathetic arousal'.

- When the *parasympathetic* subdivision is activated, this leads to the opposite picture: heart rate and blood pressure return to normal and digestion speeds up – a pattern of calm and bodily relaxation.

The adrenal medulla is controlled by the ANS, and activation of the sympathetic branch stimulates it to release the hormones adrenaline and noradrenaline into the bloodstream (in the USA these are called epinephrine and norepinephrine). Adrenaline is well known as an arousal hormone, and noradrenaline has similar effects. Together they reinforce the pattern of sympathetic activation, stimulating heart rate and blood pressure, and further mobilizing energy reserves.

So, in stressful situations, the hypothalamus activates both the HPAC and the hypothalamic–ANS–adrenal medulla pathways.

Activating the body's stress-response

Selye identified the activation of these two pathways – the HPAC and the hypothalamic–ANS–adrenal medulla – as the main components of the body's response to stressors. He also began the debate about why they should be activated under these conditions.

The key to this is to understand that the two systems, when aroused, prepare the body for energy expenditure. Corticosteroids, adrenaline and noradrenaline mobilize energy reserves and sustain blood flow and heart rate to get oxygen to the muscles. They do this under normal circumstances to supply our daily energy needs, but in stressful situations we also have to consider the role of higher brain centres.

Normally, the hypothalamus and the ANS function perfectly well without our conscious involvement, making sure that the body's physiological systems function within normal limits. However, we do need the higher centres when things happen in the world around us to which we have to respond quickly.

To our ancestors, the appearance of a sabre-toothed tiger on the horizon was a signal to run for their lives. Or, if they were hunting, the appearance of a suitable target was a signal to chase. Either way, the reaction was due to higher brain centres in the cortex and limbic system perceiving and evaluating the situation as either threatening or attractive. But to run in any direction needs energy. So, to make sure the energy was available, the higher centres would communicate with the hypothalamus and the ANS, and would stimulate a pattern of bodily arousal; ACTH would be released from the pituitary, leading to the secretion of corticosteroids from the adrenal cortex, and sympathetic ANS arousal would lead to the secretion of adrenaline and noradrenaline from the adrenal medulla. When the emergency was over, the systems would return to their normal level of functioning.

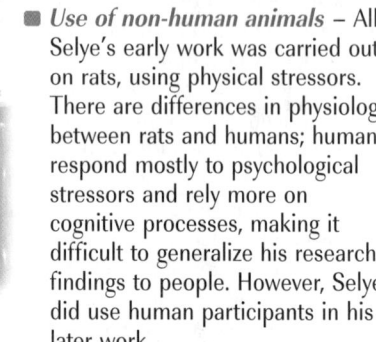

Hans Selye

Cannon (1914) called this pattern of bodily arousal the 'flight or fight' response. Selye's experimental studies showed that it was also central to the stress-response he observed in rats. Later, he proposed that any physical or psychological stressor activated the two pathways. Selye developed a model, the General Adaptation Syndrome (GAS), which explained the short-term effects of exposure to stressors, but also accounted for stress-related illnesses such as gastric ulcers.

The General Adaptation Syndrome

The GAS (Selye 1956) has three stages (see Fig. 3.2):

- In the first *alarm* stage, the presence of a stressful event is registered; this can be a threat from outside or a physical stressor, such as injury or illness affecting the body. The hypothalamus–pituitary system secretes a surge of ACTH which, in turn, releases corticosteroids from the adrenal cortex, while sympathetic ANS activation leads to increased adrenaline and noradrenaline secretion from the adrenal medulla. The body is prepared for energy expenditure, i.e. to respond to the perceived threat.

- In the second stage of *resistance*, the body's stress-response is fully activated and is apparently coping with the stressor, and so from the outside, things seem to be back under control.

- However, if the stressor is long lasting or chronic, the body enters the third stage of GAS, the stage of *exhaustion*. Selye felt that hormone reserves were depleted, and it is at this point that stress-related conditions such as raised blood pressure, ulcers, depression and anxiety may develop as stress systems become exhausted.

In evaluating the GAS, the key points are as follows:

- *Experimental support* – The GAS was the first systematic attempt based on experimental data to describe the body's responses to stress. Selye was the first to emphasize the central role of the HPAC and the hypothalamic–ANS–adrenal medulla pathways.

- *Use of non-human animals* – All Selye's early work was carried out on rats, using physical stressors. There are differences in physiology between rats and humans; humans respond mostly to psychological stressors and rely more on cognitive processes, making it difficult to generalize his research findings to people. However, Selye did use human participants in his later work.

- *Individual differences* – The GAS ignores individual differences, such as Type A behaviour (discussed on p. 95) and gender. It assumes we all respond in the same way to stressors, but we now know that personality and gender can significantly affect reactions to stress (see pp. 97–8).

The body systems underpinning the stress-response are responsible for providing energy resources whenever we need them. Most of the threats facing our ancestors

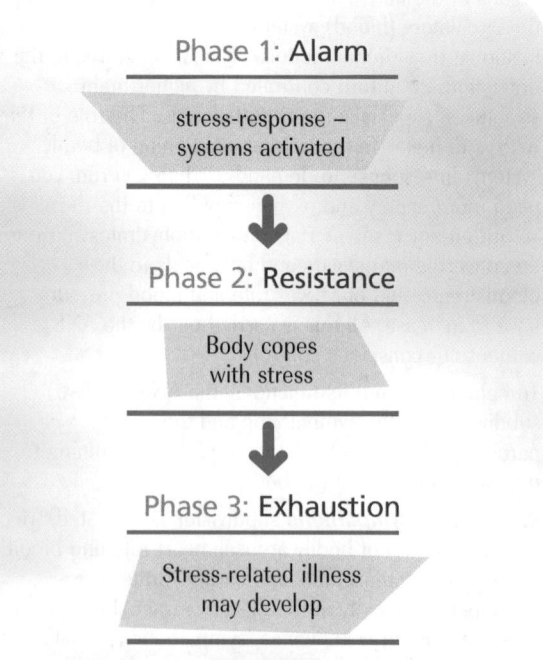

Figure 3.2 >> *The three stages of Selye's General Adaptation Syndrome*

AS Physiological Psychology

were external (e.g. large predators and other people), and for that reason a physical response that enabled them to expend energy and either fight the threat or take flight was appropriate (adaptive). It was a highly effective mechanism for survival, and this is still the case if we find ourselves in an extreme situation that requires an immediate physical response. However, our world today is very different; while physical threat and violence are still too common, they are not part of most people's daily experience. For the most part, the daily concerns we have are dominated by psychological stress involving such things as our relationships, careers, the future of the environment, pressures to be successful. Unfortunately, worrying about a big telephone bill or what we look like can trigger the same stress-response as running away from a large predator. Our stress-response is geared to providing the resources we need for physical action (such as fighting or running away) and therefore provides energy that has nowhere to go. If a psychological stressor is long lasting and the physical response to it occurs over long periods, then damaging effects of stress can occur, as we shall see in the next section. Now try the following activity.

ACTIVITY

How do you feel when you experience stress?

1 Think back to the last time that you felt stressed because you were in a frightening situation – perhaps you were walking home along an unlit street late at night? How did you feel? What happened to your heart rate? How did your mouth feel? How did your stomach feel? How did you deal with this situation?

2 Now think of the last time you were stressed because you were struggling to finish some homework by the deadline for handing it in, or you had to give a presentation, but hadn't had enough time to prepare properly. Again, how did you feel and how did you react? What are the possible signs of stress that others might notice in you (e.g. moodiness, irritability)?

3 Were there any similarities in the way that you felt about each of these situations? Did you deal with each of these in similar or in different ways?

For our ancestors most stressors were physical. Nowadays, stressors are more often psychological – and yet the stress-response prepares us for fight or flight

STRESS AND PHYSICAL ILLNESS

The last phase of Selye's GAS is the stage of exhaustion. Selye thought that the constant outpouring of stress hormones eventually depleted our stores, so that a literal state of 'exhaustion' occurred. It was this that led to stress-related illness. Nowadays, the view has changed; it is the hormones themselves that are believed to be responsible for the negative effects of stressful situations. The two main reasons for this change in view are that:

- hormone supplies are rarely exhausted – even under the most severe pressure
- we now know far more about the widespread effects of these hormones on the body.

Stress-related activation of the HPAC pathway and the sympathetic branch of the ANS leads to the increased secretion of corticosteroids, adrenaline and noradrenaline. Heart rate and blood pressure increase and energy reserves are mobilized in the form of fatty acids and glucose in the bloodstream. We will look at some of the possible harmful effects of this energy mobilization below, but another important feature of the body's stress-response is that, besides activating some systems, it shuts down others. Blood supply is prioritized, increasing to heart and skeletal muscles and the brain, whilst decreasing to systems that are of no immediate use, such as the digestive tract.

Our immune system is also inhibited in stressful situations. The immune system is an immensely complex system of cells and chemicals that protects the body from infection by viruses and bacteria, and helps to repair tissue damage. During stress, however, everything is geared to escape, so protection and tissue-repair can wait until the emergency is over.

So the picture is one in which the body's systems are totally directed to survival in the face of threat. As long as the threat is short lived, this is an excellent survival strategy. However, if the threat is long lasting, the combination of maximum activation of the stress-response arousal pathways and the shutting down of non-essential systems can lead to problems.

Stress-related illness

Many illnesses are believed to be related to stress, including the following cardiovascular disorders:

- *hypertension* – raised blood pressure due to the furring up of the cardiovascular system
- *atherosclerosis* through raised blood pressure wearing away the blood-vessel lining, scarring of blood vessels that act as a collection point for fatty acids and glucose circulating in the bloodstream, and the formation and deposit of plaques that slowly block blood vessels
- *stroke* caused by plaques blocking the tiny blood vessels in the brain
- *raised blood pressure*, which can also cause a brain haemorrhage (the breaking of a blood vessel and bleeding into brain tissue)
- *coronary heart disease* (heart attack) caused by damage to the functioning of the heart, which is responsible for pumping blood around the body.

Other illnesses related to stress include migraine, asthma, gastric ulcers and eczema.

All of these conditions can have other causes besides chronic (long-lasting) stress. Heart disease and hypertension may have a genetic component and are certainly linked to diet. Often, it may be a case of stress interacting with these other factors to make the situation worse.

Furthermore, while chronic stress may not lead to obvious illness (such as a heart attack, flu or stomach ulcers), it can damage the body, making these conditions more likely to occur. There are many stages of deterioration between a healthy heart and blood supply and an actual heart attack or stroke.

We can divide the possible ways in which stress can damage the body into four simple categories:

- direct mechanical effects (atherosclerosis)
- energy mobilization (hypertension, atherosclerosis, brain haemorrhage, stroke)
- suppression of the immune system
- other effects.

Direct mechanical effects

The body's stress-response increases heart rate, pumping blood around the body at faster speeds and at a higher pressure. At particular points in the cardiovascular system, notably where blood vessels branch, this increased mechanical pressure can simply wear away the blood-vessel lining, resulting in atherosclerosis. Like any hydraulic system, increased pressure leads to increased damage and a shorter life.

Energy mobilization

Nowadays, most of our stress comes from psychological sources, such as life events and the workplace. Physical activity is rarely the coping response to psychological stress. However, the core of stress-induced arousal is the effect of corticosteroids, adrenaline and noradrenaline in releasing stored carbohydrates and fats from their storage cells into the bloodstream in the form of glucose and free fatty acids. These are then transported to the muscles and brain cells that need them as a source of energy. If they are not burnt up in energy expenditure, the body's systems will try to restore balance by reabsorbing the excess levels back into storage cells when the current emergency passes.

If the stress is chronic, reabsorption cannot cope, so high levels of glucose and free fatty acids remain in the bloodstream, where they contribute to the 'furring up' of the cardiovascular system. This can lead to hypertension and atherosclerosis.

Suppression of the immune system

The immune system is our main defence against infection by foreign agents. It is an immensely complicated network of cells and chemicals throughout the body that functions to seek out and destroy invading particles. Any agent that stimulates an immune response is called an antigen. Familiar antigens are bacteria, viruses and fungi (such as moulds and yeasts). Sometimes particles that are normally harmless, such as dust and pollen, cause an overreaction of the immune system, and this is the basis of allergies.

Key players in our immune system are the white blood cells, which are manufactured in the bone marrow and circulate in the bloodstream. The two types of white blood cell are lymphocytes and phagocytes, and these provide three different mechanisms of immunity:

- *Non-specific immunity* – phagocytes surround and ingest foreign particles wherever they encounter them.
- *Cell-based immunity* – lymphocytes called T cells (because they mature in the thymus gland) seek out and destroy any cells recognized as foreign (e.g. in transplanted tissues) and also cells infected with antigens such as viruses and bacteria. Closely related to T cells are NK (natural killer) cells, which also seek out and destroy antigens.
- *Antibody-based immunity* – another class of lymphocytes called B cells (because they mature in the bone marrow) destroy invading agents while they are still in the bloodstream and before they enter the body's tissues. They do this by producing large proteins called antibodies which attach themselves to the virus or bacteria, slowing them down and making it easier for other immune cells such as the phagocytes to destroy them.

The immune system is complex and stress-response hormones can affect it directly. For example, high levels of corticosteroids can shrink the thymus gland, preventing the growth of T cells. The immune system is also more sensitive to stress than was originally thought. Even short-lasting life events such as brief marital strife can cause suppression of the immune system (immunosuppression), while long-term life stress causes parallel long-term reductions in immune function (Willis *et al.* 1987). On the other hand, exercise, diet and social support can improve immune function, and as a self-regulating system, it will also recover from suppression if the stressful situation is resolved (Sapolsky 1994).

Short-term immunosuppression is not dangerous, but chronic (long-lasting) suppression leaves the body vulnerable to infection and disease. The best current example is AIDS, which leaves the sufferer vulnerable to a host of possible illnesses. So we would expect chronic stress to lead to more frequent illnesses and infections. We will look at the experimental evidence in the next section.

Other effects

The stress hormones, such as corticosteroids, adrenaline and noradrenaline, have many complex effects on the body. Apart from energy mobilization and immunosuppression, they also affect many hormones released by the pituitary gland. Earlier, we referred to the role of the pituitary as a master gland, secreting many hormones, which in turn control a variety of bodily functions. Secretion of many of these hormones is disrupted by the stress-response, leading to various problems.

The pituitary controls sexual and reproductive functions. In males, testosterone production declines during the stress-response, leading to problems with erections and sexual desire. In females, menstrual cycles can be disrupted and sexual desire reduced. Pituitary release of growth hormone is inhibited, potentially affecting growth and repair of bone structure. There is a rare condition known as 'stress dwarfism', in which children suffering extreme chronic stress through deprivation or abuse fail to grow normally.

Another aspect of the body's stress-response is a loss of pain sensitivity (stress-induced analgesia). During emergencies, the release of brain neurotransmitters called enkephalins and endorphins is increased. These control our pain sensitivity, and it makes sense for this to be reduced in situations such as a battle, when people suffering severe injury only realize it when the conflict has subsided.

Complete the next activity before reading on.

ACTIVITY

How stress can indirectly affect your health and wellbeing

As we have seen, chronic stress can lead *directly* to physical illness, such as heart disease or weakening of the immune system. Sometimes, however, stress may cause physical illness *indirectly*, by altering the way a person behaves, which could in turn damage their health.

In what ways might a stressed person behave that could later increase the risk of damage to their physical health?

To help you to start thinking about this, consider the following three 'stressful' scenarios:

1 A student studying for an exam in a subject that they find quite difficult.

2 A person who has just broken up with their girl/boyfriend after several years of being together.

3 Someone who is caring for a relative who is terminally ill.

In the last activity, you identified a range of behaviours that might result from being in a stressful situation and could indirectly affect a person's health in the longer term. These probably included smoking, drinking excess alcohol, drug abuse or neglecting oneself by eating a poor diet over a period of time, making it more likely that the person will suffer from illnesses such as colds and coughs. Later in the unit we will be considering a range of techniques that can help to reduce the negative effects of stress.

RESEARCH INTO STRESS AND PHYSICAL ILLNESS

Many studies have investigated the effects of stress on:
- physical illness (including cardiovascular disorders)
- the immune system.

The key studies described below are two of the best known. See also the Western Collaborative Group Study undertaken by Friedman and Rosenman (1974), described on p. 95, for a study of the relationship between stress and cardiovascular disorders.

KEY STUDY >> STRESS AND PHYSICAL ILLNESS

the 'executive monkey' study by Brady *et al.* (1958)

Aim >>

To investigate whether the stress of receiving electric shocks would lead to stress-related illness in monkeys, and whether this would interact with the degree of control over the shocks.

Procedures >>

- Monkeys received electric shocks to their feet at 20-second intervals for periods of six hours at a time, with six hours' rest in between.
- The electric foot shocks were not signalled.
- Monkeys were run in pairs, with one in each pair – the so-called 'executive' monkey – able to press a lever to postpone shocks for 20 seconds.
- The other monkey in the pair could not press the lever, but received all the foot shocks that were delivered (this second monkey in the pair was the 'yoked' animal).

Findings >>

- Not all shocks could be avoided on this schedule.
- After 23 days the 'executive' monkeys began to die of gastric ulceration.
- The yoked control monkeys, who received shocks but could not try to avoid them, remained healthy.

Conclusions >>

- Brady concluded that the shocks themselves were not severely stressful as the yoked monkeys showed little gastric ulceration; the critical factor was the stress associated with trying to avoid the shocks.
- Having *control* was the stressful element in this study, causing gastric ulceration in the 'executive' monkeys.

Criticisms >>

- Brady used monkeys, so there is a problem of generalizing his results to humans. Monkeys have a different physiology to humans and may respond to stress in different ways. However, Brady did show that trying to cope with stressors is highly stressful for monkeys.
- Brady also chose monkeys who were the most active bar-pressers as the executives; as a group, they were more active generally than the yoked control group, and this may have made them more sensitive to the stress of the footshocks. This means that the experiment was poorly controlled, as both groups should have been made up of monkeys that were equally active.

AO2 check

Stressing monkeys (or any animals) until they die or become severely ill is highly unethical and would not be permitted today. All researchers are now obliged to follow clear ethical guidelines (see Unit 5), which ensure that such a study could not be carried out again.

AS Physiological Psychology

a study into the functioning of the immune system by Kiecolt-Glaser *et al.* (1984)

Aim >>

To investigate whether the stress of important examinations has an effect on the functioning of the immune system.

Procedures >>

- This was a natural experiment using 75 medical students.
- Blood samples were taken: (a) one month before their final examinations (relatively low stress), and (b) during the examinations (high stress).
- Immune function was assessed by measuring NK cell activity in the blood samples.
- The students were also given questionnaires to assess psychological variables such as life events and loneliness.

Findings >>

- NK cell activity was significantly reduced in the second blood sample, taken during their final examinations, compared with the first sample (taken one month before their final examinations).
- NK cell activity was most reduced in participants who also reported high levels of life events and loneliness.

Conclusions >>

- Examination stress reduces immune function, potentially leaving the individual vulnerable to illness and infections.
- Immune function is also affected by psychological variables such as the stress of life events and feelings of loneliness. These long-term stressors may make individuals more vulnerable to the added effect of short-term stressors such as examinations.

Criticisms >>

- This was essentially a correlational study, so a strong conclusion about a cause-and-effect relationship cannot be drawn.
- It was a natural experiment using a natural source of stress and therefore had reasonable ecological validity, but students may be a special group and generalizations should be made with caution.

AO2 check

However, the results are in line with other studies linking stress to reduced immune function. Kiecolt-Glaser's research group has carried out many other studies on stress and the immune system. They have shown that immune function is significantly reduced in highly stressed groups such as carers for patients with Alzheimer's disease (dementia) (Kiecolt-Glaser *et al.* 1991) and women going through divorce proceedings (Kiecolt-Glaser *et al.* 1987). Even short periods of marital conflict have been known to lead to immunosupression, with women showing a greater and longer-lasting reduction than men (Kiecolt-Glaser *et al.* 1998).

ACTIVITY

Expert interview

Read the 'Expert interview' with Janice Kiecolt-Glaser on p. 86. As you read it, pay particular attention to:

1 the effects of short-term stress on the immune system

2 the immunological consequences of personal relationships

3 any evidence of gender differences.

Stress and the *immune system*

Janice Kiecolt-Glaser is Professor of Psychiatry and Psychology in The Ohio State University College of Medicine. Working in the area of psychoneuroimmunology, she has written more than 160 articles, chapters and books, most in collaboration with Dr Ronald Glaser. Their studies have shown the important health consequences of stress, including slower wound-healing and impaired vaccine-responses in older adults. In addition, their work has focused on the ways in which personal relationships influence immune and endocrine function, and health.

Q Would the reductions you see in immune function always make people more vulnerable to infection and illness, or would it only be in chronic states, such as caring for Alzheimer's patients? Are the changes associated with *short-term* stressors (such as examinations, marital arguments) unlikely to increase vulnerability to illness?

A Even short-term, predictable and relatively benign stressors can increase vulnerability to illness. For example, dental students participated in a study in which small standardized wounds made three days before a major test healed on average 40 per cent more slowly than those made during the summer vacation; indeed, no student healed as rapidly during exams as during the vacation. Similarly, medical students who were more stressed took longer to produce a protective antibody response following hepatitis B vaccination than students who were less stressed, suggesting that the stressed students would also be slower to develop an antibody response to other pathogens. Theoretically, therefore, they could be at greater risk of developing more severe illness.

Q Have you noticed any characteristics in your participant groups that seem to protect people against the effects of stress on the immune system?

A Individuals who have stronger close personal relationships are less likely to show adverse immunological consequences when stressed. For example, when we followed students through exams, we found that lonelier students had lower NK cell activity than students who were not as lonely. Additionally, students who reported lower social support experienced a weaker immune response following hepatitis B vaccination than those with greater support. Spouse caregivers of dementia sufferers who reported lower levels of social support showed the greatest and most uniformly negative changes in immune function one year later. Lower marital satisfaction was also associated with poorer immune function.

Janice Kiecolt-Glaser

Q Have you noticed any consistent gender differences in your studies? If so, how do you explain them?

A In our studies the most consistent gender differences occurred in response to marital conflict. The relationships between adverse hormonal and immunological changes, and negative or hostile behaviors, were stronger for women than for men, and women's physiological changes following marital conflict showed greater persistence than men's.

Arguments with the spouse are more upsetting to women than men, and wives demonstrate more detailed and vivid memories of marital disagreements than their husbands. Women reminisce more frequently about important relationship events, and spend more time thinking about their marital relationships than men – all reasons to expect that women would show greater responsivity.

Suppression of the immune system need not necessarily lead to illness and disease if immune function remains within the normal range. Even if it is not, you still have to be exposed to an infectious agent for illness to develop. Cohen *et al.* (1993) demonstrated this in a classic study. Participants filled in questionnaires on negative life events, how stressed they felt, and the degree of negative emotions (depression and hostility) they felt. These scores were combined into a stress index. The participants were then exposed to low doses of the common cold virus. 82 per cent of the 394 participants became infected with the cold virus, and infection was highly correlated with their stress index score, i.e. the higher their score, the more likely they were to become infected. Although this was a correlational study, it strongly suggests that high levels of stress reduce immune function and make a person more vulnerable to viral infection.

Research evidence suggests that there is a relationship between stress and physical illnesses, and in some cases this comes about through immunosuppression. Findings on life events and workplace stress are also relevant to this area; some of these studies are reviewed in the next topic.

✓ CHECK YOUR UNDERSTANDING

Check your understanding of stress as a bodily response by answering these questions. Try to do this from memory at first. You can check your answers by looking back through Topic 1.

1 What are (a) stressors (b) a stress-response? Who did the earliest systematic studies of the stress-response?

2 Describe the transactional model of stress.

3 Outline the two main pathways of the body's stress-response.

4 Outline the three stages of Selye's General Adaptation Syndrome (GAS) to show how chronic stress may lead to illness.

5 What does the body's immune system do and what is immunosuppression?

6 Describe one important confounding variable in Brady and colleagues' 'executive' monkey study.

7 How did Kiecolt-Glaser and colleagues measure activity of the immune system?

8 Outline one strength and one limitation of Kiecolt-Glaser and colleagues' work.

9 How did Cohen and colleagues measure the stress levels of their participants and how did they test immune function?

10 Outline one strength and one limitation of Cohen and colleagues' study.

REVISION SUMMARY

Having covered this topic you should be able to:

✓ define the following terms: 'cardiovascular disorders', 'General Adaptation Syndrome', 'immune system', 'stress' and 'stressor'

✓ describe at least two ways in which the body responds to stress – these should include the two main pathways of the body's stress-response

✓ describe and evaluate the General Adaptation Syndrome

✓ outline the effects of stress on the body, including physiological arousal and immunosuppression

✓ describe and evaluate research into stress and cardiovascular disorders

✓ describe and evaluate research into stress and the immune system

✓ describe the aims, procedures, findings, conclusions and criticisms for a key study investigating stress and physical illness, and a key study investigating the effects of stress on the immune system.

GETTING YOU THINKING...

In 1967, Holmes and Rahe published a scale called the Social Readjustment Rating Scale (SRRS), reproduced in Table 3.1 opposite. This scale consists of a list of 43 major life events that were perceived as being potentially stressful because they forced people to make substantial psychological readjustments. Each life event in the list is allocated a point value to reflect the relative amount of change it requires. This is known as the Life Change Unit (LCU).

1 Look at the three photographs below. Why do you think that Holmes and Rahe included each of the events illustrated in their scale?

2 Why do you think that each event was allocated the rating it was?

Outstanding personal achievement is ranked 25 in the SRRS, with a LCU of 28.

Taking a holiday is rated 41, with a LCU of 13.

Marriage is ranked 7, with a LCU of 50.

KEY TERMS

Life changes: major life events, such as marriage, divorce, moving house and having a baby, that are scored according to their psychological impact within the Social Readjustment Rating Scale (SRRS) and used to investigate the relationship between life changes and stress-related health breakdown.

Control (psychological): the sense that we can anticipate events that occur in our environment – a feeling that we can accomplish things and are not at the mercy of forces beyond our control.

Workplace stressor: any stimulus in the workplace environment that produces the stress-response, such as work overload or role ambiguity.

RESEARCH INTO SOURCES OF STRESS

As we saw in Topic 1, the common definition of stress views it as rooted in the demands that we perceive in our environment compared with our perceived ability to cope with those demands; therefore, we can describe many sources of stress. We make many demands on ourselves – am I happy enough, rich enough, do I look okay, will I meet this deadline? Other people also make demands on us – get this job done, make me happier, earn more money, be my friend. We get stuck in traffic jams or break down on the motorway; friends and relations have accidents, become ill or even die; we all have illnesses and accidents. Whether these situations are regarded as stressful depends on our coping abilities, but some of them are almost certain to be.

Experimental approaches to the study of stress need to define and, if possible, quantify the amount of stress in people's lives, so that reliable links can be made to physical and psychological disorders. The problem is that the sources of stress are so varied that many different approaches have been developed to assess stress. We will look at some of the most popular ones.

The Social Readjustment Rating Scale (SRRS)

This scale, developed by Thomas Holmes and Richard Rahe in 1967, is also known as the Holmes–Rahe Life Events Rating Scale. Together with some later variations, the SRRS has been the most widely used of all methods for assessing life stress.

Inevitably, things happen in life that force us to make psychological adjustments. The more we have to adjust, the more stressful the event is. Holmes and Rahe made a list of major life events, based on their experience as clinicians. They then asked hundreds of men and women, of a variety of ages and backgrounds, to rate the events in terms of the amount of readjustment they would require, i.e. their psychological impact. The death of a spouse came out top, and was given an arbitrary value of 100. Other events were given ratings relative to this ranking, so that redundancy, for instance, came out as 47, a house move as 20, and holidays as 13.

Table 3.1 >> The Social Readjustment Rating Scale (SRRS)

	Life event	LCU		Life event	LCU
1	Death of spouse	100	22	Change in responsibilities at work	29
2	Divorce	73	23	Son or daughter leaving home	29
3	Marital separation	65	24	Trouble with in-laws	29
4	Jail term	63	25	Outstanding personal achievement	28
5	Death of close family member	63	26	Wife begins or stops work	26
6	Personal injury or illness	53	27	Begin or end school	26
7	Marriage	50	28	Change in living conditions	25
8	Fired at work	47	29	Revision of personal habits	24
9	Marital reconciliation	45	30	Trouble with boss	23
10	Retirement	45	31	Change in work hours or conditions	20
11	Change in health of family member	44	32	Change in residence	20
12	Pregnancy	40	33	Change in schools	20
13	Sex difficulties	39	34	Change in recreation	19
14	Gain new family member	39	35	Change in church activities	19
15	Business readjustment	39	36	Change in social activities	18
16	Change in financial status	38	37	Mortgage or loan less than US$10,000	17
17	Death of close friend	37	38	Change in sleeping habits	16
18	Change to different line of work	36	39	Change in number of family get-togethers	15
19	Change in number of arguments with spouse	35	40	Change in eating habits	15
20	Mortgage over US$10,000	31	41	Vacation	13
21	Foreclosure of mortgage or loan	30	42	Christmas	12
			43	Minor violation of the law	11

Source: Holmes and Rahe (1967)

Once the scale was constructed, it was simply a matter of asking participants to check off any of the 43 life events they had experienced over a given period – usually two years, but sometimes less. The researcher then totalled their score and used it as an index of that person's life stress. Using studies that were both retrospective (asking people with possible stress-related illnesses to look back at the previous two years) and prospective (assessing life stress and then observing participants over the following months), Holmes and Rahe proposed that a score of 150 or more increased the chances of stress-related health breakdown by 30 per cent, while a score of over 300 increased the odds by 50 per cent.

KEY STUDY >> LIFE CHANGES AND STRESS

a study by Rahe et al. into life changes as a source of stress (1970)

Aim >>

To investigate whether scores on the Holmes and Rahe Social Readjustment Rating Scale (SRRS) were correlated with the subsequent onset of illness.

Procedures >>

- 2,500 male American sailors were given the SRRS to assess how many life events they had experienced in the previous six months.
- The total score on the SRRS was recorded for each participant.
- Then over the following six-month tour of duty, detailed records were kept of each sailor's health status.
- The recorded number of Life Change Units were correlated with the sailors' illness scores.

Findings >>

- There was a positive correlation of +0.118 between Life Change scores and illness scores.
- Although the positive correlation was small (a perfect positive correlation would be +1.00), it did indicate that there was a meaningful relationship between Life Change Units and health (this is often referred to as a statistically significant correlation).
- As Life Change Units increased, so did the frequency of illness.

Conclusions >>

- The researchers concluded that as Life Change Units were positively correlated with illness scores, experiencing life events increased the chances of stress-related health breakdown.
- As the correlation was not perfect, life events cannot be the only factor in contributing to illness.

Criticisms >>

- The study does not take into account individual differences in reactions to stress.
- A correlation does not imply causality nor the direction of any effect; depression or anxiety may not be caused by life events, since depressed or anxious people may bring about life events such as separation or divorce.
- The sample was restricted to male US Navy personnel; therefore it was ethnocentric (Americans only) and androcentric (males only). This reduces the validity of the study and makes it difficult to generalize to other populations.

A02 check

On the positive side, these findings support other research that suggests that life-event scores do have a low but significant association with stress-related health breakdown.

Evaluation of the SRRS

Many studies have been done on the link between life events and health breakdown using the SRRS. Although significant correlations are often found, they tend, like the study undertaken by Rahe and colleagues outlined earlier, to be relatively small (the highest is about 0.30). This suggests a relationship between stress and health, but not a strong one. However, it also became clear that there were problems with the scale:

- *Individual differences* – The scale values for different events are arbitrary and will certainly vary from person to person. Some people really dislike holidays or Christmas, and would have them near the top of their list of stressors, rather than at the bottom. Others might find marital separation a relief from a highly dysfunctional relationship. The stress of taking out a large mortgage depends on your income. Each of us could devise a personal rating scale since the stress of an event depends upon our individual perception of it.

- *Causality* – The relationship between SRRS score and health is correlational and so tells us nothing about causality. Depression or chronic physical illness may lead to life problems rather than being caused by them.

- *Positive life events* – Some life events are positive. People getting married probably see it as a positive change, while 'change in financial state' can clearly be positive or negative. The SRRS does not distinguish positive from negative because the model assumes that any life change is stressful, without evidence to support such an assumption.

- *Self-report* – Self-report of life events can be surprisingly unreliable. Raphael *et al.* (1991) asked participants to fill out a life-events scale for the previous year, and then repeated the exercise every month for another year. As time passed, the agreement on life events between the later reports and the first declined significantly.

However, despite these criticisms, the SRRS was a major step in stress research for two main reasons:

- It was the first detailed attempt to quantify levels of stress in people's lives.
- Its use confirmed that life events can lead to health breakdown.

Life Experiences Survey

In the years following the introduction of the SRRS, refinements were made to life-event scales to try and overcome the criticisms outlined above. A popular version is the Life Experiences Survey (LES) (Sarason *et al.* 1978). Based on the SRRS, the LES has 57 items, but these can be rated in terms of their positive or negative impact on a seven-point scale (highly negative, –3, through neutral, 0, to highly positive, +3). This allows for individual differences in the perception of

events to be taken into account. There are also specialized sections that can be used for particular groups of people, such as students. The LES produces scores for positive change, negative change and total change. As you might expect, health problems correlate more highly with negative life-change scores, than with positive or total change.

One general problem with any life-event approach is that it concentrates on events that are by their very nature unusual. In any given study, 10 to 30 per cent of participants may experience none of the scale items, while still not being free of stress. This is because incidents we would not count as major events – the everyday hassles of life – can also be a source of considerable stress. These are everyday occurrences such as worrying about friendships, losing the car keys, concerns over appearance (weight, hair loss, skin condition), keeping up with college courses and minor health problems. For most people, these have more daily impact than items included in scales such as the SRRS or LES.

Hassles scale

Your hassles and uplifts

Keep a diary over the next week or so. At the end of each day, make a note of all the *hassles* that you have experienced (keeping the diary may be one of them!) and record the total number.

Beside your list of hassles for each day, make a note of all the *uplifts* you experienced on the same day and the total number.

Also, at the end of each day, give yourself a rating between 1 and 10 to indicate how you have felt that day: a rating of 1 indicates a very low sense of psychological wellbeing, while 10 indicates very high psychological wellbeing.

Finally, note down any health problems that you have experienced that day (e.g. headaches).

At the end of the week, prepare a bar chart to show the total number of hassles and uplifts for Day 1, Day 2 through to Day 7.

1 Does there appear to be any relationship between the number of hassles and uplifts on a particular day and the rating for general psychological wellbeing on that day?

2 Did you seem to experience more health problems after you had experienced a higher number of hassles?

3 How might you explain the possible relationship between the number of hassles, uplifts, general sense of psychological wellbeing and health problems?

Table 3.2 >> Examples of hassles and uplifts

Examples of hassles
>> Concerns about weight
>> Health of a family member
>> Rising prices of certain goods
>> Home maintenance
>> Too many things to do
>> Misplacing or losing things
>> Physical appearance

Examples of uplifts
>> Relating well to your spouse/partner/lover
>> Relating well to friends
>> Completing a task
>> Feeling healthy
>> Getting enough sleep
>> Eating out
>> Visiting, phoning or writing to someone

Household chores are a hassle for many people

To assess these very real sources of stress, Lazarus and colleagues devised the Hassles Scale (Kanner *et al.* 1981). The original form had 117 items, although versions can be constructed for subgroups, such as students (e.g. unfriendly classmates, boring teachers). Since they thought that positive events in life could reduce the impact of daily hassles, the group also introduced an Uplifts Scale, with 135 items that cheer people up; items include getting on well with your partner and feeling healthy. See Table 3.2 for some examples taken from the Hassles and Uplifts Scales.

Research shows that scores on the Hassles Scale can correlate with levels of depression, anxiety and health problems. DeLongis *et al.* (1982) compared Hassles scores with Life Events, and found that although both correlated significantly with health status, the association for Hassles scores was greater. No statistical relationship was found between Uplift scores and health outcomes.

In the final topic of this unit, we shall see that various factors can help protect us against the negative effects of stress. Recent variations of the life-event approach to stress include some assessment of these factors along with the life-event scale. For example, Moos and

Swindle (1990) propose eight areas of common life stressors:

- illness and other medical problems
- home and local environment (items such as safety and traffic)
- family finance
- relationship with partner
- children
- extended family
- work (discussed in the next part of this topic)
- relationships outside the family.

These areas are assessed using their Life Stressors and Social Resources Inventory, which also incorporates measures of factors that may help cope with life stressors. These include social support networks and financial state.

In evaluating research using life events scales and hassles/uplifts scales, the following points are important:

- Research using scales of major life events and daily hassles supports the idea that there are many sources of stress in life, and that they can affect physical and psychological health.
- Correlations are not huge, but are often significant. This means that in a general sense, the stress in each of our lives can potentially affect our health and how we operate from day to day.

There are also situations where stress-related problems can have more direct effects, and this brings us to the area of applied stress research.

Workplace stressors: research findings

Through its effects on psychological and physical health, stress can affect performance at work, whatever your job. All jobs involve a certain amount of stress, but there is a growing interest in work conditions that increase stress. Companies have an interest in maintaining productivity and performance, which are both affected by stress-related illness. The study of workplace stress is an area of occupational psychology and is one of the fastest growing fields of psychology.

Different types of work bring different stressors. Which of these would you find more stressful?

Sources of stress in the workplace depend on the type of work or enterprise. An assembly-line worker in a car factory has different problems from a middle-rank manager in a City bank. A fire fighter has different problems again. There are, however, some sources of stress that apply to most workers:

- *Physical environment* – Space, temperature, lighting and arrangement of an office (open plan or separate rooms) can all affect the individual. Physical stressors make work more difficult and more energy has to be expended to overcome them. The increased arousal can also lead to frustration, and many studies have shown that increased temperature (e.g. Halpern 1995) and exposure to intense noise (e.g. Evans *et al.* 1998) can lead to stress and aggression.

- *Work overload* – We seem to be moving to a culture in which long hours at work are seen as a mark of esteem, at the cost of both the individual and social structures. Overload is frequently reported as one of the most stressful aspects of the workplace (Dewe 1992). A key element in this is the impact long hours have on family life (the home–work interface).

- *Lack of control* – In many organizations, other people often determine workload and work patterns. Both animal studies (for example, the work on learned helplessness by Seligman (1975), see p. 109) and work with humans (e.g. Marmot *et al.* 1991, see p. 94) show that a perceived lack of control increases the stress-response and contributes to depression and illness.

- *Role ambiguity* – This occurs when the requirements for a particular work role are unclear or poorly defined, and is a major factor contributing to work-related stress. This sometimes results either from having no clear guidelines separating one role from another, or ones that are contradictory. Role ambiguity will also contribute to other sources of workplace stress, such as relations with co-workers and lack of control.

ACTIVITY

Categorizing workplace stressors

Four possible sources of workplace stressor are listed on the left. Spend a few minutes talking with your teachers, parents, relations and any friends with full-time jobs about what they find most stressful in their work. Include both men and women in your sample. Make a note of their answers.

When you have gathered all their responses, put each response into one of the four categories on the left. If there are answers that do not seem to fit any of the categories, try to think of a new descriptive category (for instance, home–work interface, career progression, job insecurity).

How many categories did you need to accommodate all the responses? Which category or categories had the highest number of responses? Why do you think this is?

Sources of stress are highly significant to the individual concerned, but they also affect the organization. Stress can lead to physical and psychological consequences, which, in turn, affect productivity, through decreased motivation at work and time off with health problems. In the USA, and increasingly in companies in the UK, occupational psychologists are brought in to identify sources of stress in the workplace and to advise on methods of reducing them. By assessing the organizational structure and interviewing employees at all levels of the hierarchy, they try to pinpoint key problems and identify solutions. These can involve changes in methods of communication or the physical arrangement of workplaces, or the introduction of different work schedules or management structures.

The key study on the following page (*Stress in the workplace*) describes one study of work stressors and the possible link with work-related illness.

a study by Johansson *et al.* (1978) into work stressors and stress-related illness

Aim >>

To investigate whether work stressors such as repetitiveness, machine-regulated pace of work and high levels of responsibility increase stress-related physiological arousal and stress-related illness.

Procedures >>

- The researchers identified a high-risk group of 14 'finishers' in a Swedish sawmill. Their job was to finish off the wood at the last stage of processing timber. The work was machine-paced, isolated, very repetitive yet highly skilled, and the finishers' productivity determined the wage rates for the entire factory.
- The 14 'finishers' were compared with a low-risk group of 10 cleaners, whose work was more varied, largely self-paced, and allowed more socializing with other workers.
- Levels of stress-related hormones (adrenaline and noradrenaline) in the urine were measured on work days and on rest days.
- Records were kept of stress-related illness and absenteeism.

Findings >>

- The high-risk group of 14 finishers secreted more stress hormones (adrenaline and noradrenaline) on work days than on rest days, and higher levels than the control group.
- The high-risk group of finishers also showed significantly higher levels of stress-related illness such as headaches and higher levels of absenteeism than the low-risk group of cleaners.

Conclusions >>

- A combination of work stressors – especially repetitiveness, machine-pacing of work and high levels of responsibility – lead to chronic (long-term) physiological arousal. This in turn leads to stress-related illness and absenteeism.
- If employers want to reduce illness and absenteeism in their workforce, they need to find ways of reducing these work stressors, for example by introducing variety into employees' work and by allowing them to experience some sense of control over the pace of their work.

Criticisms >>

- Some important variables, such as individual differences, are not controlled in this study; it may be that certain people who are vulnerable to stress (e.g. those exhibiting Type A behaviour – see opposite) are attracted to high-risk demanding jobs, such as finishing in a sawmill.
- In addition, the study does not identify which of the various work stressors may be the most stressful. The high-risk group was exposed to low levels of control through repetitive machine-paced work, physical isolation and high levels of responsibility. To separate out the effects of these different factors, a more controlled experimental study would have to be carried out, but this would be at the expense of ecological validity.

Many other studies have been carried out on stress in the workplace. For example, Marmot *et al.* (1991) carried out a three-year longitudinal study of over 3,000 civil servants, measuring job control and stress-related illness. They found that people with low job control (i.e. type and amount of work decided by others) were four times more likely to die of a heart attack than those with high job control (i.e. more independence in deciding the type and amount of work). Job control and illness were negatively correlated: as job control decreased, the chances of stress-related illness

increased. This was supported by a review of research that concluded that a combination of high job demands and low control is associated with an increased chance of heart disease (Van der Doef and Maes 1998).

As mentioned earlier, research on stress can be affected by individual differences. For example, not all workers with high scores on life event scales or jobs with low control and high demands become ill. The study of these individual differences is an important area of stress research and we will look at this area of study next.

Personality and Type A behaviour

From the early 1960s, Friedman and Rosenman (1974) studied the behaviour of patients suffering from coronary heart disease (CHD), and proposed that a particular behaviour pattern was associated with increased vulnerability to this stress-related illness. This pattern is known as the 'Type A behaviour pattern' and is characterized by constant time-pressure (always being in a hurry), doing several tasks at once, being intensely competitive in work and social situations, and being easily frustrated by the efforts of others. The frequency with which this pattern is observed has led to it often being referred to as the Type A personality (see Table 3.3 and the key study below – this key study is also relevant to the debate about the relationship between stress and physical illness).

Table 3.3 >> Type A behaviour pattern

Time pressure
>> working against the clock
>> doing several things at once
>> irritation and impatience with others
>> unhappy doing nothing

Competitiveness
>> always plays to win at games and at work
>> achievement measured as material productivity

Anger
>> self-critical
>> hostile to the outside world
>> anger often directed inwards

KEY STUDY >> STRESS & CARDIOVASCULAR DISORDERS

the Western Collaborative Group Study by Friedman and Rosenman (1974)

Aim >>

To investigate links between the Type A behaviour pattern and cardiovascular (heart) disease.

Procedures >>

- Using structured interviews (see p. 209), 3,200 California men, aged 39 to 59, were categorized as either Type A, Type X (balanced between Type A and Type B) or Type B (the opposite of Type A, i.e. more relaxed and not showing Type A characteristics of time pressure, competitiveness and anger).
- This large sample was followed up for $8\frac{1}{2}$ years to assess their lifestyle and health outcomes.

Findings >>

- By the end of the study, 257 men in the sample had developed coronary heart disease (CHD), of which 70 per cent were from the Type A group – twice the rate of heart disease found in the Type B group.
- This difference in the incidence of CHD between the two groups was independent of lifestyle factors, such as smoking and obesity, that are known to increase the chances of heart disease.

Conclusions >>

- The Type A behaviour pattern increases vulnerability to heart disease.
- Behaviour modification programmes to reduce Type A behaviour should result in a reduced risk of heart disease.

Criticisms >>

- Although some aspects of lifestyle were controlled for, there may have been other variables that could have affected vulnerability to heart disease, such as elements of hardiness (see p. 96).
- This was not an experimental study, so cause and effect cannot be assumed; other studies have failed to show a relationship between Type A behaviour and heart disease.

AO2 check

An example of a study that did not show a relationship between Type A behaviour and heart disease is the large-scale, seven-year longitudinal study involving 12,000 men carried out by Shekelle *et al.* in 1985.

Unit 3 // Stress

In evaluating Type A behaviour, the key points are:

- *Lack of consistent research support* – Since the original work by Friedman and Rosenman (1974), many studies have looked at the relationship between Type A behaviour and CHD. Some of these have been retrospective (looking at the previous behaviour of patients with CHD) and some prospective (measuring Type A behaviour using questionnaires and then following participants' health outcomes over months or years). Significant correlations have been found, but these are never very high, and many negative findings have been reported. Even the value of the Type A concept has been questioned (Evans 1990).

- *The role of hostility* – To try to make some sense of this, the behaviour pattern has been more closely analysed, and it turns out that a critical personality variable is hostility. When high levels of hostility are combined with high levels of Type A behaviour, correlations with CHD are significantly increased (Matthews and Haynes 1986). Particularly vulnerable are individuals who repress high levels of hostility rather than express it (although that may be better for the rest of us, of course!).

- *Type A and hardiness* – Despite the fact that Type A behaviour seems to be a risk for stress-related illness, many Type A individuals survive quite happily with their pressured and competitive lives. In the third topic of this unit, which looks at stress-management techniques, we will see that one of the key factors in managing stress is a strong sense of commitment, control and challenge. These are key elements of Kobasa's hardy personality (discussed below), which, she proposes, is resistant to the damaging effects of stress. There is no reason why Type A people should not also show high levels of commitment and control; in fact, they would be expected to. They are high achievers and so must be very committed, and they like to do everything themselves, as they do not believe anyone else can do it as well, i.e. they have a strong sense of control.

- *Protective factors* – So, along with factors which make them vulnerable, such as haste, time pressure, doing too many things at once and hostility, the Type A person may also score highly on protective factors such as control and commitment. There are also other less specific elements that have been shown to protect against stress, such as physical exercise and social support – these may also help the Type A person avoid the negative effects of stress.

Hardy personality

According to Kobasa (Kobasa and Maddi 1977), the concept of hardiness (or the hardy personality) is central to understanding why some people are vulnerable to stress and some resistant. Hardiness includes a range of personality factors that, if present, provide defences against the negative effects of stress. These factors are:

- *Control* – This is the belief that you have control over what happens in your life, rather than attributing control to outside influences. It is similar to locus of control, discussed later, and attributional style, which is the tendency to attribute causes either to yourself (dispositional attribution) or to external factors over which you have no control (situational attribution).

- *Commitment* – This is a sense of involvement in the world around you, including people as well as jobs and careers. The world is seen as something to engage with, rather than to stand apart from. It includes a strong sense of purpose in your activities.

- *Challenge* – Life changes are seen as challenges to be overcome or as opportunities, rather than as threats and stressors. Life is not about comfort and security, but change and growth.

Kobasa has presented evidence that people who have high scores on scales measuring hardiness are significantly less likely to suffer stress-related physical and psychological disorders than those with low hardiness scores. In theory, their positive approach means that life events are not seen as stressful, but as challenges and opportunities that can be overcome. This leads to less activation of the stress-response and its negative consequences.

Kobasa's studies of personality and stress have identified other factors involved in coping with stress and have implications for stress management. Using previous work suggesting that physical exercise and social support also protected against stress-related illness, Kobasa *et al.* (1985) rated participants on the presence or absence of the three factors:

- hardiness
- social support
- regular exercise.

In this prospective study, Kobasa and colleagues then followed the participants and assessed the severity of any subsequent psychological problems (depression and anxiety) or physical illnesses.

Results showed clearly that participants with no protective factors had higher scores on severity of illness scales than any other group. In addition, the presence of one, two or all three protective factors was associated with steadily decreasing illness scores. This implied that the factors acted additively in improving resistance to stress. Of the three, hardiness seemed to have the greatest impact.

In evaluating hardiness and the hardy personality, the key points are:

- *Participants* – Much of Kobasa's work has been carried out with male, white-collar workers, and so the findings may not be generalizable to other groups. Stressors and coping responses differ between men and women, for example.

- *Components of personality* – Control, commitment and challenge have never been very clearly defined, so control, for instance, may be an important part of commitment and challenge, rather than being separate from them. This would mean that Kobasa is only looking at the role of control in protection against stress rather than a full 'personality type'.

Gender

Although sources of stress may vary between males and females – especially if the female takes most responsibility for home and children – there is no evidence that the levels of stress each experience are any different. There is some evidence that physiological reactions to stressors (the stress-response) may distinguish the two groups.

ACTIVITY

Gender differences in coping with stress

It is commonly believed that men and women deal with stress in different ways. Either on your own or in a small group, ask at least 20 of your peers who are not studying psychology how they tend to deal with stressful situations.

1. What gender differences, if any, did you find to support this belief?

2. Are men more or less likely than women to use social support (such as talking through things with someone else) to help them cope with stressful situations?

3. What other ways of dealing with stress did the people in your sample use?

Evidence for gender differences includes the following:

- *Physiological reactivity* – Frankenhaeuser *et al.* (1976) measured levels of the stress hormone adrenaline in boys and girls taking an examination. The boys showed a much more rapid increase in hormone levels, which took longer to return to normal after the examination. The girls' increase was slower and smaller, and returned to baseline more quickly. Interestingly, performance in the examination was roughly the same for the two groups and so were levels of reported (subjective) anxiety and stress.

- *Support for Frankenhaeuser* – Similar results were reported by Stoney *et al.* (1990) who found that women showed smaller rises in blood pressure due to stressful tasks than did men. Possible explanations for these findings might be that:
  - the hypothalamus-pituitary and ANS stress pathways are more reactive in men than in women
  - men and women vary in their attitude to the test, and this psychological difference influences the stress-response; for instance, men may be more competitive and 'aroused' during the test, leading to more sustained physiological arousal.

- *Gender differences in coping* – On the whole, men show more stress-related physiological arousal than women across a range of psychological and physical stressors (Vogele *et al.* 1997), even though both genders report similar levels of subjective stress. This means that men should be more vulnerable to stress-induced illness but, as we shall see, other factors influence responses to stress and vulnerability to illness. Physical exercise and social support are important 'buffers' against stress-induced illness, and you can argue that these vary between the genders. Men take more physical exercise, while women make more use of social support networks, so predictions as to who should show more vulnerability to stress are very difficult.

Does your own experience support the idea that men and women make use of different buffers against stress?

One simple conclusion reached by Frankenhaeuser is that women live longer on average because they show less stress-related physiological arousal than men. One exception she found was that women in occupations traditionally regarded as 'male', such as engineering students and bus drivers, show a male-pattern physiological response to stress. Of course, we do not know if this was produced by the role or that they were attracted to such occupations because of their physiological make-up.

Look back at the expert interview with Janice Kiecolt-Glaser on p. 86 to remind yourself of what she has to say about gender differences.

See 'An eye on the exam', opposite, for an evaluation of the effects of gender.

Culture

Stress is found in all communities, but the sources can vary a great deal depending on the sort of society. In the developing world, we do not worry so much about finding food and water day by day, while people in developing countries spend less time worrying about which primary school to choose or why they haven't been promoted. However, all of these different sources of stress conform to the basic idea that stress exists when the perceived demands on you outweigh your perceived ability to cope.

Several studies have looked at different ethnic groups in Western societies and how they cope with common stressors.

■ *Cultural differences in social support* – Social support is an important protective factor against stress, and there are clear ethnic variations in how it is used. Kim and McKenry (1998) looked at social support networks in a range of ethnic groups in America. They found that African-Americans, Asian-Americans and Hispanics all used parents and children for social support more than Caucasian (White) Americans did. African-Americans were more likely to be members of religious organizations, while Asian-Americans and Caucasians took more part in recreational groups. Such cultural variations

in social networks have clear implications for coping with stress.

For instance, compared to White Americans, African-American and Asian-American carers for Alzheimer's patients report more belief in filial (children's) duty to parents, use faith and religion as part of their coping strategy, and report lower levels of depression and stress related to caring (Connell and Gibson 1997). Their lower levels of stress could be linked to the cultural differences in attitudes to social and family life, and their religious networks.

■ *Other cultural differences* – One of the difficulties in assessing cultural variations in relation to stress and responses to stress is that cultures vary along many other dimensions that can affect health. Heart disease, hypertension and depression, for instance, can be affected by your genetic inheritance, diet, general lifestyle and social organization. To isolate effects of stress is therefore virtually impossible. As an example, Weg (1983) studied the Abkarsian people of Georgia (formerly part of the USSR), who have a high percentage of individuals living beyond 100 (400 per 100,000, compared to 3 per 100,000 in the UK). Factors that emerged as important were:
– genetic inheritance
– high levels of social support
– physically active lifestyles of work and recreation
– diet high in fruit and vegetables, low in meat
– no alcohol or smoking
– low reported stress levels.

It is impossible to decide which of these factors is most important. Regardless of which culture you study, health outcomes are a complicated mix of inheritance, lifestyle, social networks and stress. Sources of stress and methods of coping will vary between cultures, but stress-related problems will still depend on available coping strategies versus the demands being made on the individual.

See 'An eye on the exam', opposite, for an evaluation of the effects of culture.

individual differences and stress

The preceding sections dealt with two of the most important factors that modify the experience of stress for an individual – gender and culture. However, this raises two important questions concerning the *nature* of such individual differences. First, *why* are there gender differences in stress reactions? Second, is cultural diversity itself a stressor? The following material constitutes AO2 *commentary* in these two areas (see pp. 247–8 for an explanation of different types of question).

Gender differences – an adaptive response to stress?

In humans and animals, biological and behavioural responses have evolved that allow the individual to maximize their chances of survival when confronted with a stressor. Traditionally, it has been adaptive for males to deal with a threat using a 'fight-or-flight' response. However, although this fight-or-flight response may be advantageous for the survival of the individual male, it puts defenceless offspring at a significantly greater risk of being harmed. Compared to males, females make a greater investment in offspring, initially in pregnancy and then in supporting them to maturity. This greater maternal investment should result in the selection of female stress-responses that do not jeopardize the safety of offspring in times of threat, and maximize the chances that they will survive. Taylor *et al.* (2000) believe that this should favour the development of biological mechanisms that *inhibit* the fight-or-flight response and shift the female's attention when faced with a threat to tending to the young (i.e. showing attachment behaviour) and seeking the company of other females as a defensive network against external threats.

Taylor and colleagues claim that high sympathetic nervous system activation (which is targeted primarily at the cardiovascular system, thereby optimizing physical performance) and high cortisol responses are characteristic biological components of the *male* stress-response. In contrast, neurophysiological mechanisms within the female brain inhibit the fight-or-flight response, and instead promote attachment behaviour – Taylor and colleagues refer to this as the 'tend-and-befriend' response to stress. It is entirely possible, therefore, that these differences also apply to the non-life-threatening stressors of daily life, and could play a role in the fact that men are more likely than women to die of cardiovascular disorders.

Cultural diversity – is diversity itself a stressor?

What we understand about the ways in which stress affects members of different cultures and, indeed, different groups within the same culture, is relatively limited. It is difficult to separate out the very different experiences of individuals within those cultures and pinpoint exactly how the experience of stress may differ for those individuals. It is possible, for example, that cultural diversity itself is a major stressor for members of minority ethnic groups within a majority culture. However, traditional stress scales (such as the SRRS developed and used by Holmes and Rahe) focus on mainstream stressors, such as divorce, bereavement and debt, and fail to address the specific situations that may affect some groups more than others. Such specific stressors might include economic marginality, unemployment and discrimination.

The major stressors for many members of minority ethnic groups are precisely those associated with their diversity and their consequent experiences of discrimination. Research is beginning to show evidence of a dual identity among diverse populations. Members of an minority ethnic group sometimes maintain two identities – one for work and the other for 'real life'. This allows them, as part of their stress management strategy, to maintain a positive self-image in their 'real world' when they believe they are subject to intolerable stress and discrimination in the workplace (Kelly-Radford 1999).

Check your understanding of the sources of stress by answering these questions. Try to do this from memory at first. You can check your answers by looking back through Topic 2.

1 What is the name of the rating scale devised by Holmes and Rahe in 1967 to investigate life stress? How many life events were on this scale and which was was given the highest score of 100?

2 Outline two criticisms of the Holmes and Rahe scale and its use.

3 Describe one difference between the Holmes and Rahe scale and Sarason's Life Experiences Survey.

4 What term is used to describe incidents that we would not call major life events, but which nevertheless can be a source of stress?

5 Why were the Hassles and Uplifts scales introduced?

6 Outline the procedures and findings of one study of stress in the workplace.

7 How did Johansson et al. (1978) measure levels of stress in their study of Swedish sawmill workers?

8 Describe two or more sources of stress in the workplace.

9 Describe the main characteristics of the Type A behaviour pattern.

10 Which characteristic of the Type A pattern seems to be especially important in increasing vulnerability to stress?

11 Of people with Type A behaviour pattern, why might some be less vulnerable to stress-related illness than others?

12 Outline some research findings that demonstrate gender differences in reactions to stress.

13 Describe two factors that might lead to gender differences in reactions to stress.

14 Describe one way in which cultural variations may affect reactions to stress.

15 Why is it difficult to investigate cross-cultural differences in the relationship between stress and illness?

REVISION SUMMARY

Having covered this topic you should be able to:

✔ define the following terms: 'life changes', 'control (psychological)' and 'workplace stressor'

✔ describe and evaluate research into life changes as a source of stress

✔ describe the aims, procedures, findings, conclusions and criticisms of a key study into life changes as a source of stress

✔ describe and evaluate research into workplace stressors

✔ describe the aims, procedures, findings, conclusions and criticisms of a key study into life changes and stress, and a key study into workplace stressors

✔ discuss the role played by personality, gender and culture in modifying the effects of stressors.

Topic 3 >> Critical issue: Stress management

GETTING YOU THINKING...

Look back to the questions in 'Getting you thinking...' on p. 77. For each of the stressors you noted there, think about how you try to cope with that particular source of stress. Create a table, using the format shown below. List each stressor, and next to it, record the ways of coping that you have found particularly successful. Then list any coping methods that have been less successful. Which ways of trying to cope with stress are better than others ?

Perceived stressors	Successful ways of coping	Unsuccessful ways of coping

KEY TERMS

Stress management: methods of managing the negative effects of stress. These include (a) the use of drugs and biofeedback (b) the use of relaxation and meditation (c) cognitive and behavioural training (d) the use of exercise and social support networks.

Physiological approaches to stress management: the use of drugs and biofeedback to target directly the stress-response systems themselves.

Psychological approaches to stress management: this includes (a) general psychological approaches such as the use of techniques of relaxation and meditation to reduce bodily arousal associated with stress (b) specific psychological approaches, such as cognitive and behavioural training, to help people control specific stressors in their lives.

The public considers stress to be one of the most prevalent 'diseases' of the past 20 years. It is also seen as fundamental to the way we live; as the pace of life increases, so, inevitably, does the stress of keeping up. In parallel with the increase in research into the negative effects of stress, such as psychological and physical disorders, so an industry has grown up devoted to methods of managing stress. These are by now many and varied, but can be divided into four major categories:

- *Physiological approaches* – The use of drugs and biofeedback to target directly the stress-response systems themselves.
- *General psychological approaches* – The use of techniques of relaxation and meditation to reduce the bodily arousal associated with stress.
- *Specific psychological approaches* – For example, cognitive and behavioural training to help people control specific stressors in their lives.
- *Aspects of lifestyle* – For example, exercise and social support.

Drugs

The most commonly used drugs to combat stress are the benzodiazepine (BZ) anti-anxiety agents and beta-blockers. BZs, such as librium (chlordiazepoxide) and valium (diazepam), are the most prescribed drugs for psychological disorders and can be very effective against states of stress and anxiety. They appear to act by reducing activity of the brain neurotransmitter serotonin and reducing central (brain) arousal. Beta-blockers, such as inderal, do not enter the brain, but directly reduce activity in pathways of the sympathetic nervous system around the body. As sympathetic arousal is a key feature of stressful states, they can be very effective against symptoms such as raised heart rate and blood pressure. (They have also been used when bodily arousal can reduce performance in groups such as musicians and snooker players.)

When evaluating the use of drugs, there are important drawbacks to note associated with their use:

- *Dependency* – Long-term use of BZs especially can lead to psychological and physical dependency. A proportion of people trying to come off BZs will experience a physical withdrawal syndrome, with symptoms such as increased anxiety, tremors and headaches. BZs should only be prescribed for short periods of a week or so, to help cope with short-term stress. Dependency is far less of a problem with beta-blockers as they do not have a significant effect on central brain mechanisms.

- *Side effects* – All drugs have side effects; BZs can cause drowsiness and affect memory.

- *Only targeting symptoms* – Drugs treat symptoms, not causes. Many stressors are essentially psychological, so while they may help in the short term, drugs may prevent the real cause of stress being addressed. They are best used to manage acute (short-lived) stressors, such as the initial shock of a bereavement or examinations (although see side effects, above). They are most effective when psychological coping techniques are employed at the same time.

However, drugs are also a vital part of the armoury against the harmful effects of stress:

- *Speed and effectiveness* – Drugs can work quickly, rapidly reducing dangerous symptoms such as raised blood pressure (beta-blockers) or reducing disabling levels of stress-related anxiety (BZs).

- *Availability* – Drugs can be prescribed immediately. In addition, the range of treatments available is increasing rapidly, with newer agents such as angiotensin-converting enzyme inhibitors (ACE-inhibitors, e.g. Captopril) providing a variety of ways of tackling the symptoms of stress.

Biofeedback

This technique involves recording the activity of the physiological systems of the body's stress-response, such as heart rate, blood pressure or tension in the neck muscles that can lead to stress-induced headaches (see Fig. 3.3 below). Recording is usually made via electrodes on the skin leading to a hand-held monitor that the person holds.

People are encouraged to try various strategies to reduce the physiological readings. These can be muscle relaxation or meditation, or even altering their posture. The aim is to find a strategy to reduce, for instance, blood pressure consistently, and then to transfer the strategy to the world outside the laboratory and to practise it regularly.

In evaluating biofeedback, the key points are these:

- *Effectiveness* – Biofeedback can be very successful for some individuals, especially children (Attanasio *et al.* 1985) who enjoy the technological aspects in controlling, for instance, migraine headaches.

- *Role of relaxation* – Biofeedback is often found to be no more effective than muscle relaxation procedures without biofeedback (Masters *et al.* 1987). This suggests that feedback on symptoms such as blood pressure is not a vital part of the procedure, but that training in relaxation techniques is.

- *Expense* – This is related to effectiveness, as biofeedback is expensive in terms of equipment and time. If relaxation is the important feature, then the cost of the equipment could be avoided and training time would be much reduced.

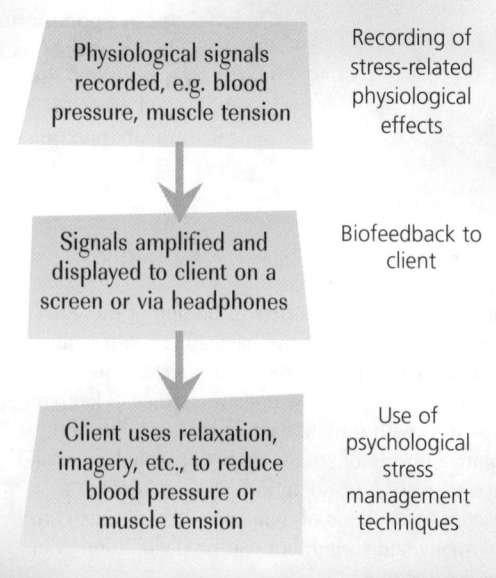

Figure 3.3 >> *Biofeedback: outline of the procedure*

Different approaches to stress management

GENERAL PSYCHOLOGICAL APPROACHES TO STRESS MANAGEMENT

Progressive muscle relaxation

Although we all think we know how to relax, effective relaxation has, in practice, to be learned. Rather than simply thinking about nice things, progressive muscle relaxation is – strange as it may sound – an active approach to reducing bodily arousal. A standard procedure would be to train clients consciously to clench and unclench muscles, to get them used to the sensations of tension and relaxation. Whole-body relaxation would begin with the muscles of the toes, tensing and then relaxing them, and then working up through the legs, body, arms, shoulders and head (facial muscles).

Eventually, the client understands the sensations well enough to use progressive muscle relaxation in everyday life as a method to reduce bodily arousal. During relaxation, stress-response mechanisms are inactive, heart rate and blood pressure fall, and the parasympathetic subdivision of the autonomic nervous system is activated (see p. 79).

The activity on the right encourages you to experience the effects of progressive muscle relaxation for yourself.

An evaluation of these techniques would focus on the following points:

- *Effectiveness* – If practised regularly, relaxation techniques are effective in reducing stress, but are not effective in all situations because of space and time constraints (see the next point).

- *Practicality* – These techniques take time and space. If you are stuck in a traffic jam or in the middle of an examination, full progressive relaxation is inconvenient, if not impossible. However, the

ACTIVITY

Relaxation techniques

It is easier to focus on your studies when you are feeling relaxed. If you find this or any other unit difficult to take in, it may be because you are feeling stressed and so find it hard to concentrate. If you are feeling stressed, then take a few minutes out to practise a relaxation technique.

The progressive muscle relaxation technique is most effective if you lie on the floor. Tense each of the areas in turn, starting with your toes and ending with your facial muscles. For each area, tense your muscles as hard as you can and count to five. Then relax the muscles, counting to five before moving on.

By the end of the process, a lot of the tension in your body will have disappeared and you should feel much more relaxed as your heart rate and blood pressure reduce. Try it for yourself and use this technique whenever you are feeling stressed.

training also involves cognitive strategies to help relaxation, such as imagining yourself in pleasant, non-arousing surroundings, taking deep breaths, and consciously telling yourself to relax. Relaxation of some muscle groups is usually possible. Taking two minutes to run through a learned procedure like this can pay dividends in many stressful situations.

■ *Targeting symptoms* – Relaxation techniques address bodily or physiological arousal by reducing activation of stress-response systems. This is undoubtedly beneficial, but long-lasting severe stressors need more than non-specific relaxation; their source has to be identified and targeted, usually via cognitive and behavioural strategies. Relaxation can still remain as an important component of stress management, but long-term adjustment requires more focused intervention as well.

Meditation

Meditation is similar to progressive muscle relaxation in that the aim is to reduce bodily arousal and to achieve a state of transcendental calm. This is achieved through sitting quietly and repeating your mantra – a single sound or word – while breathing deeply and regularly. The aim is to empty your mind of distracting and arousing thoughts. Like muscle relaxation, it can be used to combat stressful situations with a state of calm, thus preventing activation of the stress-response systems (Lichstein 1988). With your mantra readily available it may be more 'portable', but otherwise has the same problem of not addressing the source of long-term stressors. With practice, though, it gives the individual confidence in coping with short-term stress, and can be an important accessory to other methods of stress management.

In evaluating the use of meditation, the following factors are important:

■ *Effectiveness* – Meditation can be used to reduce the physiological arousal associated with stress, and can do so very effectively. It is especially effective if incorporated as a part of your lifestyle and performed regularly. It can also be used to combat immediate stressful situations, such as examinations, because it can be done anywhere, and even a short period of meditation can reduce arousal.

■ *Targeting symptoms* – With severe, long-term stressors, such as a poor marriage or problems at work, meditation does not provide a solution but only temporary respite. For this type of problem, strategies have to address the cognitive element of the stress-response using specific psychological techniques.

SPECIFIC PSYCHOLOGICAL APPROACHES TO STRESS MANAGEMENT

At the beginning of this unit we discussed the definition of stress. The trigger in stressful situations, according to the definition, is the perceived gap between the demands being made on you and the coping responses you have available. So, a straightforward approach to stress management would be either to reduce the perceived demands or to improve your coping abilities or, preferably, both. Cognitive–behavioural approaches aim to do this by encouraging clients to perceive and evaluate stressful situations accurately (often we overestimate the demands being made on us), and to improve coping skills and techniques through training and practice.

Meichenbaum's Stress-Inoculation Training

Meichenbaum's (Meichenbaum and Cameron 1983) approach has three phases:

■ *Conceptualization* – This is the main cognitive element. Clients are encouraged to relive stressful situations and to analyse various features. What was actually stressful about it? How did they attempt to cope? Why wasn't it successful? If many situations are stressful, do they have elements in common, such as the presence of strangers or the knowledge that performance is being assessed, as in exams and tests? These discussions can be individual or take place in groups, where the sharing of experience can help achieve a greater understanding of the nature of stress and the client's reactions to it. Clients are able to reach a more realistic understanding of the demands being made on them.

- *Skills training and practice* – Once the key elements of the stressful situations have been identified, clients can be taught specific and non-specific strategies for coping with them. The relaxation techniques described earlier help them to cope with the initial arousing effects of stress. Training in particular skills then helps reduce the specific demands. For instance, if examinations are the problem, knowing the syllabus in detail and developing simple strategies for learning, revision and time allocation can help to reduce stress. Relaxation techniques can be used in the examination room to keep arousal under control. Mock examinations can be taken to practise stress management. As another example, many people find social interactions stressful. Surprisingly, perhaps, social skills such as body posture, eye contact and conversational give-and-take can be taught relatively easily and practised in a therapeutic setting. Again, general relaxation techniques can help to limit stress-induced arousal.

- *Real-life application* – The final stage is for the client to go out into the real world and to put the training to the test. Contact with the therapist is maintained, and follow-up sessions and further training are provided if necessary. The reinforcement of successful coping with examinations or social interactions then becomes self-sustaining.

In evaluating Meichenbaum's approach, the key factors are as follows:

- *Targeting symptoms and causes* – Meichenbaum's programme is directed at both ends of the stress problem, i.e. sources of stress and coping strategies. By reviewing the coping methods they have used in the past, clients can gain a clearer understanding of their strengths and weaknesses. By acquiring new skills and techniques, they reduce the gap between demands and coping resources, and gain more confidence in their ability to handle previously stressful situations.

- *Effectiveness* – The combination of cognitive therapy (i.e. thinking about situations in the past and using cognitive strategies as part of a general relaxation technique) and behavioural therapy (i.e. training in new skills) makes stress-inoculation training a powerful method of stress management. However, few controlled studies of its effectiveness have been carried out, although Meichenbaum has reported some encouraging results (Meichenbaum and Turk 1982).

- *Practicality* – It takes time, application and money. Clients have to go through a rigorous programme over a long period, analysing their responses to stress and learning new techniques. This requires high levels of motivation and commitment, so it is not a quick-and-easy fix.

- *Difficulties* – There is evidence that the way we cope with life's stressors can reflect basic aspects of our personality, possibly innate or acquired during early experience. Examples include locus of control, (discussed later in this topic on p. 108). Any technique aimed at improving stress management may be acting against habits that are well established, even if they are not very effective. Changing cognitions and behaviour will always be difficult.

Increasing hardiness

Kobasa's belief that hardiness (see p. 96) is an important element in stress management led her to propose ways in which it could be increased. As with stress-inoculation training, the procedure has three aspects, the first two of which are quite similar to the first stage of stress-inoculation training:

- *Focusing* – Clients are trained and encouraged to spot signs of stress, such as muscle tension, increases in heart rate and anxiety. This allows them to recognize stressful situations and thereby to identify sources of stress.

- *Reliving stressful encounters* – Clients analyse recent stressful situations in terms of how they were actually resolved, ways in which they could have turned out better, and ways in which they could have turned out worse. This gives them insight into their current coping strategies and how they may be more effective than they imagine.

- *Self-improvement* – Central to hardiness is the belief that you can cope with life's challenges. Often, however, we are faced with stressors that cannot be easily managed. It is important, then, to recognize and to take on challenges that we *can* cope with. In this way we confirm that we still have control over some events in our lives. It is this sense of personal control and effectiveness that is fundamental to stress management. So, an essential part of hardiness training is to begin with challenges the client can cope with before moving on to more complex problems.

In evaluating Kobasa's concept of hardiness, note the following key points:

- *Theoretical issues* – The concept of hardiness itself has been criticized. The relative importance of the three factors – control, commitment, challenge – is unclear, although there is evidence for the role of control and commitment in reducing responses to stressors. As we shall see, the importance of control in stress management cannot be exaggerated, and the concept of hardiness overlaps substantially with issues of personal control.

- *Generalizability* – Kobasa's studies usually involve white, middle-class businessmen, so the results cannot reliably be generalized to women or to different classes and cultures.

- *Effectiveness and practicality* – There are few systematic studies of the effectiveness of hardiness training. As with stress-inoculation training, it is lengthy, and requires commitment and motivation. It would never be a rapid solution to stress management problems. It also has the problem of addressing basic aspects of personality and learned habits of coping that are notoriously difficult to modify.

ASPECTS OF LIFESTYLE AND STRESS MANAGEMENT

Exercise

Earlier in this unit we reviewed the physiological mechanisms of the stress-response, and the role of these systems in mobilizing energy reserves and increasing heart rate and blood pressure. Many of the damaging effects of stress are linked to energy mobilization in situations where physical action is not appropriate or possible, leading to high levels of glucose and free fatty acids floating around in the bloodstream. These can then contribute to the 'furring up' of the arteries (atherosclerosis).

If the stress is short lived, our physiological systems will restore normal blood levels by storing excess glucose and fats. If stress is long lasting (chronic), then the constant energy mobilization overwhelms our body's capacity to cope, and disease can result. Physical exercise is one way of dealing with stress-related arousal and removing excess glucose and fats. It also has significant psychological effects, and so could be seen as both a physiological and a psychological method of stress management.

When evaluating exercise, there are two key points:

- *Effectiveness* – Correlational studies, where levels of fitness and exercise are recorded, along with frequency of stress-related disorders, such as depression and high blood pressure, consistently show that exercise is associated with lower levels of depression and a lower incidence of hypertension (raised blood pressure) (Holmes 1993). But causality is a problem; perhaps depression leads to people taking less exercise, rather than vice versa?

- *Supporting evidence* – Luckily, many studies have used prospective designs. Jennings *et al.* (1986), for instance, had participants undergo physical training programmes. Separate groups followed programmes of either less than their normal physical activity, the same level as normal, above-normal levels, or far-greater-than-normal levels. Results showed clearly that regular exercise at above-normal or far-above-normal levels produced significant reductions in heart rate and blood pressure.

Social support

Although it is easy to make the assumption that having a wide network of friends and relations must make life less stressful, it is more challenging to provide convincing experimental evidence to support this claim. In their extensive work, Brown and Harris (1978) demonstrated that loneliness and social isolation were factors in causing depression in women with young children. This can be related to the idea that social support protects against the psychological effects of stress. Before looking at more recent evidence, we should first examine what social support can mean.

There are various categories of social support:

- *Emotional support* – This can provide comfort and reassurance, and, by raising the person's sense of self-esteem and self-worth, help them feel able to cope with the situation.

- *Practical support* – Friends and support groups can help in practical ways, for example by lending money or helping sort out affairs after bereavement.

- *Advice* – Friends, and especially special interest support groups, can be a source of information and advice, commenting on possible coping strategies and suggesting others. They will often have met the particular situation before and can help the individual learn from their experience.

The mechanisms underlying the protective effects of social support are unclear. Talking with other people can help the cognitive evaluation of stress-induced demands and give reassurance that friends are around who will help with coping. However, work with monkeys shows strongly that isolation is very stressful, and that the simple physical closeness of others directly reduces physiological arousal. One could speculate that with humans, we have a combination of help at the cognitive and practical level, along with a more primitive need to be close to other people. The evidence suggests that hugging children is both reassuring and stress reducing. Before reading on, try the activity at the bottom of the page.

When evaluating social support, there are several factors to take into account:

- *Effectiveness (research support)* – Most studies are correlational, assessing levels of social support through questionnaires and correlating these scores with levels of stress-induced disorder. Evidence consistently shows a significant association. Social support was used by both male and female students in reducing the effects of stress (Weinstein 2002). In the workplace, job-related stress is reduced in organizations with high levels of support from co-workers (Constable and Russell 1986).

ACTIVITY

Your experience of social support

Using the three headings – emotional support, practical support, advice – make a list of all the people you think provide you with these kinds of social support.

1 How many different names appear in your lists? This provides an indication of your perceived social support network.

2 Do some names appear in more than one of your lists? If so, why is this?

3 When do you make the greatest use of these three types of social support?

4 Which people do you, in turn, offer social support to?

6 Think of some examples where social relationships can actually harm an individual's health or increase feelings of being stressed (e.g. by providing a bad example).

When you have completed this activity, you should have an idea of the size and composition of your own social support network. Some people are very happy and feel well supported by a relatively small number of social contacts, so please don't worry if your network seems rather small; quality of support is just as important as quantity.

More direct studies have demonstrated lower levels of cardiovascular activity (heart rate and blood pressure) during difficult tasks when a friendly companion is present (Kamarck *et al.* 1998), indicating less stress-induced arousal. Even recovery from heart disease is faster when a patient has high levels of social support (Kulik and Mahler 1989). Prevention of relapse and survival rates in cancer patients are helped by high levels of social support (De Boer *et al.* 1999)

■ *Effectiveness (animal studies)* – The most convincing findings are from studies of monkeys. Some species, such as the cynomolgus monkey, are highly social animals with complex networks of relationships. If they are kept in isolation, heart rates and blood pressure immediately increase, while chronic (long-lasting) isolation leads to atherosclerosis and heart disease. When isolated animals are returned to the colony, they increase their rate of affiliative (friendly) behaviours over pre-isolation levels, as though they are compensating for the lack of social contact (Watson *et al.* 1998).

■ *Gender differences* – It is clear that the level of social support varies. For example, one study found that men seem to have larger networks, but women seem to use them more effectively (Ratcliffe-Crain and Baum 1990). This has been related to the more severe effects of bereavement stress in men than women (Stroebe *et al.* 1999). On the other hand, Weinstein (2002) reported that female undergraduates had larger networks and used them more than male undergraduates did.

■ *Types of network* – Whether people receive social support depends on the nature of the networks they have with other people. Social networks vary in their quantity and quality; for example, they differ in terms of the size of the network, the frequency of contact, the composition (who makes up the network) and the closeness of individual relationships within the network. These can vary with gender, age and the stage of one's life or career. It should also be remembered that the various types of social support (see above) could be provided by a small number of very close relationships.

CONTROL

The concept of control is central to stress and stress management. When there is a gap between perceived demands and perceived coping resources, we define it as a state of stress, but it is also a situation of being out of control. The Meichenbaum and Kobasa approaches to stress management both directly address ways of increasing the feeling of being in control. Analyses of how people try to impose control reveal that several different types of control exist:

■ *Informational* – Your train stops unexpectedly on the way to an important meeting. Informational control is finding out what the problem is and how long the delay is likely to be.

■ *Decisional* – Before you travel, there are alternatives, such as car, train or bus. Even if the decision turns out badly, you have control at that stage.

■ *Behavioural* – Is there any direct action you can take? If the train stops in a station and you know the problem is serious, are there alternative forms of transport you can take, such as a bus or taxi?

■ *Cognitive* – This refers to the use of cognitive relaxation techniques (as described earlier) to reduce the stress-induced arousal directly. Think about the meeting itself: is it absolutely critical that you be there? Will it really matter if you are late?

■ *Retrospective* – This means thinking about the stressful situation after it is resolved. How did you cope, was it effective, what would you do differently next time, e.g. leave more time, not travel by train? Explaining how things happened and how they

could be avoided in the future are important aspects of control.

When described in this straightforward manner, stress management appears simple. Unfortunately, in real life it can be hard to act so rationally, especially when it goes against aspects of one's personality.

Individual differences: locus of control

The concept of locus of control (Rotter 1966) refers to individual differences in how we see the world and our ability to control what happens to us. There are two extremes:

■ *Internal locus of control* – People attribute events that happen to them to sources within themselves; they are responsible. This can be misplaced because some events are clearly out of our control. For instance, if the train breaks down, a strong internal locus of control would lead to the assumption that the situation was a result of your choice of travelling by train. On the positive side, a strong internal locus of control is associated with the belief that you can control much of your life and succeed in difficult or stressful situations. People with a strong internal locus tend to cope well with stressful situations, showing less physiological arousal. They would be more likely to take behavioural control.

■ *External locus of control* – The person with an external locus of control attributes events in their lives to outside agencies and factors. They have a sense that 'things happen to them' and are largely uncontrollable. Luck or fate are important factors.

As you would expect, people who sense they have little control over life events confront stressful situations with a more passive or fatalistic attitude, when a more active strategy is usually better for stress management. They suffer more stress-related illness and are less active in coping (Kamen and Seligman 1989).

Most people are not located at the extremes, but can often be characterized as more internal or more external. Locus of control questionnaires are commonly used in stress research, as locus of control relates to how we cope and how we react to stress, and one of the aims of stress-management training is to internalize the sense of control. However, as a fundamental part of personality, locus of control is hard to modify. It emerges during development, probably as a mixture of inherited factors and early social experience.

Research on the role of control

Many experimental studies have examined levels of control and reactions to stress.

- *Learned helplessness* – The work of Seligman (1975) on learned helplessness is probably the best known. He demonstrated that rats that were given inescapable foot shocks failed to learn to escape from avoidable foot shocks on a later test. He called this 'learned helplessness'. It can also be demonstrated in humans. Using loud noise as a stressor, Hiroto and Seligman (1975) found that participants exposed to uncontrollable loud bursts of noise performed poorly on a later task in which the noise was controllable. They had learned from their earlier experience that they could not control the noise, so did not even try. Seligman suggests that the experience of life as uncontrollable is stressful and an important factor in the development of stress-related disorders such as depression.

- *Personal control* – The important role of control is also supported in a study that has much greater ecological validity. Langer and Rodin (1976) carried out a study in a nursing home for older people. On one floor, residents were given some control over their lives, such as arranging their rooms, and deciding when to have visitors or go to watch films. On another floor, the residents had all these decisions made for them, as is often the case in many nursing homes. After a year and a half, over 90 per cent of the group who had been given greater control were rated by the nurses as having improved; the older people themselves also stated that they were more active and much happier. On the other hand, 70 per cent of the group without control were rated as less active and generally worse than before the study began.

- *Illusion of control* – Other research shows that even the illusion of active coping can reduce stress. Rats that were given repeated and uncontrollable foot shocks developed gastric (stomach) ulcers. However, when rats were given a lever to press, even though pressing it had *no* effect on the number of shocks, they developed far fewer ulcers (Sapolsky 1994). A similar effect has been found in people exposed to uncontrollable loud noises. Glass and Singer (1972) reported that a group that was given a button to press, which had no effect on the frequency of noises, still showed a smaller activation of the stress-response than a group simply exposed to the loud noise. This can also be seen in everyday life. People tend to be far more stressed by air travel than by car travel, even though statistically you are much safer when travelling by air. One explanation may be that we have no control when flying, whereas the car is far more under our control.

ACTIVITY

Expert interview

In the 'Expert interview' on p. 110, Dr Rob Briner, a psychologist specializing in organizational psychology, tells us his views on stress and whether stress management techniques can help reduce the bad feelings that can be associated with stress.

As you read his answers to the three questions, think carefully about:

1 whether you agree with what he is saying

2 what evidence from Unit 3 you would cite either to support or challenge a particular idea.

ACTIVITY

Research studies

This final activity should help you to check your understanding of some of the research in this unit. Select a study on each of the following topics:

- individual differences in modifying the effects of stressors
- stress management
- the role of control in perception of stress.

For each study complete a table like the ones that have been developed for key studies (see, for example, p. 84), using the following headings:

- Topic
- Aim
- Procedures
- Main findings
- Main conclusions
- Some criticisms

Stress *management*

Dr Rob Briner is Senior Lecturer in Organizational Psychology at Birkbeck College, University of London, and is a self-proclaimed sceptic when it comes to the subject of stress and stress management. His research has led him to become increasingly convinced that the 'stress' concept is not only limited, but also unhelpful, in trying to understand the links between work and wellbeing.

Q **Stress is bad for us and needs to be managed, yes?**

A Maybe. The answer depends on two things: what you mean by stress and what the research shows about the effects of stress. What researchers and lay people mean by stress is wide, varied and confusing. It sometimes means something 'out there' – a situation or experience that makes us feel bad. Sometimes it refers to something inside, something we experience – a feeling such as fear, anger, tiredness, sadness or frustration. There certainly is some evidence that some of the experiences or feelings we label 'stress' can be bad for us. However, this evidence is not as strong as most people imagine. Also, some of the things we label 'stress' may also be good for us or at least not harmful.

Rob Briner

Q **Has research shown one psychological method of stress management to be more effective than others in dealing with the negative effects of stress?**

A There are many so-called stress management techniques and a booming stress management industry. However, in most cases there is no or little evidence to support these techniques. Some have been shown to make some people feel better, such as counselling and relaxation. But in claiming this, we return to the problem: what does stress mean anyway? What may be effective in dealing with feelings of fear may not be effective in dealing with anger, yet both these things can be described as 'stress'. Just as it is not possible to have one best way of treating all illnesses (as it depends on the illness), it is not possible to have one best way of managing stress because it depends on what we mean by stress.

Q **Are there any dangers in developing a culture of stress management rather than dealing more constructively with the sources of stress?**

A In general, yes, because prevention is certainly better than cure. But before we can treat the sources of stress, we need much more evidence about what kinds of situations are psychologically harmful to people, how they cause harm and the nature of that harm. Some researchers have argued that believing that 'stress' is bad for us and makes us ill, together with the general hype around 'stress', is harmful. For example, people may ignore the real causes of their illness, blame it on 'stress', and fail to seek medical care. Also, people may get quite worried that being 'stressed' is going to make them ill when there is only limited evidence to support this.

Check your understanding of stress management by answering these questions. Try to do this from memory at first. You can check your answers by looking back through Topic 3.

1   Describe one physiological approach to stress management.

2   Outline one strength and one weakness of the approach to stress management that you described in Question 1.

3   Explain the principle underlying biofeedback.

4   Describe one psychological approach to stress management.

5   Outline one strength and one weakness of the approach you described in Question 4.

6   Name and outline the three phases of stress-inoculation training.

7   Describe the three components of the hardy personality.

8   What procedures did Kobasa recommend to improve hardiness?

9   Outline two criticisms of Kobasa's concept of hardiness.

11   Why does physical exercise help in coping with the effects of stress?

11   Name three types of social support and describe how each might help in coping with stress.

12   Outline three ways in which we might try to impose control in a stressful situation.

13   What is 'locus of control'? Describe what it means for a person to have an internal locus of control.

14   Why is it difficult to change a person's locus of control?

15   Outline findings from two studies concerned with levels of control and reactions to stress.

REVISION SUMMARY

Having covered this topic, you should be able to:

✓ define the following terms: 'stress management', 'physiological approaches to stress management' and 'psychological approaches to stress management'

✓ describe physiological approaches to stress management, such as the use of drugs and biofeedback

✓ describe psychological approaches to stress management, such as stress-inoculation and increasing hardiness

✓ evaluate the strengths and weaknesses of methods of stress management

✓ discuss the role of control in relation to stress.

Unit 3 // Stress

Topic 1: Stress as a bodily response

■ A state of stress exists when there is a mismatch between the **perceived demands (stressors)** on us and our **perceived coping strategies**.

■ Stressors lead to activation of the bodily **stress-response**. This involves the **autonomic nervous system** (ANS) and the **hypothalamus–pituitary gland** link, both acting on the **adrenal gland** to release different sets of hormones that control many vital bodily functions.

■ **Selye's General Adaptation Syndrome** (GAS) has three stages: **activation** of stress-response, **resistance** (apparent coping with stressors), and **exhaustion** (through long-term or chronic stress), when stress-related conditions may develop.

■ The **relationship between stress and physical illness** involves various mechanisms. Increased heart rate affects the **cardiovascular** system, by wearing away blood vessel linings. **Corticosteroids, adrenaline** and **noradrenaline** release stored carbohydrates and fats into the bloodstream, which, if not expended or reabsorbed, remain in the bloodstream leading to **hypertension** and **atherosclerosis** (blocking of blood vessels). Stress hormones also suppress the **immune system**, which can – especially if long term or chronic (**immunosuppression**) – leave the body vulnerable to infection and disease.

Topic 2: Sources of stress

■ Research into sources of stress has produced several life-event scales, the most widely used being **Holmes and Rahe's Social Readjustment Rating Scale** (SRRS). This scores **major life events** and **life changes** according to their psychological impact, proposing that higher scores on the SRRS increase the chances of stress-related health breakdown.

■ Other scales, such as the **Hassles scale**, deal with minor, everyday stressors, which correlate significantly with health status.

■ Research into **workplace stressors** includes studies of workplace **relationships**, the **physical environment**, **work overload** and **role ambiguity**. Workplace stress significantly affects not only individuals, but also organizations and productivity.

■ **Individual differences** have been shown to relate to vulnerability to stress. **Friedman and Rosenman's** (1974) **Type A behaviour** pattern showed some correlations with increased vulnerability to stress-related illness, but Type A people may also score highly on protective factors such as control and commitment.

■ Research into **gender differences** reveals that men show more stress-related physiological arousal than women, and that sources of stress may vary between genders. However, both genders report similar levels of subjective stress.

■ **Social support** is an important protective factor against stress, and there appear to be clear cultural and ethnic variations in how it is used. However, **cultures** vary along many dimensions that affect health – such as genetic inheritance, lifestyle and diet – and in the range of stressors experienced. Therefore, assessing cultural variations to stress can be difficult.

Topic 3: Stress management

■ **Physiological approaches** to **managing the negative effects of stress** include **drugs**, such as benzodiazepines (BZ) and beta-blockers. While drugs can be effective in reducing states and symptoms of stress, they can also lead to dependency, have side effects and may prevent the real causes of stress being detected. **Biofeedback** involves recording the body's physiological systems, e.g. blood pressure, and then finding strategies to reduce the readings.

- General **psychological approaches**, such as **relaxation** and **meditation** are used to reduce the bodily arousal associated with stress. Specific psychological approaches, such as **Michenbaum's Stress-Inoculation Training** uses **cognitive–behavioural** techniques to encourage clients to relive, analyse and evaluate stressful situations more accurately. They are then taught specific and non-specific strategies for coping, which should become self-sustaining.

- **Kobasa**'s concept of **hardiness** centres on personality factors that provide defences against the negative effects of stress. These include: belief that we have **control** over our lives, **commitment** to engaging in the world around us, and seeing life changes as **challenges** rather than threats or stressors. Kobasa proposed increasing hardiness by focusing on recognizing signs of stress, reliving stressful encounters, and self-improvement, especially by taking on challenges that we can cope with.

- **Physical exercise** (to keep the cardiovascular system in shape) and using social support networks effectively are both thought to help protect against the damaging effects of stress.

- The concept of **control** is central to stress and stress management. The gap between perceived demands and perceived coping resources produces a state of stress, but also a feeling of being 'out of control'. Several different types of control exist, such as informational, decisional and behavioural. Improving the sense of being in control is an important part of cognitive approaches.

- **Internal locus of control** refers to people who attribute events that happen to them to sources within themselves. They generally cope well with stressful situations, showing less physical arousal. **External locus of control** refers to people who attribute events in their lives to outside forces. They generally suffer more stress-related illness and cope less well.

- There are **strengths and weaknesses in stress-control methods**. The difficulties include: trying to change fundamental aspects of personality, the time, commitment and money needed to follow these methods through, the few controlled studies of their effectiveness and the generalization of results across gender and cultures.

Answering exam questions on Stress

For sample examination questions and answers on Stress, together with examiner comments on the answers, see pp. 255–7.

WEBSITES

www.about.com/
A searchable site that covers (among other things) a wide range of sites about stress and stress management.

www.mentalhealth.net/
A starting point for searching the web for topics related to stress, stress management and other areas of mental health.

http://agency.osha.eu.int/publications/reports/203/en/stress.pdf
A comprehensive report on work-related stress for the European Agency for Safety and Health at Work. It includes an excellent review of the concept of stress, measuring stress, and evidence linking stress with illness, besides covering workplace stressors.

4
UNIT

Abnormality

PREVIEW

After you have read this unit, you should be able to:

>> describe attempts to define psychological abnormality

>> explain the limitations associated with attempts to define abnormality, including cultural relativism

>> discuss the assumptions made by biological and psychological models of abnormality with regard to the causes and treatment of abnormality

>> describe the clinical characteristics of anorexia nervosa and bulimia nervosa

>> explain eating disorders in terms of biological and psychological models of abnormality, and discuss research studies on which such explanations are based.

INTRODUCTION

Abnormal psychology, or 'psychopathology', is the field of psychological study that deals with mental, emotional and behavioural problems. It involves research into the classification, causation, diagnosis, prevention and treatment of psychological disorders. The range of disorders classified under this term is huge, but some well-known examples are phobias, clinical depression, eating disorders and schizophrenia.

It is difficult to define precisely what is meant by the term 'abnormality', as there is no single characteristic that applies to all instances of abnormal behaviour. Therefore, people have to make judgements about whether or not a particular behaviour is abnormal. Judgements are often influenced by social and cultural factors, and so people from different backgrounds may disagree. However, there is general agreement about certain key components of abnormal behaviour and, in Topic 1, we shall look at some of the ways these have been used in attempts to definite abnormality. Whilst most of these definitions have some practical value, we shall also consider their limitations in terms of operational or ethical difficulties. We need also to be aware that judgements about labelling human behaviour as 'normal' or 'abnormal' cannot be made in absolute terms but only within the context of a given culture (called cultural relativism).

A model of abnormality offers a complete and coherent explanation for the origins of abnormal behaviour and psychological functioning according to its own perspective. Each model leads to quite different ideas about how to treat mental disorders or psychological problems. In Topic 2, we shall consider the biological model and a number of psychological models of abnormality.

The critical issue for consideration in this unit is eating disorders and in Topic 3, we shall look at two major examples of this category of disorder: anorexia nervosa and bulimia nervosa.

Pamela Prentice

Jane Willson

GETTING YOU THINKING...

1 Look at the photos on the right. How many people do you know who dress (or don't dress!) in a similar way to the people shown in these two photos? How would you explain their behaviour?

Would you consider people who behave and dress in these ways to be abnormal or even psychologically disordered?

2 Read the descriptions below. Which of the behaviours described do you consider normal and which abnormal? How do you decide what is normal and what is abnormal?

A "Sian always puts things off until the last minute. She's always late with assignments and now she's in danger of being thrown off the course."

B "Ashok has gone to pieces since splitting up with his girlfriend two months ago. He sleeps all the time now and never wants to do anything. He often misses classes and today he told me that he couldn't see the point of going on."

C "Pete's really nervous. He hates standing up in class to read out anything – he gets all shaky. Now he's started turning down all invitations to go out. People will stop asking him soon."

D "Katie has this weird habit – she says it's really important to chew an even number of times when eating. No one talks to her at mealtimes any more because she's so busy counting that she doesn't pay any attention."

KEY TERMS

Psychological abnormality: behaviours and psychological functioning that are considered different from normal behaviour within a given society.

Statistical infrequency: in psychopathology, this term is used for behaviour that occurs rarely within the general population.

Deviation from social norms: behaviour that violates the implicit and explicit rules and moral standards of a given society.

Failure to function adequately: an assessment of an individual whose disability prevents them from pursuing normal activities and goals (e.g. alcohol addiction preventing normal performance at work or interfering with social activities).

Deviation from ideal mental health: behaviour that does not meet the six criteria relating to mental health or optimal living first proposed by Jahoda (1958).

Cultural relativism: the idea that judgements about definitions of human behaviour (e.g. abnormal behaviour) cannot be made in absolute terms but only within the context of a given culture.

In the first topic of this unit, we look at four definitions of abnormality, along with their limitations. These are:

1 statistical infrequency
2 deviation from social norms
3 deviation from ideal mental health
4 a failure to function adequately.

STATISTICAL INFREQUENCY

Using this definition, it is assumed that most people do not stray very far from the norm or average. Hence, any behaviour that is statistically infrequent is regarded as abnormal.

People who adopt the statistical approach measure specific characteristics and assess how such characteristics are distributed in the general population. One way of showing population distribution is by means of a normal distribution curve, which is bell shaped and has certain mathematical properties. It tells us, for instance, that for a given characteristic most people score around the middle.

It also tells us the percentage of the population that falls within a certain spread of scores. The spread is measured by a statistic called the standard deviation. Mathematicians have calculated that approximately 68 per cent of the population fall between one standard deviation either side of the mean, and approximately 95 per cent fall within two standard deviations either side of the mean. It follows that scores outside this range are very unusual, that is, only 2.5 per cent fall below it and 2.5 per cent score above it. A physical example of this would be, for instance, height or foot size. Shoe manufacturers will take this into account when deciding how many of each shoe size to produce. They know, for example, that 95 per cent of a given population of adult females placed into a normal distribution curve, would take a shoe size of between 3 and 9. Therefore, manufacturers produce very few adult female shoes below or above these sizes and people requiring them would probably need to find a specialist or have their shoes made to measure.

In terms of psychological attributes, it is assumed that personality traits and behaviour can also be measured and assessed in terms of population distribution. The assumption is that individuals are 'normal' if they do not deviate too far from the average on a particular trait or behaviour pattern – see Fig. 4.1, which illustrates how IQ (intelligence quotient) scores are normally distributed within the population.

Limitations of the statistical infrequency definition

To define abnormality in terms of statistical frequency seems to be common sense. However, there are several problems associated with this approach.

■ *Which characteristics to choose* – The statistical infrequency approach simply provides a method for measuring abnormality. It does not suggest which characteristics might be related to abnormal behaviour. According to the statistical frequency approach, behaviour is deemed abnormal if it is at *either* end of the normal distribution. For example, both very low scores and very high scores on an anxiety scale would be seen as psychologically abnormal. However, this is not always the case. Consider the example of IQ given above. One criterion for mental retardation, a psychological disorder, is an IQ score of 70 or under. As Fig. 4.1 shows, approximately 2.5 per cent of the population fall into this category. However, it is equally rare to have an IQ score of over 130, but exceptionally high intelligence is not classified as a psychological disorder. This raises the issue of desirability. Some behaviours are statistically rare, but would not be classified as psychologically abnormal because they are seen as desirable (for example, high levels of heroism or exceptional artistic ability).

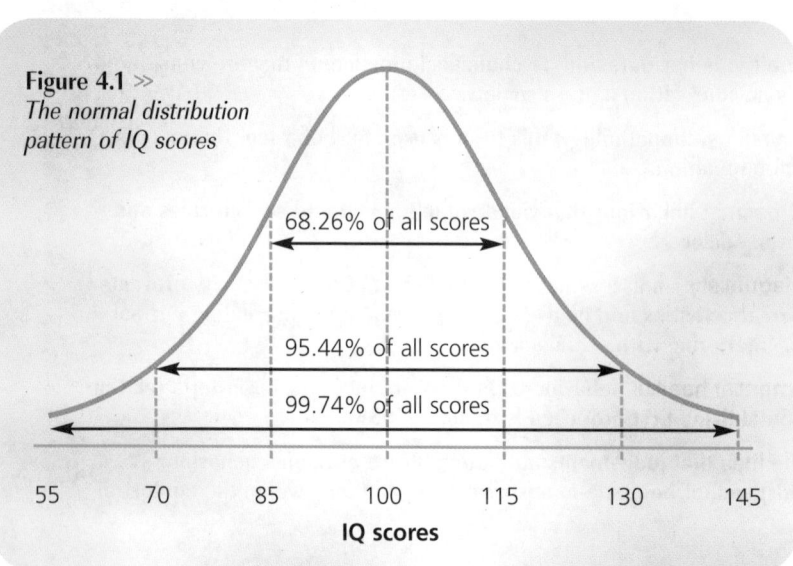

Figure 4.1 »
The normal distribution pattern of IQ scores

68.26% of all scores

95.44% of all scores

99.74% of all scores

55   70   85   100   115   130   145

IQ scores

Mozart (below) was giving keyboard recitals at the age of 5. Serena and Venus Williams (at foot of page) dominated women's tennis in the early 2000s. Are these examples of abnormality?

the statistical approach is deciding where the cut-off point is for defining abnormality. There is no agreed point on a scale at which behaviour is classified as abnormal and, in any case, it is unlikely that abnormal states can be categorized in such black-and-white terms. For example, there are degrees of severity in disorders such as depression or anxiety.

■ *Common disorders* – Problems such as depression or anxiety are classified as psychological disorders because they adversely affect normal functioning. However, in purely statistical terms, they are not particularly unusual. Angst (1992), for example, has found that one in 20 Americans is severely depressed and that there is a one-in-ten chance of having a serious depressive episode at least once in your lifetime. A large-scale survey undertaken across 48 states in the USA and reported by Kessler *et al.* (1994) found that 48 per cent of the people in their survey had suffered from at least one psychological disorder at some point in their lives.

■ *Misleading statistics* – Statistical infrequency may be a useful definition of abnormality in general terms, but it falls short when applied to mental disorders. It is only possible to determine mental-disorder statistics for those who have been diagnosed by a clinician. This may not necessarily reflect the true occurrence of any given mental disorder because many people suffer from mental disorders but do not seek professional help.

Females are more likely than males to consult their doctor for anxiety problems, whereas males are more likely to bottle up their anxiety, or try to deal with it in physical ways, such as vigorous sporting activity. Some people believe that in industrialized societies men are taught from an early age to distance themselves from their emotions. This socialization creates masculine stereotypes that alienate men from seeking help for psychological problems. Therefore, statistical data may be more a reflection of male and female socialization than a true reflection of real differences between men and women for any given mental disorder.

■ *Cultural issues* – Mental disorders appear to be statistically infrequent in some ethnic groups, but this may simply reflect a reluctance to seek professional help, owing to cultural beliefs. In India, for example, mentally ill people are cursed and looked down on. Rack (1982) points out that in China, mental illness also carries a great stigma. The Chinese are, therefore, careful to diagnose only those whose behaviour is indisputably psychotic (i.e. where thinking and emotion are so impaired that the individual is out of contact with reality).

Depression, a frequently diagnosed disorder in Western culture, appears to be absent in Asian cultures. A general explanation for this has been that Asian people tend to live within extended families with ready access to social support. However, Rack (1982) claims that depression is equally common among Asians, but that Asians consult their doctor only for physical problems and rarely with 'emotional' distress. They do not see this as the responsibility of the doctor and instead sort it out within the family. Therefore, statistical infrequency merely reflects the statistical likelihood of seeking professional help, rather than an indication of whether a particular mental disorder is really present or absent in a particular culture. A further example of this is found with Puerto Ricans, who generally react to stressful situations with severe heart palpitations, fainting and seizures, but this is regarded as a quite normal reaction in their culture (Guarnaccia *et al.* 1990).

DEVIATION FROM SOCIAL NORMS

Every society sets up rules for behaviour based on a set of moral standards. Some of these rules are explicit and to violate them can mean breaking the law, such as stealing, arson and driving on the wrong side of the road. Others rules are implicit and agreed as a matter of convention within a particular society, such as not standing too close to someone in a face-to-face conversation, dressing according to a particular code or sitting silently during a play at the theatre. These rules (codes) of conduct, whether implicit or explicit, become established as social norms and people who violate these norms are regarded as deviant or abnormal. For example, inappropriate affect (emotion) is often found in people with schizophrenia, e.g. laughing when told that someone has died or crying when watching a comedy show. Similarly, people with phobias often demonstrate bizarre behaviour when trying to escape their feared object.

At a practical, everyday level, deviation from social norms can be a useful way to identify mental problems. We learn what to expect from individuals and, if their behaviour drastically deviates from this, then we become concerned on their behalf. This may be vital in securing appropriate help because, for example, people with clinical depression are often unable to motivate themselves to seek assistance. However, there are several limitations associated with this approach.

Limitations of the deviation from social norms definition

■ *Eccentric or abnormal?* – Deviance from social norms does not always indicate psychological abnormality. We tend to make judgements about whether behaviours that deviate from the norm are merely eccentric or whether they are abnormal in a pathological sense. Running naked across a rugby pitch, or taking part in a marathon dressed as a giant rabbit may be regarded as strange or idiosyncratic, but we would not necessarily assume that the person is mentally disturbed. However, if someone is walking down the street talking out loud to an invisible person, or if someone insists that Martians have taken over their brain, then we would be more likely to suspect a mental disorder. Thus, only particular kinds of 'abnormal' behaviour tend to be regarded as pathological.

ACTIVITY

Eccentric or abnormal?

Look back at the two photographs on p. 115. What do these two photos tell us about the limitations of using deviation from social norms as a means of identifying psychological abnormality?

■ *The role of context* – Much of our behaviour is context-specific and, out of context, may seem bizarre. For example, what would you think if you were walking through the park and someone sitting on a bench suddenly jumped up and started singing and dancing? You would probably think them rather odd. But if you then saw a film crew, you would contextualize the scene, assume the person was an actor and perhaps stay around to watch.

■ *Change with the times* – Beliefs about abnormality and social norms of morally acceptable behaviour change over time, so what is regarded as deviant by one generation may be perfectly acceptable to the next. Consider the changes that have taken place in society's attitudes towards unmarried mothers and towards homosexuality (see p. 124 for more information).

■ *Abnormal or criminal?* – The behaviour of people who violate *legal* norms is usually regarded as criminal and the behaviour is rarely attributed to underlying psychological disorder. Would you consider someone convicted for fraud, for example, to be psychologically disordered? There are, however, types of behaviour that are generally regarded as unacceptable, such as rape and mass murder, where it is difficult to accept that such violation of others could possibly be normal. In such cases, there is a tendency to regard the perpetrators of the crimes as abnormal and their extreme antisocial behaviour as inherent in their personality. Otherwise, if they, as people, were regarded as 'normal' and merely their *behaviour* as 'abnormal', then the inference would be that anyone could be a potential rapist or mass murderer. This is too unsettling a notion for most people to contemplate. On the other hand, studies in social psychology have shown that, in certain circumstances, so-called 'normal' people can behave in violent and antisocial ways. A prime example is football hooliganism.

Abnormal or just criminal?

Cultural issues – In Western societies, there is a common assumption that the behaviour of the White population is the norm and that any deviation from this by another ethnic group indicates psychological abnormality.

In certain cultures with rigid political or social structures, using deviation from social norms as a means of classifying abnormality can be a form of social control. For example, political dissidents in Russia used to be seen as abnormal because they did not toe the party line; they were diagnosed as insane and often detained in mental asylums. In Japan, a diagnosis of insanity has been used as a threat to ensure a strong work ethic. According to Cohen (1988), because of Japan's drive for industrial success, 'loony-bins' are required for those who are unwilling to conform to the demands of industry. Therefore, in order to instill the appropriate terror, the 'bins' must be sufficiently unattractive. Conditions in Japanese mental hospitals are similar to the old Victorian asylums in the UK, being overcrowded, dirty and often brutal places.

Social norms vary: what is abnormal in one culture, may be acceptable in another. For example, walking around nude in public may be considered normal in some cultures and talking to an invisible person is considered normal in certain African and Indian cultures following a bereavement (where people believe it is possible to remain in contact briefly with a lost loved one).

DEVIATION FROM IDEAL MENTAL HEALTH

The notion of ideal mental health was first put forward by Jahoda in 1958. It turns the traditional notion of abnormality on its head, by looking at positives, rather than negatives – the notion of mental *health* rather than mental *illness*. Jahoda identified six major criteria for optimal living which, she believed, promoted psychological health and wellbeing. Anyone unable to show these qualities would be vulnerable to mental disorder.

ACTIVITY

Psychological health

So far, we have focused on negative aspects of life and deviations from what might be considered 'normal'. Before reading on, make a list of the qualities that you feel indicate a psychologically healthy person.

When you have done this, compare your list with the six criteria that Jahoda (1958) identified, discussed in the text below.

Jahoda's six criteria are as follows:

1 *Positive attitudes towards the self* – This means having a positive self-concept and a sense of identity. Jahoda suggested that a mentally healthy attitude towards the self included self-respect, self-confidence, self-reliance and self-acceptance; the person has learned to live with themselves, accepting both their limitations and their possibilities. What is important here, is to view oneself realistically and objectively. Unfortunately, many people develop a negative self-concept or low self-esteem because of the way they have been treated by others and perhaps made to feel small and unimportant. Jahoda claimed that to be mentally healthy, a person must know who they are and like what they see.

2 *Self-actualization of one's potential* – This idea was proposed by Abraham Maslow (1968), who suggested that we all have potential in certain directions (for example, intellectual, artistic, athletic) and that we constantly strive to fulfil this potential. mental-health problems occur when we are prevented from fulfilling our true potential.

3 *Resistance to stress* – Jahoda called this the ability to tolerate anxiety without disintegration. The mentally healthy person will have developed good coping strategies for dealing with stressful situations. Indeed, it does seem that those people who are more vulnerable to stress and anxiety are more likely to develop psychological problems. A great deal of research has been undertaken to identify effective coping strategies to reduce stress (see Topic 3 in Unit 3, starting on p. 101).

4 *Personal autonomy* – This means that the person is reliant on their own inner resources and can remain relatively stable even in the face of hard knocks, frustrations and deprivations. This is because autonomous people are not dependent upon other people. They are self-contained and depend upon their own resources. Jahoda describes personal autonomy as an ability to make our own decisions on the basis of what is right for ourselves, rather than to satisfy others.

5 *Accurate perception of reality* – This means seeing oneself and the world around one in realistic terms, rather than through either 'rose-tinted glasses' or in an overly pessimistic manner. Indeed, if someone continually distorts reality, then they are not really living in the real world and their views

and behaviours are bound to appear abnormal to others. If someone only ever sees the best in people then this may endear them to others, but it also leaves them vulnerable to those who may take advantage. Conversely, someone who is overly morbid and pessimistic is a likely candidate to develop a depressive disorder and would not endear themselves to others very easily.

6 *Adapting to the environment* – This means being competent in all areas of life: at work, in personal relationships and in leisure activities. It also involves being flexible rather than rigid, being able to adapt and adjust to change. Someone who is fixed in old ways of thinking and behaving may appear abnormal to younger people and to those who have been able to adjust to a changing environment.

Limitations of the deviation from ideal mental health definition

This is a refreshing approach in that it focuses on positive aspects of life rather than negative ones, but meeting all six criteria appears to be quite demanding. Most people are likely to fall short of 'ideal mental health'. Specific limitations include the following:

■ *The difficulty of self-actualizing* – Unfortunately, in reality, very few people achieve their full potential in life, which may be because of their own particular environment or through some failing within themselves. It would seem, then, that if self-actualization is a criterion for ideal mental health, most of us would be regarded as mentally unhealthy.

■ *Possible benefits of stress* – As far as resistance to stress is concerned, some people actually work more efficiently in moderately stressful situations. For example, many actors say that they give their best performances when they experience a certain amount of anxiety.

■ *Cultural issues* – The idea of mental health is culture-bound and Jahoda's ideas are based on Western ideals of self-fulfilment and individuality. Seeking to fulfil your own potential, for example, may be seen as a prime goal in life within some cultures but not in others. In some cultures, elders in the family plan the person's future out for them. This planning might include such things as arranged marriages, which are common in Asian cultures. It may, therefore, be regarded as 'abnormal' to pursue your own goals if they are in conflict with those of your culture. The pursuit of self-actualization or personal happiness is, perhaps, a privilege for those living in an affluent, industrialized society, where people are freed from the need to pursue the basic necessities for survival.

Similarly, with regard to personal autonomy, there is an overwhelming sense of duty to others in many cultures; it would not be regarded as 'normal' to put your own wishes before those of others.

Perceptions of reality differ over time (remember people once thought the world was flat) and also differ between cultures. For example, seeing or hearing someone who has died would be considered normal in some cultures, but regarded as psychotic hallucinations in other cultures.

Parenthood, winning awards, achieving feats of physical endurance (in 2003, Andrew Cooney became the youngest man to walk to the South Pole) – these are all self-actualizing experiences. But how many people do you know who have reached full self-actualization? If we don't, does that make us 'mentally unhealthy'?

FAILURE TO FUNCTION ADEQUATELY

People with psychological disorders often experience considerable suffering and distress, as well as a general inability to cope with their everyday activities, such as being unable to go to work or take part in social activities. Such dysfunction is so common that it is taken into account when making a diagnosis of an individual with psychological problems. There are diagnostic manuals available to doctors when they are trying to identify particular mental disorders. One of the most widely used is the Diagnostic and Statistical Manual of Mental Disorders (American Psychiatric Association 1994), which requires doctors to assess people on various psychological and physical measures. One of these measures is called the Global Assessment of Functioning Scale (GAF), shown in Fig. 4.2. This is an important part of the overall assessment, although a poor score on its own would not be seen as an indication of a psychological disorder.

The failure to function adequately view of abnormality carries certain implications. If someone's behaviour appears strange or 'abnormal' to others, then provided they are not harming themselves or others, and provided their behaviour is not dysfunctional, such as preventing them from carrying on their daily lives,

Figure 4.2 >> *Global Assessment of Functioning (GAF) Scale*

Consider psychological, social and occupational functioning on a hypothetical continuum of mental health–illness. Do not include impairment in functioning due to physical (or environmental) limitations.

Code (Note: Intermediate codes can be used when appropriate e.g. 45, 68, 72.)

100	Superior functioning in a wide range of activities. Life's problems never seem to get out of hand. Is sought out by others because of his or her many positive qualities. No symptoms
90	Absent or minimal symptoms (e.g. mild anxiety before an exam), good functioning in all areas, interested and involved in a wide range of activities, socially effective, generally satisfied with life, no more than everyday problems or concerns (e.g. an occasional argument with family members)
80	If symptoms are present, they are transient and expectable reactions to psychosocial stressors (e.g. difficulty concentrating after family argument); no more than slight impairment in social, occupational, or school functioning (e.g. temporarily falling behind in school work)
70	Some mild symptoms (e.g. depressed mood and mild insomnia) OR some difficulty in social, occupational, or school functioning (e.g. occasional truancy, or theft within the household), but generally functioning pretty well, has some meaningful interpersonal relationships.
60	Moderate symptoms (e.g. flat effect and circumstantial speech, occasional panic attacks) OR moderate difficulty in social, occupational, or school functioning (e.g. few friends, conflicts with peers or co-workers).
50	Serious symptoms (e.g. suicidal ideation, severe obsessional rituals, frequent shoplifting) OR any serious impairment in social, occupational or school functioning (e.g. no friends, unable to keep a job).
40	Some impairment in reality testing or communication (e.g. speech is at all times illogical, obscure or irrelevant) OR major impairment in several areas, such as work or school, family relations, judgement, thinking or mood (e.g. depressed man avoids friends, neglects family and cannot work).
30	Behaviour is considerable influenced by delusions or hallucinations OR serious impairment in communication or judgement (e.g. sometimes incoherent, acts grossly inappropriately, suicidal preoccupation) OR inability to function in almost all areas (e.g. stays in bed all day, no job, home).
20	Some danger of hurting self or others (e.g. suicide attempts without clear expectation of death, frequently violent, manic excitement) OR occasionally fails to maintain minimal personal hygiene (e.g. smears faeces) OR gross impairment in communication (e.g. largely incoherent or mute).
10	Persistent danger of severely hurting self or others (e.g. recurrent violence) OR persistent inability to maintain minimal personal hygiene OR serious suicidal act with clear expectation of death.
0	Inadequate information.

then no intervention is required. A failure to function adequately does, however, mean that someone with a psychological problem that falls outside the criteria for a serious mental disorder should still be given appropriate professional help if their problem is causing a dysfunction in their daily living. Unfortunately though, NHS provision (in the UK) is not always available for people with less severe psychological problems and there are generally long waiting lists for treatment.

Limitations of the failure to function adequately definition

Using the criterion of failure to function adequately as a definition of abnormality may be the most humane way of addressing psychological problems and mental disorders, as it is left to the person (or others close to them) to decide whether they need or wish to seek help. However, there are problems with this approach:

- *Not the whole picture* – This is not a true definition of 'abnormality'. Rather it is a way of determining the extent of a person's problems and the likelihood that they might need professional help. Comer (2000) points out that psychological abnormality is not necessarily indicated by dysfunction alone. For example, some people protest against social injustice by depriving themselves of necessities, such as food. It is when abnormal behaviour interferes with daily functioning, such that people lose the ability to work or the motivation to care for themselves properly, that the behaviour becomes is viewed as abnormal.

- *Exceptions to the rule* – A student experiencing anxiety and distress about a forthcoming exam may behave uncharacteristically, even inadequately, but this would not necessarily be regarded as abnormal behaviour. Conversely, *sociopaths* (people with antisocial personalities) might exhibit violent or aggressive behaviour, but be unlikely to experience personal suffering, distress or any general dysfunction, because of their amoral attitudes.

- *Cultural issues* – It may be that the inability to cope with the demands of daily living is the cause rather than the outcome of mental disorder. It might explain why statistics show a higher incidence of psychological problems among people from minority ethnic groups, owing to the exploitation, deprivation and harassment they often experience. Cochrane and Sashidharan (1995) point out that racism and prejudice have a significant impact upon psychological wellbeing. Migration from developing to developed Western countries also means that the first generation of migrants is likely to be exposed to economic uncertainty, substandard housing and harsh working conditions. These have mental-health implications for new immigrants, but their problems may mistakenly be attributed to ethnicity.

Is he 'failing to function adequately'?

CULTURAL RELATIVISM

We have looked at some of the limitations of attempts to define abnormality and found that a major problem with all of them is the fact that they are culturally specific. In other words, it is impossible to provide a clear definition of abnormality that applies to the whole of humankind because each culture has a different set of norms and expectations. It may be inappropriate for a member of one cultural group to make judgements about the behaviour of a member of another, and doctors involved in diagnosing mental disorder need to be aware of this. The implication of culture and its relationship to diagnosis is set out in DSM-IV:

<< Diagnostic assessment can be especially challenging when a clinician from one ethnic or cultural group uses the DSM-IV classification to evaluate an individual from a different ethnic or cultural group. A clinician, who is unfamiliar with the nuances of an individual's cultural frame of reference, may incorrectly judge as psychopathology those normal variations in behaviour, belief, or experience that are particular to the individual's culture. For example, certain religious practices or beliefs (e.g. hearing or seeing a deceased relative during bereavement) may be misdiagnosed as manifestations of a psychotic disorder. >>

Subculture

There can be groups of people within a wider culture that have their own particular set of norms and beliefs; these people are said to have a distinctive subculture. For example, ethnic groups within the UK, such as African-Caribbeans, while conforming to many of the norms of the wider society, often have their own particular behaviour patterns that may make them vulnerable to misunderstanding. For instance, in Britain, Black (African-Caribbean) immigrants are between two to seven times more likely to be diagnosed with schizophrenia than White people (Cochrane 1977). There are many factors that might account for this difference, but one possible reason is that cultural variations in communication style (i.e. that deviate from White social norms) may lead to mistaken diagnosis. In a broad interpretation of the term 'subculture', it is interesting to look at gender and social class issues. These are discussed in the two panels below.

Social class issues

Research has indicated that the higher prevalence of severe mental disorders in socially disadvantaged groups is largely due to their exposure to more stressful life experiences, compared with those in more advantaged social groups. The first large-scale survey to support this hypothesis was the Midtown Manhattan Study (Srole *et al.* 1961). The study found the lowest levels of psychiatric impairment in the upper classes, slightly more in the middle classes and the highest levels in the lower classes. These findings were supported in a British study (Cochrane and Stopes-Roe 1980), which also found that lower social status was associated with higher risk of psychological problems.

A major study by Brown and Harris (1978) found a high incidence of depression among working-class housewives in Camberwell, London. The main vulnerability factors they identified were long-term periods of adverse circumstances, together with the cumulative effect of short-term life events, combined with factors such as lack of paid employment. In addition, while the middle and upper classes have more 'positive' life experiences to offset the 'negative', those in the lower classes have less control over their environment.

Cochrane (1995a) points out that people living in high-rise flats are more prone to psychological problems than those in traditional accommodation. This may be because they have poorer relationships with their neighbours – an important factor in mental health, as neighbours are a potential source of social support. Of course, as Cochrane points out, neighbours can also be a source of irritation and even fear. Halpern (1995) claims that if a neighbourhood becomes labelled as a dumping ground for 'problem families', then people who did not originally experience problems may develop adverse reactions which may affect their mental health.

The *social drift* hypothesis offers another explanation for the higher incidence of serious mental disorder in lower socio-economic groups: the early onset of a major mental disorder, such as schizophrenia, might reduce the chances of establishing a career and the person may then subsequently 'drift' down the socio-economic scale. This suggests that social class is largely a consequence of, rather than a contributory factor in, mental disorder. Support for this is found in cases where the initial onset of schizophrenia has occurred later in life. It has been noted that many such individuals had previously had good careers. The higher incidence of schizophrenia in poor areas could reflect the number of people who move to those areas after the onset of their illness, because it is all they can afford (Cochrane 1983).

Gender issues

Other studies have examined reasons why certain psychological problems appear to be more prevalent in men or women. Howell (1981) points out that women's experience in British culture predisposes them to depression and therefore clinicians are diagnosing a situation rather than a person. Cochrane (1995b) explains that depression can be related to the long-term effects of child abuse and also to gender-role socialization, which produces increased female vulnerability. He points out the adverse effects on women of power relationships and sex discrimination. Despite the vast amount of evidence that relates women's depression to sociocultural factors, some clinicians continue to ignore environmental circumstances that may contribute to depressive symptoms. Johnstone (1989) believes this also applies to men. Unemployed men have a high rate of psychiatric breakdown. Johnstone explains that by labelling the problem as a mental disorder, not only does the person have the stigma of a psychiatric label, but the problem is seen only in individual terms, rather than in the wider political and social context. Furthermore, Bennett (1995) believes that the socialization of men in industrialized societies has created masculine stereotypes that alienate men from seeking help for psychological problems.

Cultural change

Attitudes, values and beliefs can change over time within a given culture and this will affect judgements about abnormal behaviour. Two examples serve to illustrate this:

- Until as recently as the early years of the twentieth century, unmarried women in the UK who became pregnant were sometimes sent to mental institutions. In many cases the babies were taken away for adoption. Some of these women were in their early teens when they became pregnant and remained in mental institutions for the rest of their lives.

- In recent centuries, homosexuality has been regarded as a deviation from social norms. In the UK, homosexual acts were criminal offences, even among consenting adults, until 1967. In the USA until 1973, the American Psychiatric Association classified homosexuality as a mental disorder.

Culture-bound syndromes

Certain psychological disorders appear to be universal and are found in cultures all over the world. However, there are a few disorders that seem to occur only within certain societies. These are called *culture-bound syndromes* (see Table 4.1). The actual symptoms described in Table 4.1 would be recognized in most cultures, but it is the unique grouping of symptoms (known as a syndrome) that marks these disorders out as culture-bound. Note that bulimia nervosa is included because, so far, it has only been observed in Western cultures.

An example of cultural change: in 2002, Alex Cannel and Ian Burford became first same-sex couple to sign the London Partnerships Register set up by the Greater London Authority.

ACTIVITY

Expert interview

Read the expert interview given by Ray Cochrane on p. 125 and answer the following questions:

1 What two examples does Ray Cochrane give to show how cultural factors may influence whether or not we class a behaviour as abnormal?

2 What are the two main dangers of ignoring culture when we define mental illness?

3 To what extent is it "impossible to escape entirely the blinkers of one's own culture when assessing abnormality"?

Table 4.1 >> Culture-bound syndromes

Diagnosis	Country/Culture	Characteristics
>> *Latah*	Malaysia, Indonesia, Bantu in Africa	Exaggerated response to a minor stimulus; tendency to mimic people nearby in speech and gesture; only occurs in females.
>> *Behainin*	Bali	Abdominal pain, headache, ringing in the ears, impaired vision, screaming, weeping and convulsions; exhaustion follows episode and individual (usually female) has no memory of what happened.
>> *Taijin-kyofusho*	Japan and some other Asian countries	Occurs mainly in males; anxiety, fear of rejection, fear of eye contact, blushing, worry about body odour.
>> *Bulimia nervosa*	North America and Western Europe	Food bingeing, self-induced vomiting; may occur alongside depression and substance abuse.
>> *Tabanka*	Trinidad	Depression in men abandoned by their wives; high rate of suicide.

Source: Based on Geiselman (1988)

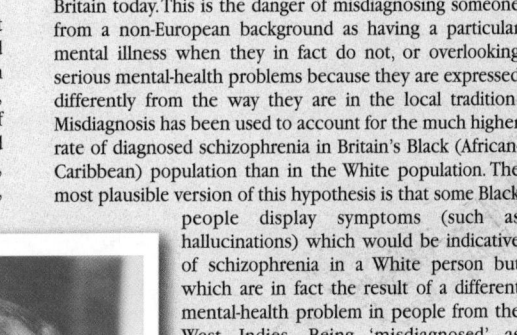
Cultural *relativism*

Ray Cochrane is Professor of Psychology at the University of Birmingham. His main interest is in the mental health of immigrants and ethnic minorities in Britain. He has also undertaken research into the delivery of mental-health care, particularly into how services relate to the needs of black and ethnic minorities.

Q In what ways do cultural factors compromise traditional definitions of abnormality?

A It is easy to forget that both the definition of what constitutes mental illness and the diagnostic schemes used to categorize patterns of symptoms were developed from within the European cultural tradition (largely in France, Germany, the USA and the UK). The operational definition of what is pathological behaviour is very strongly influenced by the culture within which the observer is embedded. So, for example, in contemporary Northern European culture, building a shrine to a dead relative in one's house and leaving food and gifts beside it each night would be seen as abnormal, whereas in another culture this might be seen as perfectly appropriate, normal behaviour.

Even where there might be a cross-cultural consensus that a particular behaviour is 'abnormal', there might be sharp cultural differences in explaining why it occurred. While there might be wide agreement that seeing visions and talking aloud to someone who is not present is very unusual, this could be attributed to either madness or extreme holiness depending on the culture in which it occurred.

Ray Cochrane

Q What are the dangers of ignoring cultural issues when attempting to define abnormality?

A There are two main dangers of ignoring culture when defining mental illness. First, when scientists, anthropologists and doctors from Europe and North America have gone looking for evidence of mental illness in other cultures, they have taken their own definitions with them and seen the culture they are exploring through Western European eyes. In most instances, there are no objective tests for the existence of mental illness. This can lead to great mistakes being made. Sometimes, it has resulted in conclusions being drawn that a particular cultural group do not have experience of a disorder – depression was believed to be rare in black Africans right up until the 1960s because it was not manifested in the same way as in Europe. On other occasions, people whose behaviour contravenes Western Europeans' social norms have been defined as mentally ill even though their behaviour was compatible with local standards.

The second danger is based on the same set of misconceptions, but is much more acute in multicultural Britain today. This is the danger of misdiagnosing someone from a non-European background as having a particular mental illness when they in fact do not, or overlooking serious mental-health problems because they are expressed differently from the way they are in the local tradition. Misdiagnosis has been used to account for the much higher rate of diagnosed schizophrenia in Britain's Black (African-Caribbean) population than in the White population. The most plausible version of this hypothesis is that some Black people display symptoms (such as hallucinations) which would be indicative of schizophrenia in a White person but which are in fact the result of a different mental-health problem in people from the West Indies. Being 'misdiagnosed' as suffering from schizophrenia means that they are unduly stigmatized and receive totally inappropriate treatment.

Q Does this mean that such attempts to define 'abnormality' are doomed to failure?

A It would be tempting to throw up one's hands in despair and agree that a universal definition of abnormality that is appropriate in all cultures is impossible. Realistically, though, we have to get on with dealing with people in distress and accept that, whatever their shortcomings, the current Western concepts of mental health and illness, and Western medicine are dominant worldwide. In certain areas, the situation is not that problematic – a syndrome that we call 'schizophrenia' is recognized in almost all cultures and is almost always considered to be abnormal and undesirable. The World Health Organization has also established through a very carefully devised programme of research that the incidence of schizophrenia is similar in most cultures. For other forms of 'mental illness' the situation is less clear cut. It has not been possible to establish that depression, or the neuroses, as defined in the West, are recognised in other cultures either as specific syndromes or as resulting from an illness.

That said, with the gradual evolution of diagnostic systems such as ICD-10 and DSM-IV, cultural factors have increasingly been taken into account, and certainly in the UK the training of all mental-health workers now includes substantial consideration of the issues discussed here. While it might not be possible to escape entirely the blinkers of one's own culture when assessing abnormality, greater awareness that one is blinkered does help.

Check your understanding of definitions of abnormality by answering these questions. Try to do this from memory at first. You can check your answers by looking back through Topic 1.

1   What do you understand by the term 'statistical infrequency'?

2   Give one limitation of this definition of abnormality.

3   What is meant by the term 'social norm' and give one example of a social norm from your own culture.

4   Give an example of a social norm that has changed over time.

5   Explain how the use of the social norm definition of abnormality can be used as a form of social control.

6   Describe the cultural issues raised by the deviation from mental health definition.

7   Describe the six criteria identified by Jahoda as being necessary for optimal living.

8   Why is the failure to function adequately definition of abnormality a humane way of defining abnormality?

9   Give two limitations of this definition of abnormality.

10 "It is impossible to define abnormality for all humankind." To what extent is this statement true?

REVISION SUMMARY

Having covered this topic, you should be able to:

✓ define the terms: 'statistical infrequency', 'deviation from social norms', 'failure to function adequately', and 'deviation from ideal mental health'

✓ describe the way in which each of these terms has been used to define abnormality

✓ explain the limitations associated with each of these attempts at definition

✓ explain how cultural relativism affects the definition of abnormality.

GETTING YOU THINKING...

Read the brief descriptions of the following terms, given in the 'Key terms' box below:

- the medical (or biological) model
- the psychodynamic model
- the behavioural model
- the cognitive model.

Now read the six cases below and decide which model is being used to determine the treatment described.

1 Rebecca has a spider phobia and is no longer able to stay in the house alone with her young daughter whilst her partner goes to work every day. She is being treated by systematic desensitization. This is teaching her to relax and confront her fear of spiders in a relaxed setting, so that she learns to associate a feeling of calm with the presence of a spider.

2 Lynda has been diagnosed as suffering from schizophrenia. She regularly takes the drug chlorpromazine that helps to keep her severe symptoms in check and enables her to live with her family and keep her job.

3 Rational-emotive therapy is being used to treat Karl's panic attacks. In his twice-weekly session with the therapist, Karl is being helped to recognize the irrational assumptions that he has about his life and change these into more positive views of himself and his situation.

4 Bill suffers from severe depression that has not improved with the drugs that he was prescribed. He has recently been admitted to hospital for electroconvulsive therapy (ECT) which involves passing an electric current through the brain.

5 Tom suffers from severe headaches that have no physical cause but leave him unable to get out of bed or go to work. His therapist encourages him to free associate on dreams and early childhood memories by letting his mind wander and saying aloud whatever comes into his mind. This may bring uncomfortable desires or repressed thoughts into conscious awareness. The therapist interprets his words, dreams and behaviour. This helps him to make sense of, and come to terms with, his experience and to work through repressed thoughts.

6 Lou is keen to give up smoking and is being treated by aversion therapy: a drug that induces sickness is given to her so that she learns to associate unpleasant feelings with cigarettes and stops smoking.

KEY TERMS

Model: a term that is used synonymously with theory. In psychopathology, it refers to an explanation of the causes of psychological disorders.

Medical model (or Biological model): a view of abnormality that sees mental disorders as being caused by abnormal physiological processes such as genetic and biochemical factors. Abnormality according to this model is seen as an illness or disease.

Psychodynamic model: a view that abnormal behaviour is caused by underlying psychological forces of which the individual is probably unaware.

Behavioural model: a view that abnormal behaviours are maladaptive, learned responses in the environment which can be replaced by more adaptive behaviours.

Cognitive model: a view that stresses the role of cognitive problems (such as illogical or irrational thought processes) in abnormal functioning.

BIOLOGICAL/MEDICAL MODEL

Models of abnormality are conceptual models, each offering a different explanation for the origins of mental disorders. Which particular conceptual model is adopted is important because it will influence the type of research that is conducted and also the methods of treatment adopted. We will start by looking at the biological/medical model.

Basic assumptions of the medical model

The medical model has dominated the field of mental health for the past 200 years. It is a biological approach that regards abnormality of mental functioning as an illness or disease. Mental disorders are thought to be related to the physical structure and functioning of the brain. Some mental disorders are thought to have an organic basis, for example, poisoning due to alcohol or drug abuse that results in anatomical deterioration. Disorders where a clear organic cause has not been identified have been traditionally referred to as 'functional disorders'. However, people who adopt the medical model believe that research will eventually show that all mental disorders have an underlying physical cause.

Advocates of the medical model are psychiatrists who are medically qualified practitioners specializing in mental disorders. They approach psychological abnormality in the same way that they would investigate physical illness: by classifying disorders, seeking the underlying cause, developing appropriate treatments and devising methods of prevention.

They consider four possible causal factors that sometimes overlap:

- *Brain damage* – Abnormal behaviour may occur if the structure of the brain is damaged in some way. Once disease or brain damage has caused mental deterioration, there is, unfortunately, little that can be done to stop it. A good example of this is Alzheimer's disease, a type of dementia caused by the malformation and loss of cells in a number of areas of the nervous system.

- *Infection* – We are familiar with the idea of bacteria or viruses causing physical illness such as flu or meningitis. It seems, though, that infection can also give rise to mental illness. Syphilis, for example, was identified in the nineteenth century as the cause of deterioration in specific regions of the brain resulting in symptoms of a mental illness known as 'general paresis'. The symptoms of this disorder were:

  - delusions of grandeur, such as believing that you are God

  - delusions of persecution, believing that everyone is plotting against you

  - other bizarre, irrational behaviours, which now come under the general heading of psychosis.

This disease is now rarely seen, as the use of antibiotics in the treatment of syphilis prevents subsequent brain damage occurring.

- *Biochemistry* – During the twentieth century, the medical profession has increasingly learned more about the role played by biochemistry in mental disorders.

Neurotransmitters, which are the chemicals that transmit nerve impulses from one nerve cell to the next, are thought to be out of balance in the nervous systems of individuals with certain psychological disorders. For example, schizophrenia has been associated with an excess of the neurotransmitter dopamine, and depression has been associated with decreased availability of serotonin.

Hormones, which are chemical messengers released by the endocrine system (see pp. 78–9), have also been implicated in the origins of some mental disorders. For example, people with depression are often found to have higher than normal levels of the hormone cortisol. The reasons why these chemical changes take place are not yet clear, but they may be due to infections, life stress or a genetic defect.

- *Genes* – Important new genetic research has highlighted the possibility that some people may be genetically at risk of developing a mental disorder, but so far the only strong evidence relates to conditions such as schizophrenia and bipolar depression (a disorder characterized by alternating periods of depression and mania). It has been demonstrated, for example, that a first-degree relative (e.g. son, daughter) has a 10 per cent chance of developing schizophrenia. This is far in excess of the 1 per cent risk to the normal population. In order to investigate genetic links, researchers do family studies to see whether particular disorders run through families. These studies can be difficult to interpret because the similarity of family members might simply reflect their shared environment rather than their shared biology. Some physical disorders, such as muscular dystrophy, appear to arise from defects in single genes. It seems unlikely that this is the case for mental disorders such as schizophrenia. In disorders such as this, it is more likely that there are defects in several genes. The Human Genome Project, which aims to determine the sequence of all human DNA, will provide the means to establish genetic linkage in psychiatric disorders.

Advances in genetic research raise ethical and practical concerns about the consequences of trying to engineer a better society by genetic means.

Treatment and the biological/medical model

Since mental problems are viewed in this model as physical illnesses, then physical treatments are regarded as the most appropriate. These physical interventions fall into three main categories:

- *Drug therapy (chemotherapy)* is the main treatment and is based on the assumption that chemical imbalance is at the root of the problem. Drugs for mental disorders range from minor tranquillizers (for anxiety disorders), to antidepressants (for depressive disorders), through to major tranquillizers (for severe psychotic disorders such as schizophrenia). These drugs have been found to be effective in relieving the symptoms of mental disorders in many, but not all, people. However, they also have side effects that may be considered worse than the original symptoms of the disorder. The fact that chemotherapy is effective in reducing symptoms of mental disorders is regarded as sufficient evidence to support the theory that chemical imbalance is the cause of the problem. Indeed, it is now known that some chemicals can affect the functioning of particular neurotransmitters, producing the symptoms of certain mental disorders. However, some psychologists disagree, believing the chemical imbalance to be the effect, rather than the cause, of mental problems.

- *Electro-convulsive therapy (ECT)* involves passing a high current through the brain for approximately half a second. This induces convulsions that last for approximately one minute. Patients are anaesthetized before the treatment and recall nothing about it once they come round from the anaesthetic. It is now used mainly for people with severe depression and can be an effective short-term treatment. However, approximately 60 per cent of patients will become depressed again within a year. It is not clear exactly how ECT works, but it may increase the availability of certain neurotransmitters in the brain.

- *Psychosurgery (brain surgery)* is the most invasive form of biological therapy because it involves removal of brain tissue and the effects are irreversible. This method is rarely used now and is only offered as a last resort.

Evaluation of the biological/medical model

- *No blame* – A diagnosis of mental 'illness' implies that the person is in no way responsible for the abnormality of functioning and as such is not to blame. The concept of 'no blame' is generally thought to be more humane and likely to elicit a much more sympathetic response from others.

- *Stigma* – However, Szasz (1972), pointed out that even more than physical illness, mental illness is something that people fear – largely because it is something they do not understand. In general, people do not know how to respond to someone diagnosed as mentally ill. There may also be fears that the person's behaviour might be unpredictable and potentially dangerous. Therefore, sympathy is more likely to give way to avoidance of the person, which in turn leads to the person feeling shunned.

- *Research* – A huge amount of research has been carried out within the framework of the medical model and this has greatly increased our understanding of the possible biological factors underpinning psychological disorders. However, much of the evidence is inconclusive and findings can be difficult to interpret. For example, in family studies, it is difficult to disentangle the effects of genetics from the effects of environment. It can also be difficult to establish cause and effect. For example, raised levels of dopamine may be a *consequence* rather than a *cause* of schizophrenia.

- *Use of drugs* – Many psychologists criticize psychiatry for focusing its attention primarily on symptoms and for assuming that relieving symptoms with drugs cures the problem. Unfortunately, in many cases where the drug treatment is ceased, the symptoms recur, suggesting that drugs are not addressing the true cause of the problem.

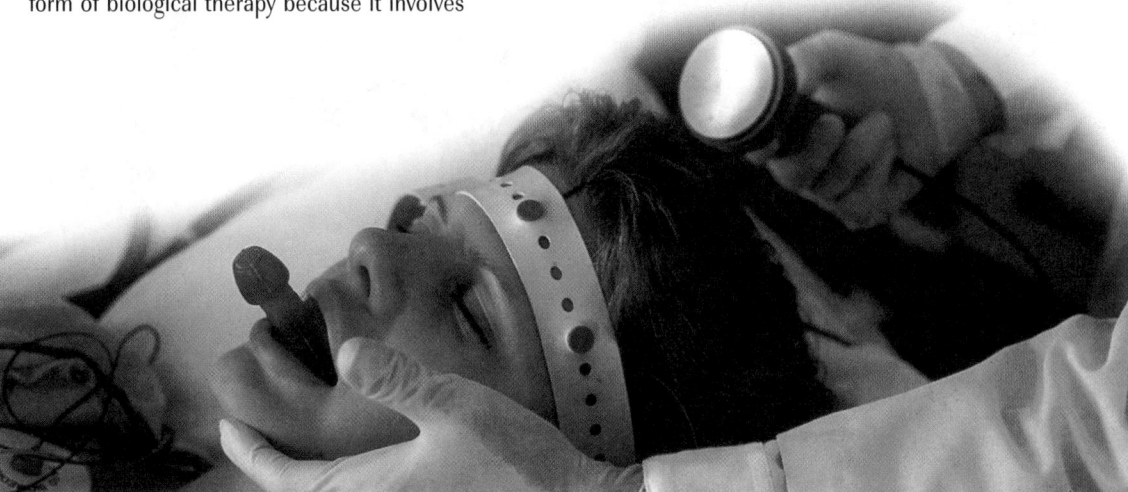

Relinquishing responsibility – Another criticism of the medical model is that people are encouraged to become patients, handing over responsibility for their 'wellness' to professionals, and so not feel responsible for their own recovery.

■ *Treatment success* – Some successful treatments have arisen from the medical model that have helped people with psychological disorders. However, many treatments have been criticized as being unethical or ineffective. Prescribed treatment may not be appropriate and yet there is an expectation that patients will comply with medication, despite the fact that, as the British National Formulary (an index of pharmaceutical drugs and preparations) indicates, most medication carries side effects and often long-term dependency upon the drugs.

■ *Reductionist* – The biological explanation of abnormality is criticized for being reductionist. This means that it attempts to explain phenomena by breaking them down to the most fundamental level, that is, it explains abnormal behaviour in terms of the activity of brain cells. It seems, however, much more likely that psychological disorders are caused by the interaction of many factors.

PSYCHODYNAMIC MODEL

Basic assumptions

Freud and others developed the psychodynamic model in the latter part of the nineteenth century through clinical work with mentally disordered patients. Freud believed that problems arose directly from the dynamics of the personality (*psyche*), rather than from physical causes. According to Freud, the psyche consists of three interrelated systems:

■ *Id* – the unconscious, insatiable set of instincts with which people are born. The id is pleasure-orientated and completely selfish.

■ *Ego* – the conscious, rational part of the psyche that has to arbitrate between the demands of the id and the demands of the superego, the last part of the psyche to develop.

■ *Superego* – the moral part of the personality concerned with right and wrong. The superego develops through the process of socialization when people learn the moral standards and expectations of their culture.

The id and the superego, therefore, are in direct conflict and need to be managed in a rational way. The well-adjusted person develops a strong ego that is able to cope with the demands of each by allowing both the id and the superego expression at appropriate times. If, however, the ego is weakened, then either the id or the superego, whichever is the stronger, may dominate the personality. If id impulses emerge unchecked, then they are expressed in destructiveness and immorality, which may result in conduct disorders in childhood and psychopathic (dangerously abnormal) behaviour in adulthood. A too-powerful superego rigidly restricts the id to such an extent that the person will be deprived of even socially acceptable pleasures. According to Freud this would create neurosis, which could be expressed in the symptoms of anxiety disorders, such as phobias and obsessions. Psychological disturbance, therefore, results from the inability of the ego to manage conflict within the psyche. Freud maintained that these internal conflicts occur at an unconscious level, so that we are unaware of their influence.

Although psychical conflict can occur at any time in our life, it is most marked in early childhood because the ego is not developed fully enough to mediate between the id and the superego. Nor is it developed fully enough to deal with external events, such as maternal

AS Individual Differences

absences, parental shortcomings or competition with siblings. Traumatic or confusing events in childhood, therefore, are pushed into the unconscious – a process which Freud called repression – because they are too painful for the ego to bear or because the child hasn't developed sufficient knowledge of the world to make sense of the event (A. Freud 1936). Distressing feelings around traumatic events do not disappear, however, simply because they are repressed. They find expression in dreams and irrational behaviour, and may eventually erupt and express themselves in psychological disorders.

Defence mechanisms

In order to balance the demands of the id and superego, the ego employs defence mechanisms (see Table 4.2). These distort or deny reality and are essential ways of protecting the ego from distress and allowing the person to cope with life. They have a powerful, yet unconscious, influence upon our behaviour, and everyone uses them. Freud said that they are perfectly natural and normal, and offer a way of satisfying the demands of the id without upsetting the superego. Whilst useful for protecting the ego, however, they do not offer a long-term solution to problems, and if defence mechanisms are adopted too frequently, or get out of proportion, they themselves can create psychological problems of their own.

According to Freud, the behaviour of all people is to some extent 'abnormal', in that none of us is free from the dynamic conflicts caused by our unconscious drives and repressed memories. Therefore it is perfectly 'normal' to experience anxiety. Abnormality is, therefore, both inevitable and beyond our conscious control. Now try the next activity at the top of p. 132.

Table 4.2 >> Defence mechanisms

Mechanism	How it works
>> **Repression**	Prevents unacceptable desires, motivations or emotions from becoming conscious. Repression does not mean that you consciously cover up guilty secrets; it means that you make them unconscious so that you are not even aware of them. The repressed drives do not disappear; they remain in the unconscious where they influence behaviour in ways that we are unaware of, and may cause emotional difficulties. *Example:* A person who is normally placid acts in a violent way towards someone else and subsequently has no recollection of this.
>> **Projection**	When people's own unacceptable faults or wishes are attributed to someone else. In the extreme, this defence mechanism can become paranoia. *Example:* Accusing someone else of being angry, secretive or thoughtless, when it is actually you who are feeling angry or being secretive or thoughtless.
>> **Denial**	People sometimes refuse to believe events or to admit they are experiencing certain emotions that provoke anxiety. *Example:* An alcoholic may deny that they are dependent on alcohol.
>> **Regression**	Sometimes people respond to anxiety by behaving in childish ways, such as adults who resort to stamping or kicking, which they may have found effective as children. People may also regress to an earlier type of behaviour when they suffer a traumatic experience. *Example:* A 9-year-old child whose parents are getting divorced may revert to thumb-sucking or bed-wetting.
>> **Displacement**	Diverting emotions onto someone else because the emotions cannot be expressed to the person concerned or because accepting faults in ourselves will cause anxiety. *Examples:* A child who feels angry towards their parents may resort to bullying a younger or weaker child at school. A student who fails an exam may blame the teacher.
>> **Sublimation**	Diverting emotions onto something else (rather than someone else). This is the socially acceptable form of displacement, and a defence mechanism that is encouraged in our society. *Example:* Playing a vigorous sport as an expression of aggressive drives.

Source: Based on Geiselman (1988)

Using defence mechanisms

1 In what way can hard physical activity be a form of sublimation?

2 Spend a few minutes identifying:
   – times when you might have used defence mechanisms
   – occasions when others might have used defence mechanisms with you.

Note down all the examples you can think of.

When you have done this, try to provide additional examples for any of the six defence mechanisms from Table 4.2 that you have not included in your examples.

Is this an example of sublimation?

Treatment and the psychodynamic model

Freud was instrumental in changing ways of thinking about people who are mentally ill, by pointing out that physical symptoms could have psychological causes. He developed a method of treatment for psychological distress, known as psychoanalysis, which is often called the 'talking cure'. From this, many other psychodynamic therapies have evolved. These therapies seek to uncover unconscious psychodynamic processes in order to facilitate insight into the conflicts and anxieties that are the underlying causes of abnormal behaviour. The belief is that if someone can better understand what happened in the past and what is going on at an unconscious level within their psyche, then they can better deal, at a conscious level, with situations that are happening in their life now.

According to psychodynamic theory, the unconscious is revealed in dreams; therefore, one of the techniques of psychoanalysis is the analysis of dreams. Another technique is free association, in which clients are encouraged to let their thoughts wander and say whatever comes into their heads. The idea is that such uncensored thoughts will reveal underlying conflicts and uncomfortable or unfulfilled wishes. The analyst is then able to offer an interpretation of the client's behaviour and make the thoughts that had been repressed available to the client's conscious mind.

Evaluation of the psychodynamic model

■ *Validity* – Freudian theory has been enormously influential and was the first model to establish talking therapy as an acceptable form of treatment in mainstream mental-health practice. However, the psychodynamic model has proved difficult to test scientifically, which has led some theorists to claim that the theory is lacking in validity. However, Kline (1988) claims that a theory is not invalidated because it cannot be tested scientifically; it merely means that no one has yet found a way to do it.

AS Individual Differences

- *Defence mechanisms* – These have been difficult to demonstrate experimentally, but there appears to be some support from everyday experience. Although early traumatic experiences may not necessarily emerge in adulthood as psychological problems, research indicates that many people with psychological problems do recollect having experienced emotional trauma in childhood. However, It is important to understand that retrospective data (i.e. information gathered from clients years after the event) may be unreliable.

- *Determinism* – The psychodynamic model claims that abnormal behaviour results from unconscious psychic conflict related to innate, biological drives. The model also claims that early relationships with parents are important to psychological development. For these reasons it has been claimed that the theory is deterministic, that is, individuals are portrayed as having very little conscious involvement in their own personality development. The implicit assumption is that people are not to blame for their own abnormal behaviour, but may be partially responsible for the development of abnormal behaviour in their offspring. This may prove a heavy burden for parents who feel they have 'done their best' and, according to the model, may also be grappling with their own inner emotional conflicts.

- *Cost and efficacy* – Critics of classical psychoanalysis, such as Eysenck (1967), have suggested that the treatment is costly, time-consuming and ineffective.

- *Relevance* – Some critics have suggested that the theory is culture-bound and that it has little relevance for modern times.

BEHAVIOURAL MODEL

Basic assumptions

This model focuses on the behaviour of an individual in order to explain psychological problems. Advocates of the behavioural model would not use the term 'mental disorder' or 'mental illness', since they have no interest in mental structures, only in overt behaviour. They claim that abnormal behaviour is quite simply learned in the same way as most other behaviour. The behavioural model explains the emergence of specific, maladaptive or dysfunctional behaviours, such as phobias, anxiety, depression and eating disorders, through the processes of classical conditioning, operant conditioning and social learning.

Classical conditioning

The theory of classical conditioning (Pavlov 1927) explains how behaviour is learned through stimulus–response associations. An event in the environment (stimulus) results in a physiological reaction (response) in the individual. The event and the reaction are then forged into an association. Phobias (pathological fears of objects or situations) are thought to develop in this way. For example, a person may climb to the top of a high building and, when looking down (environmental stimulus), experience nausea and dizziness (physio-logical response). This association may then develop into a fear of heights so strong that it becomes a phobia and the person will then be so afraid of heights that they will avoid all situations involving them.

In classical conditioning, it is not the object, nor the situation, which is the cause of the fear but the conditioned response to the object or situation. For example, it is the response of feeling sick and dizzy when looking down from a high building that causes the fear of heights, not the height itself. What is important is that the person must have first experienced a fearful reaction to the situation or event so extreme that they will avoid it (or anything similar) at all costs in the future. This may be fine if the person can avoid being in high places, but will be dysfunctional if the person works in a tall office block, for example, or has a job that involves airline travel. In such cases, the person would either have to seek alternative employment or seek help from a therapist to overcome the phobia. In a classic study, Watson and Rayner (1920) conditioned a young boy to fear white rats in order to illustrate how phobias are the consequence of learned behaviour (see panel on next page).

Are height phobias caused by classical conditioning?

Watson and Rayner attempted to show how a phobia could be conditioned. With his parents' consent, they conducted an experiment on an 11-month-old child – known as Little Albert. Albert was first introduced to a tame white rat and showed no fear. During the experiment, each time Albert reached out to touch the rat the experimenters made a loud noise by striking two metal bars together. The noise startled Albert and soon he became afraid to touch the white rat. In this classic study, Watson and Rayner showed that an association had been formed between touching the white rat and fear of the noise. This conditioned fear then became generalized to other stimuli that resembled the white rat, such as other fluffy animals and objects such as cotton wool. Unfortunately, Little Albert's parents became concerned and withdrew him from the experiment before the experimenters had the opportunity to try and countercondition him. This experience raises ethical issues around the use of humans in such experiments.

ACTIVITY

Counterconditioning

Can you think of a way in which Little Albert could have been counterconditioned? The clue lies in the way in which he was originally conditioned.

Operant conditioning

In his theory of operant conditioning, Skinner (1974) explained how our behaviour is influenced by the consequences of our actions. We learn at an early age, for example, which of our actions are rewarded and which are punished. Conduct disorders and antisocial personality disorders have been explained in operant conditioning terms. If childhood aggression is rewarded, then that behaviour is likely to be repeated and reinforced again and again. However, behaviours that may appear maladaptive to others may be functional or adaptive for the individual. For example, anxiety or depression might gain a reward in the form of attention and concern from others.

Social learning

According to social learning theory (Bandura 1973), a child learns antisocial behaviour by observing and copying violent behaviour in others. A study of monkeys by Mineka et al. (1984) showed how a phobia could be developed through observation alone. Monkeys raised by parents who had a fear of snakes did not automatically acquire this fear themselves, and so Mineka concluded that the fear was not genetically inherited. Those monkeys, however, who had the opportunity to observe their parents showing fearful reactions to real and toy snakes did acquire an intense and persistent fear themselves.

Treatment and the behavioural model

If maladaptive or dysfunctional behaviours have been learned through classical and operant conditioning, it should be possible to change them through the same processes. Behavioural therapy, therefore, takes a practical, problem-solving approach. The therapist's role is to identify maladaptive learning and then to educate the person into more adaptive learning strategies.

Does comforting simply reinforce children's anxious behaviour?

- *Therapies based on classical conditioning* – These therapies aim to replace a maladaptive response such as fear with a healthier one. The main techniques are:

  - systematic desensitization, where clients are taught relaxation techniques and are then gradually exposed to feared objects or situations until the fear diminishes

  - aversion therapy, where the therapist tries to get rid of undesirable behaviour, such as alcoholism, by presenting unpleasant stimuli to the client at the same time as the desired object, for example, giving an electric shock while simultaneously offering alcohol.

- *Therapies based on operant conditioning* – These therapies are based on the assumption that maladaptive behaviour can be reshaped through a system of rewards and punishments, known as behaviour modification. One such method is token economy – this is a procedure that is often used in institutions such as prisons or mental hospitals to discourage antisocial behaviour. Tokens, used to reward any instances of desired behaviour, can be collected and then exchanged for privileges.

Evaluation of the behavioural model

- *Focus on behaviour* – The behavioural model overcomes the ethical issue raised by the medical model of labelling someone as 'ill' or 'abnormal'. Instead, the model concentrates on behaviour and whether it is 'adaptive' or 'maladaptive'.

- *Individual and cultural differences* – The model allows individual and cultural differences to be taken into account. Provided the behaviour is presenting no problems to the individual or to other people, then there is no reason to regard the behaviour as a mental disorder. It is the behavioural model that led to the definition of abnormality previously outlined as a 'failure to function adequately' (see p. 121).

- *Underlying causes* – Those who support the psychodynamic model, however, claim that the behavioural model focuses only on symptoms and ignores the causes of abnormal behaviour. They claim that symptoms are merely the tip of the iceberg – the outward expression of deeper underlying emotional problems. Whenever symptoms are treated without any attempt to ascertain the deeper underlying problems, then the problem will only manifest itself in another way, through different symptoms. This is known as symptom substitution. Behaviourists reject this criticism, however, and claim that we need not look beyond behavioural symptoms because the symptoms are the disorder. Thus, there is nothing to be gained by searching for internal causes, either psychological or physical. Behaviourists point to the success of behavioural therapies in treating certain disorders. Others note that the effects of such treatments are not always long lasting

- *Ethical issues* – Some critics claim that behavioural therapies are dehumanizing and unethical. For example, token economy systems and aversion therapy have sometimes been imposed on people without their consent.

- *Reductionism* – Behavioural theory is accused of being reductionist and simplistic because it seeks to explain human behaviour in very narrow terms, that is, that all behaviour is learned through the processes of conditioning.

COGNITIVE MODEL

Basic assumptions

The cognitive model assumes that emotional problems can be attributed directly to distortions in our thinking processes (cognitions). These take the form of negative thoughts, irrational beliefs and illogical errors, such as polarized (black and white) thinking and overgeneralization. These maladaptive thoughts, it is claimed, usually take place automatically and without full awareness.

This approach to understanding abnormality was founded by Albert Ellis (1962) and Aaron Beck (1963), who thought that the weakness of the behavioural model was that it did not take mental processes into account. The rationale behind the cognitive model is that the thinking (cognition) processes that occur between a stimulus and a response are responsible for the feeling component of the response.

Ellis (1962) maintained that everyone's thoughts are rational at times and irrational at other times. Psychological problems occur only if people engage in faulty thinking to the extent that it becomes maladaptive for themselves and others around them (see Fig. 4.3).

According to Ellis, when we *think* rationally, we *behave* rationally, and as a consequence we are happy, competent and effective. When we think irrationally, however, the result can be psychological disturbance, because people become habituated to their disturbed thoughts. Ellis observed that irrational thinking is often revealed in the language that people use, in particular the use of words such as 'should', 'ought' and 'must'.

Examples of irrational thinking that Ellis claimed could lead to psychological problems:

- "I ought to be good for my parents."

- "David should be nice to me."

- "I must do well in all my A levels."

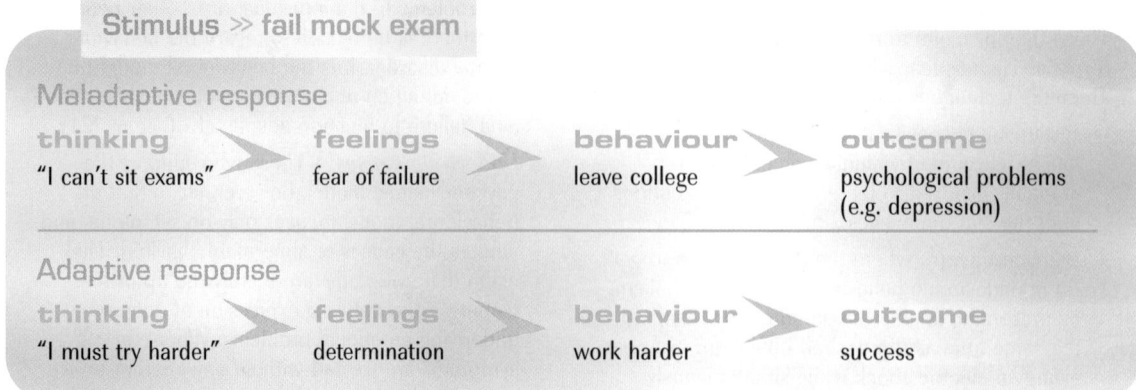

Stimulus >> fail mock exam

Maladaptive response

thinking	feelings	behaviour	outcome
"I can't sit exams"	fear of failure	leave college	psychological problems (e.g. depression)

Adaptive response

thinking	feelings	behaviour	outcome
"I must try harder"	determination	work harder	success

Figure 4.3 >> *Rationale behind cognitive theory*

Ellis also claimed that some people tend to exaggerate or 'catastrophize' events. For example: "I must be an awful person because Mary ignored me when I spoke to her this morning." They tend to fail to consider rational alternatives, for example that Mary was perhaps engrossed in thought, or was feeling ill, or may be a moody type of person.

Beck, who also believed that negative thoughts underlie mental disorder, was particularly interested in finding out why people become depressed. He found that depressed people tend to draw illogical conclusions when they evaluate themselves. Such negative thoughts lead to negative feelings, which, in turn, can result in depression. Beck identified three forms of negative thinking that he called the cognitive triad and that he thought were typical of those suffering from depression (see Fig. 4.4).

Treatment and the cognitive model

▪ Cognitive therapy is aimed at encouraging people to examine the beliefs and expectations underlying their unhappiness and to replace irrational, negative thoughts with a more positive, adaptive pattern of thinking. Therapists and clients work together to set new goals for the clients in order that more realistic and rational beliefs are incorporated into their ways of thinking.

Negative views about the future
(e.g. "I'll never be any good at anything")

Negative views about the world
(e.g. "Everyone is against me")

Negative views about oneself
(e.g. "I'm worthless and inadequate")

Figure 4.4 >>
The cognitive triad that leads to depression (Beck 1963)

ACTIVITY

The cognitive triad

Read the following case study, which is taken from Comer (2000), and try to identify the features of the cognitive triad:

1 the negative views that this woman expresses about herself

2 the negative views that she expresses about the world

3 the negative views she expresses about the future.

"I can't bear it. I can't stand the humiliating fact that I'm the only woman in the world who can't take care of her family, take her place as a real wife and mother, and be respected in her community. When I speak to my young son, Billy, I know I can't let him down but I feel so ill equipped to take care of him; that's what frightens me. I don't know what to do or where to turn; the whole thing is too overwhelming … I must be a laughing stock. It's more than I can do to go out and meet people and have the fact pointed up to me so clearly."

- Ellis developed Rational-Emotive Behaviour Therapy (REBT) based on his theoretical model of how psychological problems emerge. He claimed that REBT helps people to 'cure' themselves in an elegant way because they become less disturbed and less anxious, and they maintain this over a long period, or even permanently. The ultimate aim is that REBT should be incorporated into a person's way of life, in order to overcome procrastination and eradicate self-defeating thoughts.

- Beck's cognitive therapy is used mainly with people with depression. It is aimed at training clients to monitor situations where they make negative assumptions, and to encourage them to challenge these distorted thoughts and to take part in activities that will help them to see that such assumptions are unfounded.

- Cognitive therapies are becoming more and more popular and diverse in their applications. For example, they are increasingly being applied in stress management, as well as with marital and family problems, and in educational settings. They are also being applied to eating disorders, which will be considered later on in this unit.

Evaluation of the cognitive model

- The cognitive approach offers a 'model for living' which promotes psychological wellbeing and avoids the stigma of 'mental illness'.

- Research has shown that many people suffering from mental disorders do exhibit thought patterns associated with maladaptive functioning. For example, Gustafson (1992) found that maladaptive thinking processes were displayed by many people with psychological disorders such as anxiety, depression and sexual disorders.

- A criticism of the model is that it does not attempt to examine the origins of irrational thinking, nor does the treatment address these origins. Beck (1991) has pointed out that, although cognitive processes are involved in many psychological disorders, they may well be a consequence rather than a cause of their problems.

- The cognitive model has also been criticized because it suggests that everyone should be self-sufficient. Indeed, Ellis himself had little sympathy with those suffering from depression, regarding it as an 'indulgence' of self-defeating thoughts. A belief in self-sufficiency lays the blame for psychological problems firmly with the individual, rather than with the social environment. Consequently, attention may be drawn away from the need to improve social conditions that have a significant effect on the quality of life.

- The cognitive model also ignores the possibility that some so-called irrational thoughts might actually be true and therefore rational.

✓ CHECK YOUR UNDERSTANDING

Check your understanding of models of abnormality by answering these questions. Try to do this from memory at first. You can check your answers by looking back through Topic 2.

1 What is an alternative name for the medical model?

2 What are the four possible causal factors according to the medical model?

3 What are the three main categories of treatment suggested by the medical model?

4 Give one strength and one weakness of the medical model of abnormality.

5 Give a brief description of the process of repression.

6 Explain what is meant by the term 'defence mechanisms'.

7 Give a brief description of psychodynamic therapy.

8 What is meant by (a) classical conditioning (b) operant conditioning?

9 Give one strength and one weakness of the behavioural model of abnormality.

10 Outline the basic assumptions of the cognitive model of abnormality.

biological and psychological models of abnormality

We have just finished a fairly extensive coverage of four different models of abnormality. You will now have a good understanding of where each of these models stands on the causes and treatments of abnormal behaviour. However, as the title of this panel suggests, it is always wise to keep a careful eye on the examination. Let's review what the specification dictates for this subsection.

<< Assumptions made by biological (medical) and psychological (including psychodynamic, behavioural and cognitive) models of abnormality in terms of their views on the causes and treatment of abnormality. >>

Now let's look at some possible examination questions for this area (note, this is not meant to be an exhaustive list):

1 Outline the biological (psychodynamic, behavioural, cognitive…) model with respect to the causes of abnormality.

(6 marks)

2 Outline the biological (psychodynamic, behavioural, cognitive…) model with respect to the treatment of abnormality.

(6 marks)

3 Give two criticisms of the biological (psychodynamic, behavioural, cognitive…) model of abnormality.   (3 + 3 marks)

4 Outline and evaluate the biological (psychodynamic, behavioural, cognitive…) model of abnormality.   (18 marks)

What does this tell us? Although you may know a great deal about a particular model, in an examination you will only ever get the chance to offer a précis of that model. Can you, for example, describe Freud's psychodynamic theory (as it applies to an understanding of the causes of abnormality) in just 100 or so words? A well-prepared student thinks ahead and can fit what they know to what is required in the exam. Look again at the questions and think what is actually required in response to each.

1 requires a précis (approximately 100 to 120 words) of one of these four models concerning the **causes** of abnormality (you will, of course, need to be able to do this for all four models)

2 requires a précis (approximately 100 to 120 words) of one of these four models concerning the **treatment** of abnormality

3 requires a short description of **two** criticisms (approximately 50 to 60 words each) of one of these four models – remember these can be positive as well as negative

4 requires a précis (approximately 100 to 120 words) of one of these four models concerning the causes and/or treatment of abnormality **together with** a longer (200 to 250 words) evaluation of that model.

Performing well in an examination is only partly to do with having a good understanding of the material. It is also important to have good editorial skills, knowing what to leave out as much as what to put in. Practising these skills will pay off when you have to do it for real.

REVISION SUMMARY

Having covered this topic, you should be able to:

✓ define what is meant by the following models of abnormality:

- the medical (biological) model
- the psychodynamic model
- the behavioural model
- the cognitive model

✓ explain the assumptions of these models in terms of causes of abnormality

✓ explain the assumptions of these models in terms of the treatment of abnormality.

GETTING YOU THINKING...

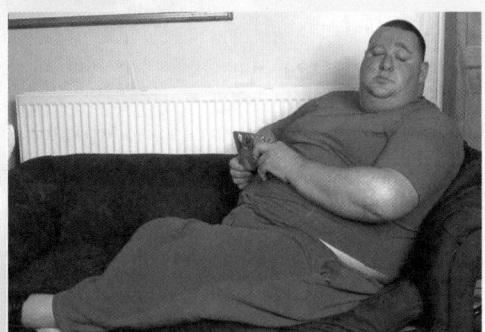

Tuesday 3 January

9st 4 (terrifying slide into obesity - why? why?), alcohol units 6 (excellent), cigarettes 23 (v.g.), calories 2472.

9 a.m. Ugh. Cannot face thought of going back to work. Only thing that makes it tolerable is thought of seeing Daniel again, but even that is inadvisable since am fat, have spot on chin, and desire only to sit on cushion eating chocolate...

Extract and photo from Bridget Jones's Diary

Look carefully at the images portrayed above.

1 What do they tell us about our attitudes to eating and body image in the Western world at the beginning of the 21st century?

2 Why do you think that the incidence of eating disorders is rising among young women and also among young men?

KEY TERMS

Eating disorder: a condition where there is serious disruption of healthy eating habits or appetite.

Anorexia nervosa: an eating disorder characterized by the pursuit of extreme thinness and by an extreme loss of weight.

Bulimia nervosa: an eating disorder characterized by secret binge eating followed by vomiting, misuse of laxatives, diuretics, excessive exercise, etc., in order to lose weight.

ANOREXIA NERVOSA

This topic looks at two subtypes of eating disorder – anorexia nervosa and bulimia nervosa. You will consider a number of explanations for the cause of eating disorders. Each explanation has its origins in one of the models of abnormality already outlined in this unit.

What is anorexia?

The term anorexia nervosa means literally a nervous loss of appetite. However, this is slightly misleading because people with anorexia usually have normal appetites and may often be very hungry, but will nevertheless behave as if they have lost their appetite – see the panel below for the characteristics of anorexia nervosa. Ninety per cent of cases of anorexia occur in females, usually between the ages of 13 and 18, and it is rarely diagnosed before puberty. The American Psychiatric Association (1994) states that anorexia occurs in 0.5 to 1.0 per cent of females in late adolescence and early adulthood. In the UK, surveys indicate that around 1 per cent of schoolgirls and female university students suffer from anorexia (Gelder *et al.* 1998). Although still low by comparison, cases of eating disorders in males are becoming more frequent. Currently in the UK, figures for men are between 5 and 10 per cent of those diagnosed with anorexia nervosa.

The course and outcome of anorexia are variable:

- Around 20 per cent of anorexics have one single episode with full recovery.
- Around 60 per cent follow an episodic pattern of weight gain and relapse over a number of years.
- The remaining 20 per cent continue to be severely affected and, in many cases, hospitalization is required to restore weight and fluid balance.

Studies with weight-recovered anorexics have found significantly reduced grey matter in the brain, which affects cognitive functioning. This brain damage is irreversible. For some people with anorexia, it is a chronic unremitting course until death. The mortality rate of those admitted to hospital is over 10 per cent, with deaths occurring from starvation, suicide or organ malfunction. See the box on p. 141 for a case study of a girl with anorexia nervosa.

Clinical characteristics of anorexia nervosa

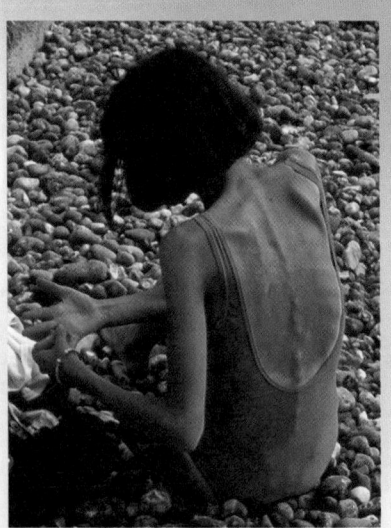

- *Refusal to maintain expected body weight* – Body weight is below 85 per cent of normal for one's height and age. Even though the person is underweight, there is an intense fear of gaining weight or becoming fat. Food intake is restricted to around 600 to 800 calories or less per day, with an avoidance of any food regarded as fattening.

- *Cessation of menstruation* – This is an early sign in females and, in about 40 per cent of cases, precedes obvious weight loss.

- *Ritualistic behaviour* – Food is often cut up into small pieces and eaten in a ritualistic way.

- *Preoccupation with food* – Anorexics like reading cookery books and preparing food for others, and often work in environments involved with food.

- *Body perception* – People with anorexia have a distorted body image and tend to believe themselves to be overweight or deny that they are seriously underweight.

- *Mood disturbance* – People with anorexia often show signs of depression, anxiety, mood swings and irritability.

- *Denial* – People with anorexia often deny the seriousness of their abnormally low weight.

- *Physical effects of starvation* – Apart from the huge weight loss which is the central feature of anorexia, there are other consequences of starvation, including dry skin, brittle nails, fine hair growth over the body, but thinning hair on the scalp.

BULIMIA NERVOSA

Bulimia nervosa was named as a condition distinct from anorexia nervosa only in 1979. Its clinical characteristics are outlined in the panel below. It is diagnosed in around 1 to 2 per cent of women aged between 16 and 40 (Gelder *et al.* 1998). Ninety per cent of cases are female, with bulimia being very uncommon in men.

Bulimia frequently follows on from months or years of anorexia. It differs from anorexia, however, in a number of ways:

- Bulimia is more common in the UK than anorexia.
- Bulimia tends to occur in older people (most sufferers are in their 20s) compared with anorexia.
- There is some evidence that people with bulimia are more likely than anorexia sufferers to engage in self-destructive or antisocial behaviours, such as drug/alcohol abuse, deliberate self-harm or shoplifting.
- Nearly all those with bulimia nervosa are within 10 per cent of their normal body weight.
- People with bulimia nervosa are not likely to die from starvation. However, their continual purging has long-term effects on their physical health.

Clinical characteristics of bulimia nervosa

- *Normal or above normal weight*
- *Binge eating* – There are recurrent episodes of uncontrollable overeating. These is usually precipitated by stress and accompanied by a loss of control.
- *Compensatory behaviour* – Binge eating is accompanied by feelings of guilt and disgust, followed by an extreme need to control body weight; in order to compensate for overeating, the person then engages in purging. This involves behaviours such as self-induced vomiting, misuse of laxatives, diuretics, enemas, medications, excessive exercise or fasting.
- *Physical effects of purging* – an increased risk of urinary infections and kidney disease and a tendency to develop epileptic fits. Repeated vomiting can cause the erosion of enamel on the teeth.
- *Body perception* – Unlike those with anorexia, the bulimic person is usually within the normal weight range. However, as with anorexia, this is accompanied by a disturbance in self-perception of body weight, size or shape.
- *Mood disturbance* – Depression is common and people sometimes feel suicidal after bingeing.
- *Awareness* – Denial is unusual in people with bulimia nervosa; they usually recognize that they need help.

What causes eating disorders

Consider the following statement:

<< Psychological processes cause eating disorders.>>

Discuss this statement with a friend. Note down any ideas that you have that support this statement and also any arguments against such a statement. On balance do you think that this statement is true?

We shall return to reconsider this statement later in the unit, once you have looked at the available evidence.

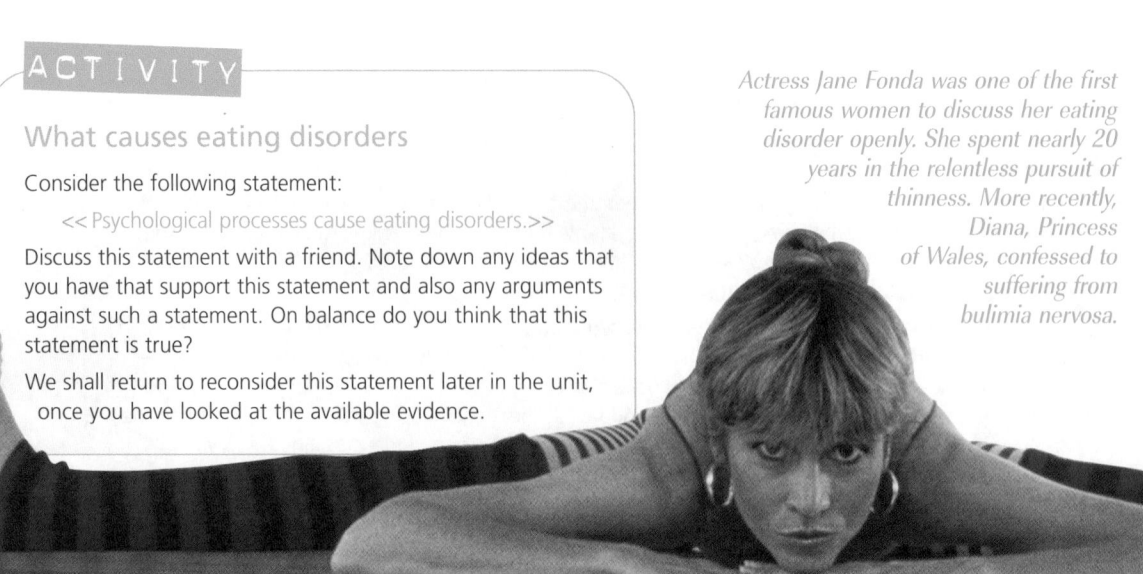

Actress Jane Fonda was one of the first famous women to discuss her eating disorder openly. She spent nearly 20 years in the relentless pursuit of thinness. More recently, Diana, Princess of Wales, confessed to suffering from bulimia nervosa.

Bulimia nervosa – a case study

Extracts from an account given by a married woman who suffers from bulimia nervosa. Her husband has left home for work and she is on her own:

<< I float to the refrigerator knowing exactly what is there. I begin with last night's brownies. I always begin with the sweets. At first I try to make it look like nothing is missing but my appetite is huge …
I know there is half a bag of cookies in the bathroom, thrown out the night before and I polish them off immediately. I take some milk so that my vomiting will be smoother. I get out six pieces of bread and toast one side, turn them over and load with butter … I take all six pieces on a plate to the television and go back for a bowl of cereal and a banana to have along with them. Before the last toast is finished, I am preparing the next batch of six more pieces. Maybe another brownie or five and a couple of bowlfuls of ice cream, yogurt or cottage cheese. My stomach is stretched into a huge ball below my ribcage. I know I'll have to go into the bathroom soon, but I want to postpone it. I am in never-never land. I am waiting, feeling the pressure, pacing the floor in and out of the rooms. Time is passing. It is getting to be time.

I finally make the turn into the bathroom. I brace my feet, pull my hair back and stick my finger down my throat, stroking twice and get a huge pile of food. Three times, four and another pile of food. I can see everything coming back. I am glad to see those brownies because they are SO fattening. The rhythm of the emptying is broken and my head is beginning to hurt. I stand up feeling dizzy, empty and weak. The whole episode has taken about an hour. >>

Source: Adapted from Comer (2000)

BIOLOGICAL EXPLANATIONS OF EATING DISORDERS

Biological explanations of eating disorders fall into two categories:

- genetic inheritance
- biochemical dysfunction of neurotransmitters in the brain.

A biochemical dysfunction or imbalance may have been genetically inherited or may be due to other causes.

Genetic explanation for eating disorders

As yet, genetic science has been unable to identify genes for specific behaviours, such as those associated with eating disorders. Research is based, therefore, on examining whether a particular disorder runs in families. The American Psychiatric Association (1994) reports that there is an increased risk of eating disorders among first-degree biological relatives of those diagnosed (parents, children and siblings), with a number of studies showing a much higher prevalence rate than in the general population. However, since relatives usually share the same environment, this does not necessarily support a genetic cause, as the behaviour may have been learned from other family members.

Twin studies provide more reliable evidence. The nature of this research is to compare monozygotic (MZ) twins with dizygotic (DZ) twins. MZ twins have identical genes, whereas DZ twins are no more alike genetically than any other siblings. Therefore, environmental factors could be largely eliminated if a significantly higher concordance rate were found among MZ twins compared with DZ twins. Concordance means that both twins have the same disorder.

Both Holland *et al.* (1984) and Kendler *et al.* (1991) claim to have found evidence in support of a genetic basis for anorexia and bulimia nervosa respectively (see the following two key studies).

KEY STUDY >> ANOREXIA NERVOSA

a study of 34 pairs of twins and one set of triplets by Holland *et al.* (1984)

Aim >>

To investigate whether there is a genetic basis for anorexia by studying identical (MZ) and non-identical (DZ) twins where at least one twin in each pair suffered from anorexia.

Procedures >>

- Participants were: 30 female twin pairs (16 MZ and 14 DZ pairs), four male twin pairs, and one set of male triplets.
- The twins and triplets were selected because one of the twins (and one of the triplets) had been diagnosed as suffering from anorexia nervosa.
- Data were collected on the other twin and triplets to check for concordance.

Findings >>

- High concordance rates were found for monozygotic female twins – 55 per cent compared to 7 per cent for dizygotic female pairs.
- Five of the non-anorexic female co-twins had either other psychiatric illnesses or minor eating disorders.
- None of the male co-twins (or triplets) had anorexia (i.e. they were discordant).
- The anorexic male twins tended to have been disadvantaged at birth and to be the less dominant of the pairs.

Conclusions >>

- Results support the view that there is some genetic basis for anorexia among females, since identical twins (who share the same genes) had 55 per cent concordance, while DZ (fraternal) twins (who share only half of their genes) showed only 7 per cent concordance.
- No conclusions can be drawn from the data from the male twins owing to small numbers.

Criticisms >>

- The higher concordance rates among identical twins may be caused by the similar ways in which they were treated by family and friends rather than by their genetic similarity.
- Holland and colleagues acknowledge that if genes do contribute to anorexia, their role is small.
- The sample size is very small and so is probably unrepresentative; other studies have not supported a genetic basis.

AO2 check

For example, Wade *et al.* (1998) studied both genetic and environmental risk factors in 325 female twins. They found a significant environmental influence in shaping women's attitudes towards weight, shape, eating and food, but little evidence of a genetic component.

a genetic epidemiology study of bulimia nervosa by Kendler *et al.* (1991)

Aim >>

To establish the prevalence (number of cases) of bulimia and to see whether there were genetic risk factors.

Procedures >>

- 2,163 female twins were given personal, structured, psychiatric interviews.
- The twins were assessed for psychiatric disorders.
- The risk factors for bulimia nervosa were recorded.

Findings >>

- The prevalence of bulimia nervosa was 2.8 per cent of those interviewed.
- Risk factors for bulimia included: being born after 1960; poor parental care; dieting and fluctuating weight; slim ideal body image; low self-esteem; feeling a lack of control over one's life.
- In identical (MZ) twins, concordance was 23 per cent.
- In non-identical (DZ) twins, concordance was 8.7 per cent.

Conclusions >>

- There are genetic risk factors involved in bulimia nervosa.
- There are also other important risk factors, for example relating to age and childhood experiences.

Criticisms >>

- Compared with many twin studies, this investigation involved quite a large number of participants.
- The higher concordance rates among identical twins may be caused by the similar ways in which they were treated by family and friends, rather than by their genetic similarity.
- People may not inherit a risk for bulimia (or anorexia), but rather a risk of developing an obsessional personality which makes them susceptible to eating disorders under certain circumstances.

There is clearly a significantly higher concordance in MZ twins compared with DZ twins in these studies, but, even with the Holland study reporting 55 per cent concordance, this still leaves 45 per cent of the MZ twins in their study who were discordant (that is, one twin had the disorder, but the other twin did not).

Hsu (1990) has suggested, on the other hand, that the genetic element may relate to personality traits such as emotional instability, which make the person more susceptible to stressful life events. These could manifest in an eating disorder or, alternatively, in some other mental disorder. In many cases of anorexia and bulimia, there is a family history of mood or personality disorders.

Biochemical explanations for eating disorders

- One view amongst the medical profession is that eating disorders may be associated with a biochemical imbalance. Research in the biological field has focused on the region of the brain known as the hypothalamus. Animals have been found to stop eating – and even to starve themselves to death – when the hypothalamus is damaged

According to Keesey and Corbett (1983) the lateral hypothalamus (LH) and the ventromedial *hypothalamus* (VMH) work alongside each other to provide a 'weight thermostat'. When activated, the LH produces hunger and the VMH depresses hunger. If weight falls below the set point on the 'thermostat', the LH is activated; if weight rises above the set point, the VMH is activated. Once either the LH or the VMH is activated, the hypothalamus will send messages to areas of the brain responsible for thinking and behaviours that will satisfy whichever is activated (LH or VMH). A malfunction in this part of the hypothalamus offers a possible explanation for eating disorders, although there is as yet no conclusive evidence to support this.

- Amenorrhoea (loss of menstrual cycle) can occur *before* weight loss, which suggests a primary disorder of low endocrine levels, again associated with a hypothalamus dysfunction. Also, the endocrine levels of anorexics of around 19 years old are similar to those of a healthy 9-year-old. However, postmortems have not revealed damage to the hypothalamus, and eating disorders do not appear to be accounted for by any known physical disease.

- More recent research has focused on certain hormonal chemicals, including norepinephrine, dopamine and, most especially, low levels of serotonin, which has been found to be associated with binge eating. The most effective drug treatment for bulimia is serotonin-active antidepressant medication which decreases binge eating. In the light of such findings, Jimerson *et al.* (1997) conducted clinical tests comparing serotonin function in patients with bulimia and in healthy controls. They found considerable differences and concluded that impaired serotonergic responsiveness may contribute to the onset, persistence or recurrence of abnormal eating patterns in people with bulimia nervosa. The problem with biochemical research is that it is difficult to differentiate between the cause and the effect, since the behavioural symptoms of anorexia and bulimia have a direct, and significant, adverse effect on the person's physiology, which, in turn, may affect their biochemistry. In simple terms, starvation may eventually cause an imbalance in biochemical functioning.

Evaluation of biological explanations

- Twin studies have provided some support for a genetic basis for eating disorders. However, most of the studies have used small samples, and it is difficult to disentangle the effects of a shared environment from a shared genetic make-up.

- Although many studies have demonstrated biochemical changes in individuals with eating disorders, it is not always easy to tell whether these changes are the cause or the consequence of the disorder.

PSYCHOLOGICAL MODELS OF EATING DISORDERS

Behavioural explanations

Advertising in teenage magazines and on television promotes the message that 'slim is beautiful'. It is not surprising, therefore, that so many people turn to diets with such frequency. This has led to the layperson's view of anorexia as 'slimming that got out of hand'.

Is it accurate to say that all teenage magazines promote the message 'slim is beautiful'?

Classical and operant conditioning

Classical conditioning incorporates the layperson's view, suggesting that slimming becomes a *habit*, just like any other habit, through stimulus-response mechanisms. The person first goes on a diet and after a while receives admiration from others, either for their endeavour or their new, slimmer appearance. In other words, they learn to associate being slim with feeling good about themselves. Operant conditioning comes into play as admiration from others further reinforces the dieting behaviour. Refusing to eat may also provide an additional reward in the form of attention gained from parents, and starving oneself can even be rewarding as an effective way of punishing parents.

Cross-cultural studies

Cross-cultural studies appear to support the behavioural explanation. It has been noted that anorexia and bulimia are more prevalent in industrialized societies, mainly Europe, USA, Canada, Australia, Japan, New Zealand and South Africa. In these societies, there is an abundance of food and yet, at the same time, being attractive is associated with being slim.

The American Psychiatric Association (1994) states that immigrants from cultures where these disorders are rare have been found to develop anorexia just as frequently as those born in industrialized societies, once these ideals of attractiveness are assimilated. A study by Nasser (1986) compared 50 Egyptian women in London universities with 60 Egyptian women in Cairo universities. Twelve per cent of those in London developed an eating disorder. None of those in Cairo did so. However, another study of Asian schoolgirls living in Bradford, found that concerns about weight and body shape were more commonly found among those girls who used Asian languages and wore Asian dress. It has been suggested that the more traditional Asian girls might be experiencing greater internal conflict about their identity as they grew up within two sets of cultural values (Mumford *et al.* 1991).

There are still very few studies conducted in non-industrialized countries, so it is quite difficult to provide adequate comparisons. The idea that pressures to be slim in Western cultures play a part in eating disorders is supported in studies conducted on groups of people for whom slimness is essential, such as gymnasts and ballet dancers. For example, Garner *et al.* (1987) found that in a group of 11- to 14-year-old ballet students, 25 per cent developed anorexia over the two-year period of their study. Other studies, such as that by Pike and Rodin (1991), have identified family pressures on daughters to be thin, particularly from mothers who are perfectionist, overly concerned with external appearance and who continually diet themselves.

In evaluating behavioural explanations for eating disorders, the following points are important:

- Operant conditioning techniques have been helpful in promoting weight gain in some people with anorexia.
- This model does not address the underlying problems of depression and loss of control apparent in people with eating disorders.
- The model has been more useful in explaining how eating disorders are maintained rather than in providing a comprehensive explanation of how they originate.

Cognitive explanation

This model focuses on the irrational beliefs that some people hold that they cannot be valued unless they have an ideal physical appearance. People with eating disorders often have a distorted body image and perceive themselves to be unattractive because they think they are fat.

A consistent pattern of distorted thinking among people with anorexia was found by Bemis-Vitousek and Orimoto (1993). They noted their cognitive convictions, which were consistent with the cognitive model of abnormality – for example, "I must lose more weight since I am not yet thin." They also found irrational attitudes about control – for example, "I must continue to lose weight so I can continue to be in control of my body" – yet at the same time, they were clearly not in control because they were losing weight to a dangerous degree. Fairburn *et al.* (1999) conducted an interview study comparing 169 people with eating disorders, 102 people with other psychiatric disorders and 204 healthy controls. They identified 'perfectionism' and 'negative self-evaluation' as high-risk factors for both anorexia and bulimia. What is not clear in the cognitive model, however, is where irrational beliefs come from in the first place.

An evaluation of the cognitive explanation for eating disorders would focus on the following points:

- This model, unlike the behavioural explanation, takes account of the way people with eating disorders think about their bodies.
- The model has suggested therapies designed to help people with eating disorders develop more realistic ways of thinking about themselves.
- The cognitive model explains how eating disorders are maintained, but does not really explain why the distorted self-image first occurs.

Psychodynamic explanations

- *Repressed sexual impulses* – Freud maintained that eating is a substitute for sexual expression and therefore, in psychoanalytic terms, anorexia could be viewed as the person's way of repressing sexual impulses. Hilde Bruch (1979) has been particularly influential in applying psychodynamic theory to anorexia. She suggested that anorexia is associated with psychosexual immaturity in a number of ways. One suggestion is that women have fantasies of oral impregnation and confuse fatness with pregnancy. They unconsciously believe that eating will lead to pregnancy and therefore starve themselves.

Another suggestion is that eating becomes equated with taking on an adult sexual role and that women who cannot face this starve themselves in order either to remain children or to regress to childhood. Bruch suggested that this provides a mutual reward for both mothers and daughters. The mother may become over-anxious about her daughter and therefore curtail her independence and thus retain her 'child'. For the daughter, her behaviour has secured a way of continuing to be dependent upon her mother.

■ *Sexual abuse and gender socialization* – Eating disorders have been strongly related to early traumatic experiences, and psychotherapy studies indicate that a large proportion of patients report early experience of sexual abuse (see also a key study below by Wonderlich and colleagues).

ACTIVITY

Childhood sexual abuse and bulimia

Wonderlich *et al.* (1996) suggest that the psychological trauma associated with childhood sexual abuse is a risk factor for bulimia.
Do you think that childhood sexual abuse might place a person at risk of a later eating disorder? If so, why?

Compare your ideas with those given in the following text.

KEY STUDY >> CHILDHOOD ABUSE AND BULIMIA

a study by Wonderlich *et al.* (1996)

Aim >>

To see whether childhood sexual abuse is a significant factor for the development of bulimia in women.

Procedures >>

■ A representative national sample of 1099 women in the United States was interviewed about:
 – their sexual experiences during childhood
 – whether they had shown bulimic behaviour at any time during their lives.
■ Calculations were carried out to find out whether sexual abuse in childhood increased a woman's risk of developing bulimic behaviour (once age, ethnic group and parents' educational level had been controlled for).

Findings >>

■ Those women who had experienced childhood sexual abuse were significantly more likely to develop bulimia nervosa than those who did not report having been abused.

Conclusions >>

■ Childhood sexual abuse is associated with dissatisfaction about one's weight and body.
■ Consequently, childhood sexual abuse is a risk factor for bulimia nervosa.

Criticisms >>

■ The data for this study came from interviews with adults who were asked to recollect childhood experiences. Such data can be unreliable, as respondents are prone to errors of memory. If they suffer from an eating disorder, they may also try harder to recollect some cause from their past to explain their adult problems.
■ However, later research by Wonderlich *et al.* (2000) using data from abused and non-abused girls between the ages of 10 and 15 confirmed these findings from the adult women; abused girls were more dissatisfied with their weight and used more dieting and purging behaviour.

A study conducted in an eating disorder clinic by McLelland *et al.* (1991) reported that 30 per cent of clients had a history of childhood sexual abuse. The suggestion is that such experiences are repressed into the unconscious and express themselves in adolescence and adulthood through the symptoms of anorexia or bulimia. Sexual abuse in childhood can lead to a rejection by victims of their own bodies; in adolescence this rejection can turn to disgust and an unconscious desire to destroy their bodies.

An interesting suggestion is that early traumatic experiences are repressed and then become expressed in later life in ways associated with gender socialization. Females are taught to be subservient and self-critical and so early trauma is turned inwards upon the self in the form of self-harm. Males, on the other hand, are taught to be dominant and outwardly expressive. Thus their early trauma is more likely to be directed outward in hostility towards others. This could explain why eating disorders are predominantly a female disorder and why most violent crimes are perpetrated by males. A study of anorexia and bulimia in males was conducted by Carlat *et al.* (1997) on 135 patients in Boston, USA from 1980 to 1994. They observed that 42 per cent of the bulimia group were either homosexual or bisexual, and 58 per cent of the anorexia group were identified as asexual. They concluded that sexual orientation was a major factor in male eating disorders.

Evaluation of the psychodynamic explanation:

- Although a number of studies have been carried out to investigate the psychodynamic explanations, it is difficult to obtain convincing empirical support.

- Not all people who have experienced childhood sexual abuse develop an eating disorder, and not all people with eating disorders report having been sexually abused as children.

Other psychological explanations

- *Individual identity* – Some psychologists suggest that eating disorders relate to family relationships, and in particular to an adolescent's struggle to gain a sense of individual identity. In some family relationships, the parents exert such a strong level of control that children grow up without a sense of their own identity and, consequently, with low self-esteem. In adolescence, this control is maintained through roles within the family, such as the mother cooking the meals and the daughter dutifully eating them. This may form the arena in which the daughter struggles for her identity by refusing to eat.

- *Pressures to succeed* – Anorexia is much more prevalent in middle-class families, particularly among those whose parents have a professional background. It is also more prevalent in those

who go on to higher education. Consequently, it is suggested that family pressure to 'succeed' may be too great for some young people and may lead to psychological problems, such as depression and anorexia.

- *Negative self-evaluation* – The study by Fairburn *et al.* (1999), mentioned previously, also supports this explanation. They found that negative self-evaluation was identified as a high-risk factor for bulimia nervosa, along with parents who had high expectations for their daughters and yet had low contact with them. The prospective study by Button and colleagues also identified low self-esteem as a risk factor for eating disorders (see key study opposite). Further support comes from Joiner *et al.* (1997) who conducted a ten-year study from 1982 to 1992 on 459 females diagnosed with bulimia, aged 18 to 22 years at the beginning of the study. What they found to be the most significant factors sustaining the disorder over the ten-year span were a drive for thinness, maturity fears, perfectionism and interpersonal distrust.

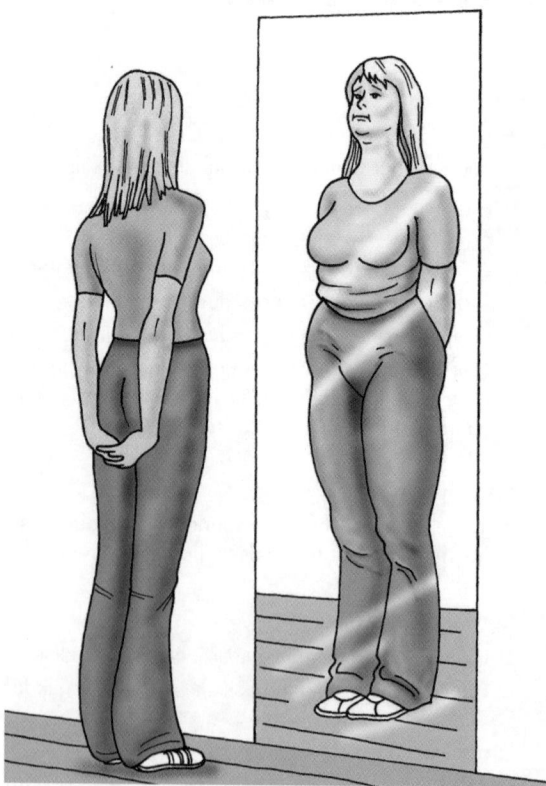

A distorted body image may contribute to the development of anorexia

- *Family conflict* – Family systems theory implicates family factors in a quite different way. Minuchin *et al.* (1978) suggest that the development of anorexia serves the function of preventing

a prospective study by Button *et al.* (1996)

Aim >>

To investigate the role of self-esteem as a cause of eating disorders (such as anorexia or bulimia nervosa).

Procedures >>

- Self-esteem was measured in 594 schoolgirls aged 11 to 12 years, using the Rosenberg Self-Esteem Scale.
- 400 girls were followed up at age 15 to 16. They completed a questionnaire about eating and other psychological problems.

Findings >>

- Those with low self-esteem at age 11 to 12 were more inclined to have low self-esteem at 15 to 16 years.
- Girls with low self-esteem at age 11 to 12 were significantly more at risk of eating disorders than those with higher self-esteem.
- Girls with low self-esteem at age 11 to 12 were more likely to display other problems at age 15 to 16 relating to health, family and school.

Conclusions >>

- Low self-esteem at age 11 to 12 is a significant risk factor for girls developing eating disorders later on.
- This study lends support to the argument that psychological factors play a part in eating disorders.
- It may be worth trying to enhance self-esteem in childhood and adolescence to help prevent eating disorders.

Criticisms >>

- This study relied on questionnaire data that may be unreliable and the sample was incomplete as some head teachers declined to let their pupils participate. This resulted in a biased sample: 60 per cent of girls' families were in social classes 1 and 2.
- We cannot be sure that the self-esteem measured at age 11 to 12 predated the onset of eating disorders. Early processes in eating disorders might have already started.

disagreements within the family. For example, it may be the adolescent's way of preventing a marriage break-up by diverting attention onto themselves. In so doing, the hope is that joint concern for the child will bring the parents back together. Other researchers have found that parents sometimes became more anxious and depressed if their anorexic child started to recover and gain weight. This finding fits in with the idea that anorexia may be a way of defusing family conflict.

Family relationships are thought to be a central feature in eating disorders, so much so that family therapy (based largely on family systems theory) is currently the most significant form of intervention for eating disorders.

ACTIVITY

The causes of eating disorders revisited

Think back to the following statement which you considered near the beginning of this topic:

<< Psychological processes cause eating disorders. >>

Now that you have read about the biological and psychological explanations of eating disorders, you should read the Expert interview by Gill Harris on p. 150. Write a short essay to answer the question:

<< To what extent can eating disorders be explained by biological factors? >>

Eating *disorders*

Gill Harris is a Senior Lecturer In Psychology at the University of Birmingham, and a Consultant Clinical Psychologist at The Children's Hospital Birmingham. Her research interests are in feeding and eating disorders in children and adolescents. She also runs a clinical service at the Children's Hospital for children and adolescents with eating problems.

Q Can we explain eating disorders such as anorexia nervosa and bulimia nervosa purely from a biological perspective?

A We can't really say that eating disorders occur irrespective of cultural and psychological factors. Eating disorders are more prevalent in cultures where a slim body shape is seen as desirable, and where the media promotes images of thin bodies as the norm. Eating disorders are also more frequently observed in women rather than in men, where the drive for thinness is greater. Having said that, eating disorders are now being reported more frequently in homosexual men, perhaps in response to an increasing preoccupation with appearance in the male homosexual community.

The best explanation, especially for AN, is that there is a predisposition for the disorder, which is triggered by environment factors and cultural norms. The genetic predisposition shows itself in certain personality traits. Girls with AN tend to be obsessive-compulsive, high-achieving perfectionists. The need to achieve in a competitive society produces stress, the response to which is dietary restraint and the control of body shape to conform with desirable norms. Those with BN tend to be more impulsive, and show more self-harming behaviour, and this might lead to the binge–purge cycle when dietary restraint cannot be maintained.

Q But could the family environment act as the trigger?

A It has been argued that the drive to succeed comes from the family of those girls who develop AN, and it is the family environment and not a genetic predisposition that triggers dietary restraint as a response to stress. Family members have been implicated in the development of eating disorders since the disorders were first recorded (Gull 1874). However, much of this work has been carried out with families after the eating

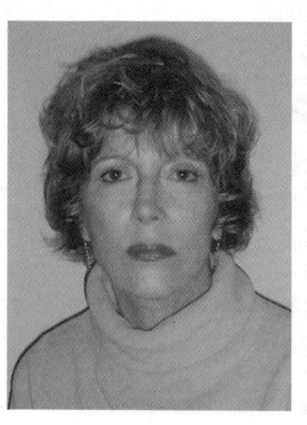

Gill Harris

disorder has developed, and the effect of caring for an adolescent who is trying to starve herself has not been taken into account. It has also been suggested that early negative experience affects core beliefs about self that are then resistant to change (Young 1994), and that it is these core beliefs that give rise to the personality profiles typically associated with the disorders.

Q Could EDs be a 'normal' reaction to dieting triggered by socio-cultural factors?

A EDs are most frequently seen in girls as they come into their pubertal growth spurt, so might it be that the disorders are just a normal biological response to dieting? Many people choose to diet or fast, for many reasons, and most of them do not develop eating disorders. For dancers and gymnasts (who have the highest incidence of EDs), there is emphasis on a slim body and low calorie intake, so do they react to stress by inhibiting signals of hunger?

There is no one pattern of eating in response to stress: some people eat less and some people eat more. This variation is possibly determined by sensitivity to stress hormones. But the differential response to stress may explain why some people can inhibit eating completely and go on to develop AN, and others to develop BN.

The normal response, if you do try to inhibit food intake, is for gut hormones to act to make you eat again, and to eat sufficient food to compensate for the calories that you have missed out. Binge eating is therefore an evolutionary determined response to periods of fasting. Those with AN are more able to inhibit signals as a response to stress and find that eating restraint improves their mood and lowers stress. Those with BN are not able to inhibit eating, and respond to this incomplete control with vomiting and purging, which in turn reduces stress.

This model does not explain, however, the extremes of binge eating seen in those with BN. It is therefore probably easier to explain AN rather than BN purely in terms of physiological factors.

✓ CHECK YOUR UNDERSTANDING

Check your understanding of eating disorders by answering these questions. Try to do this from memory at first. You can check your answers by looking back through Topic 3.

1 Identify three characteristics of anorexia nervosa.

2 What is meant by the term 'binge eating'?

3 Identify three characteristics of bulimia nervosa.

4 Give a brief description of the procedures and findings of the study by Holland *et al.* (1984) that investigated the genetic basis for anorexia.

5 Briefly outline the findings of research that has investigated biochemical factors in eating disorders.

6 Explain why cross-cultural studies lend support to the behavioural explanation of eating disorders.

7 Give one strength and one weakness of the cognitive explanation of eating disorders.

8 Give a brief explanation as to how anorexia nervosa can be linked to repressed sexual impulses.

9 What is meant by 'family systems theory'?

10 To what extent is it reasonable to claim that eating disorders are caused by psychological factors alone?

REVISION SUMMARY

Having covered this topic you should be able to:

✓ outline the clinical characteristics of 'anorexia nervosa' and 'bulimia nervosa'

✓ explain these eating disorders in terms of biological and psychological models of abnormality

✓ discuss research on which the various explanations have been based

✓ outline the aims, procedures, findings, conclusions and criticisms for one study each about a biological explanation of anorexia and of bulimia and one study each about a psychological explanation of anorexia and of bulimia.

Topic 1: Defining psychological abnormality

- There are various ways in which abnormality can be defined, including:

  - behaviour that occurs infrequently (i.e. **statistical infrequency** definition)
  - behaviour that deviates from accepted standards (i.e. **deviation from social norms** definition)
  - behaviour that that lacks the elements needed for optimal living (i.e. **deviation from ideal mental health** definition)
  - an inability to pursue normal activities and goals (i.e. **failure to function adequately** definition)

- These definitions offer a useful general guide for distinguishing forms of functioning that might be regarded as pathological. However, their use is limited because there are no universal definitions of 'normality' and 'abnormality'.

- All of these attempts at definitions, however, have limitations in terms of their relevance to people of **different cultures**.

Topic 2: Biological and psychological models of abnormality

- Biological (medical) and psychological (psychodynamic, behavioural and cognitive) models of abnormality are based on very different assumptions about the nature of human functioning, and the origins and causes of abnormality. Each model offers quite different **treatments** (or **therapeutic strategies**).

- The **biological (medical) model** claims that mental disorders should be viewed as disease or illness. This approach proposes four possible causes of mental illness: brain damage, infection, biochemical imbalance and genetic predisposition. Since mental problems are viewed as physical illnesses, it follows that they are best treated by physical means. These include: **drug treatments** (chemotherapy); **electro-convulsive therapy** (ECT) and **psychosurgery** (brain surgery).

- An advantage of the biological approach includes the increased knowledge gained from research into the possible biological factors underlying psychological disorders and the treatments that have resulted. However, disadvantages include side effects of and dependency upon drugs, as well as the stigma endured by those who have been medically diagnosed as abnormal.

- The **psychodynamic model** states that unconscious psychological forces cause abnormal behaviour. According to **Freud**, psychological disturbance occurs when the **ego** (the rational part of the psyche) fails to manage the conflict between the **id** (the insatiable set of instincts with which we are born) and the **superego** (the moral part of the psyche concerned with right and wrong). Such conflicts are most marked in early childhood when the ego is less developed. To balance the demands of the id and the superego, **defence mechanisms** (such as repression) are used, but these do not provide permanent solutions and may themselves create psychological problems. Treatments aim to uncover **unconscious psychological processes** in order to facilitate insight into the conflicts and anxieties causing the abnormal behaviour.

- The psychodynamic model has been influential but has also received much criticism. It is difficult to test scientifically and is accused of being deterministic. Critics also claim that treatments are often expensive, time-consuming and ineffective.

- The **behavioural model** views abnormal behaviours as maladaptive, learned responses, acquired through conditioning and social learning processes. If maladaptive behaviours are learned, then they can be replaced by other learned, adaptive behaviours. Main techniques include **systematic desensitization**, **aversion therapy** and the use of **token economies** to reward desired behaviour.

■ The behavioural model avoids labelling a person as abnormal; it focuses upon behaviour (which is seen as changeable) rather than the person. However, the model is accused of ignoring the possible underlying causes of abnormal behaviour. Other criticisms are that it is reductionist and its treatments have sometimes been imposed on people without their consent.

■ The **cognitive model** of abnormality assumes that emotional problems are caused by distortions in thinking processes, such as negative thoughts and irrational beliefs. According to **Ellis** we can become habituated to irrational thinking and then may tend to exaggerate the negative aspects of events. **Beck** identified the cognitive triad (three forms of negative thinking) that he claimed underlie depression: negative views about oneself, about the world and about the future. Cognitive therapy aims to help people examine their irrational thoughts and replace them with more **positive, adaptive ways of thinking**.

■ One criticism of the cognitive model is that it does not address the origins of irrational thought processes. The model has been accused of underestimating the role of social conditions in the development and maintenance of psychological disorders because it places responsibility for psychological abnormality firmly within the individual.

Topic 3: Critical issue – eating disorders

■ **Eating disorders**, such as **anorexia nervosa** and **bulimia nervosa**, have very serious consequences for physical health and so it is important to understand the causes of these disorders. Anorexia is characterised by the pursuit of extreme thinness and by an extreme loss of weight. Bulimia is characterised by secret binge eating followed by purging behaviours such as vomiting, misuse of laxatives and excessive exercise in order to lose weight.

■ Research into **biological explanations** has found no links with disease. Biochemical dysfunction is more likely to be a consequence of the disorder, rather than the cause. Genetic links have been investigated by looking at concordance rates among family members including twins. Support for a genetic basis is considered weak and difficult to prove, because members of a family tend to share the same environment.

■ **Behavioural explanations**: eating disorders originate when a person goes on a diet and is complemented (reinforced) for being slim. This results in the person associating thinness with feeling good about themselves. Operant conditioning has been helpful in promoting weight gain among some anorexia sufferers, but the approach fails to address the underlying problems of depression and loss of control.

■ **Cognitive explanations** point to the irrational beliefs that some people hold that they will not be valued unless they achieve some ideal body shape. However, the approach does not explain how these irrational beliefs come about in the first place.

■ **Psychodynamic explanations**: anorexia is viewed as a way of repressing sexual impulses or as a means by which women can remain children and so avoid adult responsibilities. Psychotherapy studies have also found that women who have experienced childhood sexual abuse are more likely to develop bulimia nervosa. However, data collected from recollections about childhood can be unreliable.

■ Other psychological explanations for eating disorders include low self-esteem, struggling for a sense of identity, pressure to succeed and family conflict.

Answering exam questions on Abnormality

For sample examination questions and answers on Abnormality, together with examiner comments on the answers, see pp. 257–9.

Unit 4 // Abnormality

5
UNIT

SOCIAL
Influence

PREVIEW

After you have read this unit, you should be able to:

>> explain why people yield to majority and minority influence, and discuss research in these areas

>> explain why people obey and how people might resist obedience

>> discuss research into obedience to authority and the issues of experimental and ecological validity associated with research in this area

>> discuss the ethical issues concerned with deception, informed consent and the protection of participants from psychological harm, particularly as these relate to research on social influence

>> discuss the ways in which psychologists try to deal with these ethical issues.

INTRODUCTION

Social influence is the process by which an individual's attitudes, beliefs or behaviours are modified by the presence or actions of others. Some forms of social influence, such as when a teacher insists that you hand in work on time, are obvious (though not always successful). Other types of social influence are more subtle, sometimes unintended and, on occasions, even unnoticed by those who are influenced.

In Topic 1, we will look at the topics of conformity (majority influence) and minority influence. Then, in Topic 2, we will explore the research studies of obedience, one of the most challenging and controversial topics in social psychology. Not only are the results of such studies unsettling, but the methods used by those who have researched this area (e.g. Stanley Milgram) have come in for much criticism. Consequently, in Topic 3, we will look at some of the ethical issues that have arisen in psychological investigations and particularly those that are evident in social influence research.

KEY TERMS

Social influence: the process by which a person's attitudes, beliefs or behaviours are modified by the presence or actions of others. There are two types of social influence that lead people to conform: normative social influence (based on our desire to be liked) and informational social influence (based on our desire to be right).

Conformity/majority influence: a form of social influence where people adopt the behaviours, attitudes and values of other members of a reference group.

Minority influence: a form of social influence where a persuasive minority exerts pressure to change the attitudes, beliefs or behaviours of the majority. Minorities are most influential when they appear consistent and principled.

Claire
Meldrum

GETTING YOU THINKING...

1 What do these photos tell us about conformity?

2 To what extent do you think that the people in the second photo are displaying anticonformity? To what extent are they actually conforming?

3 Do you think that the people in the second photo are more or less aware that they are conforming, compared with those in the top photo?

4 To what extent do *you* conform? What do you conform to?

CONFORMITY

Conformity is the process of yielding to majority influence and is defined by David Myers (1999) as "a change in behaviour or belief as a result of real or imagined group pressure". Zimbardo *et al.* (1995) defined it as a "tendency for people to adopt the behaviour, attitudes and values of other members of a reference group". You may find it easier to identify with Myers' definition because it focuses upon the kind of experience most of us have had at one time or another: the feeling that others are putting pressure on us to change our minds or behaviour. However, the Zimbardo definition proposes that when we are evaluating our status, we tend to go along with those people with

whom we compare ourselves (i.e. our reference groups). If you accept that the process of conformity can occur without your being aware of it, then you may prefer the wording of the Zimbardo definition.

Although most people think of themselves as autonomous individuals, they nevertheless tend to go along with (conform to) the social norms (rules and expectations) that their groups and societies have evolved. The social norms that indicate how we ought to behave may be explicit (such as a 'No Smoking' sign in a restaurant) or they may be implicit (such as the unspoken but well-understood norm in the UK of not standing too close to strangers).

The pressure to conform

1 Think of an occasion when you have felt under pressure to behave in a particular way because of group pressure. How did you behave? What was it about the situation that caused you to conform? In what kinds of situation do you feel under pressure to conform?

2 Was the group pressure to behave in a particular way *real* (i.e. those around you were actually telling you how you must behave) or was it *imagined* (i.e. you felt you ought to behave in a particular way in order to be seen to 'go along' with your friends, your family or a group of peers)?

3 How did it make you feel?

4 Are there situations in everyday life when it is perhaps desirable to conform, or is conforming behaviour inherently bad? What are the dangers, if any, of being overly conformist?

TYPES OF CONFORMITY

As long ago as 1958, Kelman identified three types of conformity (that is, three responses to social influence):

■ *Compliance* – publicly conforming to the behaviour or views of others but privately maintaining one's own views. For example, if you are with a group of friends who support a particular football team, you might not reveal that you support a different one, even if asked directly.

■ *Identification* – adopting the views or behaviour of a group both publicly and privately because you value membership of that group. However, the new attitudes and behaviours are often temporary and not maintained on leaving the group. For example, when young people move away from home to go to college, they may begin to question the lifestyles they had previously taken for granted. New students often enthusiastically adopt the dress and behaviour codes of their new student groups. However, on graduating and moving into employment, they often change the way they dress and behave again.

■ *Internalization* – a conversion, or true change of private views to match those of the group. What distinguishes this type of conformity from identification is that the new attitudes and behaviours have become part of your value system; they are not dependent on the presence of the group. For example, a person searching for some greater meaning to life may be influenced to convert to a religious faith if the members of that faith seem able to provide the answers being searched for. A true conversion will survive even if the person loses contact with those who influenced them originally.

Resisting majority influence

There are occasions, however, when people appear not to conform. There are at least two ways of explaining their behaviour:

■ *Independence* – being unresponsive to the norms of the group, such as a student who ignores the dress norms of her fellow students and dresses only to please herself. Note that sometimes this student might dress like her friends if their dress sense happened to coincide with hers. She is not reacting against their code; she is just unaffected by it and is, therefore, truly independent.

■ *Anticonformity* – consistently opposing the norms of the group. Anticonforming behaviour is quite common, such as deliberately choosing to dress or wear your hair in a way that is different from others. It may seem paradoxical, but anticonformity is, in fact, a type of conformity as it is determined by the norms of the group; if the group favours long hair, anticonformists will wear theirs cut short; if the group decides that short hair is cool, anticonformists will wear theirs long.

Singer and DJ, Boy George – an example of independence or anticonformity?

ACTIVITY

Types of conformity and non-conformity

Look back at the two photos in 'Getting you thinking...' on p. 155. For each one, decide whether it is an example of compliance, identification, internalization, independence or anticonformity.

What about the singer and DJ Boy George, shown opposite? Make a note of your reasons.

WHY DO PEOPLE CONFORM?

According to Deutsch and Gerard (1955), there are two types of social influence that lead people to conform:

- *Normative social influence* – based on our desire to be liked. We conform because we think that others will approve of and accept us. The conformity that results from this desire to be liked is often called compliance, that is, publicly going along with the majority but privately holding to one's own views (see p. 156)

- *Informational social influence* – based on our desire to be right. We look to others whom we believe to be correct, to give us information about how to behave, particularly in novel or ambiguous situations. Informational social influence may be particularly strong when we move from one group to another. For example, young people moving from school to university might redefine themselves as students (no longer pupils) and look to other students to learn what are acceptable ways of behaving (the norms) in this new situation. Informational social influence can sometimes lead to a genuine and long-lasting change of belief or attitude, called internalization (see p. 156)

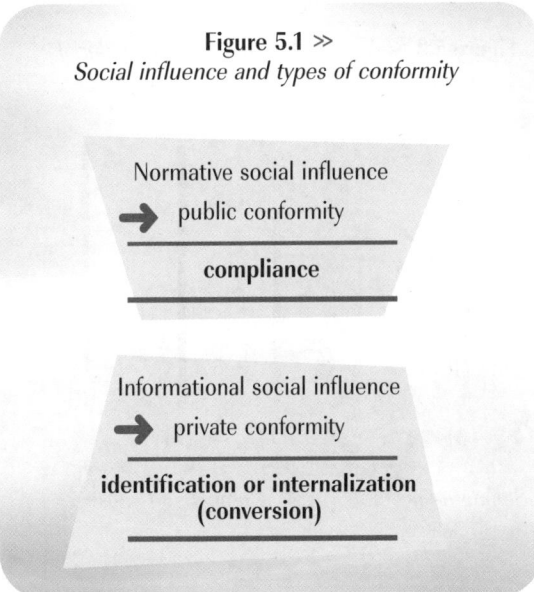

Figure 5.1 >>
Social influence and types of conformity

Normative social influence
→ public conformity

compliance

Informational social influence
→ private conformity

identification or internalization (conversion)

Deutsch and Gerard's explanation of conformity is called the dual process model because it offers two explanations as to why people yield to majority influence. It is sometimes criticized for implying that the two types of social influence are separate and independent. Instead, Insko *et al.* (1983) claimed that normative and informational influence often work together to affect levels of conformity.

ACTIVITY

Types and effectiveness of social influence attempts

1 Prepare two lists. In List A, write down at least two examples of situations where others have tried to influence your behaviour (e.g. parents trying to persuade you to stay in and work instead of going out with friends). For each example, note down the type of influence that was used (e.g. how your parent tried to persuade you). Which attempts were more successful and which ones were less successful or unsuccessful?

2 In List B, write down at least two examples of situations where those being influenced are unaware of what is happening. Under what circumstances do you feel that people might be influenced without realizing it?

3 Why do you think that some attempts at social influence succeed and others fail? Consider a range of factors, including: (a) the person(s) doing the influencing (b) the person who is being influenced (c) the circumstances that exist at the time.

4 When are people best able to resist attempts to influence their behaviour?

RESEARCH INTO CONFORMITY

Many psychologists have attempted to answer the question "Why do people conform?" by conducting research studies aimed at teasing out the different factors that cause people to yield to majority social influence.

Asch's original study (1951)

Asch (1951) wondered what would happen if participants were exposed to normative social influence in a group situation where there could be no doubt about the correct answer to a question? How many participants would conform to the group, deny the evidence of their own eyes and give the wrong answer when it was their turn?

Complete the activity on the right now.

Figure 5.2 >> *A sample of the stimulus material used in Asch's experiments on conformity*

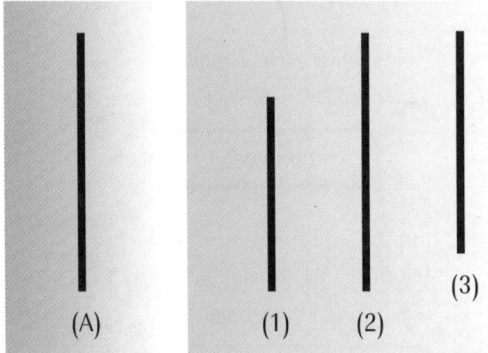

Standard line   *Comparison lines*

ACTIVITY

Identifying weaknesses of Asch's study of conformity

1 Read the key study, *Majority influence*, up to and including the Conclusions. Do not read the Criticisms. Note down any criticisms that you can identify in relation to:

  – the sample he studied

  – the time and place of the study.

2 Compare your thoughts with the criticisms at the end of the key study. When reading any research study, it is important to get into the habit of trying to identify any weaknesses. This will help you to develop your evaluation skills (referred to as AO2 skills – see p. 247).

The set-up in Asch's studies, in which a minority of one (answering last but one) faces pressure to conform to an otherwise unanimous majority

In addition to the specific criticisms made of Asch's study, he is also sometimes criticized for implying that conforming behaviour is 'bad' and that resisting (not yielding) to majority influence is somehow always good. Clearly, there are dangers involved if people are too conformist. Nevertheless, without widespread conformity, society could not function effectively. Conformity to prosocial norms, such as helping others in distress, is obviously highly desirable.

Extensions to Asch's research

In order to find out exactly which features of a situation made it more likely that someone would conform,

Asch varied some of the situational factors in his original study. He introduced the following changes and observed the effects:

■ *A non-unanimous majority* – Asch found that levels of conformity dropped dramatically (to only 5 per cent) when just one other participant dissented from the majority and supported the naive participant. A majority of three with no other dissenters was more effective in producing conformity than a majority of eight with one other dissenter.

■ *The size of the majority* – When the majority consisted of only two people, conformity responses in naive participants dropped to 12.8 per cent of their

study of conformity by Asch (1951)

Aim >>

To see if participants would yield (conform) to majority social influence and give incorrect answers in a situation where the correct answers were always obvious.

Procedures >>

- Seven male, student participants looked at two cards: the test card showed one vertical line; the other card showed three vertical lines of different length.
- The participants' task was to call out, in turn, which of the three lines was the same length as the test line. The correct answer was always obvious (see Fig. 5.2).
- All participants, except one, were accomplices of the experimenter. The genuine participant called out his answer last but one.
- Accomplices gave unanimous wrong answers on 12 of the 18 trials. These 12 trials were called the critical trials.
- In total, Asch used 50 male college students as naive, genuine participants in this first study.

Findings >>

- Participants conformed to the unanimous incorrect answer on 32 per cent of the critical trials. This might not strike you as a very high figure but remember that the correct answer was always obvious.
- 74 per cent of participants conformed at least once.
- 26 per cent of participants never conformed. Some of these 'independent' participants were confident in their judgements. More often, however, they experienced tension and doubt but managed to resist the pressure exerted by the unanimous majority.
- During post-experimental interviews, some conforming participants claimed to have actually *seen* the line identified by the majority as the correct answer. Others yielded because they could not bear to be in a minority of one and risk being ridiculed or excluded by the group. Most participants who had conformed, however, experienced a distortion of judgement: they thought that their perception of the lines must be inaccurate and for that reason they yielded to the majority view.

Conclusions >>

- Even in unambiguous situations, there may be strong group pressure to conform, especially if the group is a unanimous majority.
- However, after interviewing his participants, Asch concluded that people go along with the views of others for different reasons. Some people experience normative social influence and feel compelled to accept the mistaken majority's norms or standards of behaviour to avoid being rejected. Others experience informational pressures and doubt their own judgements – "Surely they can't all be wrong!"

Criticisms >>

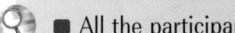

- All the participants were male college students and so a very limited sample.
- The time and place when the research was carried out might have affected the findings. In the 1950s the USA was very conservative, involved in an anticommunist witchhunt against anyone who was thought to hold left-wing views (this became known as 'McCarthyism', named after the senator who spearheaded the witchhunt) and its educational institutions were more hierarchical than they are today.

A02 check

Since all the participants were male and college students, it might not be valid to generalize the findings to a wider population. The way to check this is to rerun the study using different types of participants. Do you think that male college students are typical, or more or less conformist than the general population?

total judgements. Optimum conformity effects (32 per cent of responses) were found with a majority of three. Increasing the size of the majority beyond three did not increase the levels of conformity found. Some psychologists have suggested that people may suspect collusion if the majority rises beyond three or four. When only one confederate (accomplice) was used, no conformity effects were found.

■ *Losing a partner* – The naive participant started with a 'partner' who responded correctly to begin with but who 'deserted' to the majority in the middle of the procedure. This resulted in conformity levels of 28.5 per cent on critical judgements.

■ *Gaining a partner* – When a participant who had started the procedure as a minority of one received a 'partner' part way through, this reduced conformity responses to 8.7 per cent.

■ *The nature of the task* – The levels of conformity increased (see also Crutchfield's results in the next section) as tasks were made more difficult.

■ *Mode of response* – When Asch asked his participants to write their answers rather than call them out loud, conformity levels dropped sharply. This illustrates the difference between public compliance (overtly adhering to social norms) and private acceptance (actually thinking as others do).

Table 5.1 >> Factors affecting conformity levels

Factors increasing conformity levels	Factors decreasing conformity levels
>> Unanimous majority	>> Non-unanimous majority
>> Difficult task	>> Majority of only two people
>> Being deserted by a partner who had previously given correct answers	>> Writing responses rather than calling them aloud (i.e. private rather than public responding)

FURTHER RESEARCH ON CONFORMITY

Although many criticisms have been made of Asch's findings (see key study on p. 159), one of the strengths of his work is the amount of subsequent research it generated.

When participants can't see each other

Crutchfield (1955) thought that the face-to-face arrangement of participants in the Asch procedure might be responsible for the levels of conformity found. Therefore, he arranged his participants in booths out of sight of each other, but all able to see the stimulus cards (see Fig. 5.3). This enabled him to collect data more economically by running several naive participants at the same time. Participants sat individually in booths with a row of switches and lights in front of them. They had to press the switch that corresponded to their judgement when their turn came to answer. They were told that the lights on the display panel showed the responses of the other participants. In fact, the experimenter controlled these lights and each participant saw an identical display. Despite the absence of an actual face-to-face group, Crutchfield found the following:

■ Conformity levels were 30 per cent when using Asch's line comparison tasks.

■ When the task was made more difficult, conformity increased.

Figure 5.3 >>
Crutchfield's conformity-testing procedure: people sit in adjacent booths and answer questions shown on the wall in front of them after being told of other people's apparent responses

Research into individual differences

Crutchfield was also interested in individual differences and how these might affect conformity. He found that participants with high scores in intelligence and leadership ability displayed less conformity. However, there has been a lack of evidence subsequently to support any idea of a 'conforming personality'. Crutchfield's studies can also be criticized for their artificial setting. The findings do, however, support those of Asch, suggesting that conformity pressures operate on people other than students.

Furman and Duke (1988) looked at how lack of confidence might make people more likely to conform. They asked students to listen to two versions of each of ten musical excerpts. On their degree programme the students were majoring either in music or in another subject. Each student, on their own, selected a preferred version for each of the ten pairs. They were then individually tested in the presence of three confederates who unanimously stated a verbal preference from each pair of excerpts. Their findings were as follows:

- Music majors were not influenced to change their already stated preferences.
- However, the publicly stated preferences of non-music majors were significantly affected by the preferences of the confederates.

Research into historical and cultural contexts

Some observers have suggested that Asch's findings tell us more about the historical and cultural climate of the USA in 1951 than they do about fundamental psychological tendencies. Some more recent studies of conformity have failed to confirm Asch's findings:

- Perrin and Spencer (1980) replicated Asch's procedure, using 33 British students. They found only one conforming response in 396 trials. They concluded that cultural changes over 30 years had led to a reduction in the tendency of students to conform. Another factor that might have influenced the results is the type of students used. They were drawn from engineering, chemistry and mathematics courses, and it is possible that the knowledge and skills acquired in their courses had equipped them to resist conformity pressures during a task of this sort. Another study by Perrin and Spencer (1981) using youths on probation as participants and using probation officers as the confederates demonstrated levels of conformity similar to those found by Asch in 1952. The researchers concluded that where the perceived costs for people of not yielding were high, conformity effects would still be demonstrated.

- Nicholson *et al.* (1985) compared conformity levels in British and in American students using the Asch procedure. They found no significant differences between the two groups, suggesting some similarity in British and US student cultures, at least at that point in history. The students in 1985 were found to be significantly less conformist than their 1951 American counterparts but more conformist than the British students in 1981. Nicholson and colleagues have suggested that the experience of the Falklands War (when Britain went to war with Argentina over the occupancy of the Falkland Islands) might have contributed to group cohesiveness and, in turn, to a higher degree of conformity. (The war took place in 1982, between the collection of Perrin and Spencer's data and the collection of their own data.)

ACTIVITY

Conformity and war

Look at the two photos below: one of a woman buying food using government-issued ration coupons, the other of Londoners taking shelter in Picadilly Underground station during the London Blitz of the 1940s. Why might people be more likely to conform during times of war?

- Finally, Smith and Bond (1998) reviewed 31 studies of conformity conducted in different cultures using Asch's procedures. They concluded that people in collectivistic cultures show higher levels of conformity compared with those who live in individualistic cultures. In collectivistic cultures, people emphasize loyalty to the group and being concerned about the needs and interests of others. Group decision-making is preferred to individual decisions. In individualistic cultures, people are more concerned with their own and their family's self-interest, and individual initiatives are valued.

Zimbardo's prison simulation study (1973)

Philip Zimbardo and colleagues conducted one of the best-known and most controversial studies in psychology. They looked at how people conform to the expectations they have about social roles. He used a simulated prison set-up to see to what extent normal, well-balanced people would conform to new social roles. For example, Zimbardo wondered whether participants who were assigned the role of guards would act in a way that conformed to their stereotyped view of how prison guards should behave. (In a simulation, participants are asked to act (role-play) as though the simulation is real. Simulations are used to study behaviours to which psychologists would not normally have access.)

According to Zimbardo, his results demonstrate how easily people can come to behave in uncharacteristic ways when placed in new situations and given new roles. Another possible explanation is that the volunteers might have tried to be 'good subjects' and behaved in the ways they thought the researcher wanted (called demand characteristics).

Ethical issues in Zimbardo's prison study are discussed further on p. 186.

MINORITY SOCIAL INFLUENCE

Minority influence is a form of social influence where a persuasive minority exerts pressure to change the attitudes, beliefs or behaviours of the majority. If people simply went along with the majority all the time and minority viewpoints never prevailed, there would be no change, no innovation. There are, of course, many instances where small minorities – or even lone dissenters – have influenced majority opinion. Nemeth (1986) believes that even when minorities are wrong, their views can stimulate productive thinking. Small minority groups may be dismissed initially by the majority as eccentrics or extremists. However, under certain circumstances and over a period of time, these small groups or even individuals can eventually become very influential. The dissociation model (see p. 166) offers one explanation for the slowness of minority influence.

Moscovici's (1969) 'blue–green' slide study

Moscovici and colleagues carried out one of the best-known studies of minority influence and one that led to a great deal of subsequent research. They asked six participants to estimate the colour of 36 slides. All the slides were blue but adding filters varied their brightness (see key study, *Minority influence*, on p. 164). Clearly, consistency on the part of the minority is important. Although the levels of yielding found in the consistent condition are nothing like as high as those found by Asch in his studies of majority influence, they do indicate that minorities can exert some degree of influence, even when yielding is measured publicly and immediately after the influence attempts. Furthermore, minorities may be even more influential with the passage of time provided they adopt the appropriate style of behaviour.

> ## ACTIVITY
>
> ### The ethics of the study by Moscovici and colleagues
>
> Reread the key study on p. 164, this time thinking about the ethics of the experiment. For example, how do you think that the participants might have felt when they were told about the true purpose of the study?

Behavioural styles of minorities

Following many investigations, Moscovici (1985) identified the behavioural styles that minorities must possess if they are to exert social influence on majorities:

- They must be consistent in their opposition to the majority. Consistency, according to Moscovici, comprises "resolution, certainty, clarity of definition, and coherence". Consistency is generally recognized as the single most important factor for a minority to be influential.
- They must not appear dogmatic by rigidly reiterating the same arguments. They need to demonstrate a degree of flexibility.

Others psychologists (e.g. Hogg and Vaughan 1998) have also claimed that minorities are more likely to be influential if they:

- appear to be acting from principle (not out of self-interest)
- are seen to have made sacrifices in order to maintain their position

Stanford prison simulation study by Zimbardo *et al.* (1973)

Aim >>

To investigate how readily people would conform to new roles by observing how quickly people would adopt the roles of guard or prisoner in a role-playing exercise that simulated prison life. Zimbardo was interested in finding out whether the brutality reported among guards in American prisons was due to the sadistic personalities of the guards or had more to do with the prison environment.

Procedures >>

- Well-adjusted, healthy male volunteers were paid $15 a day to take part in a two-week simulation study of prison life.
- Volunteers were randomly allocated to the roles of prisoners or guards.
- Local police helped by 'arresting' nine prisoners at their homes, without warning. They were taken, blindfolded, to the 'prison' (actually the basement of Stanford University), stripped, sprayed with disinfectant, given smocks to wear and their prison number to memorize. From then on they were referred to by number only.
- There were three guards, who wore khaki uniforms, dark glasses and carried wooden batons.
- No physical aggression was permitted.

Findings >>

- The guards, who were permitted to devise most of the rules, harassed the prisoners and conformed to their perceived roles with such zeal that the study had to be discontinued after six days.
- Prisoners rebelled against the guards after only two days. Guards quelled the rebellion using fire extinguishers.
- Some prisoners became depressed and anxious; one prisoner had to be released after only one day. Two more prisoners had to be released on the fourth day.

Conclusions >>

- The 'prison environment' was an important factor in creating the guards' brutal behaviour (none of the participants who acted as guards had shown sadistic tendencies before the study).
- People will readily conform to the social roles they are expected to play, especially if the roles are as strongly stereotyped as those of prison guards.
- The roles that people play shape their attitudes and behaviour. If it took only six days to alter the behaviour of the participants in this study, then the roles we play in real life will have even more far-reaching effects.

Criticisms >>

- The study has received many ethical criticisms, including those about lack of fully informed consent by participants and the humiliation and distress experienced by those who acted as prisoners.
- Zimbardo was wrong to act as both prison-superintendent and chief researcher as this produced a conflict of roles whereby he lost sight of the harm being done to the participants.

AO2 check

Participants did not know, for example, that they would be arrested at home. Zimbardo thought, however, that withholding this type of procedural detail was justifiable given the nature of the study. Those acting as guards had to face up to the unpalatable fact that they had been willing to mistreat their prisoners. They, as well as the 'prisoners', might have suffered psychological harm. However, Zimbardo's follow-up interviews with participants found no lasting negative effects.

experiment by Moscovici *et al.* (1969)

Aim >>

To see whether a consistent minority of participants could influence a majority to give an incorrect answer in a colour perception task.

Procedures >>

- 172 participants in total were involved. All had good eyesight.
- Six participants at a time were asked to estimate the colour of 36 slides.
- All the slides were blue, but of differing brightness.
- Two of the six participants were accomplices of the experimenter.
- There were **two conditions**:
  - consistent: the two accomplices called the slides green on all trials
  - inconsistent: the two accomplices called the slides green 24 times, and blue 12 times.

Findings >>

- Participants in the consistent condition yielded and called the slides green in 8.4 per cent of the trials.
- 32 per cent of participants in the consistent condition reported a green slide at least once.
- Participants in the inconsistent condition yielded and called the slides green in only 1.3 per cent of the trials.

Conclusions >>

- It is important that those in a minority behave consistently if they are to influence a majority to change its viewpoint.
- Individual members of a minority must maintain a consistent viewpoint and there needs to be agreement among the different members of the minority group.
- Inconsistent minorities lack any real influence on majorities. Their opinions are viewed as groundless.

Criticisms >>

- The artificiality of the laboratory setting is unlike real-life situations where minorities such as pressure groups exert their influence on the prevailing majority opinion.
- Later research, using similar procedures, found that consistency alone was not sufficient to ensure minority influence. Minorities must also avoid appearing rigidly inflexible.

A Suffragette march in the early 1900s (below) and a gay rights parade (right). How can these situations be seen as minority social influence?

- are seen as similar to the majority in terms of class, age and gender
- advocate views that are consistent with current social trends (e.g. as our society becomes more concerned with environmental issues, so the views of certain minority groups, once derided, attract a wider audience and become more persuasive).

Clark's (1994) *Twelve Angry Men* study

Clark carried out an unusual experiment to see what aspects of minority influence had the greatest effects on an individual's views. He asked 270 college students to role-play the part of jurors and read a summary of a court case presented in the film *Twelve Angry Men*. The students, who were unfamiliar with the film, had to decide whether or not the accused was guilty.

Clark gave his participants a summary of a murder case and of the jury's discussions about key pieces of evidence. The persuasiveness of the arguments and the views of the jury were manipulated. The participants were asked their views about the guilt of the defendant at various stages. Clark found that participants were most persuaded when they heard consistent persuasive arguments from the minority jury members and when they learned that more than one juror had defected

from the majority position. He concluded that it was a combination of convincing arguments and a shift by other majority members that resulted in the minority exerting the greatest influence.

In the film, Twelve Angry Men, *Henry Fonda played a member of a jury in the trial of a young man accused of stabbing his father to death. At the start, Fonda's character alone held to the belief that the man was innocent. Gradually, by sticking to his guns, he persuaded his fellow jurors to re-examine the evidence. Eventually he succeeded in persuading the other jurors to change their minds and the innocent young man was found not guilty.*

ACTIVITY

Do minorities really exert influence on jury decision-making?

Read the accounts of the Tanford and Penrod experiment, and the Chicago Jury Project. Then answer the following questions:

1. To what extent do these studies reflect the outcome of *Twelve Angry Men*?
2. Do these laboratory studies of juries' behaviour resemble what happens in real juries?

Tanford and Penrod (1986) designed an experiment where six-person juries watched videotapes of a trial being re-enacted. The jurors voted immediately after the trial before any discussion, and then after they had talked about it. Results showed that after the discussion:

- The view first held by the majority always prevailed if initially only one person disagreed. This evidence is similar to the results that Asch found when he investigated majority influence. Therefore, it would appear from this study that when people are discussing serious issues, it is majorities, not minorities, that are influential.
- In only 7 per cent of cases did an initial minority of more than one manage to persuade the majority to change its verdict.

The Chicago Jury Project (Kalven and Zeisel 1966) interviewed jurors and used tape recordings of actual jury deliberations. Although the real juries studied in this project differed in some respects from the experimental juries used by Tanford and Penrod, there were similar findings concerning the lack of influence by minority jurors. In only 5 per cent of the cases did an initial minority prevail and then only if the minority began with at least three members of the jury.

This does not mean that an articulate and determined person who holds a minority viewpoint can never persuade others to change their minds. However, the dramatic example of the Henry Fonda character in the film *Twelve Angry Men*, in which one courageous, lone juror sways the majority by his intelligent questioning, is almost absent from the historical record.

WHY DO PEOPLE YIELD TO MINORITY INFLUENCE?

The following explanations have been proposed for minority influence.

Consistency

There are two types of consistency:

- *intra-individual* – where a person maintains a consistent position over time
- *inter-individual* – where there is agreement among members of the minority group.

If members of a minority fail to demonstrate either of these forms of consistency, the majority is unlikely to pay them much attention. However, a consistent minority punctures any illusion of unanimity among the majority and so it becomes easier for majority members to express any doubts they may have.

The snowball effect

The term 'snowball effect' (Van Avermaet 1996) is used to describe what sometimes happens in minority influence. Once a few members of the majority start to move towards the minority position, then the influence of the minority begins to gather momentum as more people gradually pay attention to the potential correctness of the minority view. Recall what Clark (1994) found in his jury study: once a few people had begun to defect from the majority viewpoint, the student participants were increasingly influenced by the minority arguments to find the defendant not guilty.

Group membership

According to Hogg and Vaughan (1998), we are most likely to be influenced by those we perceive to be like us (called our in-group). For example, the attitudes of straight men towards gay men are more likely to become more liberal if other straight men (the in-group) express liberal attitudes than if only gay men (the out-group) express such attitudes. However, even within an in-group, minority influence works slowly. The dissociation model provides one reason for this.

The dissociation model

Mugny and Perez (1991) propose that minority groups influence majority group members through a process called social cryptoamnesia, meaning that minority ideas are assimilated into the majority viewpoint without those in the majority remembering where the ideas came from. In other words, the content and the source become dissociated. According to this model, minority ideas are so strongly associated with their source that to adopt the message risks assuming the negative identity of the source. If, on the other hand, the ideas can be dissociated from their source, the majority can resist overt identification with an out-group while still drawing inspiration from their ideas.

This may account for why the conversion effect (outlined by Moscovici) generated by minority groups is often delayed. The process of assimilating ideas is slow because initially they have been resisted vigorously, purely because of their source. Over time, the ideas become detached from their source and begin to reappear in the individual's mind as their own.

The dissociation model does not lend itself to experimental testing, but it does provide an appealing explanation as to how dominant ideas or trends within a culture (*zeitgeists*) can be launched by minority groups despite the strong resistance they encounter from majority positions.

Differences between majority and minority social influence

Different processes

According to Moscovici (1980) majorities and minorities achieve influence through different processes. Majority influence, he claimed, involves public compliance (rather than private acceptance) where the person is more concerned with how they appear in front of others than with the issue itself. The majority, therefore, exerts normative social influence (as seen in Asch's experiments) to exact compliance from the minority.

By contrast, minorities use informational social influence to persuade those in the majority to change their views. Minorities are aiming for conversion rather than compliance. They hope that by focusing on the issue, the majority will come to examine the arguments proposed by the minority. In turn, this may start the process of conversion whereby, at least in private, attitudes genuinely begin to shift.

Instant vs delayed effects

Majority social influence may produce instant effects where people conform rather than appear foolish or risk rejection. However, there is no such risk in the case of minority influence. After all, who cares what a small minority thinks and, furthermore, minorities are often ridiculed for their unpopular positions. In fact, many people holding mainstream views would wish to avoid being associated with oddball minorities (see 'The dissociation model', left). Nevertheless, by using informational social influence, a consistent minority may plant the seed of doubt in the mind of someone holding a majority viewpoint. Over time, that doubt may lead to a change of view, albeit delayed, especially if others from the majority are seen to be wavering or converting to the minority position.

Minority *influence*

Charlan Nemeth is a Professor of Psychology at the University of California at Berkeley and received her PhD in Social Psychology at Cornell University. Professor Nemeth has written and spoken extensively on the positive contribution of dissent within groups and its role in creativity. These research interests have many applied aspects, including jury deliberations, innovation in organizations, and the value of diversity.

Q **What do you consider to be the main lessons learned from minority influence research?**

A First, I think the research shows us that people holding minority viewpoints are not just passive recipients of influence. Their choices are not simply to conform or to be independent (or to be silent). They can actively promote a differing viewpoint and they can prevail. The important ingredient is that they need to be consistent in their position. If they capitulate to the majority, they tend not to exert influence. Second, we need to realize that, even with consistency and commitment, minority views do not often prevail. And - regardless of whether they prevail or not - the person holding the minority (dissenting) viewpoint is often disliked, seen as incompetent and rejected. Third - and I think this is the most important lesson from my own work over the past 25 years - we profit from minority views. Even when they are wrong and even though we find them to be incompetent or even immoral, exposure to dissenting minority views stimulates us to be better decision-makers and more creative in our thought. We search for more information on all sides of the issue; we consider more alternatives in our problem-solving and decision-making; and our thinking is even more creative. Thus, we should learn to "welcome and not fear the voices of dissent".

Charlan Nemeth

Q **Is minority influence potentially more powerful than majority influence?**

A Yes, but not in terms of direct influence, but rather in terms of indirect influence and the stimulation of thought. Majorities have much more power when it comes to 'winning'. Many people will adopt the majority opinion because they assume that the majority is right and, further, they don't want to incur the rejection that maintaining a minority viewpoint brings. Thus, you will find that people will conform to error, even on issues that have an objectively clear and correct answer, when a majority takes that erroneous position. This is far less likely when we are faced with a minority viewpoint. However, the minority's power comes from our reflection on the issue after the confrontation. Sometimes, we change our opinions to that held by the minority - but we do it in private, or later, or on related topics. Often, we think differently about the issue as a result of exposure to that minority view and, in general, we think more broadly, more deeply and come up with better judgements and decisions.

Q **How successfully do the insights from minority influence research extend beyond the laboratory?**

A I will give you two examples, as these are areas in which I have taught and published related work. One is the law, especially trial by jury. As you know, juries are lay people who decide on conviction as a group. The important issue here is NOT who wins (the majority or the minority position) but, rather, how do we best achieve the 'truth'. How do we serve the aims of justice? Given that minority viewpoints stimulate better decision-making (but are often not given credit for such stimulation and, in fact, are derided), they need to be protected. We have substantial research showing that a requirement of unanimity (rather than some form of majority rule) provides some protection. It increases the likelihood that the minority views will be expressed and maintained and, further, it increases the perception of justice.

A second example, one that I teach executives in Business Schools, is that flexibility and innovation are indispensable elements in a global economy and that, in this context, dissent should be protected and valued. Many times, executives would rather learn how to get power and keep it, how to get their employees to do their bidding and 'like it'. If they want people to implement their ideas, that is fine. However, if they want an organization which anticipates changes in products or the marketplace, if they want one that is flexible and able to innovate, they must harness the power of dissenting views for the stimulation of thought that this provides.

And finally, perhaps the best application of all is the value of dissent for democracies. As John Stuart Mill noted, diversity, variety and choice, the allowance of refutation and the airing of differing views are great strengths of democracies. They serve as a safeguard against tyranny but, importantly, they serve the detection of truth and the vitality of our beliefs.

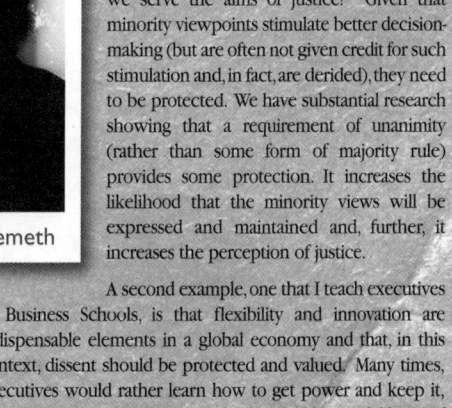

Expert interview: Charlan Nemeth

This activity aims to boost your all-important AO2 evaluative skills. Using the material from the Charlan Nemeth interview on p. 167 and other material on minority influence, complete the following sentences. Using lead-in phrases such as these will help you to focus on what is AO2 material and will make your intentions explicit to the examiner.

- ■ "Nemeth believes a particular important lesson from minority influence research is ..."
- ■ "Minority influence has the potential to be more powerful than majority influence because ..."
- ■ "However, studies of jury decision-making ..."
- ■ "An important application of minority influence research is ..."
- ■ "This is particularly important because ..."

✓ CHECK YOUR UNDERSTANDING

Check your understanding of conformity and minority influence by answering these questions. Try to do this from memory at first. You can check your answers by looking back through Topic 1.

1 What do you understand by the terms: 'social influence', 'conformity' and 'minority influence'?

2 Give two reasons why people conform.

3 Explain the difference between compliance, identification and internalization.

4 Give the main findings and the main conclusions of Asch's study of conformity.

5 How did the results found by Perrin and Spencer in Britain in 1981 differ from those found by Asch in 1951? What explanation did Perrin and Spencer offer for this?

6 In what ways did the participants in Zimbardo's prison simulation study demonstrate conformity?

7 Give two explanations for people yielding to minority influence.

8 Outline the procedures and conclusions of one study of minority influence.

9 Outline two differences between minority and majority influence.

10 To what extent does research on conformity tell us anything about conformity in the real world?

REVISION SUMMARY

Having covered this topic, you should be able to:

✓ define 'social influence', 'conformity' and 'minority influence'

✓ explain why people yield to majority influence

✓ explain why people yield to minority influence

✓ describe and evaluate the research that has been carried out into majority and minority influence

✓ describe the aims, procedures, findings, conclusions and criticisms of a key study in the areas of majority and minority influence

✓ outline differences between majority and minority influence.

Topic 2 >> Obedience to authority

GETTING YOU THINKING...

A guard supervises inmates of a Nazi concentration camp during World War II

A lone Chinese student protester faces up to tanks in Tianenman Square, Beijing, 1989

During the Vietnam War, American soldiers rounded up hundreds of women, children and old men from My Lai village – and were ordered them to kill them. Mike Wallace from CBS News interviewed one of the soldiers, reported in *The New York Times*, 25 November 1969:

Q: *How many people did you round up?*

A: Well, there was about 40, 50 people that we gathered in the center of the village...

Q: *What kind of people – men, women, children?*

A: Men, women, children.

Q: *Babies?*

A: Babies. And we huddled them up. We made them squat down and Lieutenant Calley came over and said, "You know what to do with them don't you?" And I said yes. So I took it for granted that he just wanted us to watch them. And he left, and came back about 10 or 15 minutes later and said, "How come you ain't killed them yet?" And I told him that I didn't think you wanted us to kill them, that you just wanted us to guard them. He said, "No, I want them dead." So – ...

Q: *And you killed how many? At that time?*

A: Well I fired on them automatic, so you can't – You just spray the area on them and so you can't know how many you killed 'cause they were going fast. So I might have killed 10 or 15 of them.

Q: *Men, women, and children?*

A: Men, women, and children.

Q: *And babies?*

A: And babies ...

Q: *Why did you do it?*

A: Why did I do it? Because I felt like I was ordered to do it, and it seemed like that, at the time I felt like I was doing the right thing, because, like I said, I lost buddies...

Q: *What did these civilians – particularly the women and children, the old men – what did they do? What did they say to you?*

A: They weren't much saying to them. They [were] just being pushed and they were doing what they was told to do.

Q: *They weren't begging, or saying, "no ... no," or ...?*

A: Right. They were begging and saying "no, no". And the mothers was hugging their children, and ... but they kept right on firing. Well, we kept right on firing. They was waving their arms and begging ...

Some questions for you to think about or debate:

1 Why do you think that people obey orders from others?

2 Why do you think people obeyed orders in the situations depicted above?

3 Think of a situation when you obeyed an order and, as a consequence, you did something that you felt to be wrong. Why did you choose to obey? Why did you choose not to stick up for what you felt to be right?

Obedience to authority: an outcome of social influence where an individual acts according to the orders of some authority figure. It is assumed that without such an order the person would not have acted in this way.

Ecological validity: the degree to which the findings from a study can be generalized beyond the context of the investigation. Problems with ecological validity tend to emerge only when other researchers try to rerun the study in different situations.

Experimental (internal) validity: a measure of whether the experimental procedures actually worked and the effects observed were genuine (i.e. caused by the experimental manipulation). The conclusions of a study are justified when there is a high level of experimental validity.

WHAT IS OBEDIENCE?

Obedience is the result of social influence where somebody acts in response to a direct order from an authority figure (Cardwell 2000). It is assumed that without such an order the person would not have acted in this way. (The panel below explains how obedience differs from conformity.) Obedience may sometimes be destructive, as when people comply with the orders of a malevolent authority.

>> Obedience as a determinant of behaviour is of particular relevance to our time. It has been reliably established that from 1939 to 1945, millions of innocent persons were slaughtered on command; gas chambers were built, death camps were guarded, daily quotas of corpses were produced with the same efficiency as the manufacture of appliances. These inhumane policies may have originated in the mind of a single person, but they could only have been carried out on a massive scale if a very large number of persons obeyed orders. >> (Milgram 1963, p. 371)

Similarly appalling events have occurred since then (e.g. the My Lai massacre during the Vietnam War, the slaughter of Kurds in Iraq and ethnic cleansing in

Kosovo). The list goes on. What induces people to obey their leaders' orders to torture and kill innocent human beings? Milgram was one of the first psychologists who tried to answer this question. He placed the issue of obedience in a social-psychological context, proposing that it is a normative process, a basic feature of human interaction.

The differences between conformity and obedience

Both obedience and conformity are outcomes of social influence. In the case of obedience, social influence takes the form of orders from an authority figure. In the case of conformity, the social norms of the majority exert influence on an individual to go along with the behaviour and attitudes of the group.

Public compliance and private change

Obedience often involves no more than public compliance, with private attitudes left unchanged. Conformity, however, may involve a long-lasting and fundamental shift of attitudes and beliefs, if the conformity takes the form of identifying with the group or internalizing the views of the majority.

Conscious vs unconscious effects

Figures who command obedience often display signs of their authority (e.g. uniforms) and individuals are usually well aware when they have obeyed such a figure. Indeed, many people have pleaded "I just did what I was told" as an excuse for carrying out reprehensible acts.

In the case of conformity, however, individuals are often unaware that they have been subjected to conformity pressures and may refute the idea that others have influenced them to modify their views or behaviour.

MILGRAM'S STUDIES OF OBEDIENCE

Stanley Milgram carried out a series of studies to try to shed some light on this aspect of human behaviour. In all, he studied over 1,000 participants who were representative of the general population. He discovered that, under certain situational influences, most of us would obey orders that went against our conscience.

His original study took place in a laboratory at Yale University in the USA (see key study, *Obedience*, on p. 172). The experimenter, who wore a grey laboratory coat to reinforce his status and authority, introduced two participants to each other and they each drew lots to determine who would be the 'teacher' and who would be the 'learner'. The learner-accomplice was a mild-mannered 47-year-old man who mentioned that he had had a heart complaint in the past, but that he was willing to participate in the study nonetheless.

As the learner-accomplice began making mistakes, the level of shock administered increased and he was heard to protest until, at 180 volts he shouted that he could bear the pain no longer. At 300 volts he screamed and complained that his heart was troubling him. At 315 volts he refused to continue and from then on he made no responses to the teacher's requests that he answer. In reality, of course, the accomplice never received any shocks. His responses and pleadings were prerecorded.

You will not be surprised to learn that this procedure was very stressful for the 'teacher' participants. Most protested and wanted to stop. Many showed signs of extreme anxiety, biting their lips and trembling. However, whenever the teacher hesitated, the experimenter gave standardized prompts to encourage him to continue:

Prod 1: "Please continue" or "Please go on"

Prod 2: "The experiment requires that you continue"

Prod 3: "It is absolutely essential that you continue"

Prod 4: "You have no other choice, you must go on".

ACTIVITY

Other people's estimates of Milgram's results

Milgram described this experiment to three different groups of people: psychiatrists, college students and middle-class adults. He asked them to guess how people would respond.

1 Before reading on to find out what they said, how do *you* think that people would be likely to respond? The maximum number of shocks that could be delivered to the 'learner' was 30, starting at 15 volts and going up to 450 volts. How many shocks do *you* think the participants would be prepared to deliver?

2 Describe the study to at least ten other people (class members, friends or family members). Ask them how many shocks they think someone would be prepared to deliver in this kind of situation. Note down each of their answers.

3 Now calculate the average score (the mean score) by adding up all the scores (including your own) and dividing by the total number of scores, or combine your answers with those collected by other members of your class so you have many more scores and then calculate the average. What is your answer?

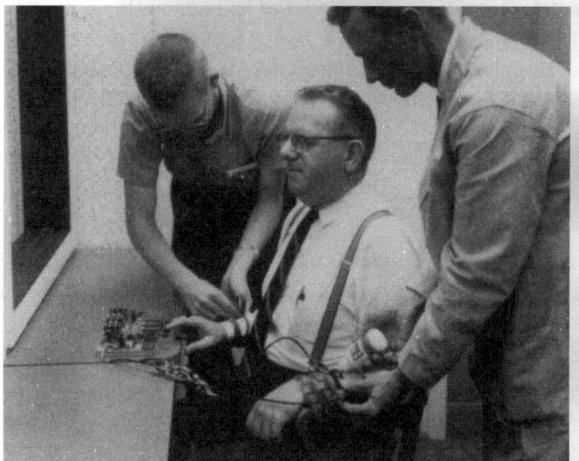

The learner-accomplice is strapped to the 'shock generator'

On average, the people Milgram spoke to estimated an average of 9 out of the possible 30 shocks (i.e. 135 volts) and predicted that the participants would rebel against the instructions once that level was reached. Only a tiny handful predicted that participants would administer the maximum shock of 450 volts, which was labelled 'Danger, severe shock'.

Now read on to find out just how many shocks the participants actually delivered in Milgram's study.

original study by Milgram (1963)

Aim >>

To find out whether ordinary Americans would obey an unjust order from a person in authority to inflict pain on another person. Milgram wanted to discover what factors in a situation led people to obey.

Procedures >>

- 40 male volunteers, each paid $4.50, were deceived into thinking they were giving electric shocks.
- The participants were told that the study concerned the role of punishment in learning. The genuine participant always had the teacher's role and a confederate played the part of the learner. His task was to memorize pairs of words. When tested, the 'learner' would indicate his choice using a system of lights. The 'teacher's' role was to administer a shock every time the learner made a mistake. The teacher sat in front of the shock generator that had 30 levers, each of which indicated the level of shock to be given. The participant watched the confederate being strapped into a chair in an adjoining room with electrodes attached to his arms.
- To begin with the accomplice answered correctly and then began to make mistakes. Every time he made an error, he was to be given an electric shock administered by the participant. Shocks started at 15 volts and rose in 15-volt increments to 450 volts. If the teacher hesitated in administering the shocks, the researcher encouraged him to continue.
- No shocks were actually administered.
- The experiment continued either until the teacher refused to continue or until 450 volts were reached and given four times. The participant was then debriefed and taken to meet the learner–accomplice (as shown in the photo).

Findings >>

- All participants went to at least 300 volts on the shock generator.
- 65 per cent of participants went to the end of the shock generator. That is, they believed they had administered the full 450 volts!
- Most participants found the procedure very stressful and wanted to stop, with some showing signs of extreme anxiety. Although they dissented verbally, they continued, however, to obey the researcher who prodded them to continue giving the shocks.

Conclusions >>

- Under certain circumstances, most people will obey orders that go against their conscience.
- When people occupy a subordinate position in a dominance hierarchy, they become liable to lose feelings of empathy, compassion and morality, and are inclined towards blind obedience.
- Atrocities such as those carried out in World War II may be largely explained in terms of pressures to obey a powerful authority.

Criticisms >>

- The study has received many criticisms, most relating to the potential harm that might have been done to participants.
- Did participants really believe that they were giving electric shocks? Orne and Holland claimed that the study lacked experimental (internal) validity; participants were only 'going along with the act' when they 'shocked' the learner, that they were not really distressed, just pretending in order to please the experimenter. Orne and Holland also claimed that the situation within Milgram's laboratory bore little resemblance to real-life situations where obedience is required and so it lacked ecological validity (see p. 175 for a fuller discussion of the experimental and ecological validity of this study).

The potential harm to those participating in Milgram's study

In the key study opposite, the first criticism of Milgram's study is about the potential harm to participants.

Pause for a moment to imagine what it might have felt like to participate in this study and make a note of the ways in which you feel those involved might have been harmed by the experience. Think especially about the issues of respect, deception and any possible long-term harm.

Milgram's main results

Although most participants dissented verbally, they obeyed behaviourally, and 65 per cent of participants went to the end of the shock generator, believing they had administered 450 volts to the 'learner'. Milgram was as surprised by these results as anyone since the people he had spoken to about the procedure before carrying out his study thought only a tiny handful would proceed to 450 volts. They were wrong. What was it about the situation that caused the participants to obey?

You may be surprised that Milgram claimed that he had no way of knowing beforehand that his study would cause distress. His follow-up procedures with his participants also showed that many said they were glad that they had taken part because they felt they had learned something important about themselves. (See p. 184 for a more detailed discussion of the ethical issues raised by Milgram's study.)

Variations on Milgram's basic procedure

Milgram systematically varied a number of the features of his procedure in order to discover what elements of the situation made it more or less likely that participants would obey. These variations and their consequences for the participants' behaviour are listed in Table 5.2. It is clear from these results that obedience levels in a laboratory setting can be manipulated by controlling situational variables:

- When participants were relocated to less prestigious surroundings, obedience levels fell.
- When the participant knew that the learner had agreed to only a limited contract, obedience levels fell.
- When participants were forced to see, as well as hear, the pain and distress caused by their actions, obedience levels fell.
- When participants were required to use physical force personally to administer the shocks, obedience levels fell even further. As the participants became increasingly aware of the pain and distress inflicted on the learners, they were more likely to disobey the experimenter's orders to continue giving shocks (see photo on p. 181).
- When others modelled disobedience for them, participants conformed, followed suit and obedience levels fell.
- When the experimenter supervised participants less closely, obedience levels fell.
- When someone else 'did the dirty work' of throwing the switches, obedience levels soared.

Now read the 'Expert interview' with David Mandel on p. 174 for a discussion about the limited applicability of these findings to what actually happened during the Holocaust (the genocide of European Jews).

Table 5.2 >> Variations on Milgram's basic procedure

Variation	Obedience rate (those going to 450 volts)
>> Original experiment	65%
>> Venue moved to seedy offices in nearby town (Bridgeport)	47.5%
>> Learner agreed to participate on the condition that "you let me out when I say so"	40%
>> Teacher and learner in the same room	40%
>> Teacher had to force learner's hand on to plate to receive shock	30%
>> Teacher given support from two other 'teachers' (confederates) who refuse	10%
>> Experimenter left the room and instructed the teacher by telephone from another room	20.5%
>> Teacher paired with an assistant (confederate) who threw the switches	92.5%

Source: Milgram (1963)

The obedience *alibi*

Dr David R. Mandel is an Associate Professor of Psychology at the University of Victoria (British Columbia, Canada). His academic background is in the fields of cognitive and social psychology. Dr Mandel's current research interests focus on the social psychology of collective violence and on topics in decision science that address how (and how well) people make judgements and decisions.

Q What aspects of Milgram's research have been used to explain events in the Holocaust?

A In Milgram's best-known 'voice feedback' experiment, 62.5 per cent of participants obeyed the experimenter's request to administer shocks to the 'learner' even at dangerously high voltage levels that apparently caused the learner harm. This key finding has been used as evidence in support of the idea that Holocaust perpetrators, like Milgram's participants, were ordinary citizens who succumbed to the influence of malign authority figures. According to this explanation, Holocaust perpetrators were motivated primarily by a need to fulfil their duties to their superiors. In short, they were 'just following orders'.

Q Are these conclusions justified?

A No, they are unjustified for several reasons. First, there is the obvious difference that whereas Milgram's participants were told that the shock procedure was not harmful, Holocaust perpetrators knew that they were killing unarmed civilians. Second, when Milgram's participants were subtly made aware of limits that the learner put on his consent to participate, obedience rates declined substantially. Holocaust victims obviously did not consent to be tortured and murdered, and any reasonable extrapolation suggests that very few of Milgram's participants would have tortured victims against their will. Third, when participants had discretion over the shock levels they administered, the vast majority were unwilling to give shocks that (apparently) caused the learner pain. In contrast, historical records reveal that Holocaust perpetrators were willing – sometimes eager – to torture and humiliate their victims before killing them. This finding alone suggests that perpetrators' motives to kill went far beyond 'just following orders'.

David Mandel

Q What potential harm is there in trying to use Milgram's research in this way?

A Although Milgram's findings are an important contribution to social psychology, their relevance to explaining the Holocaust has been greatly overstated. One danger is that an exclusive focus on obedience to authority detracts attention from other important factors including racism, prejudice and discrimination. Another danger is that the obedience explanation can be easily misused as an alibi to exonerate perpetrators of the Holocaust or other genocides.

ACTIVITY

David Mandel speaks out!

Exam questions in social psychology occasionally ask you to consider how far the conclusions drawn from a particular research area apply to the real world. The interview with David Mandel gives you some insights into the problems of extending Milgram's research to the behaviour of Holocaust perpetrators. Mandel's account of the Holocaust and the relevance of Milgram's work to it is available on the Internet at http://web.uvic.ca/psyc/dmandel/ak98paper.html Read this article and answer the following questions:

■ Draw up a table that shows some of the variations of Milgram's basic study (e.g. the presence of an authority figure, the proximity of the victim) and equivalent Holocaust events. Do Milgram's findings reflect what actually happened in these Holocaust events?

■ What does this tell us about the external (ecological) validity of obedience research?

■ What, according to Mandel, are the theoretical limitations of an obedience perspective to explaining events in the Holocaust?

Evaluating Milgram's work

Ethical issues about deception, consent and protection of participants are dealt with on pp. 182–4.

Orne and Holland (1968) have criticized Milgram's studies on two other counts:

- lacking experimental (internal) validity
- lacking ecological validity.

Read the panel on the right for an overview of these aspects of Milgram's research.

Hofling *et al.* (1966) – obedient nurses

The situation used was a hospital. They arranged for a nurse (the participant) to receive a phone call from an unknown doctor who asked her to administer 20 milligrams of a drug called Astroten (a drug not known to these nurses) to a patient so that it would have taken effect before he arrived. If the nurse obeyed, she would be breaking several hospital rules:

- giving twice the maximum dose allowable for the drug
- administering a drug that was not on the ward stock list for that day
- taking a telephone instruction from an unfamiliar person
- acting without a signed order from a doctor.

Despite all this, 21 out of 22 of the participants started to give the medication (which was in fact a harmless placebo) until another nurse, who had been stationed nearby but out of sight, stopped them.

When interviewed afterwards, all the nurses said that they had been asked to do this type of thing before and that doctors became annoyed if they refused. These results are important as they highlight that pressures to obey are greater than most people imagine. When Hofling and colleagues asked nurses (not those in the study) what they thought the rate of obedience would be in this situation, they were all convinced that nurses would refuse to obey!

This study showed that high levels of obedience can be obtained in real-life settings and so appeared to provide support for the ecological validity of Milgram's findings. However, not all studies conducted in real-life settings do so.

Experimental (internal) validity

Experimental (internal) validity is a measure of whether experimental procedures actually work and whether the effects observed are genuine (i.e. caused by the experimental manipulation). Orne and Holland claimed that the participants in Milgram's studies were 'going along with the act' when they 'shocked' the learner. They argued that participants did not believe they were really giving electric shocks and that they were not really distressed, just pretending in order to please the experimenter and to continue to play their role in the study.

Milgram disputed both these claims. He cited evidence from films made of some of his investigations that clearly showed participants undergoing extreme stress. He also referred to evidence from post-experimental interviews and questionnaires to support his belief that the majority of participants believed they were administering real shocks. Furthermore, Orne and Holland do not explain why some participants refused to continue giving shocks if they were merely role-playing in the first place or why altering the location of the study (to run-down Bridgeport) reduced the levels of obedience.

Ecological validity (mundane realism)

Ecological validity is the degree to which the findings from a study can be generalized beyond the context of the investigation. Milgram's procedures have been replicated in other countries, with higher levels of obedience found in Germany and lower levels found in Australia (see p. 177). In a Jordanian study, children aged between 6 and 16 exhibited high levels of obedience, with 73 per cent believing that they were administering the full 450 volts (Shanab and Yahya 1977). Therefore, there is plenty of evidence to support Milgram's contention that high levels of obedience can readily be obtained in laboratories other than his own.

However, Orne and Holland have challenged the generalizability of Milgram's findings, claiming that the situation within Milgram's laboratory bore little resemblance to real-life situations where obedience is required. Given this criticism, the results of the study by Hofling *et al.* (1966) are interesting. This study appeared to provide support for the ecological validity of Milgram's findings by showing that blind obedience to an authority figure could occur just as readily in real life. However, Rank and Jacobson's later study (1977) called into question the ecological validity of the Hofling study!

Criticism of the study by Hofling and colleagues

1 Did you notice any weakness in the way that Hofling and colleagues designed and carried out their study? Clue: think about the way that nurses might normally operate when asked to administer a drug that they did not know about from a doctor who was not known to them.

2 If the design of the study was changed to enable nurses to respond as they would normally, do you think the results would be any different?

3 If your answer is 'yes', what does this tell us about the importance of the design of a study and the conclusions that are drawn?

Rank and Jacobson (1977): not so obedient nurses

Rank and Jacobson were uneasy about two aspects of Hofling's study – that the nurses had no knowledge of the drug involved and that they had no opportunity to seek advice from anyone of equal or higher status. In most hospital situations, they argued, nurses would either have knowledge about a drug or would have time to seek advice. Therefore, they replicated the procedure, but this time the doctor required the nurse to use the common drug Valium at three times the recommended level. The doctor who telephoned gave the name of a real doctor on the staff and nurses were able to speak to other nurses before they proceeded. Results showed that only two out of 18 nurses proceeded to prepare the medication as requested. Rank and Jacobson concluded that "nurses aware of the toxic effects of a drug and allowed to interact naturally ... will not administer a medication overdose merely because a physician orders it" (p. 191).

Bickman (1974): the power of uniforms!

Before reading any further, do the activity below.

In this interesting field study, Bickman found that visible symbols of authority, such as uniforms, increased levels of obedience. Three male experimenters dresser either in uniform (as a milkman or a guard) or as a civilian (in a coat and tie) made requests of passers-by in a street in New York. For example, they asked them to pick up a bag for them or provide money for a parking meter. People were most likely to obey the experimenter who was dressed as a guard and least likely to obey the experimenter dressed as a civilian. A strength of this study is its real-life setting. However, the opportunity sample of participants (i.e. those people who just happened to be available) may have affected the findings. The results, nevertheless, supported those of Milgram who found higher levels of obedience at the visibly prestigious Yale University than at the run-down office in Bridgeport.

The power of uniforms

In these photographs the same man is dressed in three different ways. If he asked you to do something, such as wait inside a shop and stay there until told to, in which situation would you be most likely, and least likely, to obey? Explain your answer.

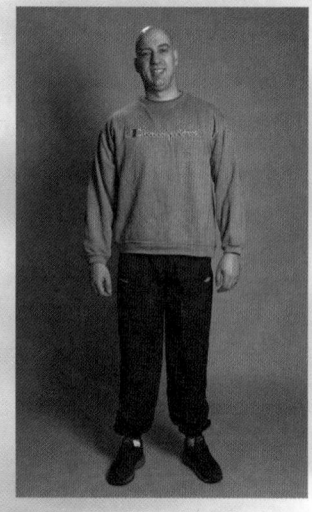

WHY PEOPLE OBEY

Why do people obey? A number of explanations have been offered that look at the psychological processes involved in obedience.

Legitimate authority

One suggestion is that we feel obligated to those in power because we respect their credentials and assume they know what they are doing. Legitimate social power is held by authority figures whose role is defined by society. This usually gives the person in authority the right to exert control over the behaviour of others, and others usually accept it (see the study by Hofling and colleagues described on p. 175). Although respect for authority permits orderly social interaction, there is the danger that it may be so deeply ingrained in us that we obey, even when we believe we are being asked to do something unethical or immoral. Clearly, the authority conveyed by a legitimate researcher at a prestigious university impressed the participants in Milgram's original experiment. When the location of the study was moved to a run-down office building, the level of obedience dropped (see Table 5.2, p. 173). Bickman's study also showed that people are more inclined to obey those who display visible symbols of authority such as uniforms.

Respect for authority varies from country to country. For example, in a study in Australia, where there is a greater tradition of questioning authority than was the case in the USA in the early 1960s, only 40 per cent of participants went to 450 volts on the shock generator. On the other hand, Mantell (1971) found 85 per cent obedience levels in Germany.

Gradual commitment

An important feature of Milgram's procedure was the gradual way in which participants became sucked into giving greater and greater levels of shock. They found it difficult to decide when to disengage from the procedure because each voltage increment was fairly small. Psychologists call this gradual commitment the 'foot-in-the-door' effect. Once people comply with a trivial, seemingly harmless, request they find it more difficult to refuse to carry out more serious, escalating requests. This is explained by the desire to appear consistent. Milgram also pointed out that participants felt that they had 'contracted' to help with the study. By coming along to the laboratory, they saw themselves as helpful people, willing to aid scientific research. If they then were to refuse to continue, they might have to re-evaluate this flattering self-perception.

Agency theory

Milgram's agency theory states that people operate on two levels:

- as autonomous individuals, behaving voluntarily and aware of the consequences of their actions
- on the agentic level, seeing themselves as the agents of others and not responsible for their actions.

The consequence of moving from the autonomous to the agentic level (known as the agentic shift) is that individuals attribute responsibility for their actions to the person in authority. At this agentic level, Milgram argued, people mindlessly accept the orders of the person seen as responsible in the situation. Milgram believed that this explained the behaviour of the participants in his study; they denied personal responsibility, claiming that they were merely "doing what they were told". You probably know that when those responsible for atrocities during World War II were asked why they did what they did, their answer was simply: "I was only obeying orders" (Arendt 1963). Similar defences have been offered more recently by ex-torturers at the South African Truth and Reconciliation Commission.

What causes people to undergo the agentic shift? Milgram suggested that it is part of the socialization process: we train children from a very early age to be obedient to authority at home, in school and in society. Many rules and regulations exist to reinforce obedience, so that eventually we tend to accept unquestioningly what we are told to do because most requests are perceived to be both reasonable and appropriate. Additionally, there are factors that operate to keep one in the agentic state. These are known as binding factors. They include:

- fear of appearing rude or arrogant by disrupting a well-defined social situation such as a laboratory experiment – this would involve a breach of etiquette and require courage
- fear of increasing one's anxiety levels (likely to be high already among Milgram's participants) by challenging the authority figure.

Buffers

The term 'buffer' is used here to describe any aspect of a situation that protects people from having to confront the consequences of their actions. Remember that the participants in Milgram's studies did not enjoy what they were doing. Why then did they continue? Milgram suggested that buffers acted as a mechanism to help people reduce the strain of obeying an immoral or unethical command. In turn, these buffers served to facilitate obedience. In the original Milgram study, the 'teacher' and 'learner' were in different rooms; the teacher was buffered (protected) from having to see his victim. In some real-life situations where obedience is required, the person merely has to press a button – the resulting destruction may not even be observed. In other cases, those carrying out orders are not told full details of their mission. This was the case with the aircrew who dropped the atomic bomb on Hiroshima.

Personality factors

Unlike the preceding situational factors, some dispositional (personality) factors have been proposed to explain Milgram's findings.

- *Authoritarian personality* – An authoritarian person has rigid beliefs, is intolerant and yet submissive to those in authority. Milgram (1974) found that participants who were highly authoritarian tended to give stronger shocks than those who were less authoritarian.

- *Psychopathic personality* – Miale and Selzer (1975) claimed that the obedience of Milgram's participants was a socially acceptable expression of their psychopathic (violent and psychologically disordered) impulses. Milgram refuted this account completely. He reminded us that when participants were able to select their own voltage levels, they gave lower levels of shock. Hannah Arendt agreed with Milgram. She covered the trial of the Nazi war criminal Adolf Eichmann for crimes against humanity. She wrote:

«It would have been comforting indeed to believe that Eichmann was a monster ... The trouble with Eichmann was precisely that so many were like him and the many were neither perverted nor sadistic ... [but] terribly and terrifyingly normal.**»**
(1963, p. 276)

Remember that the main conclusion of Milgram's findings is that situational factors are important in derailing normally decent people from the moral straight and narrow.

Adolf Eichmann as a young officer in the Austrian army and on trial in 1961. Is this the face of a monster? Would you have 'followed orders' in the same way as so many Nazi officers did?

RESISTING PRESSURES TO OBEY

So far in this topic, we have focused on the power of social influence to make people obey, but it is important to remember that some participants did actually disobey the instructions given them. The panel below lists describes how and when people resist obedience to a malevolent authority.

People resist obedience to a malevolent authority:

- when they feel responsible for their own actions
- when they observe others being disobedient (conformity effects)
- by questioning the motives of those giving the orders
- when they have time to think about what they are being asked to do
- when orders are so heavy handed and restrictive that people react against their freedom being threatened
- by using high levels of moral reasoning (though this does not guarantee moral actions).

The following paragraphs look in more detail at these types of situation.

Feeling responsible

In Milgram's study, some participants disobeyed the experimenter and refused to continue giving shocks when they thought the learner was in distress. One such participant in a follow-up study, when asked why, said that she had experienced too much pain in her own life, having grown up in Nazi Germany, and did not wish to inflict pain on someone else. According to Milgram, the triggering of painful memories had 'awakened' her from her agentic state. She felt responsible for any harm produced. The arrangement whereby the learner was in a separate room was an insufficient buffer for this particular participant who could imagine all too clearly the pain he must be suffering.

Disobedient models

Exposing people to the actions of disobedient models, i.e. seeing others refuse to obey instructions from an authority figure, encourages disobedience. For example, when confederate teachers refused to continue giving shocks, only 10 per cent of participants in Milgram's experiment continued (see Table 5.2 on p. 173).

Questioning motives

Questioning the motives, legitimacy and expertise of authority figures has been proposed as a way to prevent automatic obedience. Remember that when Milgram's study was transferred to a run-down office block, the levels of obedience dropped (see Table 5.2). The lack of prestigious surroundings made it easier for participants to question the legitimacy of the experimenter. See also the study by Gamson and colleagues that follows next.

Time for discussion

In a study conducted by Gamson *et al.* (1982) to investigate under what circumstances people will refuse to go along with an unjust authority, participants were involved in making a video and signing statements that could be used in court proceedings. Participants, who worked in groups, gradually became suspicious about the true purpose of the study and refused to obey the requests of the experimenter. They realized that they were being manipulated into producing tapes that an oil company could exploit in court. However, in this study, participants had plenty of time to share information and to discuss their suspicions. They eventually began to question the legitimacy and the motives of the authority figures. One explanation given for their disobedience was the psychological process called reactance (see below).

Participants reported feeling very anxious and stressed in this study. Therefore, the research raises ethical concerns about protecting participants from psychological harm. After running 33 groups the researchers felt obliged to abandon their plans to run the 80 groups they had originally intended.

Reactance

The process of reactance may occur when we want to protect our sense of freedom. Gamson and colleagues found in their study that once someone had voiced their concern about what they were being asked to do, others quickly joined in and this was the start of rebellion against the unjust authority.

Blatant attempts to restrict people's freedom can sometimes produce a boomerang effect, causing people to do the opposite of what is being asked. It has been suggested that reactance might contribute to underage drinking and the increase in cigarette-smoking among young people, although peer pressure and conformity effects probably play a part as well.

Individual differences

- *Moral reasoning* – Kohlberg (1969), a colleague of Milgram's, found that those who used more advanced stages of moral reasoning were more able to resist the exhortations of the experimenter and so showed higher levels of disobedience. However, other research has shown that there is not an exact correspondence between moral reasoning and moral actions: "One can reason in terms of principles and not live up to those principles" (Kohlberg 1973).

- *Gender differences* – Milgram reported no differences between men and women's levels of obedience to authority. Most of the research investigating gender differences has looked at differences in levels of conformity (rather than obedience). Overall there appears to be no difference in the susceptibility of males and females to social influence.

✓ CHECK YOUR UNDERSTANDING

Check your understanding of obedience to authority by answering these questions. Try to do this from memory at first. You can check your answers by looking back through Topic 2.

1 What do you understand by the terms 'obedience to authority', 'ecological validity' and 'experimental validity'?

2 Outline two differences between conformity and obedience.

3 Describe the procedures and conclusions from Milgram's original study of obedience.

4 What effects did changing situational factors make on the levels of obedience Milgram found?

5 Outline the criticisms levelled against the experimental validity of Milgram's studies.

6 How did Milgram respond to this criticism?

7 To what extent does later research support the ecological validity of Milgram's studies?

8 Describe two psychological processes that help explain why people obey authority.

9 Outline two reasons why people sometimes resist obedience.

10 To what extent do Milgram's findings on obedience provide a credible explanation for atrocities committed in the real world?

REVISION SUMMARY

Having covered this topic, you should be able to:

✓ define 'obedience to authority', 'ecological validity' and 'experimental validity'

✓ explain why people obey

✓ outline differences between conformity and obedience

✓ describe and evaluate research carried out into obedience to authority, including issues of experimental and ecological validity

✓ describe the aims, procedures, findings, conclusions and criticisms of a key study in obedience.

✓ explain how people might resist obedience.

AS Social Psychology

GETTING YOU THINKING...

Milgram's well-known study of obedience continues to stimulate heated debate between psychologists. Consider the following statement:

«In Milgram's research on obedience, the ends justified the means.»

1 If you are working in a group, you could debate this statement with other members of your class. Divide yourselves into two groups, one supporting the statement and the other opposing it, with each group preparing arguments to present to the other group. Use this textbook as a resource. Include an opportunity for each group to ask the other group questions on their arguments.

At the end of the debate, take a vote to see how many people support the statement and how many are opposed to it. Find out whether or not anyone has changed their views as a result of the debate.

2 If you are working on your own, prepare your own summary of arguments for and against the statement. Which arguments do you find most compelling? Do the ends justify the means?

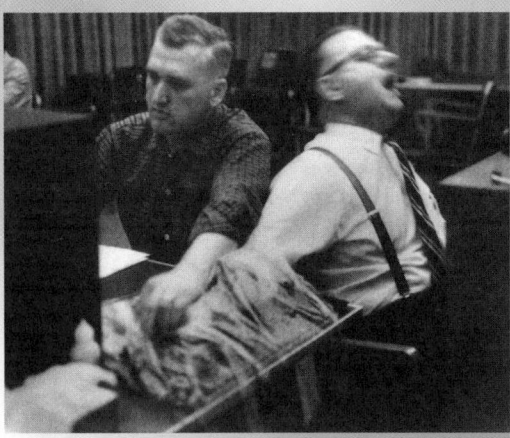

In one of the variations to Milgram's original procedure, participants were required to use physical force to administer the shocks

KEY TERMS

Deception: withholding information or misleading research participants. Deception may be trivial when only a few details of a hypothesis are withheld. On the other hand, deception is of more ethical concern when it involves deliberately providing false information that may influence a participant's willingness to take part.

Ethical issue: an ethical issue will arise in research where there is a conflict between the rights and dignity of participants and the goals and outcomes of research. For example, there may be conflict between the rights of participants to give fully informed consent and the importance of studying behaviour in as natural a setting as possible.

Ethical guidelines: the prescriptive guidance given by professional associations (such as the British Psychological Society) on how psychologists should practise (e.g. as clinical psychologists) or carry out their research. Guidelines attempt to deal with the key issues that face psychologists in their work with humans and animals. They are regularly updated by the organizations that issue them.

Informed consent: an ethical requirement that participants should have sufficient information about a research study to enable them to make an informed judgement as to whether or not to take part.

Protection of participants from psychological harm: an ethical requirement that research participants should be protected from undue risk during an investigation. Risks they should be protected from include humiliation, embarrassment and loss of dignity or self-esteem.

Ethics can be defined as a consideration of what is acceptable or right behaviour in the pursuit of a particular personal or scientific goal (Cardwell 2000). Because human participants are used in much psychological research, ethical issues are a major concern within psychology and have primarily been about the dignity and rights of participants. The need for a clear and unambiguous set of guidelines for research psychologists led to the development of the ethical principles that underlie all psychological research today. To describe something as unethical, therefore, not only describes a practice that is morally wrong, but also one that is professionally unacceptable. The guidelines drawn up by the British Psychological Society (BPS) (2000) stress that psychologists must carry out their work in a way that respects the rights and dignity of all research participants.

The work of Milgram and Zimbardo, in particular, has raised many ethical issues, including concerns about:

- the inability of participants to give fully informed consent
- the use of deception
- the adequacy of the debriefing process
- the possible harm that might be done to participants.

Informed consent

Informed consent is an ethical requirement that participants should have sufficient information about a research study to enable them to make an informed judgement about whether or not to take part. Gaining a participant's informed consent is a very important aspect of any research investigation. Without full disclosure prior to obtaining their consent, it becomes impossible for participants to make a fully informed decision about their willingness to take part. Sometimes, participants who initially give their consent to take part in a study, later wish to withdraw that consent and have their own data destroyed. They must be free to do so, even if they have previously accepted payment for their participation. Of course, we might argue that full disclosure (of procedures to be used, reasons for the research, and so on) might invalidate some psychological research. One way that psychologists have tried to deal with the problems associated with getting fully informed consent is by finding alternatives to it (see the panel below, *Alternatives to fully informed consent*).

Deception

Deception involves withholding information or misleading research participants. By deceiving research participants, we may also remove their ability to give fully informed consent to take part in the investigation we have in mind. This is not an open and shut case, however, as total honesty throughout an investigation may lead participants to modify their behaviour in some way because of the knowledge they have about the real aims of the investigation. Social psychologists face particular ethical dilemmas over the use of deception in their research. Consider the implications of complete research honesty in the investigation carried out by Milgram on obedience to authority.

There are clearly some situations where deception is inappropriate and some where it may be acceptable. There is a difference, for example, between withholding some of the research details and deliberately misleading the participants into believing the purpose of the research is more innocent than it actually is.

Alternatives to fully informed consent

There are alternatives to informed consent that may be used in situations when revealing the purpose of the investigation to participants would invalidate the study:

>> Presumptive consent

For example, we may take a large random sample from the population to be studied and introduce them to the research design, including the use of deception. If they agree that they would still have given voluntary informed consent had they known the true aims of the investigation, then we may assume that they represent the views of that population group. Another sample from that population would then be selected for use in the study without being told its true purpose.

>> Prior general consent

In this case, people who might be used as participants in a study are told that *sometimes* participants are misinformed about the true purpose of a study. Only those who agree that such a practice is acceptable would be selected as participants for this type of study. Therefore, they have given general informed consent, but they do not know whether or not the actual study they participate in uses misleading information.

There are a number of issues here:

- Some deceptions have more damaging consequences than others. The amount of discomfort or anger expressed by participants when deception is revealed is normally a good guide to this. The majority of psychologists believe that some temporary deception is justifiable provided safeguards are adopted. When participants have been asked, most report that they think minor deception is acceptable.

- Deception in investigations of a trivial nature is less acceptable than in investigations that make significant contributions to psychological knowledge. Although this may seem a case of the ends justifying the means, it should be clear that the importance of some research means that the ethical concerns spread far beyond the immediate context of the investigation. Consider how Milgram might have justified deceiving his participants.

Some psychologists have tried to deal with the ethical problems that arise when participants are deceived by using alternative strategies (see the panel on the right).

Debriefing

An important aspect of any research design, *especially when deception has taken place*, is the process of debriefing. This is an ethical requirement where participants are aware that they have taken part in an investigation. Debriefing is carried out after data have been collected. It involves providing information to participants and discussing their experience of the research. Sometimes it is seen as sufficient merely to inform participants of the true nature of the investigation, but at other times such perfunctory debriefing would be inadequate. Consider again Stanley Milgram's research into obedience. His research participants either obeyed (i.e. gave the maximum electric shock) or disobeyed and declined to give further shocks. Either way, the participants had done something they may have perceived as being wrong. (See p. 185 for an account of the debriefing measures used by Milgram.)

Debriefing is an essential part of research. What would the effect be on a participant if they took part in upsetting or challenging research and were sent home without any chance to talk through their experience?

Alternatives to using deception

>> Complete information

Provide participants with *complete information* about the purpose of the investigation. In a study by Gallo *et al.* (1973), participants were told that the study concerned the extent to which people would conform. The results for these informed participants were no different from those for deceived participants who thought they were involved in an investigation of depth perception. However, a second study by the same researchers produced opposite findings.

>> Prior general consent

Tell participants about the general nature of the study (though not the detailed hypothesis being tested) and ask them to role-play the experimental procedure as though they were naive participants. Mixon (1972) used this method in a set-up similar to that used in Milgram's obedience studies. He found that provided the role-playing participants were led to believe that the experimenter carried the responsibility for any distress caused to the 'learner', they behaved much as Milgram's participants did. However, if the role-players were led to assume responsibility, their levels of obedience were significantly lower than those found by Milgram. More often than not, studies using role-play procedures result in different findings from those where investigators have concealed their true purpose from participants.

As a general rule, debriefing aims:

- to restore participants to the same state as when they entered the investigation. Take a situation, for example, where participants arrived in a happy mood to take part in an experiment. If the experiment resulted in participants becoming upset or agitated, it is important that they receive adequate explanation and reassurance before leaving the experimental setting so that their previous happy mood is restored
- to provide an opportunity for the researcher to give participants additional information about the research so that the whole thing becomes an educational experience for them.

Debriefing does not, of course, provide a justification for any unethical aspects of the investigation. A good researcher regards participants as colleagues, not as objects to be used solely for the purposes of research.

Protection of participants

Protecting participants from psychological harm is an ethical requirement that research participants should be protected from undue risk during an investigation. Thus, the risks that an individual may be exposed to during a psychological investigation should not be greater than the risks they might already be expected to face in their everyday life. Risks they should be protected from include humiliation, embarrassment and loss of dignity or self-esteem. You might like to consider whether the risks to self-esteem encountered by Asch's, Milgram's or Zimbardo's participants were greater than those you would expect them to meet in their normal life.

The question is often asked whether the scientific knowledge gained or the moral lessons learned by social influence research have outweighed the costs and potential harm done to participants. The studies carried out by Milgram and Zimbardo have received most attention.

ACTIVITY

The case for and against the research of Asch, Zimbardo and Milgram

Reread the descriptions of three well-known studies – Asch's study of conformity which involved accomplices, Zimbardo's prison simulation study and Milgram's research on obedience. Think carefully about issues such as informed consent, the use of deception, the use of debriefing, and possible harm to participants. Make a list of all the reasons you can think of why it was important for them to carry out their studies.

Now, make a second list of any reasons why you think that these three psychologists should not have been allowed to carry out their research.

When you have done this, compare your ideas with the points made below.

ETHICS IN MILGRAM'S OBEDIENCE STUDIES

Milgram's procedures have attracted much criticism. His work, however, has also received considerable support and has been stoutly defended by Milgram himself.

The case for the prosecution

- Baumrind (1964) believed that Milgram showed insufficient respect for his participants, that there were inadequate steps taken to protect them and that his procedures had the potential for causing long-term harm. The studies, it has been claimed, involved lack of informed consent, deception and possible psychological harm to his participants.
- Voluntary informed consent and lack of deception are important principles to be adhered to if psychological research is to be ethical. Without doubt, Milgram's participants did not know the true purpose of his experiment and therefore they could not give informed consent. For the experiment to work, deception was essential. The point at issue, however, is whether or not the deception can be justified in this case. Some researchers have

advocated the use of role-playing to avoid the need for deception (see p. 183).

- The criticism most often levelled against Milgram's experiments concerns the psychological harm that might have been done to participants. This harm, it is claimed, could result from several aspects of the procedure, including the stress of carrying out the instructor's orders to continue giving the shocks to the learner. For example, Milgram (1963) recorded that his participants often trembled, stuttered and sweated. Furthermore, there were the possible long-term psychological effects of learning that they had been willing to give potentially lethal shocks to fellow human beings, and feeling stupid and 'used' when they learned the true nature of the experiment and how they had been deceived. Allied to this is the likelihood that they would not trust psychologists or people in authority in the future.

- John Darley (1992), in his thought-provoking paper, *Social organization for the production of evil*, argues that the possibility of being evil is latent in all of us and it can be made active by a conversion process. He invites us to consider the possibility that Milgram may have begun the process of converting innocent participants into evil people. To support this theory, he points to Lifton's (1986) interviews with physicians who participated in the Nazi death camps. He reported that the Nazi doctors were initially banal, ordinary individuals. What they did, however, was not ordinary, and in performing their evil acts, they changed. Their encounter with a 'demonic killing machine' began a process that morally altered them. Could the same be true of those people who gave 450-volt shocks to the learners in Milgram's experiments?

- David Mandel (1998) has argued convincingly that the misapplication of Milgram's findings has led to an oversimplified explanation of the atrocities committed during the Holocaust. According to Mandel, to attribute the horrors of the Holocaust entirely to the sort of situational factors that caused obedience in Milgram's laboratory is oversimplified and misleading (see the Expert interview on p. 174). It ignores other important factors that motivated the perpetrators of atrocities, including the chances for professional advancement and the opportunities for lucrative personal gains by plundering Jews and their corpses. Analysis of the behaviour of those who killed and tortured Jews has revealed some facts that do not accord with Milgram's laboratory findings:

  - Perpetrators did not require close supervision by their superiors.
  - They were not inhibited by seeing the pain (and even the death) of those they victimized.
  - They were often willing to continue killing even when offered the opportunity to quit.

Case for the defence

Milgram has responded to his critics. The major plank of his defence is that participants themselves do not agree with the criticisms.

- Milgram responded to Baumrind's accusation that he had not respected his participants sufficiently by drawing attention to the questionnaire distributed to participants. Eighty-four per cent replied that they were glad they had been involved. Seventy-four per cent said they had learned something of personal importance. Only 1.3 per cent reported negative

Stanley Milgram with the 'shock' generator

feelings. Furthermore, one year after the study, a university psychiatrist interviewed 40 participants and reported no evidence of emotional harm that could be attributed to participation in the study.

- After each experimental session, a careful debriefing session was held when the reasons for the deception were explained and the true purpose of the study was revealed. Milgram claimed that the debriefing process was instrumental in helping to reassure and protect the participants. Obedient participants were reassured that their behaviour was the norm in that investigation (i.e. there was nothing wrong with them). Disobedient participants were reassured that their behaviour was actually socially desirable, because they had stood up against a malevolent authority figure trying to coerce them into doing something they felt was wrong.

- As regards the criticism that people might be distrustful of psychologists or others in authority in the future, Milgram (1964) replied that he thought it would be "of the highest value if participation in the experiment could inculcate a scepticism of *this* [inhumane] kind of authority" (p. 852).

- Supporters of Milgram have rallied to his defence, agreeing with him that if the results of his studies had been different, with participants declining to continue at the first sign of learner discomfort, no one would have protested. But, of course, we cannot be sure what the results of research will be. Milgram had not intended to cause discomfort to his participants. Indeed, the survey carried out beforehand predicted that few people would give shocks after the learner began to protest. Therefore, few participants should have experienced any discomfort. Even when participants did show distress, however, Milgram did not believe it sufficient to justify stopping the experiment. After Milgram's research was published, the American Psychological Association investigated it and found it ethically acceptable. He was, in fact, awarded a prize for his outstanding contribution to social psychological research.

- Elliot Aronson (1999) has suggested that psychologists face a particularly difficult dilemma when their wider responsibility to society conflicts with their more specific responsibilities to each individual research participant. This conflict is greatest when the issues under investigation are issues of social importance. Do the potential benefits of the research outweigh the costs to the individual participants? Unfortunately this 'costs–benefits' dilemma is not easy to resolve, as it is difficult to predict either costs or benefits before a study begins. Also, participants and investigators may have very different views as to what is an acceptable cost or a worthwhile benefit.

- Darley's proposition that those who took part in Milgram's experiments may have stepped onto the slippery slope towards evil was made after Milgram's death (1984) and so Milgram did not have an opportunity to respond. He did, however, as already mentioned, arrange for a psychiatrist to interview a sample of his participants to see if any psychological damage could be detected. None was reported.

- A positive outcome of Milgram's experiments has been the increased awareness among *psychologists* since then concerning how they should treat their participants. This, in turn, has led psychologists to draft guidelines to be used for research. Remember that the sort of ethical guidelines used by research psychologists today were not formulated when Milgram carried out his research.

ETHICS IN ZIMBARDO'S PRISON SIMULATION STUDY

Harm to participants

Savin (1973) criticized Zimbardo's prison simulation study for the way it humiliated its participants (see p. 163 for more detail). After six days the simulation, originally planned to last two weeks, was ended because of the unexpectedly extreme emotional and behavioural effects. Did the knowledge gained justify the means by which it was acquired? Savin thinks not; Zimbardo thinks it did. He reports that follow-ups over many years revealed no lasting negative effects; that student participants were healthy and able to bounce back from their 'prison' experience; that they had learned the important lesson that even the most intelligent and well-intentioned among us can be overwhelmed by social influences.

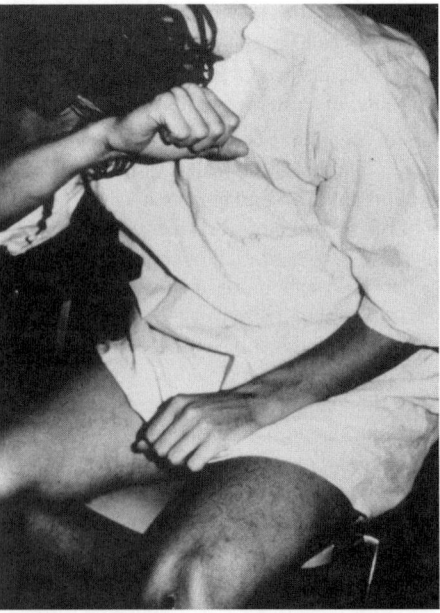

Did the knowledge gained from Zimbardo's prison simulation justify the emotional distress caused to participants during it?

Need for independent surveillance

In recent years, Zimbardo has acknowledged that he should not have acted as 'prison superintendent' as well as principal researcher, because he became trapped by the day-to-day business of his superintendent role, rather as the 'guards' and 'prisoners' became trapped in their roles. However, he argues that instead of banning research of this type, what is needed is better research – that is, where experiments are ethically sensitive, there should be an independent monitor and more vigilant surveillance by the institution concerned. In this way, he claims, participants could be protected while valuable information was acquired.

Deceiving participants

Some critics of both Milgram and Zimbardo have suggested that deceiving participants is really not necessary in research and is particularly unethical when it might leave them feeling foolish or humiliated. They have proposed that other more ethically acceptable methods could be used, such as asking people to imagine how they or others would behave in certain situations. However, you may recall that Milgram did this by asking people how many participants they thought would go to 450 volts on his shock generator. Their predictions grossly underestimated the levels of obedience found by Milgram in his actual experiments. Zimbardo is scathing about the use of 'as if' procedures to replace simulations or experiments. Read what he has said in the panel on p. 187.

Zimbardo: Ethics and research in social psychology

In an interview with Mark McDermott (1993), Zimbardo said:

« One of the subtle dangers arising out of the increase in concern for the ethics of experiments is it gives social psychologists an easy out. To do behavioural experiments is very difficult. Its time consuming, it's labour intensive and you can replace it with an 'as if' paper-and-pencil, 30-minute self-report. The question arises, 'is that the same thing?' If, in fact, you could discover the same things about human nature from asking people to imagine how they would behave in a situation instead of observing how they do, it clearly doesn't make sense to do the behavioural simulation. I think what you get from the Milgram study and my Prison study is very different from self-report-based ones. Indeed, Milgram asked 40 psychiatrists how people would behave in his conformity experiment. To a person they all got it wrong: they predicted that fewer than one per cent of the subjects would go all the way in shocking the innocent victim, when in actuality two-thirds blindly obeyed the unjust authority figure. There are situations you cannot imagine what it would be like until you are in them. So, if we are going to have a psychology of 'as if', of 'imagine this were the situation and how would you predict you would behave?', I think you are missing out on some of the powerful yet subtle dynamics of situational control ...»

« The contribution social psychologists make is [in] understanding what people will or won't do in certain situations. Typically, even if you describe the situation, people will underestimate its power. There is no way until you are in it, that you begin to feel and become entrapped in the power of the situation.»

ETHICAL GUIDELINES

As well using strategies such as role play and prior general consent (see p. 183), psychologists have also attempted to deal with ethical concerns by devising sets of ethical guidelines.

Ethical guidelines (the guidance given by professional associations, such as the British Psychological Society, on how psychologists should carry out their research) are necessary to clarify the conditions under which psychological research is acceptable. Nowadays, psychology departments in universities, colleges and hospitals have ethical committees that approve or reject proposed research. The decisions of these committees are strongly influenced by the criteria laid down in the ethical guidelines published by bodies such as the British Psychological Society (BPS). A summary of the BPS guidelines is shown in Table 5.3. This provides an outline of the guiding principles or 'rules' by which research psychologists operate.

Unfortunately, the mere existence of ethical guidelines does not guarantee ethical practice. Ethical codes have to be implemented conscientiously for this to happen. Furthermore, our views of what constitutes ethical conduct are not fixed for all time and so ethical guidelines require updating from time to time.

(see p. 183)

ACTIVITY

Your views on the BPS ethical guidelines

After you have read Table 5.3, *A summary of the ethical guidelines for research with human participants* (BPS 2000), discuss the following questions with others in your class.

1 To what extent do you think that the BPS Ethical Guidelines adequately protect the interests of those who choose to participate in psychological research?

2 These guidelines were published in 2000 and they were a revision of those published in 1993. Why do you think that ethical guidelines need to be revised at fairly regular intervals?

3 Should all psychologists who undertake research be compelled to follow a strict ethical code? If so, how could this be done? What do you think should happen to anyone who does not follow the code?

Table 5.3 >> A summary of the ethical guidelines for research with human participants (BPS 2000)

1 Introduction

Psychologists owe a debt to all those who take a part in their studies and so all participants should be treated with consideration and respect. This is reflected in the change from the term 'subjects' to 'participants'. Good psychological research is possible only if there is mutual respect and confidence between investigators and participants. Although investigators are potentially interested in all aspects of human behaviour, for ethical reasons some areas of human experience and behaviour may be beyond the reach of psychological investigation. Ethical guidelines are necessary to clarify the conditions under which psychological research is acceptable.

2 General

In all circumstances investigators must consider the ethical implications and psychological consequences for the participants in their research. The essential principle is that the investigation should be considered from the standpoint of all participants; foreseeable threats to their psychological wellbeing, health, values or dignity should be eliminated. Where investigations involve individuals of different ages, gender and social background, the investigators may not have sufficient knowledge of the implications of any investigation for the participants. The best judges of whether an investigation will cause offence may be members of the population from which the participants in the research are to be drawn.

3 Consent

Whenever possible, investigators should inform all participants of the objectives of the investigation and of all aspects of the research or intervention that might reasonably be expected to influence their willingness to participate. Research with children or with other vulnerable participants requires special safeguarding procedures. Where possible, the real consent of children and of adults with impairments in understanding should be obtained. In addition, where research involves people who are under 16 years of age, consent should be obtained from parents or from those *in loco parentis*. If this is not possible, approval must be obtained from an Ethics Committee. Investigators are often in a position of authority or influence over participants who may be their students, employees or clients. This relationship must not be allowed to pressurize the participants to take part in, or remain in, an investigation. The payment of participants must not be used to induce them to risk harm beyond that which they risk without payment in their normal lifestyle.

4 Deception

Withholding information or misleading participants is unacceptable if the participants are typically likely to show unease once debriefed. Where this is in any doubt, appropriate consultation must precede the investigation. Intentional deception of the participants over the purpose and general nature of the investigation should be avoided whenever possible, although it may be impossible to study some psychological processes without withholding information about the true object of the study or without deliberately misleading participants.

5 Debriefing

In studies where the participants are aware that they have taken part in an investigation, when the data have been collected, the investigator should provide the participants with any necessary information to complete their understanding of the nature of the research. The investigator should discuss with the participants their experience of the research in order to monitor any unforeseen negative effects or misconceptions. Debriefing does not provide justification for unethical aspects of an investigation.

6 Withdrawal from the investigation

At the outset, investigators should make plain to participants their right to withdraw from the research at any time, irrespective of whether or not payment or other inducement has been offered. In the light of experience of the investigation or as a result of debriefing, the participant has the right to withdraw retrospectively any consent given, and to require that their own data, including recordings, be destroyed.

7 Confidentiality

Except in circumstances specified by the law, information obtained about a participant during an investigation is confidential unless otherwise agreed in advance. Participants in psychological research have a right to expect that information they provide will be treated confidentially and, if published, will not be identifiable as theirs. Where confidentiality or anonymity cannot be guaranteed, the participant must be warned of this in advance of agreeing to participate.

8 Protection of participants

Investigators have a primary responsibility to protect participants from physical and mental harm during the investigation. Normally the risk of harm must be no greater than in ordinary life. Where research may involve behaviour or experiences that participants may regard as personal and private, the participants must be protected from stress by all appropriate measures, including the assurance that answers to personal questions need not be given. In research involving children, great caution should be used when discussing results with parents, teachers or those in *loco parentis*, since evaluative statements may carry unintended weight.

9 Observational research

Studies based upon observation must respect the privacy and psychological wellbeing of the individuals studied. Unless those being observed give their consent to being observed, observational research is only acceptable in situations where those observed would expect to be observed by strangers. Additionally, particular account should be taken of local cultural values and of the possibility of intruding upon the privacy of individuals who, even while in a normally public space, may believe they are unobserved.

continued on next page

Table 5.3 >> Summary of ethical guidelines continued

10 Giving advice

During research, an investigator may obtain evidence of psychological or physical problems of which a participant is apparently unaware. In such a case the investigator has a responsibility to inform the participant if the investigator believes that by not doing so the participant's future wellbeing may be endangered. If the issue is serious and the investigator is not qualified to offer assistance, the appropriate source of professional advice should be recommended.

11 Colleagues

Investigators share responsibility for the ethical treatment of research participants with their collaborators, assistants, students and employees. A psychologist who believes that another psychologist or investigator may be conducting research that is not in accordance with the principles above should encourage that investigator to re-evaluate the research.

Source: British Psychological Society (2000)

Evaluation of ethical guidelines

- *Only guidelines* – Guidelines are simply guidance (not hard-and-fast rules) and they are sometimes accused of being vague and difficult to apply.

- *Guidelines across cultures* – Different guidelines exist in different countries, e.g. the guidelines of the American Psychological Association (APA) are more detailed than those drawn up by the BPS. Most codes concentrate on the protection of participants from physical and psychological harm and on the confidentiality of the data they provide. On other matters, however, there is more variation between codes. In Holland, the guidelines deal with general advice to investigators, while the British guidelines are more concerned with the details of research procedures. In Canada, the guidelines advise going beyond the immediate concerns of the participants to analysing any long-term risks or benefits to both groups and individuals that might be affected. Therefore, we see that there is no universal set of guidelines applied to all psychologists worldwide.

- *Limited scope of BPS guidelines* – Condor (1991) has criticized the BPS guidelines for limiting its concerns to the relationship between the investigator and the participant and for ignoring the role of psychologists in society at large. Others accuse psychologists of perpetuating negative stereotypes (e.g. of elderly people) in books and research papers, and believe that ethical issues in psychology go beyond the traditional issues of confidentiality, deception or privacy (Gale 1995).

- *Role of ethical committees* – Most universities and other institutions that carry out research have ethical committees to scrutinize research proposals to ensure the rights of participants are being respected. The effectiveness of ethical guidelines and codes of conduct depends upon the rigour of these ethical committees. It is important that such committees include non-psychologists within their membership to represent the lay person's point of view.

- *Enforcing the guidelines* – Enforcement of ethical standards depends upon psychologists being willing to punish those who contravene the guidelines. The BPS and the APA impose penalties on their members if they infringe the ethical codes. However, every year A-level psychology students carry out investigations and these are not always supervised by BPS members or even psychologists. Therefore, there is potential for ethical guidelines to be breached. (Examination bodies, of course, provide guidance for conducting psychology practicals.)

- *Revising the guidelines* – Ethical codes are revised regularly to keep pace with social change. This is essential as society's views about morality change over time. The interests of psychologists also change, so that new ethical issues may arise (e.g. when to maintain confidentiality in research in the area of child abuse). The need for such revisions reminds us that ethical codes are not entirely dependent upon universal, unchanging truths.

ACTIVITY

Eliot Aronson on ethical issues

In the interview with Elliott Aronson on p. 190, you will learn the views of one of psychology's most distinguished scholars concerning the ethics of social influence research. Aronson focuses on the ethical dimension of these studies, but also makes the point that we have learned a great deal from such research.

Justifying individual studies in terms of a cost–benefit analysis is not always a straightforward task. Look again at the key studies you have covered in this unit.

- What were the 'costs' to the participants in each study, and what were the 'benefits' of the research?
- Did the benefits justify the costs?
- What other precautions might have been used to protect the participants in each study?

Ethical *dilemmas*

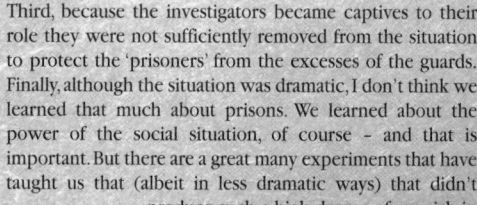

Elliot Aronson is Distinguished Visiting Professor at Stanford University. He graduated from Brandeis University in 1954, where he was influenced by Abraham Maslow. He has published 18 books (including the Handbook of Social Psychology *and* The Social Animal*) and more than 130 research articles. He is the only person in the 109-year history of the American Psychological Association to have been awarded all three of its highest academic prizes: For Distinguished Teaching (1980), for Distinguished Writing (1973) and for Distinguished Research Contributions (1999). In 2002 he was named as one of the 100 most eminent psychologists of the twentieth century.*

Q Does the importance of social influence research justify the methods used in its investigation?

A First, let me state that I believe that much (but certainly not all!) of the research on social influence is extremely important.

Second, I believe that we human beings are not fragile. Rather, we are extraordinarily resilient organisms. By that, I mean we can absorb an enormous amount of emotional discomfort without long-lasting negative effects.

Putting these two beliefs together, leads me to the following conclusions:

1 If the research is important, and well designed, and

2 If it is the best and perhaps the only way to get a peek at the phenomenon, and

3 If the degree of discomfort imposed by the experimenter on the participant is not extreme and is of short duration, then

4 I would conclude that the research is justified.

Elliot Aronson

For example, in Solomon Asch's experiment on conformity, we learned something both new and important: ordinary people will conform to implicit group pressure. I believe the research was justified because the question was an important one, the experiments were well designed, the results were clear – *and* the participants suffered a minimum of discomfort. Yes, it is discomforting to be in the minority, to have the data from your visual sense disconfirmed by the behaviour of others. But as discomforts go, this is minor. To spend an hour wondering about where you stand *vis-à-vis* the group is not an earth-shattering experience. Moreover, in the real world, we frequently find ourselves in disagreement with others, and it is no big deal.

At the other extreme, let us look at Philip Zimbardo's research on a simulated prison. I like to discuss this research in class because it is highly dramatic. But I don't think the experiment was justified. First, the discomfort was enormous. Second, the discomfort went on for six full days.

Third, because the investigators became captives to their role they were not sufficiently removed from the situation to protect the 'prisoners' from the excesses of the guards. Finally, although the situation was dramatic, I don't think we learned that much about prisons. We learned about the power of the social situation, of course – and that is important. But there are a great many experiments that have taught us that (albeit in less dramatic ways) that didn't produce such a high degree of anguish in the participants.

Q What about Stanley Milgram's experiment on obedience?

Here I am not quite sure. I think the research is extremely important. We learned for the first time that ordinary people (not just Nazis!) will go to great lengths in blind obedience to authority.

I also believe that there is no better way to get at the idea of obedience to authority than by doing it experimentally in a way similar to what Milgram did. Whenever I outline the situation to students in my class and ask them how they think they would have behaved, only 1 per cent think they might have gone all the way – while, as you know, in Milgram's experiments, about two out of three go all the way.

Thus, for me, the key issue is: "Did Milgram cross the line and make his participants too uncomfortable?" We know they sweated, strained and stuttered. We know many felt awful afterwards about what they had done. Yet, we also know that almost all of them were glad they participated. They felt they learned something extremely important. None suffered emotional disturbances.

Q Did Milgram have the right to provide them with this learning experience without their informed consent?

I think not. But I am glad he did! As a soft humanist, I think he went too far. But as a scientist interested in human behaviour, I am pleased that we have learned what we now know about obedience. In the balance, my belief in the resiliency of human beings tips the balance. No one was damaged by Milgram's experiment. I'm glad he did it – but I don't want anyone going quite that far again.

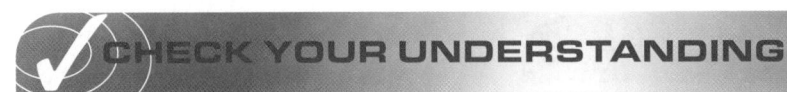

Check your understanding of ethical issues in psychological research by answering these questions. Try to do this from memory at first. You can check your answers by looking back through Topic 3.

1 What do you understand by the terms: 'ethical issues', 'ethical guidelines', 'deception', 'informed consent' and 'protection of participants from psychological harm'.

2 Describe one alternative procedure that is used when it is not possible to gain fully informed consent.

3 Give two reasons why it is unwise to deceive participants.

4 Describe a procedure used to avoid deceiving participants.

5 What does the term 'debriefing' mean? Give its main aim.

6 The BPS guidelines state that participants should be protected from undue risk. What is meant by 'undue risk'?

7 Outline and evaluate two ethical criticisms made of Milgram's procedures.

8 Outline Milgram's response to one of these criticisms.

9 Are the studies of Milgram and Zimbardo justified in terms of the ethical issues that they raise?

10 To what extent have psychologists been successful in resolving the ethical issues raised by social influence research?

REVISION SUMMARY

Having covered this topic, you should be able to:

✓ define the following terms: 'ethical issue', 'ethical guidelines', 'deception', 'informed consent' and 'protection of participants from psychological harm'

✓ describe the key ethical issues associated with research on social influence

✓ discuss whether social influence research is justified in terms of the ethical issues that it raises

✓ outline and evaluate ways in which psychologists have dealt with ethical issues.

Topic 1: Conformity and minority influence

■ **Conformity** is the process of yielding to **majority influence**.

■ **Compliance**, **identification** and **internalization** are types of conformity.

■ People yield to majority influence because they wish to be liked (**normative social influence**) and because they wish to be right (**informational social influence**).

■ Research into majority influence has found that there is strong group pressure to conform, especially if the majority is **unanimous** (**Asch**).

■ **Zimbardo's prison simulation study** has shown that conformity to social roles plays an important part in shaping behaviour.

■ More recent research has underlined the importance of **historical** and **cultural factors** in levels of conformity.

■ **Minority influence** is a form of social influence where a persuasive minority successfully exerts pressure to change the attitudes, beliefs or behaviours of the majority. Those who yield to minority influence undergo a process of conversion.

■ The **dissociation model** explains why minority influence may work slowly. Time is needed for minority ideas to become detached from their source before they are adopted openly by the majority.

■ Research into minority influence has shown that minorities must behave **consistently** if they are to be influential (**Moscovici**).

■ The **behavioural style** required for a minority to be influential is as follows:
   – consistent but not rigid
   – principled and willing to make sacrifices
   – similar in age and social standing to the majority
   – espousing views in line with current social trends.

■ Some psychologists believe that majority and minority influences involve **different psychological processes**: majorities use normative processes to achieve compliance; minorities use informational processes to achieve conversion. Majority influence may produce quick effects, but minority influence may have more long-lasting effects.

Topic 2: Obedience

■ **Obedience** is a type of social influence where somebody acts in response to a direct order from an authority figure.

■ **Explanations** offered for obedience include:
   – gradual commitment to a legitimate authority
   – an agentic shift whereby individuals surrender autonomy and see themselves as agents of the person giving orders
   – the effect of buffers to protect individuals from the consequences of their actions
   – passivity that arises from a desire to avoid confrontation or upset
   – personality factors such as authoritarianism and psychopathy.

■ **Differences** between obedience and conformity include:
   – different types of social pressure (orders in the case of obedience and social norms in the case of conformity)
   – different outcomes: public compliance (obedience) and private change (conformity where it takes the form of internalization)
   – conscious versus unconscious effect: we know when we have obeyed but we may not be aware of having conformed.

- **Milgram's** research on obedience found that when people occupy a subordinate position in a dominance hierarchy, they are inclined to blind obedience and that manipulating situational factors can influence obedience levels.

- Some psychologists have challenged the experimental (internal) validity of Milgram's studies but he has refuted any notion that his participants were merely role-playing.

- There is evidence from later studies (e.g. **Hofling and colleagues**) to support the ecological validity of Milgram's research.

- **Explanations** for resisting obedience include:
  - feeling responsible for one's own actions
  - observing others being disobedient
  - questioning the motives of those giving orders
  - having time to think about what is being requested
  - reacting against too blatant attempts to restrict one's freedom
  - high levels of moral reasoning.

Topic 3: Ethical issues in psychological research

- **Ethical issues** arise in research when there is a conflict between the rights and dignity of participants and the goals and outcome of research.

- Key ethical issues associated with social influence research include:
  - **informed consent**: an ethical requirement that participants should have sufficient information about a research study to enable them to make an informed judgement about whether or not to take part
  - **deception**: withholding information or misleading research participants
  - **protection of participants from psychological harm:** research participants should be protected from undue risk during an investigation.

- Is social influence research justified? Critics of Milgram and Zimbardo have accused them of deceiving and subjecting their participants to psychological harm. Others have defended their actions by referring to the importance of the findings and the extensive debriefing and follow-up procedures.

- Ways of dealing with ethical issues include:
  - gaining **prior general consent** or **presumptive consent** as ways of replacing the need for fully informed consent in situations where this is problematic
  - development of **ethical guidelines** by professional bodies to provide guidance on how psychologists should carry out research ethically.

- Guidelines, however, only offer guidance, and rigorous ethical committees are required to implement them. Society's views about what is moral continue to evolve and so ethical guidelines need to be updated periodically.

Answering exam questions on Social influence

For sample examination questions and answers on Social influence, together with examiners' comments on the answers, see pp. 259–61.

6
UNIT

QUANTITATIVE & QUALITATIVE
Research Methods

PREVIEW

After you have read this unit, you should be able to:

>> describe three main types of experiment – laboratory experiments, field experiments and natural experiments – and discuss the main advantages and weaknesses of each

>> describe investigations using correlational analysis, and discuss the advantages and weaknesses of this research method

>> describe three non-experimental research methods – naturalistic observation, questionnaire surveys and interviews – and discuss the advantages and weaknesses of each

>> discuss the use of ethical guidelines in psychology.

INTRODUCTION

Psychologists use a wide range of research methods and techniques that allow them to gather and make sense of the data they produce. The data can be either quantitative or qualitative. Quantitative data have a numerical basis (e.g. time in seconds, stress ratings), whereas qualitative data are non-numerical (e.g. verbal reports of how research participants feel about something).

This unit is divided into two topics. Topic 1 focuses on the different types of experimental research, while the second topic examines the nature of non-experimental research. For many years the experiment, and in particular the laboratory experiment, has been the main research method used by psychologists. However, increasing dissatisfaction with the lack of realism of the findings from experimental research carried out in laboratories and their lack of relevance to everyday life has led psychologists to use alternative methods. This has resulted in an increase in the use of non-experimental methods producing qualitative data. It is now recognized that both experimental and non-experimental research methods have their place and can be considered to complement to each other.

As we examine the different research methods, we will consider the major ethical issues associated with each one. You will already appreciate the importance of ethical questions, for example, from reading about Milgram's studies of obedience and Zimbardo's prison simulation study in Unit 5, *Social influence*). These are two of the most hotly debated studies in psychology, because people disagree about whether they should have been carried out.

This unit discusses only some of the research methods that you are likely to meet as an AS-level student. Although research methods can be divided into specific categories, these methods can merge into each other. For example, the boundary between experimental and non-experimental research is far from clear cut. What really matters is that the most appropriate research method is used to investigate a particular problem or research question.

Graham Davies

Topic 1 >> Experimental investigations in psychology

GETTING YOU THINKING...

The range of research methods psychologists use to study aspects of human and non-human behaviour include experiments, observations, questionnaire surveys and interviews. Which research method would you use to investigate each of the areas listed below? Note down the reasons for your choice:

1 the effects of day care on children's social and cognitive development

2 the effect of learning multiplication tables by heart on children's ability to solve mathematical problems

3 children's views on pocket money

4 the effect of playing violent computer games on levels of aggression in adolescents

5 children's behaviour in school playgrounds.

What problems might arise when using your chosen research method? How could you overcome these problems?

KEY TERMS

Quantitative data: information collected in the course of a research study that is in a quantified (numerical) form (e.g. speed of response in milliseconds).

Qualitative data: information collected in the course of a research study that is in non-numerical, narrative form, such as the transcript of what was said during a series of interviews.

Experiment: an investigative technique involving changes to one variable (the independent variable) in order to see its effect on another variable (the dependent variable), and to establish cause-and-effect relationships.

Laboratory experiment: an experiment carried out in a laboratory, allowing the researcher to exert a high level of control over the independent variable, and to eliminate or control for confounding variables.

Field experiment: an experiment carried out in a real-world setting (such as a classroom) rather than the more artificial setting of the laboratory.

Natural experiment: a type of quasi-experiment where the allocation of participants to the different experimental conditions is outside the control of the researcher, but rather reflects naturally occurring differences in the independent variable (e.g. two schools using different methods to teach reading).

Ethical guidelines: prescriptive guidance given by professional associations (e.g. the British Psychological Society) on how psychologists should practise or carry out their research.

When carrying out an experiment, a researcher intervenes directly in the situation being investigated. The experimental method is regarded as being the most powerful research method used by psychologists because of its potential to investigate the causes of events, and thus to identify cause-and-effect relationships. A true experiment has three key features:

- The researcher manipulates an independent variable (IV) in order to investigate whether there is a change in a second variable, known as the dependent variable (DV).
- All other variables, which might influence the results, are either held constant or are eliminated.
- Participants are allocated to the experimental conditions randomly.

A variable is simply anything that can change (or vary). Examples include weight, response times, reading scores and IQ scores. In the simplest experiments, the researcher deliberately changes the IV, in order to see whether this manipulation affects the DV. For example, consider an experiment set up to investigate which of two methods is more successful at teaching young children to read. The IV would be the teaching method that the participants (i.e. the children taking part in the study) were exposed to. The DV would be some measure of their reading ability (for example, scores derived from a standard test of reading ability).

To be sure that it is the IV that has produced any change in the DV, the researcher must ensure that all other variables are held constant. If they cannot be held constant, then the effect of these variables needs to be eliminated. These unwanted variables are known as confounding variables, and might include the following:

- differences in the instructions given by an experimenter or in the stimulus materials being used – this can be overcome by standardizing the instructions and materials for all participants in the experiment
- differences between participants, e.g. in their age – this can be eliminated by using a single age group, or can be held constant by ensuring that the age structure of each of the groups taking part in the experiment is similar).

The logic of the true experiment is that, if all variables other than the IV have either been controlled or eliminated successfully, then any change that is produced in the DV must be the result of manipulating the IV.

As a principle of good experimental design, researchers must either allocate participants randomly to groups (i.e. give all those taking part an equal chance of being selected for each group) or permit all participants to experience each condition.

Sometimes, however, it is not possible to meet all three of the requirements for a true experiment. The term 'quasi-experiment' (the prefix 'quasi' means 'resembling but not really the same as') is used to describe an experiment where the investigator lacks complete control over the IV and/or the allocation of participants to groups. For example, if a psychologist was interested in studying the effectiveness of an anti-truancy strategy in schools, it probably would not be possible to introduce the strategy for some pupils but not for others. An alternative approach would be to undertake a quasi-experiment by comparing the truancy levels in schools where the strategy has been applied with the truancy levels in similar schools where it has not. This is a quasi-experiment because the researcher has no control over the allocation of participants to the two conditions – exposure to the anti-truancy strategy or no exposure to the anti-truancy strategy.

Evaluation of the experimental method

- By holding all variables constant between groups except for the IV, an experimenter may be able to establish a cause-and-effect relationship between the IV and the DV. No other research method can do this directly.

- The use of experiments means that researchers do not have to wait for natural events to reproduce the appropriate scenario needed to investigate a particular issue. It allows psychologists to study behaviour that rarely occurs or that cannot easily be studied in another way, such as bystander attitudes to an emergency. Also, it allows the researcher to select when, and possibly where, to undertake an experiment.

- An experiment generates quantitative data (numerical measures of the DV) which can be analysed using inferential statistical tests. These statistical tests (which are beyond the specification requirement for AS) allow the researcher to state how likely the results are to have occurred by chance, rather than by manipulating the IV.

- Once the data have been obtained and analysed, it is possible to generalize the findings from experimental research to the rest of the population from which the sample of participants has been drawn, provided that a representative sample of participants was selected to take part in the original study. However, the participants in many experimental investigations reflect an over-representation of males and of specific cultures, and have often been volunteers drawn from university campuses. You may, therefore, question how far it is reasonable to generalize the results of such experimental studies to groups of people beyond those represented by those taking part.

ACTIVITY

Identifying independent and dependent variables

After reading the brief descriptions below of three memory studies, identify the IV and DV in each one. The answers to this activity can be found on p. 211.

1 Baddeley (1986) investigated the effects of acoustic similarity on serial memory recall performance by presenting participants with a list of five short words that sound alike (e.g. *man, mat, map, can, cap*) and five short words that do not sound alike (e.g. *pen, day, few, cow, pit*).

2 Tyler *et al.* (1979) gave participants two sets of anagrams to solve: one set was easy (e.g. *doctro*), while the other was more difficult (*cdrtoo*). They were then unexpectedly asked to recall as many of the words as possible. The aim was to test the hypothesis that it is the amount of processing effort, rather than depth of processing, that affects memory retention.

3 Psychologists have been interested in the effects of the learning environment on memory recall. Smith (1979) gave participants a list of 80 words to learn while sitting in a distinctive basement room. The following day he tested some of the participants in the same basement room, others in a fifth-floor room with very different décor, and a third group in another upstairs room where participants were instructed to imagine themselves back in the basement room.

LABORATORY EXPERIMENTS

Laboratory experiments provide psychologists with the highest level of control over variables and are widely used in psychology. The psychology laboratory may be the only place where some sophisticated technical equipment can be used and accurate measurements made. Researchers interested in memory and cognitive processes often carry out laboratory experiments. For example, Stroop (1935) carried out a well-known series of laboratory experiments. He studied how colour-name words have an interfering effect on the time taken to name the ink colours of non-matching colours. For example, naming the ink colour of the word 'blue' written in green ink takes longer than it does for the same word written in blue ink. This effect has become known as the Stroop effect (see the activity below).

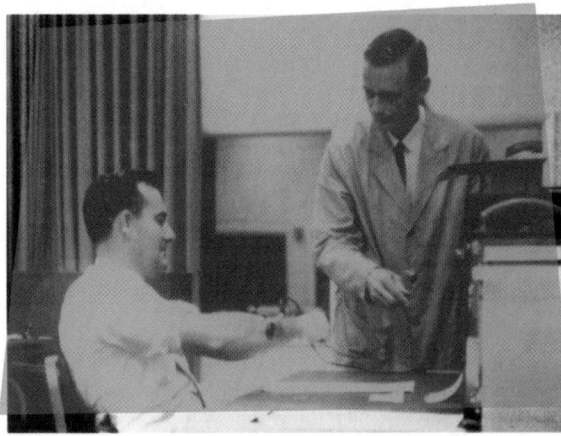

A participant is briefed in Milgram's research into obedience (see p. 171) – a classic laboratory experiment

ACTIVITY

The Stroop effect

In one experiment, Stroop (1935) selected five colour names – red, blue, green, brown and purple. For the experimental group, each word was printed several times in a grid, but never in the colour it named; instead, it appeared an equal number of times in each of the other four colours. A second sheet was produced of the same words in reverse order.

The control group experienced the same arrangement of ink colours, but this time each ink colour was represented by a coloured block. The researcher manipulated whether the stimulus sheets consisted of words in ink colours that conflicted with the colour names or were in the form of colour blocks.

The times taken to name the ink colours for each condition were compared. On average, it took participants 47 seconds longer to name the ink colours of a stimulus sheet in the experimental condition than in the control condition.

1 What is the IV in this experiment?

2 What is the DV?

3 How many conditions are there in this experiment?

4 Are the data collected quantitative or qualitative?

5 What cause-and-effect relationship does this study investigate?

Compare your answers with those on p. 211.

Advantages of laboratory experiments

- *Replicability of procedures* – A laboratory experiment that is well carried out and clearly reported can easily be repeated (replicated) by other researchers to see if they obtain similar results. If this happens and the findings are similar, then confidence is increased in the results. Without this ability to replicate studies fairly easily in a laboratory setting, researchers would have to wait indefinitely for the precise set of circumstances required for a particular experiment to recur.

- *Control over variables* – It is easier to control potential confounding variables in the laboratory than in any other setting or with any other research method, so high levels of precision can be achieved. If all variables other than the IV are controlled successfully or eliminated, then cause and effect can be established.

Weaknesses

- *Loss of validity* – By establishing high levels of control, and narrowly defining IVs and DVs, an experimental situation can become artificial and recognizably different from real-life situations. Laboratory studies were originally designed for use in the natural sciences such as chemistry and physics, where matter reacts in exactly the same way to external events under a given set of conditions. Human behaviour is far more complex and is affected by internal factors such as awareness, emotions and motives relating to human consciousness, as well as external variables that can be manipulated by the researcher.

Ecological validity is concerned with the extent to which results may be generalized to settings other than the one in which the research took place, such as those outside the laboratory. For example, memory experiments have often been conducted using word lists, which are rarely learned in everyday life. However, in some research the artificiality of the laboratory situation may not really matter, such as when carrying out research on newborn infants or on auditory perception. Ecological validity is discussed more fully in Unit 7 (see p. 227).

- *Demand characteristics* – These occur when participants try to make sense of the research situation they find themselves in and act accordingly (Orne 1962). These can seriously threaten the validity of an experiment. The demands placed on participants in a laboratory situation are not helped by the experimenter sticking rigidly to a standardized procedure and acting in an unemotional way, which is necessary if confounding variables are to be avoided. Participants may respond to specific cues made by an investigator, such as differences in the tone of voice used or non-verbal signs of encouragement. Participants may also try to behave in a way that they believe will be helpful to the researcher. Or, if feeling awkward or irritated by what is happening, they may set out deliberately to confound the results.

Other potential problems include evaluation apprehension, where participants demonstrate concern over what an experimenter might find out about them, or social desirability effects, where participants change their everyday behaviour so that they may be perceived more favourably by others.

Ethical issues

- *Consent* – In all psychological research, the fully informed consent of all the participants must be obtained. However, once in the laboratory setting, participants might become so overawed by the environment that they feel unable to withdraw from the procedure even if they wanted to. So, it is vital to abide by the guidelines about participants' right to withdraw from an investigation (see p. 188).

- *Deception* – Some experiments undertaken by social psychologists involve deception; in these situations, it is important to debrief participants about the true nature of the study and to obtain their consent to use the data collected (for example, turn to pp. 184–6 to remind yourself of the ethical issues raised by Milgram's research on obedience).

- *Use of animals* – Animals are often used in laboratory experiments as this offers greater opportunities for experimental control in research procedures, compared to research with humans. For example, Harlow and Harlow's deprivation studies with rhesus monkeys (see p. 53), could not have been carried out on humans. Since animals are not able to consent to their involvement in research, they must not be subjected to unnecessary suffering.

AS Research Methods

FIELD EXPERIMENTS

Field experiments are experimental investigations carried out in the natural environment of those being studied, e.g. in homes, schools or on the street. These experiments attempt to improve the realism of the research. As with the laboratory experiment, an IV is still deliberately manipulated by the researcher to produce a change in a DV. Therefore, much of what has been written in the previous section about the laboratory experiment also applies to the field experiment, so here we focus on the key differences.

The field experiment is used in situations where it is considered particularly important for research to take account of the natural environment. For example, the method is used widely when studying non-human animals.

Field experiments are often more costly to undertake than those carried out in laboratory settings and may also take longer to complete. In addition, it may be more difficult to use sophisticated technical equipment outside a laboratory.

Advantages of field experiments

- *Improved ecological validity* – By avoiding the artificiality of the laboratory environment, the field experiment helps to eliminate the common criticism made of the laboratory experiment that it may be difficult to generalize the findings to real-life situations.
- *Reduction of demand characteristics* – Participants may be unaware that they are taking part in a research study, and so the influence of demand characteristics may be minimized.

Weaknesses

- *Establishing controls* – It is difficult to establish high levels of control in a field experiment, not only over IVs and in measuring DVs, but also over any potentially confounding variables. For example, non-participants may intrude through conversation

ACTIVITY

Field experiments

Read the accounts of the two field experiments below. In each case, why do you think that a field experiment was used in preference to a laboratory experiment?

Two examples of field experiments

Mating success of long-tailed widow birds (Andersson 1982)

In this experiment, Andersson demonstrated the importance of tail length to the mating success of the long-tailed widow bird, a species in which the males have very long tails (see photo right). The IV was tail length – some birds had their tails lengthened, others had them shortened and some had normal-length tails as controls. Mating success was measured by the average (mean) number of nests per male (this was the DV). Those with the longest tails were the most successful in terms of their mating success, whilst those with the shortest tails had the least mating success.

Bonding between mother and infant (Klaus and Kennell 1976)

In this field experiment, the IV was the random allocation of mothers to one of two groups, following the birth of their babies. In one group, mothers were allowed extra contact with their babies immediately following the birth. In the second group, the babies were separated from their mothers until the time for their first feed (the standard hospital procedure). The DV was how the mothers subsequently reacted towards their babies. Amongst the findings from this research study were that mothers in the group who had had extra contact reacted more positively to their babies in a number of ways (e.g. holding their babies closer and establishing eye contact more often) compared with mothers in the other group.

or simply by being present where the experiment is taking place. Because of the increased difficulty of establishing controls, it may be more difficult to replicate precisely a field experiment than a laboratory experiment.

■ *Generalizing to other situations* – Although realism is high in a field experiment, the results cannot be generalized to other real-life situations that differ from the one in which the field experiment took place.

Ethical issues

■ *Consent* – Ethical issues relating to informed consent and participants' right to withdraw are similar to those for laboratory experiments.

What steps can researchers in field experiments take to minimize disruption to the natural environment?

■ *Confidentiality* – Since field experiments are undertaken in real-world settings, such as schools and hospitals, the identity of any organizations and participants involved must be protected. Simply removing the names of organizations or people, and substituting descriptive characteristics (such as 'a large teaching hospital in Nottingham', or by referring to the age, gender of participants) may not be good enough to guarantee anonymity. Where confidentiality or anonymity cannot be guaranteed, the participants must be warned of this in advance.

■ *Use of animals* – When animals are used in field experiments, their natural environment is being altered in some way because of the very nature of a field experiment. Such tampering with nature in order to understand it places great responsibilities on researchers to ensure that they minimize the disruptive effects of any manipulation.

NATURAL EXPERIMENTS

In a natural experiment, the researcher exploits naturally occurring differences in the independent variable; the researcher does not directly control the IV. The approach is therefore best described as a quasi-experiment (see p. 196), although some purists might even regard it as non-experimental.

Examples of natural experiments can be found in the adoption studies discussed in Unit 2 (see p. 62, for example). Occasionally, an unforeseen event in the environment permits a natural experiment to be undertaken, such as the effect of widespread witnessing of violent crime on levels of violence subsequently recorded. Berkowitz (1970) hypothesized that witnessing violence makes people more violent. He recorded and examined data on violent crime before and after the assassination in 1963 of President Kennedy in the USA, which appeared on TV in America and throughout the world. Berkowitz was able to demonstrate a sudden rise in violent crime after the assassination, thereby supporting his hypothesis.

Advantages of natural experiments

■ *Reduction of demand characteristics* – Participants may be unaware that they are taking part in an experiment, and so demand characteristics are avoided.

■ *Lack of direct intervention* – The experimenter does not intervene directly in the research situation, although it is possible that the researcher's mere presence may still produce an effect on the participants' behaviour.

Weaknesses

■ *Loss of control* – Since the IV is not directly controlled by the investigator, the degree of control exercised is less than in either the laboratory experiment or the field experiment. This reduces the likelihood of cause and effect being established.

- *Likelihood of the desired behaviour being displayed* – The naturally occurring situation that the researcher wishes to study may occur only rarely, thus reducing the available opportunities for research. This is illustrated in the study of violent crime by Berkowitz (1970) outlined above.

Ethical issues

- *Consent* – Ethical issues relating to obtaining fully informed consent and safeguarding participants' right to withdraw from a natural experiment are similar to those for field experiments.

- *Protection of participants* – This is also essential. For example, probing participants' views about the death penalty, following an increase in widely reported murders or terrorist atrocities might increase anxiety levels and lead to unwarranted distress associated with the study.

- *Confidentiality* – Participants in natural experiments have the right to expect that information they provide will be treated confidentially and, if published, will not be identifiable as theirs. Where confidentiality or anonymity cannot be guaranteed, participants must be warned of this in advance.

CHECK YOUR UNDERSTANDING

Check your understanding of the nature of experimental research by answering these questions. Try to do this from memory at first. You can check your answers by looking back through Topic 1.

1 What are (a) qualitative data (b) quantitative data?

2 Why are ethical guidelines important?

3 List the three key features of a true experiment.

4 What is meant by the term 'demand characteristics'?

5 Give two advantages and two weaknesses of laboratory experiments.

6 What is a field experiment?

7 Give two advantages and two weaknesses of field experiments.

8 What is a natural experiment?

9 Give two advantages and two weaknesses of natural experiments.

10 Define what is meant by (a) an independent variable (b) a dependent variable.

REVISION SUMMARY

Having covered this topic you should be able to:

✓ define the following terms: 'quantitative data', 'qualitative data', 'experiment', 'laboratory experiment', 'field experiment', 'natural experiment', 'ethical guidelines'

✓ distinguish between quantitative and qualitative data

✓ identify three main types of experiment – laboratory, field and natural experiments

✓ describe the key features of a laboratory experiment

✓ describe the key features of a field experiment

✓ describe the key features of a natural experiment

✓ discuss the main advantages and weaknesses of these three types of experiment

✓ describe the ethical issues associated with laboratory experiments, field experiments and natural experiments.

Dramatic Increase in Bullying in Local School

Imagine that you have just read a newspaper article with this headline. It reports that a short questionnaire was circulated to pupils of all the five secondary schools in your town. Sixty-five per cent of respondents stated that they had been bullied at school during the past two years. The article suggests that this dramatic increase is the result of poor discipline in the schools and holds the teachers responsible for this terrible state of affairs.

You have decided to contact the researcher and ask some questions, in order to prepare a report for your school magazine about this research.

1 Make a list of questions to ask the researcher who carried out the study. You want to find out whether you can be confident that the findings reflect the true incidence of bullying in the schools.

2 The newspaper article accuses teachers of using poor discipline. How might you go about researching whether or not this is true?

3 Imagine you discover that bullying is more common in schools with poor discipline. Can you be sure that the poor discipline causes the bullying? If not, why not and what other factors might be involved?

Investigation using correlational analysis: an investigation using a type of analysis that measures the extent of the relationship between variables that are thought likely to co-vary (e.g. height and weight).

Naturalistic observation: an observational technique where behaviour is observed in its natural context without intrusion by the person who is doing the observing.

Questionnaire survey: a technique, using a structured set of questions, for asking a large sample of people about their views and behaviours, etc. Questionnaire surveys may be conducted in person, by telephone, by post, via the Internet, etc.

Interview: any face-to-face situation where one person (the interviewer) asks a series of questions of another person (the respondent). These questions may be structured, semi-structured or unstructured.

In this topic we will examine research in which an IV is not deliberately manipulated by a researcher. Each of the research methods outlined here allows psychologists to study behaviour in more natural settings. However, this potential benefit has its costs – as a result of reduced levels of control, it is not possible for the researcher to reach any definite conclusion concerning cause-and-effect relationships, which is important if we are to understand behaviour as fully as possible.

The non-experimental methods discussed here are investigations using:

- correlational analysis
- naturalistic observations
- questionnaire surveys
- interviews.

CORRELATIONAL ANALYSIS

The term 'correlation' refers to a descriptive statistical technique that measures the relationships between variables. Literally, these techniques measure co-relationships between variables – that is, the extent to which high values on one variable are associated with high values on another (known as a positive correlation), or the extent to which high values on one variable are associated with low values on another (a negative correlation). Many correlational techniques calculate a correlation coefficient, a statistic that has a value on a scale between +1 (known as a perfect positive correlation) and –1 (known as a perfect negative correlation). The strength of a correlation (i.e. the degree of the relationship) increases as a calculated correlation coefficient moves away from zero and becomes closer to +1 or –1. Correlation coefficients are discussed more fully on pp. 241–2.

As it is a statistical technique, correlation is not strictly a research method, but the term is also used to refer to the overall design of non-experimental investigations that specifically try to identify relationships between variables.

Uses of correlational analysis

Correlational research is often used to investigate the extent of relationship between variables that are thought likely to co-vary. For example, Murstein (1972) was interested in whether we select partners who are of similar physical attractiveness to ourselves (see the panel below).

Another major use of correlation is in the early stages of research into a particular area, especially where it is desirable to isolate relationships from a web of complex variables. For example, studies using Holmes and Rahe's Social Readjustment Rating Scale (1967) have found a correlation between Life Change Units (scores derived from using the scale) and the incidence of illness (see p. 89).

Correlational techniques also play a major role in establishing the reliability and validity of psychological measuring instruments, such as psychometric tests of intelligence and personality. The concepts of reliability and validity are discussed further in Unit 7 (pp. 226–8).

Physical attractiveness and marital choice (Murstein 1972)

Murstein hypothesized that individuals tend to select marital partners of comparable physical attractiveness to themselves. He set out to investigate whether partners forming premarital couples were more similar in terms of their physical attractiveness than one would expect by chance.

Ninety-eight couples who were described as 'engaged' or 'going steady' participated as paid volunteers in his research. All participants were asked to rate the physical attractiveness of their partner and also to estimate their own physical attractiveness using a five-point scale.

Photographs were also taken of all the participants. Independent judges were asked to rate the physical attractiveness of each pair of couples.

The following correlation coefficients were obtained:

Relationship between:	Correlation coefficient
Male participants' perception of their own and their partners' attractiveness	+0.50
Female participants' perception of their own and their partners' attractiveness	+0.45
Independent judges' ratings of the physical attractiveness of partners	+0.38

All the correlation coefficients were highly significant (p < 0.01), meaning that the likelihood of these results occurring by chance was highly unlikely, at less than 1 in 100. The data therefore supported Murstein's hypothesis about the relationship between physical attractiveness and marital choice.

Does Murstein's research explain why highly attractive celebrity figures are often attracted to each other?

Analysis of Bowlby's '44 thieves' study

Reread the description of Bowlby's (1944) study of 44 juvenile thieves on p. 60. Then answer the questions below:

1 What type of study did Bowlby undertake?

2 What hypothesis was being tested?

3 Did the findings support the hypothesis?

4 What type of data did Bowlby collect in this study?

5 Do the results allow us to conclude that there was a link between frequent early separations and emotional maladjustment, or that frequent early separations cause emotional maladjustment?

6 Would it be possible to design an experiment to demonstrate a causal relationship between early separation and subsequent emotional maladjustment? Give reasons for your answer.

Advantages of correlational analysis

■ *Measuring the strength of relationships* – Correlational techniques provide a precise quantitative measure of the strength of the relationship between specific variables.

■ *Value to exploratory research* – Correlational techniques allow for the measurement of many variables and the relationships between them at the same time. They are useful, therefore, when trying to unravel complex relationships and are a powerful tool for exploratory research.

Weaknesses

■ *The issue of causality* – It is impossible to establish cause and effect through research investigations using correlational analysis; it can only measure the degree of interrelationship between different variables. For example, Snedecor (1956) reported a near perfect negative correlation of -0.98 between the production of pig iron in the USA and the birth rate in Britain for the years 1875 to 1920! This ability to identify spurious relationships is a real drawback of the technique.

To illustrate the problem, there is a well-established correlation between the presence of symptoms of schizophrenia and the high availability of the neurotransmitter dopamine. However, there is insufficient evidence to state that excess dopamine causes schizophrenia. It remains possible that it is schizophrenia that causes the increase in available dopamine or, indeed, that there may be other links in the causal chain which have yet to be discovered. Nevertheless, the existence of this correlation has provided a useful avenue for further research.

■ *Measurement of non-linear relationships* – Non-linear relationships cannot be measured by commonly used correlational techniques. For example, Fig. 6.1 shows the relationship between time of day and attention level in a group of students. Initially, there is a positive correlation between the two variables, but as lunchtime approaches this changes into a negative relationship. The result is that when such data are analysed statistically, the positive and negative relationships tend to cancel each other out, with the result that no meaningful relationship is indicated by the calculated correlation coefficient. It is important therefore to plot non-linear relationships visually in order to understand better what is happening.

Figure 6.1 >>
Relationship between time of day and attention level in students

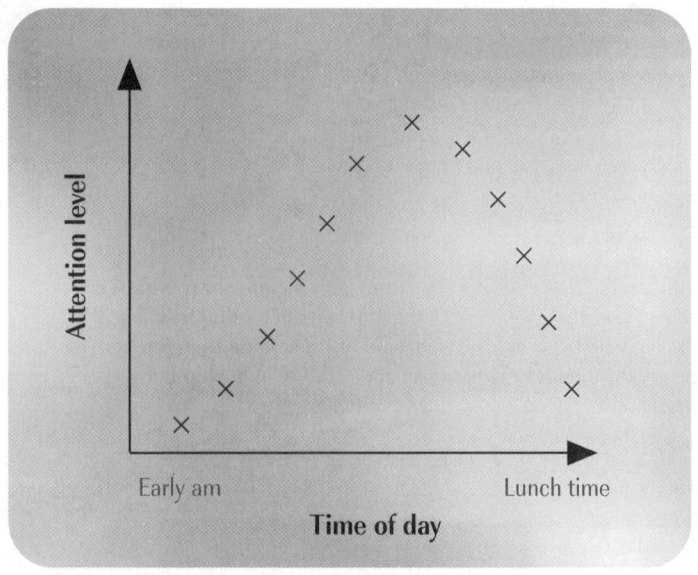

Ethical issues

- *Consent* – The same issues of fully informed consent and right to withdraw (as discussed under 'Natural experiments') apply here.

- *Use of findings* – In socially sensitive research, such as an investigation of sexual offences against children or drug abuse, the question of who 'owns' the data is very complex. It raises possible concerns about research findings being used for reasons other than those for which they were originally intended. Researchers must, therefore, consider in advance how their research might be used. Participants can then give their informed consent not only to their participation in the study, but also to the ways in which the findings will be disseminated and used.

NATURALISTIC OBSERVATION

In naturalistic observation, behaviour is observed and recorded in its natural setting and there is no deliberate manipulation of variables. This research method provides a counter to tightly controlled research methods such as the laboratory experiment. The emphasis is placed on how people or non-human animals behave in natural situations; no attempt is made to influence the behaviour being investigated. The method can therefore be used in situations where intervention would be inappropriate (e.g. when studying weddings or funerals) or unethical (e.g. interventions with children).

Naturalistic observation may nevertheless be laboratory based. Some species (e.g. rats) appear to adapt well to laboratory conditions and the behaviour displayed in psychological laboratory settings may be considered sufficiently natural for naturalistic observational research to be undertaken.

Psychological laboratories can also be designed to resemble playrooms. Once children have become completely accustomed to such a room, their behaviour there may be sufficiently natural for naturalistic observational research to be undertaken.

A distinction is often made between participant observation, in which the observer actually joins the group of people being studied, and non-participant observation, in which the observer remains external to those being observed. Observers may choose whether to remain disclosed or undisclosed, so that participants are either made aware or remain unaware of the research taking place.

Uses of naturalistic observation

The wide range of uses of naturalistic observation includes topics such as driver behaviour, the behaviour of children in school settings and studies of the workplace. It is also useful where behaviour might be difficult to recreate in a laboratory setting or as a preliminary to laboratory investigation. An example of naturalistic observational research is that by Rosenhan (1973) described in the panel on the right.

Naturalistic observation has always been popular in research carried out on non-human animals. Examples include the classic research by Lorenz on imprinting (see p. 54). The method is particularly useful when studying

On being sane in insane places (Rosenhan 1973)

Eight people who were entirely free of any psychiatric symptoms presented themselves to different psychiatric hospitals in the United States of America. All reported the same symptom – they said that they heard a voice say "dull", "empty" and "thud". Apart from this single symptom they were all instructed to behave normally and to give honest answers to any other questions they were asked. All were believed to be genuine patients and were admitted to the psychiatric hospitals concerned, seven with a diagnosis of schizophrenia. Once admitted into hospital, they immediately stopped reporting that they had been hearing voices. They were later discharged 7 to 52 days later with diagnoses of "schizophrenia in remission". Rosenhan attributed these diagnoses to the context in which their behaviour was observed. None actually displayed symptoms of schizophrenia, but the context in which the symptoms were reported led to an expectation that these 'pseudopatients' were indeed mentally ill.

species that do not thrive in, or adapt to, laboratory conditions (e.g. red deer or marine mammals).

Advantages

- *Value as a preliminary research tool* – Careful use of naturalistic observation can lead to the identification of appropriate hypotheses for further investigation or may, on the other hand, help to prevent time being wasted in carrying out unrealistic experiments. It is a useful technique for studying unknown or little-known behaviours. For example, Clutton-Brock and colleagues have provided much of our knowledge about the behaviour of red deer through their pioneering studies carried out on the island of Rum in the Hebrides (e.g. Clutton-Brock and Albon 1979).

Why is naturalistic observation a popular method for research into the behaviour of non-human animals?

■ *Validity* – Naturalistic observation can provide a useful check on whether experimental findings apply outside laboratory conditions. Realism and ecological validity can be good, provided that the observer remains undetected. The overall quality of the research may be improved through increased familiarity with the research setting, i.e. the researcher can become a "predictable and familiar part of the environment" with both human and non-human participants (Coolican 1999). Demand characteristics are minimized because behaviour is not affected either by anxiety or by inhibition that results from being in a laboratory situation. Also, with undisclosed naturalistic observation, there will be no feeling of a need to impress the researcher, as long as the observer remains undetected.

Weaknesses of naturalistic observation

■ *Control* – The level of control over potentially confounding variables is poor, although some degree of control is often possible by, for example, limiting the focus of the study. This means that cause-and-effect relationships cannot be established with any certainty. Replication may be difficult, due to the problems that arise in controlling variables such as differences between naturalistic settings. Problems may sometimes be minimized with the appropriate use of sound or video recordings, so that a record exists that can be used by others to check the researcher's own interpretation of observed behaviours.

■ *Observer effects* – It is possible that the presence of an observer may change participant behaviour, especially when a small group is being studied. This can also be an issue when observing non-human animals. For example, breeding patterns may be disturbed by the mere presence of an observer. Additionally, the potential exists for bias on the part of observers themselves, deriving from their expectations or interpretations of events.

■ *Costs* – There may be problems with costs, such as those for travel or of transporting equipment.

■ *Categorization of data* – There may be limitations concerning how the data gathered are categorized, affecting the interpretations of behaviour made – a behaviour may be observed that does not easily fit into the categories used. For example, identical behaviour in children might be classified as 'aggressive' by one researcher and as 'rough and tumble play' by another.

■ *Replicability* – Because of the uniqueness of each observational situation, it may be difficult or even impossible to generalize results to other occasions or other settings.

Ethical issues

■ *Privacy* – Studies based on observation must respect the privacy and psychological wellbeing of the individuals studied. Unless those being observed give their consent to being observed, observational research is only acceptable in situations where those observed would expect to be observed by strangers (e.g. in the high street of a major town). Particular account should be taken of local cultural values and of the possibility of intruding upon the privacy of individuals who, even while in a normally public space, may believe they are unobserved. Those observed have the right to expect that any information they provide will be treated confidentially and, if published, will not be identifiable as theirs.

■ *Confidentiality and consent* – If researchers do not disclose that they are undertaking observational research and collect data in a non-public setting, such as a hospital ward or a school playground, they should subsequently inform those who were observed about the study and obtain their consent to use the data collected. If confidentiality or anonymity cannot be guaranteed, the participant must be warned of this in advance.

■ *Use of findings* – The same issues arise as discussed under 'Correlational analysis' on p. 203.

QUESTIONNAIRE SURVEYS

A survey involves the systematic gathering of data from large numbers of people, usually by means of questionnaires. Vast amounts of data are regularly collected by large-scale surveys from households across the UK and are published in tables and charts in reports such as *Social Trends*. This provides a range of fascinating social and economic data about British society today, including population statistics, data about households and families, education, the labour market, health and lifestyles. You can access *Social Trends* electronically via the National Statistics website (see p. 213 for address).

Most surveys are carried out on carefully selected representative groups (referred to as 'samples') so that the researcher can generalize to the wider population from which any such group was drawn. The main exception is the national census that is carried out every ten years and involves every adult in the UK (i.e. the total adult population) and not a sample.

Questionnaire surveys can be used in a wide range of research situations. They allow researchers to ask participants questions about, for example, their attitudes, behaviours or intentions. They can be used where a pen-and-paper method is appropriate, allowing the researcher to gain information from a large sample of participants relatively quickly and efficiently. The researcher does not need to be present when the questionnaire is administered, although the researcher's presence may be helpful to answer any queries that the respondent has. Questionnaire surveys can be conducted face to face, by post, by telephone, via the Internet or left for participants to collect from some central point. As we shall see, both qualitative and quantitative data may be produced.

Questions can be of two broad types:

- *Closed questions* are those where the researcher determines the range of possible answers; respondents often reply by ticking boxes or circling appropriate answers. These questions are best used when factual information is required. They produce information that is easy to quantify and analyse, but which may lack realism due to the forced choices of answers available to the respondents. Examples of different forms of closed questions are shown in the panel below.

- *Open-ended questions* are those in which the researcher does not restrict the range of available answers. So, for example, a researcher might start an interview by asking: "What are your views on the use of corporal punishment by parents?" Open-ended questions produce a greater depth of qualitative information, but at a cost – answers are more difficult to analyse because the range of possible answers is so wide.

Some examples of closed questions

- *Checklists* – respondents tick any items that apply.

  For example: Please tick the subjects in the following list that you studied at GCSE level.

☐ Art	☐ English	☐ History
☐ Geography	☐ Mathematics	☐ Psychology
☐ Science	☐ Sociology	

- *Placing items in rank order*

  For example: Place a number against each of your GCSE subjects, placing them in rank order from most liked (given the number 1) to least liked.

- *Attitude scales*

  For example: Underline the response that best reflects your attitude to the statement: "A university education is essential if you are to succeed in the employment market.

  Do you: – strongly disagree?
  – disagree?
  – neither disagree or agree?
  – agree?
  – strongly agree?

- *Likert scales* – based on a numerical rating.

  For example: How important are the following factors to the relationship between you and your partner? (Please circle the appropriate number.)

	Very Important		Neither important nor unimportant		Very unimportant
Sense of humour	1	2	3	4	5
Common interests	1	2	3	4	5
Mutual respect	1	2	3	4	5

- *Semantic differential scales* – where respondents are asked to rate items on scales based on a series of pairs of opposite adjectives.

  For example: How would you rate your feelings about your AS-level Psychology course? (Place a tick at the appropriate point on each scale.)

Warm	I I I I I I I I	Cold
Satisfied	I I I I I I I I	Dissatisfied

When carrying out questionnaire surveys, it is good practice to keep the number of questions to a minimum, use short questions and phrase these questions very clearly in order to avoid any ambiguity or misunderstandings. Questions that are emotionally charged should be avoided.

Ideally, any questionnaire should be carefully piloted before it is administered (pilot studies are discussed in Unit 7, see p. 226).

Questionnaire surveys produce descriptive and/or explanatory information that can be tailored to fit a wide range of research situations. They can be carried out as a 'one-off' or, more powerfully, they can be conducted both before and after some event in order to examine the impact of that event. Their flexibility means that they are valuable both as a preliminary research tool and as a source of in-depth information on some topic of interest.

Examples of well-known questionnaires include the Social Readjustment Rating Scale (Holmes and Rahe 1967; see pp. 89–91) and the Hassles and Uplifts Scales developed by Kanner *et al.* (1981; see pp. 91–2).

What factors might influence the respondent in this survey setting?

Advantages of questionnaire surveys

- *Simplicity* – Once constructed and piloted, questionnaires can be carried out with a minimum of training. Quantitative data obtained from closed questions are usually straightforward to analyse, so it is often easy to compare answers from different individuals or groups of respondents.

- *Speed* – Response rates (i.e. the proportion of people sent the questionnaire who choose to respond) tend to be quite low – around 30 per cent or fewer of those who were sent the questionnaire. However, large amounts of information can be gathered cheaply from a large number of respondents within a fairly short period of time.

Weaknesses

- *Problems with question wording* – If the wording of questions is ambiguous, then respondents may interpret the question in different ways and their answers may reflect this. Meaningful analysis of the responses therefore becomes difficult.

  Leading questions may also influence the responses given. For example, it is clear what answer is being encouraged by the question: "Don't you think that spending money on education is good?" Different interpretations of language can also be problematic. For example, there may be different interpretations of the term 'rarely' when used in a question about days off work due to illness. To one person, 'rarely' may mean once or twice a month; to another, once or twice a year. Finally, social desirability bias may be an issue – respondents may not provide truthful answers, especially to personal or potentially

embarrassing questions. They may wish their answers to be seen in the best possible light.

- *Researcher effects and biases* – If a researcher administers the questionnaire personally, then respondents may be influenced by factors such as the researcher's ethnic origin, age, appearance, gender or mode of dress. Even unintentional nods, smiles or frowns can have an effect on the results.

  Researcher bias may be a problem when analysing the data. For example, a researcher might interpret one possible answer option on a questionnaire as being more socially desirable than other possible answers. Responses in this category might be wrongly interpreted as providing genuine support for the researcher's particular (biased) viewpoint. (See Unit 7 for further detail about the wording of questionnaires.)

Ethical issues

- *Privacy* – Studies based on questionnaire surveys must respect the privacy and psychological wellbeing of all those who agree to complete the questionnaire. Those responding have the right to expect that any information they provide will be treated confidentially and, if published, will not be identifiable as theirs. If confidentiality or anonymity cannot be guaranteed, the participant must be warned of this in advance.

- *Consent* – Researchers need to safeguard respondents' right to withdraw some or all of their data from the study, and respondents should give their consent for their data to be included in the findings.

- *Risk of harm* – Investigators have a primary responsibility to protect respondents from psychological harm during an investigation. Normally, the risk of harm must be no greater than in ordinary life. Where a questionnaire probes behaviour or experiences that respondents may regard as personal and private, the respondents must be protected from stress by a range of appropriate measures, including the assurance that answers to personal questions need not be given. In research involving children, great care should be taken when discussing results with parents, teachers or those *in loco parentis*, since

evaluative statements may carry unintended weight and, again, may cause distress.

- *Debriefing and support* – Questions on socially sensitive topics can cause distress to respondents, and appropriate debriefing and support mechanisms must be made available. However, survey researchers must also be vigilant regarding any questions that could appear straightforward, such as asking parents about their views on disciplining children. Such questions could trigger psychological distress in some respondents, who may subsequently require debriefing and support.

INTERVIEWS

<< Conducting interviews is a complex, labour intensive and uncertain business, fraught with tricky issues that social scientific researchers, and particularly psychologists, are often ill-equipped to address.>> (Banister *et al.* 1994)

Despite these difficulties, the interview is a common way of carrying out research; it may form the basis of a case study or may be used as one of the ways of conducting a survey.

Most research establishes some kind of distance between the researcher and the researched, but this kind of approach is challenged by the face-to-face nature of the interview, which is both personal and public. In order to encourage the flow of information from the interviewee to the interviewer, the interview needs an explicit purpose and aims.

Interviews also need very careful planning and piloting (see Unit 7). In some instances the focus of an interview is determined by the researcher; in others it may be negotiated between the interviewer and the interviewee.

- *Structured interviews* usually aim to produce quantitative data and include questions that are decided in advance with the aim of structuring the interviewee's responses. In this sense, they are similar to experimental research because the researcher largely determines the focus.

The structured approach has several advantages. The interviewer and interviewee are less likely to deviate from the topic that is the desired focus of the interview. Also, data analysis may be simpler, results are easier to generalize, less training is needed for interviewers, and there is less risk of the results being affected by interviewer bias, since the interviewer is more likely to be objective. However, there are costs as well as benefits. The researcher cannot follow up any new lines of enquiry that become apparent during the interview, and validity may be threatened by participants reacting to the formality of the research situation.

- *Unstructured interviews* are far less rigid and very little, if anything, concerning their nature will be decided in advance. They often start with one or two set questions, with further questions picking up on issues that the interviewee raises. These interviews can be more difficult to analyse, but have greater validity, as interviewees will be more likely to report whatever they wish to say and the interviewers can be flexible in their approach.

- The *semi-structured interview* is often the most successful approach, with the use of some prepared questions by the interviewer, supplemented by opportunities for the interviewee to expand on their answers.

The diversity of interviews also means that interviewing is a skill that requires careful development in those using this research method.

Interviews may be used to provide information in addition to that obtained by other research methods. For example, Milgram (1963) enriched his work on obedience (see Unit 5) by interviewing his participants after the experiment. Two areas where the approach has been of particular value are social psychology (see, for example, the use of interviews in the research on conformity by Asch, also discussed in Unit 5) and psychopathology (for example, in exploring the family histories of sufferers from anxiety disorders).

ACTIVITY

Interviews

Carry out two interviews on a topic of your choice. Use a structured interview with one person (i.e. a set series of five or six questions about the chosen topic) and an unstructured interview with another person.

What differences do you note in your findings?

The description of Lynch's (1960) work on 'Cognitive maps' (on the right) provides another example of the practical use of interviews.

Cognitive maps (Lynch 1960)

Lynch was interested in environmental perception and, in particular, in the cognitive maps people create of their home areas. He carried out a series of interviews with the residents in three US cities – Boston, Jersey City and Los Angeles – about their feelings about local landmarks, and also about major routes and the areas that they passed through when driving around. He used the interview data to produce a general image of each city that identified the basic units of the urban landscape. Participants often mentioned distinctive features of their urban landscape that were not always the tallest or skyline features, but rather things on a more human scale, such as a well-known building or open space. Some interviewees had been to areas in their local city which they were unable to describe. Information gathered through such interviews has been used in urban planning.

Advantages of interviews

- *Flexibility* – Interviews can enable the researcher to explore complex issues that may be difficult to investigate through experimental techniques, questionnaire surveys or observation research. The interviewer can tailor questions to the responses of an interviewee so that issues can be explored in depth.

- *Tackling sensitive topics* – Interviews allow researchers to identify aspects of behaviour that are private or personal to the individuals concerned. This can be difficult with more impersonal research methods.

Weaknesses

- *Interpreting data* – Misinterpretation or partial interpretation of data may take place. Ideally, the interviewer needs to be detached from the interviewee, which can be difficult to achieve in face-to-face situations with their potential for bias. Qualitative data obtained from unstructured interviews can also be difficult to analyse.

- *Limitations in interviewees' responses* – Interviewees may be unable to articulate their thoughts clearly. Demand characteristics may also occur, such as social desirability bias.

Qualitative data comes in many forms and can be difficult to analyse

Ethical issues

The ethical issues associated with interviews are similar to those associated with questionnaire surveys (see p. 208), expecially with regard to the following:

- respecting the privacy and psychological wellbeing of interviewees
- obtaining informed consent from participants and respecting their right to withdraw some or all of their data
- maintaining confidentiality and anonymity
- protection from harm
- debriefing and support.

ANSWERS TO ACTIVITIES

Activity, p. 197 (top)

1 IV – the acoustic similarity of the words

DV – serial memory recall scores

2 IV – level of difficulty of the anagrams (i.e. easy or difficult)

DV – memory retention (i.e. memory scores)

3 IV – location of the memory test/instructions to imagine a particular environment

DV – the number of words correctly recalled.

Activity, p. 197 (bottom)

1 The IV is whether the stimulus sheets consisted of coloured words printed in conflicting coloured inks or coloured ink blocks.

2 The DV is the time taken to name the ink colours.

3 There were two conditions: experimental and control.

4 The data were quantitative.

5 The relationship investigated is that colour names written in a conflicting ink colour affect the length of time it takes to read the colour names.

✓ CHECK YOUR UNDERSTANDING

Check your understanding of non-experimental investigations in psychology by answering these questions. Try to do this from memory at first. You can check your answers by looking back through Topic 2.

1 What is correlational analysis and when is it used in psychology?

2 Give two advantages and two weaknesses of using correlational analysis.

3 What is naturalistic observation and when is it used in psychology?

4 What is meant by the term 'participant observation'?

5 Give two advantages and two weaknesses of using naturalistic observation.

6 What is a questionnaire survey and when is it used in psychology?

7 What is meant by an 'open-ended question' in a questionnaire?

8 Give two advantages and two weaknesses of using a questionnaire survey.

9 Define what is meant by an interview and describe when it is used in psychology.

10 What are the main differences between structured, unstructured and semi-structured interviews?

11 Give two advantages and two weaknesses of using interviews.

REVISION SUMMARY

Having covered this topic you should be able to:

✔ define the following terms: 'correlational analysis', 'naturalistic observation', 'questionnaire survey', 'interview'

✔ describe the key features of investigations using correlational analysis, and discuss their main advantages and weaknesses

✔ describe the key features of naturalistic observations, and discuss their main advantages and weaknesses

✔ describe the key features of questionnaire surveys, and discuss their main advantages and weaknesses

✔ describe the key features of interviews, and discuss their main advantages and weaknesses

✔ describe the ethical issues associated with investigations using correlational analysis, naturalistic observations, questionnaire surveys and interviews.

UNIT SUMMARY

Topic 1: Experimental investigations in psychology

■ Psychologists use a range of research methods to investigate their subject matter. For many years the **experiment**, and in particular the **laboratory experiment**, has been their main research method. However, no single method is appropriate or successful in all circumstances and in all contexts.

■ When carrying out an experiment, a **researcher intervenes** directly in the situation being investigated. The experimental method is regarded as being the most powerful research method because of its potential to identify **cause-and-effect relationships**.

■ The true experiment has three key features:

 (a) The researcher manipulates an **independent variable** (IV) in order to investigate whether there is a change in the **dependent variable** (DV).

 (b) **All other variables** that might influence the results are either held constant or are eliminated.

 (c) Participants are **allocated randomly** to the experimental conditions.

■ Experiments provide the highest levels of control, but at the possible cost of a reduction in the **ecological validity** of the research and the **generalizability** of the findings.

■ The experimenter usually has greatest control when undertaking a laboratory experiment. **Field experiments** can give greater validity, but usually this is achieved at the cost of some degree of control over the key variables and possibly ease of replicability.

■ The term **quasi-experiment** is used to describe an experiment where the investigator lacks complete control over the IV and/or the allocation of participants to groups. **Natural experiments** are sometimes regarded as quasi-experiments because they use naturally occurring events over which the researcher does not have full control.

■ **Ethical guidelines** provide guidance on how psychologists should carry out experimental research in order to protect the people or animals that take part in their studies.

Topic 2: Non-experimental investigations in psychology

- **Non-experimental research methods** enable psychologists to study behaviour in more **natural settings**. However, this potential benefit has its costs – as a result of reduced levels of control, it is not possible for the researcher to reach any definitie conclusions concerning cause-and-effect relationships.

- Investigations using **correlational analysis** allow researchers to obtain measures of the relationship between variables, but do not allow the research to establish cause-and-effect relationships.

- In **naturalistic observation**, behaviour is observed and recorded in its natural setting and there is **no deliberate manipulation of variables**. Studies involving naturalistic observation provide the researcher with an **ecologically valid technique**. However, establishing controls may be difficult, making it difficult to generalize the results.

- **Questionnaire surveys** allow the researcher to ask people questions about, for example, their attitudes, behaviour or intentions, and to gather large amounts of information quickly and efficiently. Most surveys are carried out on carefully selected representative groups (referred to as **samples**) so that the researcher can generalize to the wider **population** from which the subgroup was drawn.

- **Interviews** need careful planning and piloting, but allow the flexible exploration of detailed issues, including complex ones. Interviews may be **structured**, **semi-structured** or **unstructured** and may generate **quantitative** and/or **qualitative data**.

- **Ethical guidelines** provide guidance as to how psychologists should carry out non-experimental research in order to protect the people or animals that take part in their studies.

Answering exam questions on Research methods

For sample examination questions and answers on Research methods, together with examiner comments on the answers, see pp. 262–5.

WEBSITES

www.statistics.gov.uk/socialtrends
Fascinating social and economic data about British society today.

http://universe.indiana.edu/clp/RF/experiment.htm
Useful guidance on a range of issues relating to experimental design.

http://kancrn.kckps.k12.ks.us/guide/nonexperimental.html
A site focusing on descriptive surveys.

www.mapnp.org/library/evaluatn/intrview.htm
Information on different types of interview, and how to prepare for and carry out inteviews.

www.slais.ubc.ca/resources/research_methods/question.htm
A range of resources relating to questionnaire survey research.

http://writing.colostate.edu/references/research.cfm
A range of guides on quantitative and qualitative research methods addressing research issues relevant to Units 6 and 7.

7
UNIT

RESEARCH DESIGN & IMPLEMENTATION
& Data Analysis

PREVIEW

After you have read this unit, you should be able to:

>> describe how aims are generated and how hypotheses are formulated

>> describe different research designs: experimental (independent groups, repeated measures and matched participants) and non-experimental (naturalistic observational studies, questionnaire surveys and interviews)

>> outline factors associated with research design: the control of variables, operationalization of independent and dependent variables, conducting pilot studies, techniques for assessing and improving reliability and validity, ethics

>> discuss different methods of selecting participants

>> explore the relationship between researchers and participants

>> describe the analysis of qualitative data derived from naturalistic observational studies, questionnaire surveys and interviews

>> use descriptive statistical techniques, including measures of central tendency and measures of dispersion

>> use and interpret graphs and charts

>> discuss the nature of positive and negative correlations, and the interpretation of correlation coefficients.

INTRODUCTION

Unit 6 discussed some of the research methods most widely used by psychologists. This unit covers a wide range of issues associated with the design and implementation of these research methods. You will start in Topic 1 by considering how to generate appropriate aims and formulate appropriate hypotheses. The unit then moves on to examine different experimental designs, as well as the design of non-experimental investigations. A range of factors associated with research designs are discussed, including the operationalization and control of variables, the nature of pilot studies and how two extremely important factors in research – reliability and validity – can be assessed and improved. The major sampling methods that psychologists use to obtain their participants are discussed. The unit continues by examining the relationship between researchers and participants in psychological research.

Topic 2 examines some of the ways in which psychologists analyse their data, and some of the issues that arise from this analysis. It examines how quantitative data can be interpreted using descriptive statistical techniques, as well as how qualitative methods of analysis are used in association with naturalistic observational studies, questionnaire surveys and interviews.

Graham
Davies

GETTING YOU THINKING...

Look at this image from the popular comic *2000 AD*. Do comics such as this increase levels of violence in children? How could you find out?

Imagine that you have been commissioned to find out whether there is any link between reading 'violent' comics and levels of aggression in children.

Think of as many different ways as possible of researching this topic and write brief notes about what each study would involve. This activity will revise the material you studied in Unit 6. If possible, discuss your ideas with your teacher or other students in your class.

Keep your notes safely because you will be returning to your ideas later in this unit.

KEY TERMS

Aim: the intended purpose of an investigation, i.e. what the research investigation is actually trying to discover.

Hypothesis: a testable statement. A research hypothesis is a general prediction made at the beginning of an investigation about what the researcher expects to happen.

Null hypothesis: predicts no differences between the results from the different conditions of an experiment (it predicts no correlation in an investigation using correlational analysis). Under the null hypothesis, any difference (or correlation) found is due to chance alone.

Alternative hypothesis (may be referred to as the experimental hypothesis in an experiment): predicts that something other than chance alone has produced the results obtained; in a well-designed experiment this should be the effects of the independent variable.

Directional hypothesis: an alternative hypothesis which predicts the direction in which any differences (or any correlation in an investigation using correlational analysis) in the results of an investigation are expected to occur.

Non-directional hypothesis: an alternative hypothesis which does not predict the direction in which any differences (or any correlation in an investigation using correlational analysis) in the results of an investigation are expected to occur.

Independent groups design: an experimental design which involves using different participants in each condition of the experiment.

Repeated measures design: an experimental design which involves exposing every participant to each of the experimental conditions, so, in effect, participants are used as their own controls.

Matched participants design: an experimental design which involves matching each participant in one of the experimental conditions as closely as possible with another participant in the second condition on variables considered to be relevant to the experiment in question.

Operationalization: the process of achieving precise descriptions of particular key terms in research – for example, what researchers understand by key variables such as the independent variable and the dependent variable. Operationalizing these variables usually results in a narrowing down of the research focus.

Pilot study: a small-scale prototype of a research investigation. It is carried out on a small number of participants in order to find out whether there are any problems with the design, the instructions for participants, the measuring instruments used or any other aspect of the proposed study.

Ethics: in psychology these are fundamental principles that respect the rights and feelings of those taking part in research.

Reliability: a term that means dependability or consistency. If the findings are replicated consistently, then the outcome can be said to be reliable.

Validity: a concept that is concerned with the extent to which a research instrument measures what it sets out to measure. A distinction may be drawn between different types of validity, including internal validity, external validity and ecological validity.

Internal validity: is concerned with the extent to which we can be sure that research findings are due to the mechanisms suggested, such as manipulation of the independent variable in an experiment, and not to the action of some other unwanted variable, such as individual differences or the effects of practice.

External validity: is concerned with the extent to which results can be generalized to other settings beyond that of the study concerned. A distinction can be drawn here between population validity (the extent to which results from research can be generalized to other groups of people) and ecological validity (the extent to which research findings can be generalized to situations outside the research setting).

Target population: a group of people that share a given set of characteristics, about which a researcher wishes to draw conclusions.

Sample: a subset of a target population which shares the characteristics of the population despite its smaller size.

Random sample: a subset of a target population in which every person or item stands an equal chance of being selected for inclusion. This requires the researcher to be able to identify every person or item in the target population before selection of a sample takes place. The selection process therefore takes place in a completely unbiased way.

Opportunity sample: a type of sample where the researcher selects anyone who is available to take part from a given population.

Demand characteristics: occur when participants try to make sense of a research situation that they find themselves in and act accordingly.

Investigator effects: result from the effects of a researcher's behaviour and characteristics on an investigation. They include expectation effects and the effects that the presence of a researcher can have on the behaviour of participants, resulting in their behaving in ways different from those that would normally be displayed.

AIMS AND HYPOTHESES

Generating appropriate aims

The starting point for any psychological research study is to generate appropriate aims for the idea that you wish to investigate. In order to generate these aims successfully, you need to know the intended purpose of the investigation, i.e. what the research investigation in question is actually trying to discover. In some non-experimental studies, the aims may be fairly broad, particularly in investigations in which qualitative data are being analysed. For example, the aim might be: "To describe the incidence of cigarette smoking in 10- to 16-year-olds living in Greater Manchester". In experimental investigations and, indeed, in others where quantitative data are produced, the aim may be to test one or more hypotheses.

Formulating hypotheses

A hypothesis can be defined simply as a testable statement. A research hypothesis is a general prediction made at the beginning of an investigation about what the researcher expects to happen. However, in order to

assist the analysis of data obtained from any research investigation, it is essential to phrase the hypothesis carefully, so that it is both clear and testable. This is the process of hypothesis formulation, i.e. refining the hypothesis so that it is stated in precise terms.

For example, consider the research hypothesis that "leading questions affect eyewitness testimony". In the form presented here, this begs too many questions to be tested precisely. For instance, what kind of leading question are we talking about, or in what ways is the testimony of witnesses affected? If this statement is to be converted into a format useful for the analysis of results data, then its wording must be completely unambiguous. A more tightly worded statement would be: "More witnesses report seeing a knife in a given scene when a leading question suggests the existence of a knife as a murder weapon." This formulation process highlights a fundamental issue concerning experimental research. On the one hand, the original research hypothesis is so general in its nature that it is difficult to test precisely. On the other hand, the version based on operationalized variables may be more clearly defined and testable, but may lack more general application (see p. 225 for a discussion of the operationalization of variables).

Researchers refer to two different hypotheses when analysing their data – the alternative hypothesis and the null hypothesis.

Alternative hypothesis

The alternative hypothesis (in an experiment this may be termed the experimental hypothesis) predicts that something other than chance alone has played a part in producing the results obtained. For example, imagine an experiment investigating the effect of an mnemonic on memory recall (a mnemonic is a device for aiding memory, such as using the phrase 'Richard Of York Gave Battle In Vain' to remember the order of colours in a rainbow). In such an experiment, the alternative hypothesis would predict a difference between the results from the two conditions, where those in the experimental condition would use a mnemonic and those in a second group would not. Only if the design of an investigation is completely watertight will the researcher be left with just one explanation for the results (i.e. that the independent variable is responsible for the outcome). In practice, reaching such a definite conclusion can be difficult.

An alternative hypothesis can be described as being directional or non-directional:

- A *directional hypothesis* predicts the direction in which results are expected to occur. For example, "More words are recalled from a list when using rehearsal as a mnemonic technique than when no mnemonic technique is used". In this case, we are predicting not only that there will be a difference in the number of words recalled, but that more will be recalled in one condition, i.e. when a mnemonic technique is used.

- A *non-directional hypothesis*, on the other hand, does not predict the expected direction of outcome. For example, "There is a difference in the number of words recalled from word lists presented with or without the presence of background music". Here a difference is predicted, but no prediction is made as to which of the two conditions results in a greater number of words recalled.

Directional and non-directional hypotheses are sometimes referred to as 'one-tailed' and 'two-tailed' hypotheses respectively. However, the terms 'directional' and 'non-directional' hypothesis are preferred.

Null hypothesis

The null hypothesis predicts that the results obtained from an investigation are due to chance alone. For example, in an experiment investigating the effect of an mnemonic on memory recall, the null hypothesis would predict no differences between the results from the two conditions. If any differences in observed outcome do occur, these are due to chance, rather than to the effect of the independent variable (in this case the use of a mnemonic). The researcher's task is to decide whether their null hypothesis should be retained or rejected. If the likelihood of the results occurring by chance is remote, then the null hypothesis can be rejected and we may prefer to accept the alternative hypothesis.

The null hypothesis can thus be regarded as the hypothesis which states that the alternative hypothesis is untrue. It is the more important of the hypotheses, because it is the null hypothesis that is actually tested when the quantitative data are analysed statistically.

ACTIVITY

Writing hypotheses

For each of the following studies, write a suitable alternative hypothesis and null hypothesis, and indicate whether your alternative hypothesis is directional or non-directional.

1 Tulving and Osler (1968) – experiment on retrieval cues (Unit 1, p. 24)
2 Brewer and Treyens (1981) – schemas and memory errors (Unit 1, p. 32)
3 Harlow and Harlow (1962) – formation of love in infant monkeys (Unit 2, p. 53)
4 Cohen et al. (1993) – study on stress (Unit 3, p. 86)
5 Johansson et al. (1978) – stress in a Swedish sawmill (Unit 3, p. 94)

An example is given below.

Study	Alternative hypothesis	Directional (D) or Non-directional (ND)	Null hypothesis
Baddeley (1966) – acoustic coding in short-term memory (Unit 1, pp. 8–9)	Words that sound different will be recalled better than words that sound similar.	D	Words that sound different will not be recalled better than words that sound similar.

RESEARCH DESIGNS: KEY DECISIONS

When undertaking research, a number of key decisions need to be taken. These may include the following:

- Deciding on an *appropriate research method* – Unit 6 focuses on the most appropriate research methods for different types of research and how they can best be used.

- Deciding *how many participants* to use – Researchers conducting an experiment or questionnaire survey usually have a choice when deciding how many participants to use. As a general rule, the larger the sample, the less biased it is likely to be; a sample of 25 or 30 participants is often regarded as a reasonable number in a small-scale study when quantitative data are to be collected and analysed. However, the non-experimental researcher sometimes has no control over sample size and may need to use whoever is available. Indeed, in some examples of qualitative research (e.g. research based on unstructured interviews), there may be only a few participants.

- Using an *appropriate sampling method* – This is essential where a sample of participants is selected to represent a larger population. The researcher also needs to decide how representative the participants are of a particular target population. (Sampling methods are discussed later in this unit.)

- Deciding *how to brief participants* – An important question is whether participants should be aware or unaware of taking part in research, or of the specific nature of the investigation. This raises the ethical issue of informed consent (see Units 5 and 6). Sometimes researchers disclose their intent to participants (this is usual in the case of questionnaire surveys, interviews and many experiments). They may even spend a period of time getting to know them before the research is carried out. It is hoped that this process encourages more natural behaviour. With naturalistic observation, the researcher may choose whether or not to let participants know that an investigation is being carried out on them. Where informed consent is not given, the researcher needs to consider very carefully the ethical issues that arise.

- Deciding the *medium for recording data* – A written record may be made (often by the participant in the case of questionnaire surveys and some experiments), or behaviour may be recorded for subsequent analysis, e.g. on video/audio tape or via computer. A combination of these methods is commonly used. The researcher also needs to decide which behaviour to record and which to ignore. If a written record is made, the researcher may need to devise an appropriate coding system for recording behaviour (an example is provided later in this unit in Fig. 7.2, p. 222).

- Deciding the *techniques for recording behaviour* – The method used may be highly structured (as in many experiments, questionnaire surveys and some naturalistic observational studies), or it may be unstructured (as in some interviews). The aim is to obtain data that are sufficiently explicit to enable appropriate analysis of the results.

A combination of different methods can be used for recording data ... the key is choosing the most suitable

DESIGNING EXPERIMENTS

Selecting an appropriate experimental design is essential for the success of any experimental investigation. It involves balancing the advantages and disadvantages of the different designs available. The aims of a successful experimental design are to:

- provide an overall plan for the experiment
- ensure precision of measurement
- enable results to be analysed to their full potential
- avoid potential sources of ambiguity or confusion
- ensure high levels of control over the different variables.

When deciding on an appropriate design, the researcher must consider carefully the precise nature of the experimental task, how to control relevant variables and the availability of participants. This section considers three experimental designs that you are likely to come into contact with:

- the independent groups design (different participants are used in each condition of the experiment)
- the repeated measures design (the same participants are used in each condition of the experiment)
- the matched participants design (participants are matched in each condition on variables relevant to the experiment).

Independent groups design

An independent groups design involves using different participants in each condition of the experiment (this may also be referred to as an 'independent measures/participants/subjects/samples design', or as a 'between groups/participants/subjects/samples design').

Experiments with this design may consist of:

- a control condition and one or more experimental conditions, or
- two (or more) experimental conditions.

See Table 7.1 for an example of how this design might appear in practice. In the former case, the group of participants that is given the experimental treatment is referred to as the 'experimental condition', and the group that exists for comparison and which receives no experimental treatment is the 'control condition'. Participants should be allocated randomly to each of the conditions (i.e. allocated in such a way that each participant stands an equal chance of being selected for each condition).

This procedure aims to ensure that characteristics of the participants (the participant variables) do not differ systematically between each condition. Otherwise, individual differences relevant to the experiment concerned might lead to results being confounded. (A discussion of confounding can be found on p. 225.) For example, in an experiment on learning ability it would be undesirable to have all the fastest learners

allocated to the same condition. This does not mean that random allocation will produce groups of participants that have identical characteristics. You may still, through chance, fail to eliminate individual differences as a factor and allocate all the fastest learners to one group. However, the chance of this happening is minimal. For example, imagine the likelihood of the numbers 1 to 6 inclusive coming up in that order on the National Lottery, or the probability of dealing out all four suits of a pack of cards in both suit and number order. The chances of events such as these happening are extremely remote, but of course any single combination, such as those just described, is as likely to happen as any other single combination.

By randomly allocating participants, researchers avoid any conscious or subconscious bias in participant allocation. Provided that an independent groups design is suitable for the proposed experiment and that enough participants have been used, then individual differences are unlikely to be significant as a confounding factor.

Table 7.1 >> Allocation of participants in three different experimental designs

1 The independent groups design:

Participants (Ps) may be allocated to the conditions randomly. For example:

Condition A	Condition B
P1	P3
P2	P5
P4	P6 ... *and so on.*

2 Repeated measures design:

Each participant undertakes all conditions of the experiment. For example:

Condition A	Condition B
P1	P1
P2	P2
P3	P3 ... *and so on.*

3 Matched participants design:

Pairs of participants are matched on appropriate variables relevant to the experiment; the members of each pair are then allocated to each condition (sometimes randomly). For example:

Condition A	Condition B
P1a	P1b
P2a	P2b
P3b	P3a ... *and so on.*

The random allocation of participants to conditions can be achieved in several ways. The simplest method is to draw names from a hat. More sophisticated ways include use of a random number table or a computer programme capable of drawing and allocating random numbers.

In natural experiments (see p. 200), the allocation of participants to conditions is decided by the naturally occurring event that is treated as the independent variable. For example, if the independent variable is the management style of two different hospital wards, then the experimenter does not have complete control over the allocation of participants to conditions.

See Table 7.3 for the advantages and disadvantages of an independent groups design.

Repeated measures design

A repeated measures design involves exposing every participant to each of the experimental conditions, so, in effect, participants are used as their own controls. (You may also see this referred to as related measures/samples, or within participants/subjects design.) Table 7.1 gives an example of how participants might be arranged in an experiment using this design. One of the conditions in experiments using this design may be a control condition, which serves the same purpose as the control condition in an independent groups design, i.e. to provide a baseline against which responses from any experimental condition can be compared.

Table 7.3 summarizes the advantages and disadvantages of a repeated measures design. The disadvantage associated with order effects can be minimized in two ways: counterbalancing and randomization.

■ *Counterbalancing* involves equal numbers of participants undertaking the tasks required of them in different orders. Table 7.2 shows two examples of how this might take place, with participants performing the conditions alternately until all participants have been tested. Note that there needs to be an even number of participants if counterbalancing is to be implemented fully. In the first example in Table 7.2, a multiple of two participants would be required and in the second a multiple of six, reflecting in each case the number of possible task orders.

Occasionally, however, it is not possible to apply counterbalancing as a strategy for minimizing order effects. Problems can occur, for example, when performing one condition helps the performance of another more than the other way round.

Consider the following memory experiment:

- Condition A: Learning a set of words presented randomly

- Condition B: Learning a matched set of words using a mnemonic technique to assist memory.

Table 7.2 >> Examples of counterbalancing in two- and three-condition experiments

Counterbalancing in a two-condition experiment:

Participant number	First condition undertaken	Second condition undertaken	
1	A	B	
2	B	A	
3	A	B	
4	B	A	*... and so on*

Counterbalancing in a three-condition experiment:

Participant number	First condition undertaken	Second condition undertaken	Third condition undertaken
1	A	B	C
2	B	C	A
3	C	A	B
4	A	C	B
5	B	A	C
6	C	B	A
			... and so on

There may be no problem when participants undertake Condition A first, followed by Condition B. However, when Condition A is presented after Condition B, it is likely that participants still have the mnemonic technique fresh in their minds. As a result, Condition B might help performance on Condition A more than A helps B, which is likely to lead to confounding of the results. In such circumstances, counterbalancing would be inappropriate and a researcher would be advised to use an independent groups design.

■ *Randomization* involves adopting a random strategy for deciding the order of presentation of experimental conditions by, for example, drawing lots or tossing a coin. This procedure, however, fails to provide a guarantee that presentation order of conditions will not influence results, because it is still possible, through chance, that differences will remain in the numbers of participants experiencing the conditions in particular orders.

Randomization can also be used as a technique for deciding the order of presentation of, for example, individual stimuli within experimental conditions. It works best when there is a large number of items within each condition. For example, suppose an investigation involves each participant rating 20 photographs for their attractiveness. If the same presentation order is followed by all participants, then some biases in rating may occur (for example, the picture presented first is likely to be given an average rating by many participants, simply because they are rating this picture averagely as they feel they may wish to use more extreme ratings for subsequent photos).

Finally, it is possible to combine an independent groups and a repeated measures design. For example, children from two different age groups might be given two different cognitive tasks. The independent groups element of the design would involve a comparison of the two age groups, and the repeated measures element would be a comparison of performance on the two cognitive tasks.

Matched participants design

A matched participants design (or matched subjects or matched pairs design) aims to gain the key advantages of both an independent groups design (i.e. no problems

with order effects as different people are used in each condition), and a repeated measures design (i.e. a greatly reduced risk of problems resulting from individual differences as participants are matched). It involves matching each participant in one of the experimental conditions as closely as possible with another participant in the second condition on all the variables considered to be relevant to the experiment in question. For example, pairs of participants might be matched for age, gender and their scores from intelligence and reading tests. Once pairs of participants have been identified, members of each pair can be randomly allocated to the conditions (see Table 7.1). The assumption made is that members of each pairing are so similar on the relevant variables that they can, for research purposes at least, be treated as if they are the same person. At the same time, however, participants perform in one condition of the experiment only, thereby eliminating the problem of order effects. See Table 7.3 for the advantages and disadvantages of a matched participants design.

Table 7.3 >> Advantages and disadvantages of different experimental designs

Independent groups design

>> *Advantages*   There is no problem with order effects, which occur when participants' performance is positively or negatively affected by their taking part in two or more experimental conditions. For example, performance in a second or subsequent condition may be improved through practice of a task done in a previous condition. Equally, negative effects may result from fatigue or boredom. Independent groups design has a wide range of potential uses and can be used where problems with order effects would make a repeated measures design impractical.

>> *Disadvantages*   There is the potential for error resulting from individual differences between the groups of participants taking part in the different conditions. Also, if participants are in short supply, then an independent groups design may represent an uneconomic use of those available to participate, since twice as many participants are needed to obtain the same amount of data as would be required in a two-condition, repeated measures design.

Repeated measures design

>> *Advantages*   Individual differences between participants are removed as a potential confounding variable. Also, fewer participants are required, since data for all conditions are collected from the same group of participants.

>> *Disadvantages*   The range of potential uses is smaller than for the independent groups design. For example, it is inappropriate to use two different reading schemes to teach young children to read within the same group of children – only an independent groups design could be employed in this case.

Order effects may result when participants take part in more than one experimental condition.

Matched participants design

>> *Advantages*   A matched participants design combines the advantages of both an independent groups and a repeated measures design.

>> *Disadvantage*   Achieving matched pairs of participants is difficult and time-consuming. It depends on the use of reliable and valid procedures for pretesting participants to obtain the matched pairs. Complete matching of participants on all variables that might affect experimental performance can rarely be achieved. Matched participants designs are, therefore, relatively uncommon, with their use being restricted to specific situations where a matching process is highly desirable in order that experimental success can be achieved.

DESIGNING NON-EXPERIMENTAL RESEARCH

The non-experimental methods of naturalistic observations, questionnaire surveys and interviews were introduced in Unit 6.

Naturalistic observational studies

A key design issue with naturalistic observational studies is deciding how to sample the behaviour to be studied. The possibilities include:

■ *time interval sampling* – observing and recording what happens in a series of fixed time intervals

■ *time point sampling* – observing and recording the behaviour that occurs at a series of given points in time

■ *event sampling* – observing and recording a complete event each time it occurs.

A further issue is how data are to be recorded. Likely methods are written notes, producing a checklist or tally chart, or using a rating scale. Figure 7.1 shows a simple tally chart, developed for an observational study on the state of a baby. Figure 7.2 is a simplified example of the tally chart devised by Bales (1970) as part of his technique of Interaction Process Analysis (IPA) and is used for plotting changes in the interactions within small groups.

Figure 7.1 ≫ *Specimen checklist of behaviours and tally chart (behaviour categories taken from Bee 1999)*

State of baby during 30-second time period	No. of observations
Deep sleep:	ЈНЇ ЈНЇ I
Active sleep:	ЈНЇ ЈНЇ ЈНЇ ЈНЇ I
Quiet awake:	ЈНЇ ЈНЇ ЈНЇ ЈНЇ ЈНЇ II
Active awake:	ЈНЇ III
Crying, fussing:	ЈНЇ ЈНЇ III

Figure 7.2 ≫ *Simplified version of a tally sheet used by Bales (1970)*

Each observer records the interactions of one participant for the period of the discussion, which lasts for 10 minutes. This 10-minute period can be divided into two 5-minute halves to allow comparison between behaviours over time. From this sheet, the total number, type and direction of a participant's interactions can be calculated and compared with those of other participants.

Name of observed person _____

	Person being addressed											
	Person A		Person B		Person C		Person D		Person E		The group	
Categories	1st half	2nd half	1st half	2nd half	1st half	2nd half	1st half	2nd half	1st half	2nd half	1st half	2nd half
Seems friendly												
Jokes												
Agrees												
Gives suggestion												
Gives opinion												
Gives guidance												
Asks for guidance												
Asks for opinion												
Asks for suggestion												
Disagrees												
Shows tension												
Seems unfriendly												

Questionnaire surveys and interviews

Questionnaire surveys and interviews can produce qualitative and/or quantitative data, and the range of design options available to the researcher is wide. Some of the design decisions that need to be taken into account when designing questionnaires are outlined in Table 7.4 below.

Table 7.4 >> Design issues in questionnaire surveys

Open or closed questions?
See Unit 6, p. 207, if you need to remind yourself of this issue or the different types of closed question available.

Question order
It is usual to ask questions on demographic data (e.g. age, gender) at the end of a questionnaire. Questions asking about any highly sensitive issues are rarely placed right at the start.

Avoid unnecessary jargon
For example: "Do you favour affirmative action in employment practices?" Your respondents need to be familiar with the language used for phrasing the questions. Plain English should be used wherever possible, or an explanation of terms given before the question is asked.

Avoid leading questions or value judgements
For example: "Was the suspect's shirt blue or green?" A question should not lead the respondent towards a particular response.

Avoid double-barrelled questions
For example: "Do you think that life is generally more stressful than it was 30 years ago, or do people find that modern technology reduces the stresses of life?" Don't include more than one item within the same question, as participants may wish to give different answers to each part.

Avoid emotive questions
For example: "Do you think that the killing of defenceless animals in laboratories should stop?" Emotive language may bias the response made.

Avoid vagueness or ambiguity
For example: "Do you take time off work? (please tick one)"
Never ☐   Rarely ☐   Sometimes ☐   Often ☐
These categories may mean different things to different people. All participants need to treat any particular question in the same way if the data collected are to be meaningful.

Avoid inappropriate assumptions
For example: "What is your occupation?" may cause embarrassment if people are unemployed.

ACTIVITY

Asking suitable questions

1 Look at each of the questions included in Table 7.4 and see if you can suggest a more suitable question wording in each case.

2 Prepare a brief questionnaire (no more than ten questions) designed to investigate the respondent's health over the last six months. Check all the design issues raised in Table 7.4 and review your questions. Have you asked each question in the best possible way?

Table 7.5 below contains a checklist for interview planning, while Fig. 7.3 overleaf shows an example of an interview schedule prepared for a study of gender identity that would produce qualitative data. This schedule of questions is on the subject of the

Table 7.5 >> A checklist for planning interviews (based on Dyer 1995)

1   The preliminaries to the interview
Have you:
    clearly described the research problem?
    stated the aim of the interview?
    linked the problem to an appropriate theory?
    identified the general categories of data that you will need to collect?

2   The questions
Have you:
    generated an appropriate set of questions?
    planned the order in which the questions will be presented?
    planned the interview to obtain the required balance between structured and unstructured interviewing?

3   The interview procedure
Have you:
    considered the issues of self-presentation?
    identified and approached potential respondents?
    planned the pre-interview meeting?
    planned the post-interview debriefing?
    decided how the information is to be recorded in the interview?
    considered the ethical issues raised by the proposed research and sought advice if necessary?

contribution of early school experience to the development of gender identity. The extreme right-hand column is used to place a tick against each question as it is asked, to prevent the embarrassing possibility of asking the same question twice. The clear heading ensures that you have a record of the basic details of the research stored with the questions, and the range of question types covered.

Figure 7.3 ≫ *An example of an interview schedule (Dyer 1995, p. 72)*

Title of project: A study of the development of gender identity

Topic: Contribution of early school experiences

Date of interview:

1 Can you begin by giving me a general description of the school you attended at the age of 5, so I can begin to understand what kind of a place it was?

2 Looking back, how did your school deal with the issue of gender in general?
For example, were boys and girls treated in different ways?
Could you give me some examples of that?

3 How did this compare with what you experienced at home?

4 How was children's behaviour dealt with? For example, was a clear distinction made between what was considered appropriate behaviour for boys compared to girls?

5 Did the school generally reinforce or challenge stereotyped gender definitions?
Can you give me some examples of that?

6 How do you now think this affected you during your early school life?
Can you give me some examples?

7 Can you give me some examples of the kind of thing that would have happened if a boy behaved in a way the teachers thought was more appropriate to a girl?

8 Can you give me any examples of the ways in which the rules about appropriate behaviour were enforced? How do you feel about them now?

9 What would have happened if you had been found breaking a rule like that?

FACTORS ASSOCIATED WITH RESEARCH DESIGN

This section examines some of the key factors that are associated with research design. It looks at:

- how variables in research can be defined, controlled and operationalized
- how pilot studies help to improve research quality
- techniques for assessing and improving reliability and validity
- ethical issues associated with research.

Defining variables

As you will be aware from Unit 6, a variable is anything that may change or alter in any way. The control, manipulation and observation of variables are central to psychological research. Psychologists need to be able to define variables successfully if their research is to be treated as scientifically worthwhile. This is by no means an easy task.

Try the next activity for yourself.

ACTIVITY

Defining variables

What do you understand by the term 'aggressive behaviour'? Imagine that you are one of a team involved in designing an observational study of aggressive behaviour in young children in school playgrounds. You have been asked to prepare a definition of the term 'aggressive behavior' that could be used by the research team.

When you have decided on your definition, compare your ideas with those of another psychology student. How are they similar and how do they differ? Try to agree a single definition that you are both happy with.

When you thought about your definition, you probably included different forms of violent behaviour – but did you include things such as spitting, swearing, glaring or invading personal space? Even a smile can sometimes have aggressive intent! It is even harder to define variables when they are less tangible – for example, 'stress' or 'concentration levels'. We may be able to measure the visible signs of their effect on a person, and we may strive to measure their effects on an aspect of behaviour, but can we be confident that we are actually measuring the variable itself?

Operational definitions of variables or factors being investigated are precise descriptions of what researchers understand by particular terms.

Operationalizing variables

In experimental research, the key variables are the independent variable and the dependent variable (see Unit 6). Operationalizing these variables usually results in a narrowing down of the research focus. For example, the general statement that 'mnemonics improve memory' might be refined into an independent variable that specifies the presence or absence of imagery, and a dependent variable that specifies the number of words correctly recalled. This process has important implications for the extent to which research findings can be generalized because the narrower the research focus, the more limited the extent to which results can be generalized.

ACTIVITY

Operationalizing definitions

Refine the definition of 'aggressive behaviour' that you generated in the previous activity into a fully operationalized definition that could be used in an observational study of aggressive behaviour in young children.

The control of variables

Unwanted variables (i.e. those that cause the potential confounding of results) are also known as extraneous variables. They may obscure the effect of an independent variable on a dependent variable, or provide a false impression that an independent variable has produced changes when in fact it has not. If a variable other than the independent variable produces a change in a dependent variable, then results are said to be confounded. Unwanted variables can result from either random error or constant error, and need to be eliminated or controlled as far as possible.

■ *Random errors* – The effects of random errors cannot be predicted. Possible sources of random errors might include:

– a participant's state of mind

– a participant's level of motivation

– incidental noise

– room temperature

– previous experiences on the day of the experiment.

It is hoped that random errors that might result from variables such as these will not systematically affect one condition of an experiment more than another. By allocating participants randomly to experimental conditions, psychologists will assume that random errors balance out across the experimental conditions. Such errors might, however, result in some loss of sensitivity.

The effects of random errors cannot be predicted ...

■ *Constant errors* – Constant errors affect the dependent variable in a consistent way and are, therefore, a much more serious problem for the researcher than random errors, since they may not affect all conditions of an experiment equally.

Constant errors might include:

– a failure to counterbalance or randomize the presentation order of experimental conditions

– participant differences

– errors of measurement that affect one condition more than another.

Wherever possible, such sources of error should be eliminated by good experimental design.

Conducting pilot studies

A pilot study is a small-scale prototype of a particular research investigation, carried out on a small number of participants. The aim is to find out whether there are any problems with the design, the instructions for participants or the measuring instrument(s) used. Also, a pilot study may provide information on how long the study takes to complete, and enable the researcher to practise carrying out the research task.

The researcher can inform participants that it is a pilot study, and may ask them to draw attention to any problematic areas or ambiguities that they come across. In the light of experience gained with the pilot study, the researcher can make revisions before the final research is carried out.

A questionnaire survey or interview-based investigation will need to be piloted on people from the appropriate target population.

ACTIVITY

Piloting your questionnaire

Pilot the short questionnaire that you prepared as part of the activity on p. 223 with two or three members of your family or friends.

What did you learn from this pilot? How would you change the questions in the light of your pilot? Why is it important to carry out a pilot before embarking on a research project?

Assessing and improving reliability

The term 'reliability' means dependability or consistency – vital if the psychologist is to obtain meaningful data. The term can be applied in a general way to the findings from psychological research. If the findings are replicated consistently, then the outcome can be said to be reliable. The term is also used in specific contexts. There are several ways in which reliability can be assessed and improved, and this section will consider some of these. Assessing reliability often involves using a correlational analysis in order to assess the consistency of observer ratings, or psychological measuring instruments such as psychometric tests. Check that you know the meaning of the term 'correlation' (including 'positive correlation') before reading on (refer back to pp. 203–5, if necessary).

Assessing and improving observer reliability

Observer reliability is assessed by measuring the extent to which researchers, scoring the same participants, achieve consistency of measurement between each other. Scorers record their own data individually, and then the sets of data obtained from each scorer are correlated. Observer reliability is achieved if highly significant positive correlations are obtained between the scorers.

Ideally, in observational studies, more than one observer should be used. 'Inter-rater reliability' is a procedure that allows a researcher to measure the extent to which observers agree on the behaviours they have observed. Independent checks for reliability can often be made easier by the use of audiotaping or videotaping. Correlational analysis is often used to establish inter-rater reliability.

There are ways of improving observer reliability. For example, observers should be trained thoroughly in the techniques being used. Also, operational definitions of the key terms involved in the research should be both clear and understood fully by all the observers involved in gathering data. Consider, for example, an observational study of aggressive behaviour in children's playgrounds. If more than one observer is being used, it is important that they all understand exactly which behaviours can be categorized as examples of 'aggressive behaviour'. In other words, they need to operationalize the term 'aggressive behaviour', as you were asked to do in the activity on p. 225.

Assessing and improving test reliability

Another important aspect of reliability concerns the reliability of tests, such as those which attempt to measure intelligence or personality. Several methods are used by psychologists, including the split-half method and the test–retest method.

- *The split-half method* – This can be used as a way of assessing the extent to which individual items in a particular test or questionnaire are consistent with other items in the same test. The method involves splitting the test or questionnaire concerned into two parts after data have been obtained from the participants. This splitting might be done by, for example:

  - comparing the results obtained from odd- and even-numbered questions

  - comparing the results from the first half of the test with those from the second half

  - splitting the test into two at random.

  The two sets of responses (however they are obtained) are then correlated. A highly significant positive correlation between the two sets of responses would indicate reliability. If the correlation is not high enough, the researchers would need to check the procedure used for constructing the test carefully and very possibly revise the test items. The aim of the revision would be to produce an improvement in the reliability of the particular test or questionnaire.

- *The test–retest method* – This is used to assess another important aspect of consistency – the stability of a test or questionnaire over time. This method involves presenting the same participants with the same test or questionnaire on different occasions, with no feedback given after the first presentation. The time interval between presentations needs to be selected carefully. If it is too short, participants may remember their previous answers, but if it is too long, then the participants may possibly have changed in some way relevant to the test or questionnaire. Once again, correlational techniques are used to indicate the test stability. If there is a highly significant positive correlation between the scores obtained from the test and retest phases, then the test is deemed to be stable. Test items and/or testing procedures can be revised (e.g. by rephrasing instructions) if a sufficiently high correlation is not obtained.

Assessing and improving validity

Validity is concerned with the extent to which something measures what it sets out to measure. This is not as simple as it might first appear. For example, there is considerable debate over issues such as whether personality tests are valid measures of personality, or whether diagnostic classification schemes used in the mental-health field really are valid. A distinction may be drawn between internal validity, external validity and test validity.

Internal validity

Internal validity is concerned with the extent to which we can be sure that research findings are due to the mechanisms suggested. For example, in an experiment the key issue might be whether we can be certain that differences in the results obtained are due to manipulation of the independent variable and not to the action of some other unwanted variable, such as individual differences or the effects of practice. Internal validity is also compromised if no effect is found within research when in fact an effect actually exists.

External validity

External validity is concerned with the extent to which results can be generalized to other settings beyond that of the study concerned. A distinction can be drawn here between the following:

- *population validity* – the extent to which results from research can be generalized to other groups of people

- *ecological validity* – the extent to which research findings can be generalized to situations outside the research setting.

Note that laboratory experiments do not automatically lack ecological validity by the mere fact that they are carried out in laboratories. They sometimes do, but many laboratory studies are ecologically valid and have results that can be generalized beyond the lab. Similarly, the fact that research is carried out in a natural setting does not guarantee ecological validity. This may or may not be achieved – it all depends on whether or not the results can be generalized.

Test validity

There are several different techniques available to help the psychologist assess test validity, including:

- *Face validity* – the simplest technique is concerned with assessing whether a measuring instrument looks correct in the eyes of independent experts, who may suggest improvements to the researcher. Because of its subjectivity, assessment of face validity usually only takes place in the earliest phases of constructing a measuring instrument, e.g. when a draft examination paper is submitted for approval.

- *Content validity* is superficially similar to face validity. Again, independent experts are asked to assess the validity of the measuring instrument concerned. This time, however, the procedures are more rigorous, and there is a detailed and systematic examination of all the component parts of the measuring instrument concerned.

- *Concurrent validity* involves obtaining two sets of scores at the same time: one from the new procedure with unknown validity, and the other from an alternative procedure or test for which validity has already been established. The scores obtained from both of these measures will be correlated with each other to assess the validity of the new procedure. A highly significant positive correlation would suggest that the new procedure or test is valid. For example, a new procedure for the diagnosis of a psychopathological condition might be compared with an existing method of diagnosis for which the success rate is already known. Further refinement of the criteria in order to improve concurrent validity might be necessary if the correlation obtained is not sufficiently high.

- *Predictive validity* involves a similar strategy, but this time the two sets of scores are obtained at different points in time. An example from abnormal psychology might be correlation of initial diagnoses with information gained in the light of experience with the patients concerned over a period of time. In other words, a diagnostic procedure or test with high predictive validity would allow fairly accurate forecasts to be made about future behaviour. If the test indicates that certain behaviours should occur, and they do not occur, then the test has low predictive validity.

Ethics

The ethical issues associated with research are dealt with in other units. Topic 3 in Unit 5 includes a section on ethical guidelines and Unit 6 discusses particular issues in association with the different research methods. The next activity will enable you to check your memory of key ethical issues. If you find this activity difficult, then be sure to go back and reread the relevant sections of Units 5 and 6.

ACTIVITY

Ethical issues

Describe in as much detail as you can at least one ethical issue that is important in relation to each of the following research methods:

1 laboratory experiment

2 naturalistic observation

3 questionnaire survey

4 interview.

Select a different ethical issue for each method.

SELECTING PARTICIPANTS

A 'target population' is a group of people that share a given set of characteristics about which a researcher wishes to draw conclusions (e.g. all students registered for AS-level Psychology examinations in a given year). However, a target population is usually too large for each individual to be investigated, so a subset of the population – a sample – is investigated instead. A 'representative sample' forms part of a target population, sharing the characteristics of the population despite its smaller size. If, and *only* if, a sample is truly representative, can it be used by psychologists as a basis for generalizing their conclusions to the remainder of the target population. It follows from this that a sample that is not truly representative may result in wasted time and effort.

A general principle is that the larger the sample, the more likely it is to give an accurate estimate about the nature of the population from which it has been drawn. Deciding sample size, therefore, reflects a delicate balancing act between the need to represent accurately the target population on the one hand, and practical considerations, such as saving time and money, on the other. In practice, some degree of sampling error is likely to result – the researcher's task is to minimize this error. Statistical tables can be used to advise on the sample size needed to achieve acceptable levels of

sampling error in target populations of different sizes. Samples can be taken in several different ways. We shall discuss two main methods of sampling below: random and non-random.

Random sampling

In a random sample, every person or item in a given target population stands an equal chance of being selected for inclusion. This means that it is necessary to have a list that identifies every person or item in the target population in order to generate the random sample. Selection then takes place in a completely unbiased way. However, selecting a random sample does not guarantee the researcher a sample that is totally representative of the population concerned. Nor does it mean that any two random samples drawn from the same target population will share identical characteristics. By its very nature, a random sample can only come with a guarantee that it has been selected in an unbiased manner (e.g. by using one of the techniques for randomly allocating participants to conditions described earlier on p. 219). However, as long as the target population and sample size have been chosen carefully, the laws of probability predict that the chance of selecting a biased sample through random sampling techniques is minimal.

Non-random sampling methods

There are other possible sampling methods, most of which are beyond the requirements of the AS Psychology specification. Two that you may come across, however, are the 'self-selected (or volunteer) sample' and the 'opportunity sample'.

- *Self-selected samples* – This involves participants selecting themselves for the research concerned, often by replying to an advertisement. This type of sampling is widely used in university research. A well-known example was in Milgram's research on obedience in the 1960s (see Unit 5). Potential disadvantages of using a self-selected sample are that the majority of a given target population are unlikely to respond, and that those who do respond may be atypical of the target population in some way. Thus, the data gathered from this potentially biased sample are unlikely to be representative of the target population.

- *Opportunity (or opportunist) sample* – This is a widely used but easily biased method, involving the researcher selecting anyone who is available to take part from any given population, such as available staff or students within a college. Again, data gathered from an opportunity sample are unlikely to be representative of the target population because certain subgroups may not be available for inclusion – for example, if a researcher was selecting an opportunity sample from a school on a day when all Year 6 pupils were away on a field trip.

THE RELATIONSHIP BETWEEN RESEARCHERS AND PARTICIPANTS

The research situation is not without a social dimension, and it is to be expected that a relationship will develop between researchers and participants. As a social situation, a research investigation is liable to be influenced by those taking part in it. Research participants may be affected by demand characteristics, while investigators themselves may have unintended effects on the outcome of research – known as 'investigator effects'.

Demand characteristics

Demand characteristics occur when participants try to make sense of the research situation that they find themselves in and act accordingly. These characteristics have already been described in the section on laboratory experiments (Unit 6, p. 197), but they may occur in any research scenario in which the participants are aware of taking part. They become a problem as soon as participants act differently from the way that they would outside the research situation. Well-designed research will aim to minimize their effects as much as possible.

Demand characteristics might include the following participant behaviour:

- *trying to guess the purpose of the research* and acting in a way that they feel is helpful to the researcher – or indeed, unhelpful

- *acting nervously and out of character* because of being in a research situation – for instance, participants may feel that they are being evaluated in some way (e.g. that their personality is being assessed) and feel worried about this

- *displaying a social desirability bias*, wishing themselves to be seen in the most favourable light possible, e.g. in the responses given to a questionnaire on moral standards.

Investigator effects

Investigator effects result from the effects of a researcher's behaviour and characteristics on an investigation. There is a wide range of possibilities here. Expectation effects can occur where a researcher is deeply committed to achieving a particular outcome. This may be a particular problem when observing events that can be interpreted in more than one way (an example might be the difficulty in distinguishing between children fighting or indulging in rough-and-tumble play). Alternatively, even overt fraud ('massaging the data') is a possibility, however remote.

In naturalistic observational studies, the presence of the observer can cause participants to behave in ways different from those that would normally be displayed. For example, behaviour may be more restrained than usual. When research is carried out using questionnaire surveys or interviews, then many different aspects of the investigator may have an influence, including the investigator's age, gender, ethnic group, appearance, expression and communication style.

Check your understanding of research design and implementation in psychology by answering these questions. Try to do this from memory at first. You can check your answers by looking back through Topic 1.

1 What is a research hypothesis?

2 What is a null hypothesis?

3 Name the experimental design where all participants take part in all the conditions of the experiment.

4 Give one advantage and one disadvantage of an independent groups design.

5 What does the term 'event sampling' mean in observational research?

6 What is a pilot study and why is it important to carry one out?

7 Describe one way in which observer reliability can be assessed.

8 Suggest one way in which observer reliability might be improved.

9 Name two techniques for assessing test reliability.

10 Explain what the term 'external validity' means.

11 Name three of the techniques that can be used by a psychologist to help assess test validity.

12 What does a 'target population' mean in the context of psychological research?

13 Define the term 'random sample'.

14 Why is an opportunity sample likely to be unrepresentative?

15 What is meant by the term 'demand characteristics'?

REVISION SUMMARY

Having covered this topic you should be able to:

✓ define all the key terms listed on pp. 215–16

✓ describe the following experimental designs – independent groups, repeated measures and matched participants designs

✓ discuss key design issues in non-experimental research – naturalistic observations, questionnaire surveys and interviews – including deciding how behaviour is sampled, the method(s) used for recording data, and the phrasing and organisation of questions

✓ explain why independent and dependent variables need to be operationalized

✓ describe the importance of conducting pilot studies and controlling variables

✓ outline techniques for assessing and improving reliability

✓ discuss the ethical issues relating to psychological research and the importance of respecting the rights and feelings of those taking part

✓ describe different sampling techniques to select participants for research investigations from the target population of interest

✓ discuss the relationship between researchers and participants, including demand characteristics and investigator effects.

GETTING YOU THINKING...

Look at the two graphs carefully and answer the questions that follow:

1 Describe in words what Graph A tells you.

2 Describe in words what Graph B tells you.

3 Which graph do you find the more accurate and informative? Why?

4 What changes would need to be made to the graph you considered less informative in order to make it more informative?

Look at some newspapers or magazines and try to find at least one good example of graphical presentation of numerical data and one poor example. Write a few notes about each one, highlighting what you feel to be the good and less good features of each example. Discuss these with another student on your course and/or your teacher.

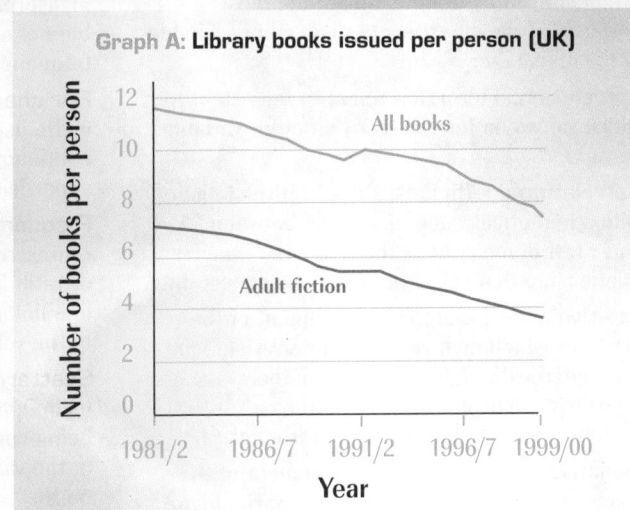

Graph A: **Library books issued per person (UK)**

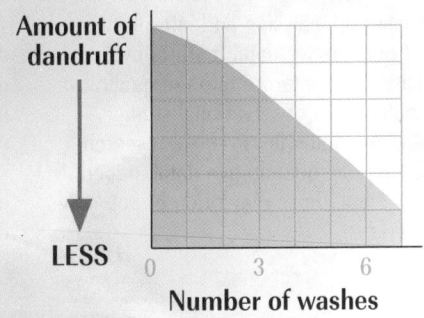

Graph B: **Long-lasting efficacy** – The best way to eliminate dandruff and prevent it recurring

KEY TERMS

Measure of central tendency: a descriptive statistic that provides a single value which is representative of a set of numbers by indicating the most typical (average) value. The mode, median and mean are measures of central tendency.

Mode: the most frequently occurring value in a data sequence.

Median: the middle value of a set of scores arranged in ascending or descending order.

Mean: the arithmetic average of a set of scores, calculated by adding all the scores together and dividing by the number of scores.

Measures of dispersion: descriptive statistics that enable us to examine the variability within sets of data; they help us to understand whether scores in a given set of data are similar to, or very different from, each other. The range and standard deviation are measures of dispersion.

Range: the difference between the highest and lowest scores in a given set of data.

Standard deviation: used to measure the variability (i.e. the typical deviation) of a given sample of scores from its mean; the most powerful of the measures of dispersion available to the researcher.

Correlation: a term that refers to the extent to which values on (usually two) different variables co-vary.

Correlation coefficient: a descriptive statistic with a numerical value on a scale between −1 and +1. It demonstrates the strength of any relationship that exists between two sets of data.

Positive correlation: a measurement of the extent to which high values on one variable are associated with high values on another. A positive correlation is indicated by a correlation coefficient between zero and +1.

Negative correlation: a measurement of the extent to which high values on one variable are associated with low values on another. A negative correlation is indicated by a correlation coefficient between zero and −1.

Histogram: a form of graphical representation used to present data on interval or ratio levels of measurement. It consist of a series of vertical bars of equal width, which represent the frequencies of the variable placed on the x-axis.

Bar chart: a series of vertical bars of equal width used to illustrate the frequencies of a non-continuous variable displayed on the x-axis. It is superficially similar to a histogram.

Frequency polygon: a form of graphical representation used to present data on interval or ratio levels of measurement. It consists of a line linking points that represent the frequencies of the variable placed on the x-axis.

Scattergraph (or scattergram): a graphical technique used to illustrate sets of data that are being correlated with each other. Data from one of the variables being correlated are presented on the x-axis, and data from the same individual for the second variable on the y-axis.

This topic looks at ways of analysing and interpreting both qualitative and quantitative data. It starts by focusing on the analysis and interpretation of qualitative data derived from naturalistic observational studies, questionnaire surveys and interviews. These research methods often also produce quantitative data; indeed, with questionnaire surveys, these may often be the only kind of data produced.

The final section of this topic introduces the use of descriptive statistical techniques to analyse quantitative data. Further analysis of quantitative data using inferential statistical tests is outside the scope of the AS-level Psychology specification. If you continue your study of psychology to A level, you will be using inferential statistical tests to help you analyse your coursework data.

ANALYSING QUALITATIVE DATA

Qualitative data include data generated from observational research, interviews and questionnaires that are not in the form of numbers. The task of the researcher, therefore, is to analyse large volumes of narrative accounts, including transcripts from interviews, detailed descriptions of what was observed or the written answers to questionnaires.

When analysing qualitative data, the researcher is usually concerned with searching for the underlying meaning in what people do or say, and this relies heavily on the researcher's interpretive skills. Researchers use a number of different techniques to analyse qualitative data, involving categorizing the data and trying to identify themes within the data. This is very different from the use of statistical tests to analyse quantitative (numerical) data.

Data from naturalistic observational studies

The use of naturalistic observational techniques is discussed in Unit 6. These techniques differ widely both in terms of the approaches used and in the ways in which behaviour is recorded and classified, so it is hardly surprising that they also differ widely in terms of how behaviour is analysed and presented. Data interpretation may also produce ideas for hypotheses that can be tested using other research methods.

When qualitative data are obtained, these may be presented in different ways, including diary descriptions and specimen descriptions of behaviour. An example of a diary description from an observational study is shown in the panel opposite; it illustrates the social rituals through which a child's ability to name can arise.

Diary description

Mary, aged 11 months: Mother takes Mary out of her high-chair and puts her on the potty. Her toys are all in a box on the table in front of her chair.

Mother (spontaneously): "Do you want Teddy?"

Mary: "aah"

Mother: "Where is he?"

Mary looks around and makes to get off her potty and go to the table, but Mother restrains her. Mary looks at the table and points.

Mother (going to table opposite and bringing down the box of toys): "That's right, he's there, isn't he? Here he is. What does he say? What does Teddy say?"

Mary: "aah"

Mother: "Yes, he does, doesn't he?"

Mary: "aah"

Mother pats Teddy.

Mary: "aah"

Mary's attention moves to the box containing her other toys, which Mother has placed on the floor near her.

Mother: "Oh, what can you see in there? Doggie? (takes doggie out) Let's see who else is in here. Who's that? Is it duckie? and what does the duck say?"

Mother squeaks the duck.

Mary: "aah"

Mother: "He doesn't! What does the duck say? What does he say?"

Mary: "argh" *(reaching towards it)*

Mother: "Yes, I know you want it. What does he say?"

Mary: "woraghagh"

Mother: "He doesn't, he says *(she squeaks it concurrently)* 'quack, quack, quack', doesn't he? 'quack, quack, quack'."

Mary: "gh, gh"

Mother: "Yes, he does."

Mary (looking at Teddy): "aah"

Mother: "And that's aah is it, that's aah Teddy?"

Mary: "aah"

Mother: "And who's this, what does he say? What does duck say? What does duck say?"

No response from Mary. Mother squeaks duck.

Mary: "gah"

Mother: "Quack!"

Mary: "gah"

Mother: "Ooh, aren't you clever."

Source: Lock (1980, p. 110)

Although ecological validity may be a strength of observational studies, the categorization of behaviours that takes place in them (and also in interview-based research, discussed later) may challenge their validity. Are the operational definitions used the best ways of defining behaviours? For instance, are the definitions comprehensive enough, or too comprehensive? It is important, therefore, that the structure of a study is fully justifiable in terms of its theoretical basis, and also sufficiently complete, i.e. it should include all the behaviours of interest.

Other potential threats to validity are:

- *inadequate sampling* (e.g. too few samples, or sampling undertaken at inappropriate times)
- *mishandling* or *inadequate handling* of the system used (e.g. through pressure or lack of familiarity in a research situation).

These challenges to validity highlight the need for careful analysis and presentation of observational data if the potential benefits from the richness of the data gathered are not to be compromised.

Data from questionnaire surveys

Much of the information that is gained from conducting research using questionnaire surveys is analysed using quantitative methods. However, data from appropriate open questions that invite participants to give different responses may be analysed qualitatively. In contrast to closed questions, the use of open questions may serve to reduce researcher bias and the impact of the researcher's own views on the design of the survey. The result is a means of analysis that is both flexible and interpretative.

A further possibility for the analysis of data derived from questionnaire surveys is to convert qualitative data to quantitative by, for example, counting the number of times that a particular item is mentioned. This is a fairly common way of analysing data and shows the extent to which qualitative and quantitative data may be interdependent.

Data from interviews

Interviews are often just one of the techniques used by the researcher in association with other methods in a particular piece of research. As such, they may help to provide a validity check on the results obtained. Interpreting the information gained from interviews is a complex procedure.

Qualitative data might include many elements which need to be taken into account when interpretation takes place. These include description of features of interest, such as:

- the actual behaviour observed by the interviewer
- the context(s) in which the behaviour occurs
- self-reports of behaviour by the participant(s)
- self-reports of cognitions that cannot be observed directly – for example, the feelings, thoughts and attitudes of the participants in the study
- interpretations made by the researchers
- implications of the study for any theory.

From this list it can be seen that distinctions need to be made between the aspects of a report that:

- describe what actually happened
- are based on the interpretations and inferences made by the researcher
- are based on the interpretations and inferences of the participant(s).

If reporting is to be objective, the distinctions between these need to be made clear to the reader when a report of an investigation is published. Inevitably, the potential for bias in reporting is considerable. For example, researchers might report only those aspects of behaviour that support their own theoretical standpoint, or are particularly relevant to their research. Also, decisions about what information to include and what to leave out may be subjective. Carefully reported investigations should always make clear to the reader the criteria used to select participants and how decisions were made about what information to present.

The close, and often prolonged, relationship between the researcher and the participant(s) in interview-based research may heighten the importance of interpersonal interaction. This interaction may be very productive or it may reduce objectivity by introducing subjectivity.

Whilst the qualitative data generated by interview-based research may add to our existing understanding, they can also produce evidence that challenges theory or our existing understanding, thereby stimulating further research and, perhaps, a new theoretical perspective.

The nature of the data obtained often reflects the extent to which the interview was structured or unstructured (see Unit 6, p. 209). Where data are qualitative, the researcher is able to present results more flexibly, but the problem exists of how to organize and present a mass of descriptive data in a meaningful way. Some of the issues the researcher might consider are listed below.

- Examine carefully the background theory for a study involving interviews before the research is undertaken, and then decide how the data can be categorized appropriately.
- Solicit opinions from the interviewees on how they would wish the material to be presented. Has material been presented in the spirit in which it has been told?
- Decide how any selection or paraphrasing of material is going to be undertaken. (Particular care needs to be taken with this if bias in reporting is to be avoided.)
- Decide whether quotations will be used to enrich the presentation of data. If so, how will they be selected?

Categorization of qualitative data is an important task for the person reporting an interview. It involves the grouping of like items together, e.g. statements by the interviewee concerning particular subjects. A good computer database can be helpful when doing this.

Perhaps inevitably, because of their nature, the interpretation of interview data is partial or incomplete. Something may be lost in terms of reliability, and something gained through the sensitivity and depth of the approach. They may have the important benefit of providing a new basis for interpretation. See the panel opposite for an example that provides interesting insights on the Bristol riots of the early 1980s derived from interviews.

DESCRIPTIVE STATISTICAL TECHNIQUES

Descriptive statistical techniques provide ways in which the researcher can obtain summary descriptions of sets of quantitative data. Two types of descriptive statistical techniques are measures of central tendency, which give average values, and measures of dispersion, which look at the variability of scores. Each of these techniques provides a single value that can help us to summarize a set of data which might otherwise be difficult to interpret. This potential benefit, however, is not without its cost. When any single value is obtained, the process of summation inevitably produces a loss of individual information.

Measures of central tendency and measures of dispersion are also valuable to the psychologist in that they form the basis for analyses using inferential statistics.

Riots and representations: the Bristol riots of the 1980s

In-depth interviews that generate qualitative data can add a great deal to our understanding of social processes, and can illuminate events that appear, at first sight, to be incomprehensible. A series of street disturbances in Britain in the early 1980s, for example, raised the spectre of 'mob rule', and the idea that people who get together in crowds are overtaken by a 'group mind'.

Journalists tend to see people in crowds (particularly when they attack the police) as if they were animals who have been stripped of the veneer of civilization that usually holds them in check. Social psychologists who have been influenced by the theories of the French writer, Gustave LeBon, have been just as negative. LeBon (1947, but first published in 1895) argued that the behaviour of people in crowds fell several rungs down the evolutionary ladder, to the level of "beings belonging to inferior forms of evolution, women, savages, and children, for instance" (LeBon, 1947, p. 36). These ideas take on a quite nasty political flavour when they are used to describe 'riots' by black people in inner-city areas, and the task of the psychologist should be to look at how popular images work, and how people in the crowd understand their actions. In-depth interviewing can move to an 'insider' perspective on these events, and so assist in this task.

One of the first 'riots' in the 1980s, in the St Paul's area of Bristol, was studied by Reicher (1984), a social psychologist whose training had been in the experimental tradition. Reicher was carrying out research on social identity at Bristol University when the April 1980 'riot' broke out, and he was able to interview participants. Their accounts did not correspond with either standard social psychological or journalistic images of people who had lost their minds, and the 'inside' story was of a community trying to defend itself against the police. One of the striking aspects of the insider accounts was that both black and white people who were in the crowd refused to accept the outsider claims that this was a racial disturbance.

Private homes and shops within the community were left untouched, whereas the banks and the unemployment office were seen as legitimate targets. The stories collected in these interviews also corresponded with the descriptions of the damage given by the authorities. An examination of the accounts of outsiders and insiders by Reicher and Potter (1985) illustrated the ways in which traditional 'scientific' explanations of crowd behaviour fail to account for the insider perspective which, in the case of St Paul's, stressed the meaningfulness of crowd action, and the feelings of solidarity and emotional warmth that came with defence of the community.

Source: Foster and Parker (1995)

Measures of central tendency

You are probably already familiar with measures of central tendency and refer to them as averages. A measure of central tendency provides a single value that is representative of a set of numbers by indicating the most typical value. Three measures of central tendency are discussed here:

- The *mode* is the most frequently occurring value.
- The *median* is the middle value of scores arranged in ascending or descending order.
- The *mean* is the arithmetic average.

Each has its own particular uses – and hence advantages and disadvantages – for particular sets of data.

The mode

The mode is the value in any set of scores that occurs most frequently. For example, with the following series of numbers:

2   4   6   7   7   7   10   12

the most frequently occurring number is 7, and so the mode = 7.

Although the mode provides information on the most frequently occurring value, it has its limitations and is not widely used in psychological research. One reason for this is that when there are only a few scores representing each value, then even very small changes in the data can radically alter the mode. For example:

3	6	8	9	10	10	Mode = 10
3	3	6	8	9	10	Mode = 3

A further possible problem is that there may not be a single modal value. For example, take the series of numbers:

3 5 8 8 8 10 12 16 16 16 20

In this situation, there are two modal values (8 and 16), known as the 'bimodal values'. With cases such as this, the bimodal values may still provide a useful summary statistic. It is, of course, possible to have several modal values, in which case the distribution is referred to as 'multimodal' and the value of the statistic becomes even more limited. For example:

2 2 4 7 7 8 8 10 11 11 13 13

Here, five values occur twice.

The mode has an advantage in that it is a figure that actually does always occur in a given sequence, which may not be true of other measures of central tendency. However, its disadvantage is that it tells us nothing about the other values in the distribution concerned.

The median

The median is the middle value of a set of numbers that has been placed in numerical order (i.e. in order from lowest to highest score, or highest to lowest). Therefore, half of the scores in a given set of data will lie above the median, and half below it. When there is an even number of scores, however, there will be two middle values. In these circumstances, the median is calculated by adding the two central values together and dividing by two. The panel below provides an example of both situations.

When calculating the median, you may find it helpful to cross out the lowest and highest values alternately until you are left with the middle value(s).

Calculating the median

To calculate the median when there is an odd number of scores:

Place scores in numerical order

2 4 5 (6) 8 10 11

Median = 6

To calculate the median when there is an even number of scores:

Place scores in numerical order

2 4 5 (6 8) 10 11 13

Median = $\dfrac{6 + 8}{2}$

Median = 7

The main advantage of the median is that it remains relatively unaffected by any outlying values. It is therefore a safe measure of central tendency to use when we are unsure about the reliability of extreme values. Also, it can be used with data from skewed distributions – that is, where there is a cluster of values at one end of the range (see the panel opposite). Unlike the mean, it can be used when data are on an ordinal level of measurement: first, second, third, etc. (for example, rating scales where data are not measured in fixed units with an equal distance between each point on the scale concerned).

A disadvantage of the median, however, is that it does not work well with small data sets and is affected by any alteration of the central values in a set of values. For example: if we have two sets of data:

10	12	13	14	18	19	22	22	**and**
10	12	13	14	15	19	22	22	

the median would be 16 in the first case and 14.5 in the second, despite only one value being different in the two sets of data.

The mean

The mean is the arithmetic average of a set of data, and is probably the measure of central tendency with which you are most familiar. It is calculated by adding all the values together and dividing the total by the number of scores. An example is shown in the panel below.

The main advantage of the mean is that it makes use of all the available data. As such, it is the most powerful of the measures of central tendency available. However, it needs to be used with a certain amount of caution. One limitation of the mean is that when it has been calculated, decimal points may be less meaningful if all the data consist of whole numbers (as in the example shown below).

Also, the distribution of values needs to be taken into account. The mean can be used appropriately as the measure of central tendency with sets of data (such as

Calculating the mean

To find the mean of:

2 4 5 5 6 6 6 7 8 10

Add all the values together:

2 + 4 + 5 + 5 + 6 + 6 + 6 + 7 + 8 + 10 = 59

Divide this sum by the number of scores (there are 10 scores):

Mean = $\dfrac{59}{10}$

Mean = 5.9

Normal and skewed distributions

A normal distribution curve is a bell-shaped curve which is symmetrical about its mean, median and mode (see diagram below). It is called 'normal' because it describes the theoretical distribution of a great many naturally occurring variables. Various characteristics of individuals are considered to be normally distributed (e.g. height and body weight) and sometimes a particular measure is deliberately constructed in a way that a normal distribution of scores results (e.g. some intelligence tests). In theory, a normal distribution curve should result when a large random sample of measurements is taken from an appropriate population. In practice, however, it would be very rare for a distribution to fit a normal distribution curve precisely – there are always likely to be at least some minor irregularities.

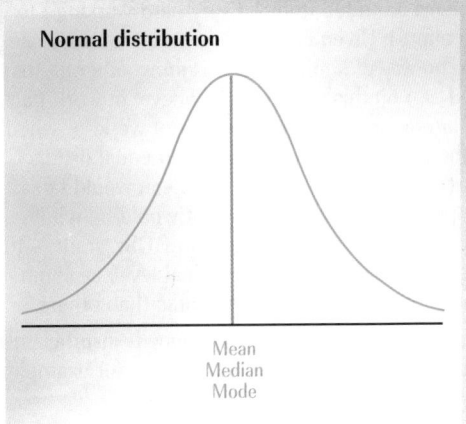

Notice the key features of this curve:

- The curve is symmetrical about its mean value, which occurs at the central point of the distribution. (This value is also the median and mode.)
- The curve has a characteristic bell shape, curving downwards close to the mean and outwards further away.
- The outer extremities of the distribution (known as the tails) will never touch the horizontal axis.
- The properties of this distribution mean that certain statements about probability can be made – a very important feature when a researcher wishes to express clearly the relationship between sample data and data from the population that the sample represents.

However, all variables are not normally distributed; some distributions can be best described as skewed (see below).

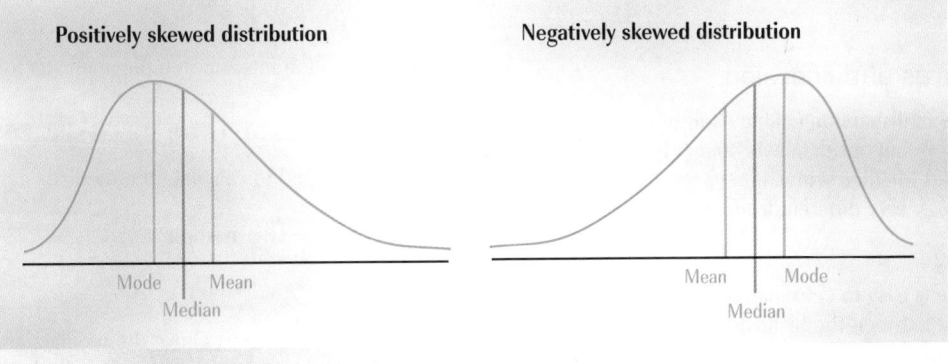

normally distributed data – see the panel above) which do not have extreme outlying values. When such extreme values are present, the median should be used instead.

For example, calculate the mean of 8, 10, 10, 12, 60. What does the mean tell us about any of these scores?

In this example, the mean is 20, which tells us very little about the four low scores and the single high score. In circumstances where such 'outliers' occur, it would be more appropriate to use the median (10), which at least would summarize the first four values

reasonably successfully (coincidentally, 10 is also the mode in this example).

The mean can be used most successfully with data on interval or ratio levels of measurement (i.e. data measured in fixed units, where each point on the scale of measurement concerned is an equal distance apart). Caution needs to be used if the mean is used with data on ordinal levels of measurement, where data are capable of being placed in rank order, but no assumptions can be made about points on the scale concerned being an equal distance apart.

For example, consider the situation where a teacher rates pupils on a seven-point scale that measures how hard they have worked on their psychology coursework. Students are rated from 1 ('very hard-working') to 7 ('no effort'). Given the arbitrary nature of the scale, we have no way of knowing for certain whether all those rated at 4 on this scale ('average level of work') actually put in precisely the same amount of work, or whether all the points on the scale are at an equal distance apart. Therefore calculating the mean would be inappropriate. In a similar way, it would be wholly inappropriate to work out a mean GCSE grade – these grades are measured on an ordinal level, as some mark bands cover a wider range of marks than others.

Using a measure of central tendency is insufficient on its own to describe a set of data. Take, for example, the following scenario:

Data set A	Data set B
100	100
101	40
99	120
102	60
98	180
100	100

The mean for each set of data is 100, yet the distribution of scores is very different in each case. In data set A, the scores are all very close to 100, while in data set B, they are dispersed much more widely. This is where measures of dispersion have an important role to play.

Measures of dispersion

Measures of dispersion enable us to examine the variability within our data sets, and help us to understand whether scores in a given set of data are similar to, or very different from, each other.

The range

The range is easy to calculate because it is simply the difference between the highest and lowest scores in a given set of data, with 1 added if the scores are all whole numbers. A sample calculation is shown in the panel below.

Calculating the range

To calculate the range of:

3 7 8 10 11 16 18 21 22 26

Find the difference between the highest score (26) and the lowest (3), and add 1.

Range = 26 – 3 + 1 = 24

Similarly, if values are recorded to one decimal place, then the range is the difference between the lowest and highest values with 0.1 added (to two decimal places, it is the difference plus 0.01, and so on). If values are recorded to the nearest half unit, then the range has 0.5 added to the difference between the lowest and highest value.

The range has the advantage of being quick to calculate, but has some important limitations. It does not provide any idea of the distribution of values around the centre, nor does it take individual values into account (remember that the only values used when the range is calculated are the two most extreme values). Following on from this point, the range is therefore seriously affected by any outlying values in a given set of data.

The interquartile range

In an attempt to overcome the potential effect of outlying values, calculating the interquartile range is often preferred. The interquartile range measures the spread of the middle 50 per cent of values when they are placed in numerical order. The top 25 per cent and the bottom 25 per cent of values are ignored, which has the effect of removing the influence of outlying values, and providing an indication of grouping around the central value. The panel below explains how this is calculated.

Calculating the interquartile range

Calculate the interquartile range for the following data:

2 3 7 8 10 11 16 18 21 22 26 26

We first need to calculate the median:

$$\text{The median} = \frac{11 + 16}{2}$$

$$\text{Median} = 13.5$$

There are six scores above the median, and six below it. The interquartile range will therefore include the six scores that lie closest to the median, and exclude the remaining six. So, for the scores lying above the median, this means that 16, 18 and 21 will be included within the interquartile range, and 22, 26 and 26 excluded.

The upper boundary of the interquartile range will therefore be the mean of the values immediately below it (21) and immediately above it (22), i.e. 21.5. Similarly, the lower boundary will be the mean of 7 and 8 (i.e. 7.5). The interquartile range is, therefore, the difference between 21.5 and 7.5 (i.e. 14).

The standard deviation

The standard deviation is a measure of the variability (i.e. of the typical deviation) of a given sample of scores from its mean. Calculation, as with the mean, involves using all the scores in a given set of data; this makes the standard deviation the most powerful of the measures of dispersion available to the researcher. Calculation is beyond the scope of the AS-level Psychology specification, although if you continue to A level, you may need to calculate it for data sets in your coursework.

The standard deviation allows us to make statements of probability about how likely (or how unlikely) a given value is to occur. This ability to make inferences is based on the relationship between standard deviation and a normal distribution curve (refer back to p. 237). The meaningful use of the statistic not only requires data that are approximately normally distributed, but also data measured on interval or ratio levels of measurement (i.e. data measured in fixed units, where each point on the scale of measurement concerned is an equal distance apart). Standard deviation becomes a less effective measure when there are any outlying scores that skew the data distribution.

The percentages of values that lie between the mean and a given number of standard deviations above and below the mean are fixed properties which help to make the standard deviation a particularly useful measure. These fixed properties are:

- 68.26 per cent of all values lie within one standard deviation either side of the mean
- 95.44 per cent of all values lie within two standard deviations either side of the mean
- 99.74 per cent of all values lie within three standard deviations either side of the mean.

Figure 7.4 illustrates how this works with some data where the calculated standard deviation is 10. As the mean value is 100, this means that 68.26 per cent of the psychology test scores in the population can be inferred as lying between 90 (minus one standard deviation from the mean) and 110 (plus one standard deviation from the mean), while the percentage of test scores lying between 70 and 130 is 99.74 per cent (three standard deviations either side of the mean).

Figure 7.4 >>
The percentage of scores that lie between a given number
of standard deviations either side of the mean

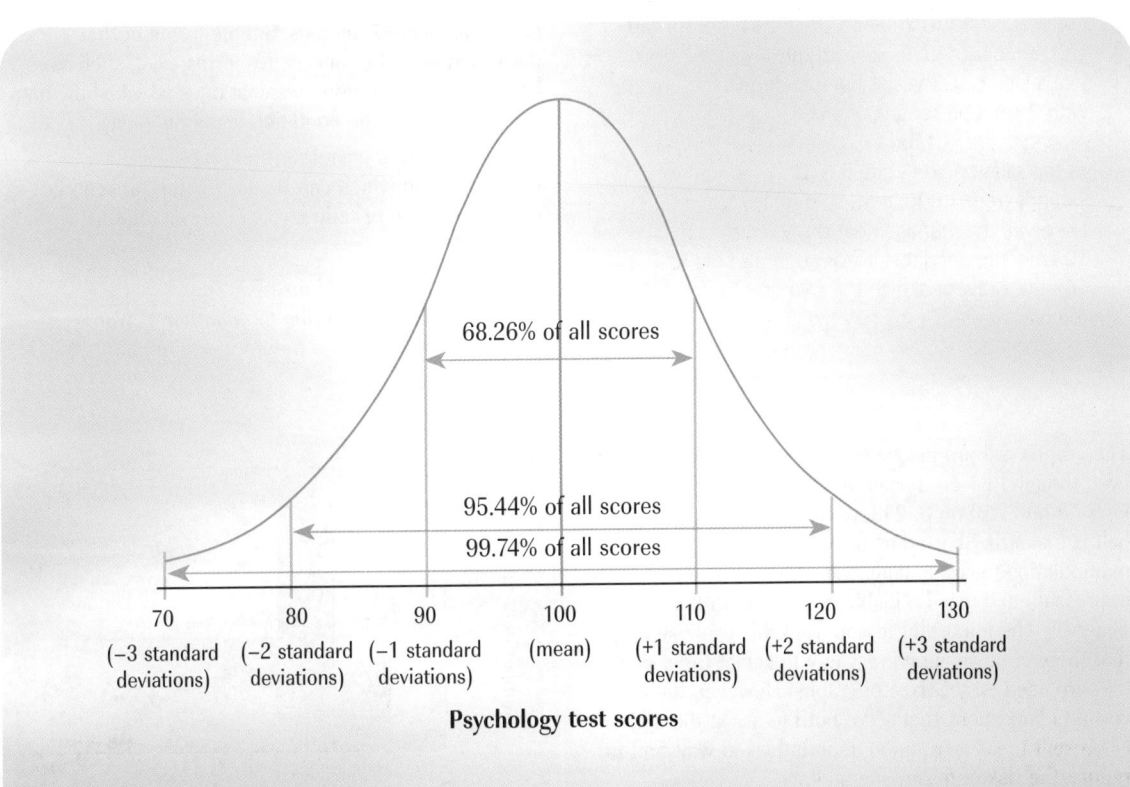

USING AND INTERPRETING GRAPHS AND CHARTS

Graphs and charts act as visual aids which help to make sense of the data obtained from psychological investigations. They aim to provide an overall picture that helps to summarize the results; when well constructed, they can show us at a glance any patterns which occur in the data.

Be warned, though, that the careful manipulation of the way that the axes in graphs or charts are drawn can easily bias the interpretation. Before reading on, try the activity below, which illustrates the kind of visual deception that can occur.

ACTIVITY

Presenting data

A psychology software publisher asks one of its sales representatives to present her sales figures for the last three years to the company's senior management. Her sales are:

2000	1,000 items
2001	1,001 items
2002	1,002 items (evidently a sales boom!).

The company is dissatisfied with the sales performance, but the sales person is desperate to keep her job. Both parties decide to present the sales figures by means of a line graph, with the years 2000 to 2003 on the x-axis (horizontal) and number of items sold on the y-axis (vertical). The sales person draws a graph with 3 cm representing one year, the management opt for 4 cm = one year. The y-axis of the sales person's graph is 16 cm long and extends from 1,000 items sold to 1,002. However, the management draw their y-axis 10 cm long, and label it from 0 items sold to 10,000. Draw or sketch the two graphs and see the bias created.

The graphs will produce very different impressions, even though they are based on identical data – see Figs 7.9 and 7.10 on p. 243, which show the graphs at half actual size. Shortening or extending the axes, or manipulating their labelling, can convey a desired impression and may be highly misleading to the observer. The important lesson from this exercise is that there is no single correct way to select the scales that are used on the axes of graphs. However, there are certain conventions that serve both to assist the author to present their information in an unbiased way, and to reduce the risk of misunderstandings.

- Plot frequency of scores on the y-axis (as in the examples that you have just drawn). This is the conventional mode of presentation, but is not a hard and fast rule – sometimes horizontal bars can provide a pleasing alternative.

- Adopt the three-quarter high rule. This states that when frequencies are plotted, the length of the y-axis should be determined in the following way. It should be organized so that the distance of the highest point on the graph (i.e. the point that represents the score with the highest frequency) from the x-axis is approximately equal to three-quarters of the total length of the x-axis.

- It is possible to break the x-axis or y-axis of a graph if labelling of the axis from zero would give a poor visual impression due to the large amount of empty space that would result.

- Remember that all graphs and charts need to have each axis clearly labelled and have an informative title.

Ideally, someone looking at a graph or chart should be able to understand what it is about without any additional explanation. It is also important when reading other people's work to look out for examples of graphs and charts that are misleading.

Histograms

Histograms and bar charts are two of the most widely used graphical techniques. Simple forms of these are discussed here, but alternative forms exist, such as compound or three-dimensional ones which show data from more than one condition simultaneously.

Histograms are a useful form of graphical representation which can be used when presenting data on interval or ratio levels of measurement.

Figure 7.5 >>
Histogram showing the number of words recalled in a memory experiment

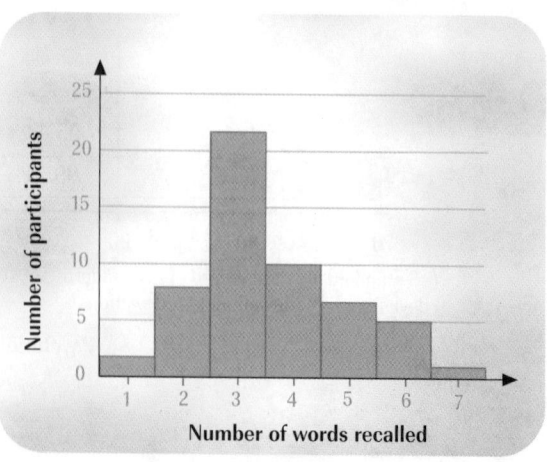

A histogram consists of a series of vertical bars of equal width, which represent frequencies of the variable placed on the *x*-axis. The height of each bar represents the frequency of occurrence for each point on the scale or each category. A histogram is drawn with the bars representing the frequencies actually touching each other. An ideal number of bars to use is between six and eight. Sometimes, single values can be used for each bar, but if the scale used on the *x*-axis has a large number of points, then the data can be placed into class intervals.

Bar charts

A bar chart is superficially similar to a histogram, and consists of a series of vertical bars of equal width, which can be used to illustrate the frequencies of a non-continuous variable on the *x*-axis. They are often used to depict data measured on nominal (placed in categories) or ordinal levels of measurement or, for example, to illustrate the means from different samples. Unlike the histogram, it is usual to draw each bar separated from each of the others so that a continuous variable is not implied on the *x*-axis (as in Fig. 7.6).

Figure 7.6 >>
Bar chart showing the number of observations of different behaviours in a group of children

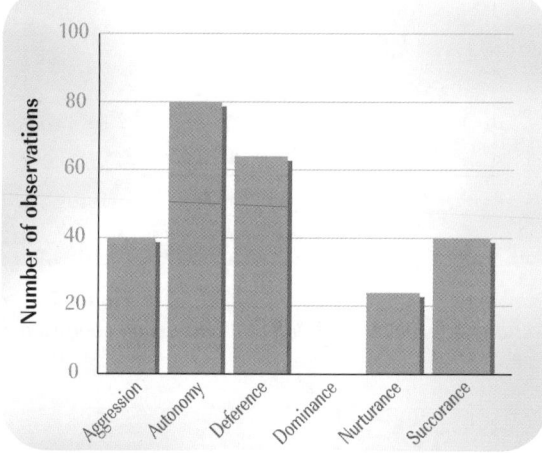

When data are at a nominal level, bias should be avoided in the order in which the bars are presented, as these can logically be presented in any order. They are often presented in alphabetical order to avoid such bias. However, when data are treated at an ordinal level, the *x*-axis can be drawn using the order of the points on the scale concerned.

Frequency polygons

The frequency polygon is a particularly useful technique when you want to compare two or more frequency distributions. It is used as an alternative to the

Figure 7.7 >>
Frequency polygon showing the number of words recalled in a memory experiment

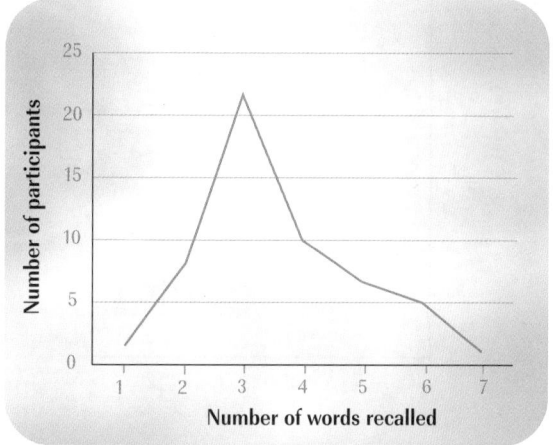

histogram. Indeed, a frequency polygon can be drawn by linking the midpoints from the top of each bar contained in a histogram, as in the example in Fig. 7.7. A frequency polygon may be the preferred technique when you need to depict results from two or more conditions of an investigation at the same time; this is because two or more lines can be drawn on the same graph to show direct comparison of results.

Scattergraphs and the interpretation of correlation coefficients

Before reading on, try the activity on the next page.

The term 'correlation' was introduced in Unit 6 (pp. 203–5), where the concepts of correlation coefficients, and positive and negative correlations were introduced. Reread that section now to refresh your knowledge of these terms. As far as interpreting correlation coefficients is concerned, the strength of a correlation increases as the obtained coefficient becomes closer to +1 or −1. An important way of depicting correlational relationships is the scattergraph (or scattergram). Data from one of the variables being correlated are presented on the *x*-axis and data from the second variable on the *y*-axis (see Fig. 7.8).

Study the examples of scattergraphs in Fig. 7.8 and then try the activity on interpreting scattergraphs on p. 243.

In order to interpret a correlation coefficient fully, it is necessary to test the correlation coefficient obtained for statistical significance. This is because the significance of a correlation coefficient is linked directly to the key variable of the number of pairs of scores being correlated. If you go on to study psychology at A level, you may have the opportunity to carry out a correlational study and to analyse the results taking this factor into account.

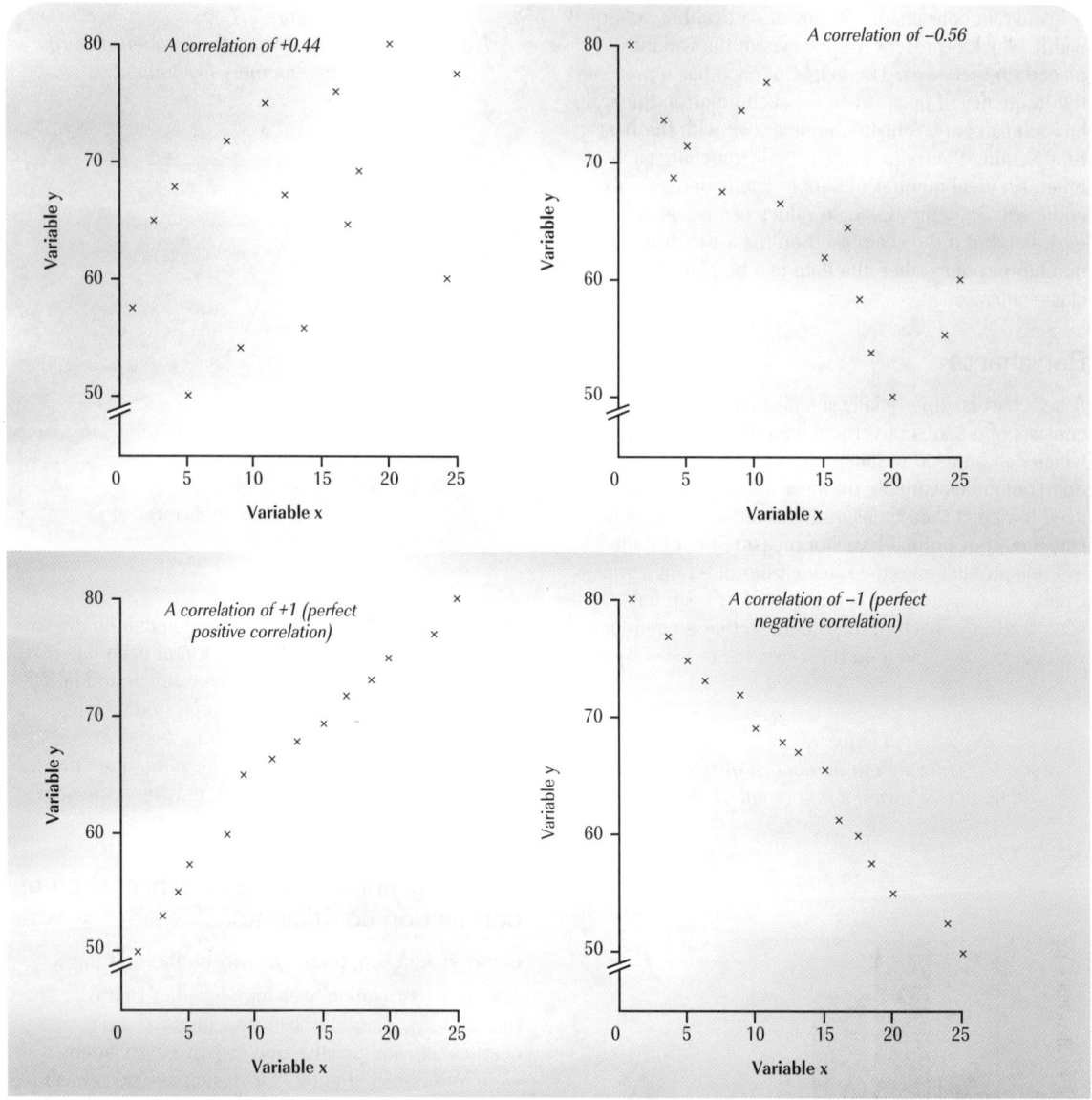

Figure 7.8 >>
Scattergraphs illustrating different correlation coefficients

ACTIVITY

Correlations

For each of the following correlations (relationships), decide whether they are positive or negative.

1. The more aggressive parents are, the more aggressive their children tend to be.

2. The hotter the weather, the fewer the clothes people wear.

3. The more expensive the petrol, the less petrol people buy.

4. The hotter the weather, the more clothes people remove.

5. The fewer sweets eaten, the fewer fillings needed.

6. The colder the weather, the higher people's fuel bills.

7. The more people exercise, the less risk they have of a heart attack.

8. More extrovert people get more party invitations.

9. The shorter the hours of daylight, the greater the incidence of depression.

10. As children grow older they become more independent.

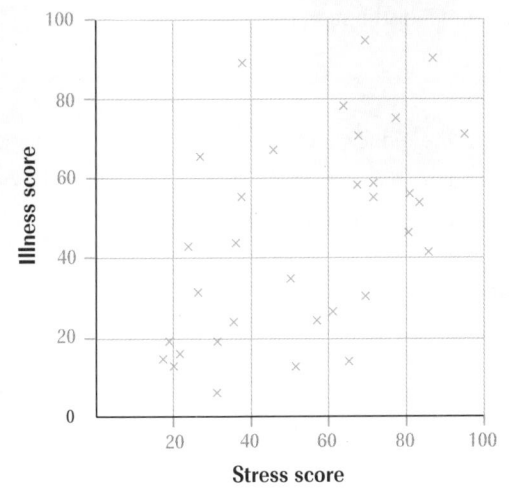

ACTIVITY

Interpreting scattergraphs

Below is a scattergraph showing the relationship between scores derived from questionnaires measuring ill health and stress levels. How would you interpret this correlation?

(See below for answer.)

ACTIVITY

Planning a study

Now that you have reached the end of this unit and have learned more about the factors involved in designing research and analysing data, look back to the 'Getting you thinking...' on p. 215. Choose just one research method to investigate whether there is any link between watching violent cartoons and levels of aggression in children.

Use what you have learned in this unit to prepare a plan. Issues to consider when planning a research study are:

1 the aim of the study and any research hypothesis (for experimental research)

2 who the participants will be – how many and how you would select them

3 what design you will use, if you plan to undertake experimental research

4 whether you will need to carry out a pilot study

5 what the main ethical issues associated with the proposed study and are how you would address them (Units 5 and 6 should help you)

6 what type(s) of data you will collect and how you will analyse the data.

ANSWERS TO ACTIVITIES

Activity, p. 240

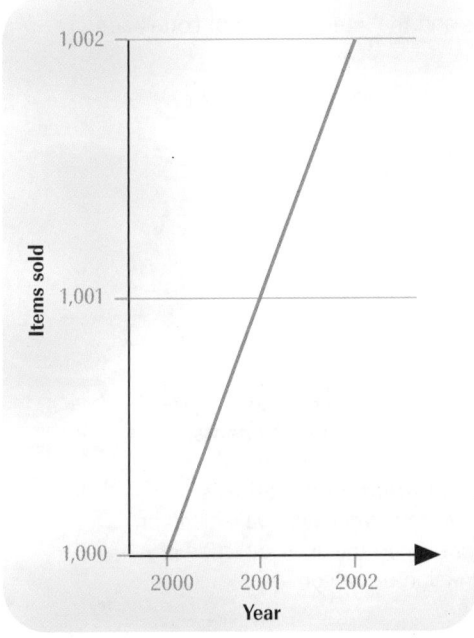

Figure 7.9 »
Graph produced by salesperson

Figure 7.10 »
Graph produced by management

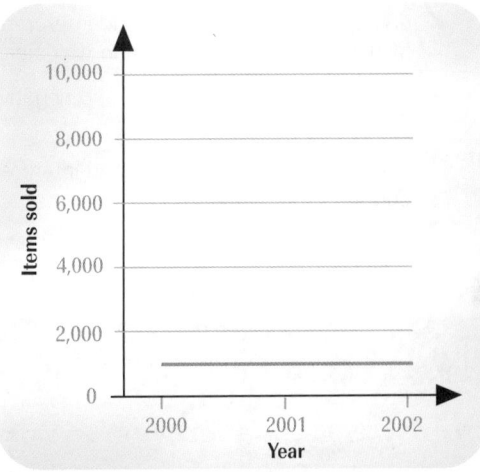

Activity, this page (top left)

The scattergraph illustrates that stress and illness scores tend to be positively correlated. In other words, when stress scores increase, then so, generally speaking, do illness scores. The correlation coefficient is in fact around +0.6.

Check your understanding of data analysis by answering these questions. Try to do this from memory at first. You can check your answers by looking back through Topic 2.

1 Name three measures of central tendency.

2 Which measure of central tendency is the middle value of a set of numbers placed in numerical order?

3 What are the main properties (characteristics) of the normal distribution curve?

4 Explain what is meant by the term 'measure of dispersion'.

5 Name two measures of dispersion.

6 When might the interquartile range be used rather than the range?

7 What is the main difference between a histogram and a bar chart?

8 When might a frequency polygon be used instead of a histogram to present frequency data?

9 Does the following statement indicate a positive or a negative correlation?

   << The more people exercise, the less risk they have of a heart attack. >>

10 What is a scattergraph (or scattergram)?

REVISION SUMMARY

Having covered this topic you should be able to:

✓ define the key terms listed on pp. 231–2

✓ describe ways in which qualitative data from naturalistic observations, questionnaire surveys and interviews may be analysed

✓ discuss the appropriate use and interpretation of three measures of central tendency – median, mean and mode – and two measures of dispersion – range and standard deviation

✓ explain the nature of positive and negative correlations and the interpretation of correlation coefficients

✓ describe the appropriate use and interpretation of histograms, bar charts, frequency polygons and scattergraphs.

UNIT SUMMARY

Topic 1: Research design and implementation

● At the start of any psychological investigation, appropriate **aims** and **hypotheses** of the study should be **generated** and clearly stated. Hypotheses are **testable statements**. A **null hypothesis** predicts no difference or no correlation, and if any difference or correlation is found, it is due to chance variation alone. An **alternative hypothesis** attributes results to some factor other than chance, such as the independent variable in an experiment. Alternative hypotheses may be **directional** (predicting the likely direction of outcome) or **non-directional** (not predicting the likely direction of outcome).

■ The **experimental designs** available to the researcher include independent groups, repeated measures and matched participants designs. Key design issues with **non-experimental** research (e.g. naturalistic observations, questionnaire surveys and interviews) include deciding how behaviour is sampled, the method(s) used for recording data, and the phrasing and organization of questions.

■ The **control of variables** is fundamental to scientific research in psychology. Psychologists need to **define precisely** all the variables that they are investigating to ensure that these are properly **operationalized**, including both **independent** and **dependent variables**.

■ Small-scale **pilot studies** can be carried out before research takes place in order to identify any potential problems.

■ Researchers need to **assess** and, where necessary, **improve** the reliability and validity of their research measures and techniques. **Reliability** refers to the consistency of a test or procedure. Key aspects of it are observer reliability and test reliability. The **validity** of measuring instruments can be established by the extent to which they measure what they set out to measure. Key aspects are internal, external (ecological) and test validity.

■ It is essential that all psychological research is carried out **ethically**, i.e. it respects the rights and feelings of all those taking part.

■ Different sampling techniques can be used to **select participants** for research investigations from the **target population** of interest. In a **random sample**, every person in the target population has an equal chance of being selected. In an **opportunity sample**, the investigator chooses whoever is available from the target population.

■ The **relationship** between researcher and participant can affect an investigation. **Demand characteristics** occur when research participants attempt to make sense of the research situation that they find themselves in. **Investigator effects** result from the effects of a researcher's behaviour and characteristics on an investigation.

Topic 2: Data analysis

■ **Naturalistic observational studies, questionnaire surveys** and **interviews** may produce **qualitative** (non-numerical) or **quantitative** (numerical) data. Qualitative data can provide a richness of detail which may not be achievable with quantitative data. However, quantitative data are often easier to analyse.

■ Descriptive statistical techniques used to analyse quantitative data include **measures of central tendency** (averages). These are the **mode** (the most frequently occurring value), the **median** (the middle value when data are placed into rank order) and the **mean** (where all values are added together and divided by the number of scores).

■ **Descriptive statistical techniques** also include **measures of dispersion**, such as the **range** (a measure of the difference between highest and lowest values in a data set) and **standard deviation** (the average deviation of scores from the mean).

■ **Graphs and charts** that can be used by a researcher include **histograms, bar charts, frequency polygons** and **scattergraphs**.

■ **Correlation** is a statistical technique for measuring relationships between sets of data. Correlations can be described as **positive** (high scores on both variables) or **negative** (high scores on one variable, low scores on another). The strength of a positive or negative correlation increases as the obtained **correlation coefficient** becomes closer to +1 or −1 respectively. The nature of the relationship (correlation) can be shown on a **scattergraph**.

Answering exam questions on Research methods

For sample examination questions and answers on Research methods, together with examiner comments on the answers, see pp. 262–5.

8
UNIT

PREPARING FOR THE
AS Examination

PREVIEW

In this unit you will be looking at:

>> the nature of the AS examination

>> how your examination work will be marked

>> sample examination answers and examiner comments

>> how to perform to your full potential in the examination.

INTRODUCTION

The Advanced Subsidiary (AS) is set at a level midway between GCSE and GCE Advanced Level, and the skills that you will need to demonstrate will be different from those at these other levels. It is our aim here to give you the fullest possible understanding of how the examination 'works' – for example, by looking at how questions are set and marked, so that you can prepare for the exam with these factors in mind. If you use this unit in conjunction with the other units that contain the psychological knowledge, topic by topic, you should be ideally prepared to achieve your best possible grade.

You will start, in Topic 1, by looking at the nature of the AS examination. Here, we focus on the different types of questions that are set in the exam and the different skills they are designed to test: labelled AO1, AO2 and AO3. Topic 2 goes on to describe what examiners will be looking for when they mark your answers.

In Topic 3, we see how this works in practice by looking at some sample exam questions, together with two candidates' responses to these questions. By examining what these candidates have done right and wrong, you will see how to score well in the answers you write.

Finally, Topic 4 contains ten top tips for doing well in psychology.

Paul
Humphreys

Mike
Cardwell

AO1, AO2 AND AO3

AS-level questions set for AQA Psychology Specification A assess three types of skill. These skills, known as 'Assessment Objectives' are as follows:

- *Knowledge and Understanding* (AO1)
- *Analysis and Evaluation* (AO2)
- *Designing, Conducting and Reporting* (AO3).

AO3 questions are restricted to Research Methods questions, but AO1 and AO2 questions are present in all other sections. Each question is worth 30 marks, with the AO1 parts of the question being worth 18 marks and the AO2 component of each question being worth 12 marks.

The first two parts of each question (except for Research Methods) are always AO1 and the last part always AO1 *plus* AO2. This is important because different types of question require different types of answer. AO1 questions require more *descriptive* responses, whereas AO1 + AO2 questions require more *evaluative* responses.

Assessment Objective 1 (AO1)

AO1 is the demonstration of knowledge and understanding through clear and effective communication. Are knowledge and understanding the same thing? No, they are not! I know that in order to make my car go faster, I have to press my foot down on the accelerator pedal, but I must confess I don't understand how this 'works'. By same token, I may 'know' what the main features of Bowlby's theory of attachment are (pp. 53–6), but this knowledge may be quite superficial with no real understanding underpinning it. Take the non-understanding student away from their rote-learning list, and they're lost.

Conversely, if you really understand something, you can look at it from any angle – not just a prelearned sequence – and still feel totally at ease with it. Understanding leads to insight: having a real grasp and comprehension of the thing in question. If you depend on memory, it may well let you down, especially if you are anxious about it; understanding will never let you down.

Assessment Objective 2 (AO2)

AO2 is analysis and evaluation. We are using the term 'analysis' in the same sense as it is used in psychoanalysis. Freud was interested in analysing the psyche, or the mind, using such questions as:

"What are the elements that make it up?" – "How do they work together?" – "How do they interrelate?"

In the same way, we can take any theory apart, examine the individual parts of it, and then put it back together. Think of analysis as taking something apart, stripping it down to its basic elements and then carrying out a detailed examination of these.

There is another aspect of analysis that is not immediately apparent from a literal definition of the word. Imagine you go to see your football team play a match. The odds are you will get sucked into the 'theatre' of the match, and will watch it with the heart more than the mind. A football writer, on the other hand, will be watching your team and the game *analytically*. There is, then, a component of critical consideration to analysis too.

What about evaluation? By this term we mean making an informed judgement about the value or worth of something. It is one thing to know the 'factual features' of Bowlby's theory of attachment, quite another to make an informed judgement about its quality or worth.

Two important points need to be made. You may have noticed that the phrase used was *informed* judgement. This means the judgement is not a whim or 'pulled out of thin air', but is based on solid information and can be substantiated. "Milgram's work was ethically unforgivable" is an evaluation of sorts, but has no substance.

The second point is that evaluation should be *two-sided*. Few things in psychology and life are so one-sided that they have nothing that can be said in their favour or nothing that can be said against them. In most circumstances, there are two sides to a question and both need evaluating. Evaluation does not mean 'slagging off'; it means giving a balanced appraisal. Try always to give both the pros and the cons.

Assessment Objective 3

Assessment Objective 3 (AO3) relates only to the Research Methods questions. In each Research Methods question, all but 9 of the marks are awarded for AO3 skills. This assesses your ability to think on your feet concerning the stimulus material rather than trotting out some rote-learned material without considering the context of the question. For example, *why* did the researchers use a matched participants design, or *how* could the design of this study be improved?

TYPES OF QUESTIONS

The following are *examples* of the types of questions that are used to assess AO1 and AO2 (this book contains many more such examples). At the end of each topic we have given you a revision summary so you know the specific question types that will apply to that topic. Remember that each mark is equivalent to approximately one minute of thinking and writing, so it is vital to use this time wisely, neither extending it nor skimping on it.

AO1

These questions assess your *knowledge and understanding* of the specification material. They are the first two parts of each question (except Research Methods). There is also an AO1 component in the final part of each question. We will deal with that later. Examples of these questions are shown in the panel on p. 248.

Examples of AO1 questions

- **What is meant by** the terms conformity, minority influence, and obedience? (2 + 2 + 2 marks)
- **Outline two reasons why** people yield to majority influence. (3 + 3 marks)
- **Describe two differences** between short-term (STM) and long-term (LTM) memory. (3 + 3 marks)
- **Describe the aims/procedures/findings/ conclusions/criticisms*** of one study of majority influence. [*any combination of two of these aspects of the study] (6 marks)
- **Outline findings of research** into the effects of day care on children's social development. (6 marks)
- **Describe one explanation** of attachment (e.g. Bowlby's). (6 marks)
- **Outline two explanations** of forgetting in short-term memory. (3 + 3 marks)
- **Outline two limitations** of the definition of abnormality as 'deviation from ideal mental health'. (3 + 3 marks)
- **Give two criticisms** of the levels of processing theory of memory. (3 + 3 marks)

AO1 + AO2

The AO1/AO2 question is your chance to show that you can *think* about the specification content in such a way as to answer a slightly more challenging question about the topic in question. This final part is assigned 18 of the 30 marks available for the total question. Six marks are given for the AO1 content and 12 are for the AO2 content. It is vitally important to remember this mark division when planning your response, so that one-third of your answer is AO1 and two-thirds AO2.

What do they look like?

The AO1 + AO2 questions tend to follow a fairly similar format in that you are asked to do something descriptive for 6 marks and then something more evaluative for the remaining 12 marks. Sometimes this AO1 division is fairly obvious, as in the following examples:

- 'Outline and evaluate ...'
- 'Give a brief account of and evaluate ...'

Sometimes it is up to you how you will divide your answer into AO1 and AO2. For example:

- 'To what extent does research support ...'
- 'Consider the view that ...'

It is always worth spending a couple of minutes 'deconstructing' the question so that *you* are clear what is the AO1 requirement and what is the AO2 requirement, and planning your response strategically along these lines. Take a look at the three questions in the panel below, and decide what the AO1 and AO2 requirements of each question might be.

Examples of AO1 + AO2 questions

- To what extent has psychological research shown eyewitness testimony to be unreliable? (18 marks)
- Give a brief account of, and evaluate the use of ethical guidelines as a way of resolving ethical issues in psychological research. (18 marks)
- *"What is considered 'normal' or 'abnormal' cannot be understood without also considering the cultural context of the behaviour being evaluated."*

  Consider how attempts to define abnormality might be influenced by cultural differences. (18 marks)

WHAT IS THE EXAMINER LOOKING FOR?

There is no one right route through these questions, but, as we shall see in the next topic, examiners have different criteria that they use when deciding how many marks to award for a particular answer. For these questions, they have separate criteria for the AO1 component and the AO2 component.

AO1 (0–6)

- *Accuracy* – is the material accurate, partially accurate or inaccurate?
- *Detail* – is the material sufficiently elaborated or does it lack detail?

AO2 (0–12)

- *Informed commentary* – are you saying something about the material that is both psychologically informed and shows engagement with the material?
- *Analysis* – what are the raw ingredients of your argument and how do these blend together?
- *Effective use of material* – have you made the most of your material?

AO3 questions

The Research Methods question carries 30 marks, as do all the questions, but there are some key differences. For example, there is no choice – just the one question, which you will be required to answer. Perhaps more importantly, there is no guaranteed structure to the Research Methods, as there is with the others. What we can say with confidence is that some of the questions will require very short answers (1 or 2 marks) whereas others will require more from you and may carry, say, 6 or 7 marks. Bear in mind that the higher the number of marks allocated to each question, the more time you spend answering it. The notional idea of 'a mark a minute' discussed earlier is still a good rule of thumb. The Research Methods question will always begin with a short piece of stimulus material – usually describing a hypothetical study – and the questions will then be based around this.

A key determinant of success is having a sound understanding of what the examiner is looking for – or to put it another way, how they mark your work. The uninformed student will write *hoping* that this is what the examiner is looking for; the informed student will write *knowing* that it is what the examiner is looking for.

Before they mark any exam papers (or *scripts,* as they are technically known), all examiners attend a full day's standardization meeting in which they work through a large number of candidates' answers. They work alongside all the other examiners and are led by the Principal Examiners who set the question papers. Two factors that will be significant to you emerge from this:

- This process ensures that all examiners mark to the same standard, so it makes no difference which examiner marks your work. There are no hard or soft markers!

- All the examiners mark to the same set of criteria or guidelines. This is the critical factor, because these criteria are made public by the examining board so you can know in advance what the examiners are looking for.

We will look at the marking criteria shortly, but three other important general points need to be made first.

- Examiners mark according to a standard that it is reasonable to expect a notional 17 year old to display working under exam conditions. They appreciate that you will be anxious and tense, have limited time, are answering questions that you have only just seen and are not allowed to consult your books, notes, etc. Clearly, an exam is a very different exercise from writing an essay for classwork, and you can rest assured that the examiner will always be mindful of this.

- In psychology there are rarely single, right answers (other than occasionally for Research Methods questions). The consequence of this is that there is no single answer to learn when preparing for questions and, perhaps most importantly, no single answer that the examiner is looking for.

- Examiners do not mark with pass or fail in mind. They do not even mark with grades in mind. Grades are decided by an Awarding Committee of examiners and teachers after the marking has been completed. Examiners award marks solely according to the marking criteria, which we will now explore.

HOW ARE THE MARKS AWARDED?

Here, we give an insight into how the marks are awarded for the most common of the AQA Specification A question types used in the AS-level psychology exam. These are summaries of the marking allocation tables used by examiners, but they contain the same mark divisions and criteria.

In the AO1 questions, the emphasis is on the amount of relevant material presented (e.g. 'limited' or 'basic'), the amount of detail given (e.g. 'lacking detail') and the accuracy of the material (e.g. 'muddled').

In the AO1 + AO2 part of the question, the emphasis is not only on the descriptive content (AO1), but also on the amount and level of the critical commentary (e.g. 'superficial'), its thoroughness (e.g. 'reasonably thorough') and how effectively it has been used (e.g. 'highly effective'). This is the AO2 component of the question, and in the final part of each question this is worth 12 of the 18 marks available.

AO1 questions

The table on the right and the one on p. 250 show how marks are awarded for different AO1 questions.

AO1: 2-mark questions

Example

"What is meant by the terms conformity, minority influence, and obedience? (2 + 2 + 2 marks)"

- >> **2 marks**   Accurate and detailed
- >> **1 mark**   Basic, lacking detail, muddled or flawed
- >> **0 marks**   Inappropriate or incorrect

AO1: 3- and 6-mark questions

Examples

Outline two explanations of forgetting in short-term memory.   (3 + 3 marks)

Outline findings of research into the effects of day care on children's social development.   (6 marks)

3-mark questions	6-mark questions	Criteria
3	6–5	>> Accurate and detailed
2	4–3	>> Limited, generally accurate but less detailed.
1	2–1	>> Basic, lacking in detail, muddled or flawed.
0	0	>> Inaccurate or inappropriate

AO1 + AO2 questions

As all AO1 + AO2 questions are worth 18 marks (6 marks for AO1 and 12 for AO2), the following table applies to the AO2 component in all the questions that you will meet in the exam. The heading 'commentary' applies to the specific AO2 requirement of the question (e.g. 'evaluate' or 'to what extent?').

AO1 + AO2 questions

Marks	Commentary	Analysis	Use of material
12–11	>> Informed	>> Reasonably thorough	>> Effective
10–9	>> Reasonable	>> Slightly limited	>> Effective
8–7	>> Reasonable	>> Limited	>> Reasonably effective
6–5	>> Basic	>> Limited	>> Reasonably effective
4–3	>> Superficial	>> Rudimentary	>> Minimal interpretation
2–1	>> Just discernible	>> Weak and muddled	>> Mainly irrelevant
0	>> Wholly irrelevant	>> Wholly irrelevant	>> Wholly irrelevant

Quality of Written Communication (QoWC)

As indicated earlier, all examinations now include an assessment of your written communication skills. There are up to two marks awarded in each unit paper. That isn't a great deal, but it helps to know that they are there and how you can make sure you get them! The table on the right may help in this respect.

Quality of Written Communication

>> **2 marks**	Accurate and clear expression of ideas, a broad range of specialist terms and only minor errors in grammar, punctuation and spelling.
>> **1 mark**	Reasonable expression of ideas, a reasonable range of specialist terms and few errors of grammar, punctuation and spelling.
>> **0 marks**	Poor expression of ideas, limited use of specialist terms and poor grammar, punctuation and spelling.

MODULE 1: COGNITIVE & DEVELOPMENTAL PSYCHOLOGY

Cognitive psychology: Human memory

(a) Give three differences between STM and LTM. (2 + 2 + 2 marks)

Answer 1

STM has limited capacity but LTM is unlimited.

STM stores information for a brief period, but LTM stores it forever.

STM is encoded in sounds and LTM is what they mean.

Answer 2

The capacity of STM is limited (7 ±2 items) whereas the capacity of LTM is thought to be unlimited.

STM stores information for a very short period of time unless it is rehearsed, whereas LTM stores information more or less permanently.

STM involves acoustic coding (i.e. by sound) whereas material in LTM is encoded semantically (i.e. by meaning).

■ *Answer 1:* Each of these differences is generally accurate, but lacking in detail. Each of these would get 1 mark, for a total of 3 marks.

■ *Answer 2:* Not a lot more words, but greater clarity and the right amount of elaboration mean that this answer gets all 6 marks available.

(b) Outline two explanations of forgetting in LTM. (3 + 3 marks)

Answer 1

One reason for forgetting in LTM is through decay. Over time we lose the ability to remember things that we have learned when we were younger. They just decay from memory.

Another reason is displacement. New memories displace older ones, so we forget them.

Answer 2

One explanation of forgetting in Long Term Memory is interference. One set of information interferes with another. Sometimes interference is proactive, where previously remembered information interferes with new information, making it more difficult to remember. Sometimes it is retroactive, where new information makes it more difficult to recall older, similar information already in memory.

A second explanation is retrieval failure, where forgetting is a result of the absence of appropriate retrieval cues. If we are in a different psychological state (e.g. sober) or the context in which we try and remember is different (e.g. in an examination), we find it more difficult to recall information than if we were in the same state and context as when we first learned it.

■ *Answer 1:* The first explanation is generally accurate but lacks the precision necessary for full marks. The term 'decay' is never really explained. The second explanation is wrong – they might have been describing interference, but they have used the term 'displacement' which is an explanation of STM forgetting. These answers would be worth 2 + 0 marks, for a total of 2 marks.

■ *Answer 2:* These are two accurate and detailed accounts of forgetting in LTM. This answer makes full use of the time available and contains an appropriate amount of elaboration for the full 6 marks. The use of appropriate examples in the second explanation helps to demonstrate the difference between internal and external cues.

Answer 1

The multi-store model was proposed by Atkinson and Shiffrin (1968). It suggests that memory flows through the system going through sensory memory (SM), short-term memory (STM) and finally long-term memory (LTM). Atkinson and Shiffrin found that at each of these three stages, information can be lost through forgetting. They found that in SM information is lost because of decay. In STM, information is lost through displacement, and in LTM it is lost through interference.

Atkinson and Shiffrin also found that there were differences in the way the information was coded in each of the stores. In the STM, for example, they found that coding was acoustic (the way things sounded) and in LTM it was semantic (the meaning of things). Many other studies have demonstrated this distinction between STM and LTM, and so support the multistore model.

Other research findings have also supported Atkinson and Shiffrin. For example, the case of KF, who had become brain injured after an accident showed that he could remember some things in his long-term memory and also remember new things, but he could not remember things in the short term. This supported the idea that LTM and STM are different parts of the memory, because KF had damaged the part of his memory connected with STM, but the part of his brain connected with LTM was undamaged, so accounting for his memory impairment.

Answer 2

Atkinson and Shiffrin (1968) explained memory in terms of three distinct stores. These were the sensory memory, which holds information for a very brief period, short-term memory (STM), which has limited capacity and relatively short duration, and a long-term memory (LTM) which has potentially unlimited capacity and duration. If a person's attention is focused on material in the sensory memory, then this material would get transferred to STM. Atkinson and Shiffrin claimed that information was transferred from STM to LTM through the process of rehearsal. They proposed a direct relationship between rehearsal in STM and the strength of the long-term memory – the more the information is rehearsed the better it is remembered.

Research studies have supported Atkinson and Shiffrin's view that the stores are different in terms of capacity, encoding and duration. The existence of separate stores in memory is also supported by the use of modern brain scanning techniques (such as PET scans). These have shown, for example, that the prefrontal cortex is active when individuals are working on a task in immediate (i.e. short-term) memory whereas the hippocampus is active when LTM is engaged. The idea that there is a different physiological basis for short-term and long-term memory is further supported by the study of a man called HM (Milner 1966) who had to have both hippocampi removed due to a tumour. After this surgery he was unable to form any new long-term memories though he could perform STM tasks.

Despite this research support, the multi-store model is probably an oversimplification of memory processes. The multi-store model just proposes one long-term store whereas research suggests several different forms of LTM (e.g. episodic, semantic and procedural memory). This model also proposes just one short-term store whereas Baddeley and Hitch's working memory model shows that this too is an over-simplification. Finally, the multi-store model proposes one mechanism for how data is stored in LTM – rehearsal. Despite Atkinson and Shiffrin's claim, it is unlikely that rehearsal is the only way that information finds its way into LTM. Flash-bulb memories, for example, are extremely long-lasting, without any form of rehearsal taking place.

■ *Answer 1:* Most of this material is descriptive, so it picks up fairly decent marks for the AO1 component of this question (accurate and detailed, so 5 of the 6 marks available), but there is little evidence of AO2 material. Some of this is speculative (e.g. "many other studies have demonstrated this distinction"), and is not particularly effective as 'commentary' on the multi-store model. The material on KF does address the validity of this model, but overall the AO2 material is superficial and would only receive 3 of the 12 marks available.

■ *Answer 2:* This answer is clearly divided into three distinct paragraphs. The first of these is an accurate and well-detailed précis of the multi-store model. The next two paragraphs are purely evaluative, the first being evidence for the multi-store model and the second evidence against. This is very effective evaluation. The entire answer is extremely well organized and is structured so as to capture the full 6 marks available for AO1 and the full 12 marks available for AO2.

Developmental psychology: Attachments in development

> **(a)** Explain what is meant by the terms 'secure' and 'insecure' attachment.   (3 + 3 marks)

Answer 1

Secure attachment means that the child is better balanced and happier than an insecurely attached child. They are more likely to cope better with relationships later on in their life compared to insecurely attached children who lack the security of having someone they can trust to look after them.

Answer 2

Securely attached infants feel content to explore a strange environment using their caregiver as a safe base. They show some distress when left by their caregiver but are relatively easily comforted and greet the caregiver enthusiastically at reunion.

Insecurely attached children show disturbed behaviour during separation from the caregiver and also when reunited. 'Resistant-insecure' children are distressed on separation and resist attempts at reunion with their caregiver. 'Avoidant-insecure' children are indifferent at separation and avoid contact on reunion.

■ *Answer 1:* These explanations have a 'whiff of truth' about them so are obviously worth more than zero marks, but the lack of detail and the general imprecision means that they are restricted to 1 mark each. The student has presented a comparison by way of explaining each of these terms, but may have been better off explaining each term independently.

■ *Answer 2:* Although relatively brief, these two explanations are accurate and detailed. This demonstrates a good understanding of the terms and would be worth the full 3 marks for each term.

> **(b)** Outline research into the effects of privation.   (6 marks)

Answer 1

Rutter studied privation to see if its effects were far reaching. He found that privation could produce a number of different types of retardation including intellectual retardation and possible anti-social behaviour later in life. The case of Genie found that she too suffered later in life as a result of her earlier privation, and failed to recover once the privation was removed. The Czech twins (Koluchova, 1976), despite extreme privation when young, nevertheless recovered well when placed in a foster home at the age of 7 years. Tizard and Hughes studied children who were put in a childrens home before they were 4 months old. Those who were later adopted fared much better than those who were not.

Answer 2

Spitz (1945) discovered, that despite hygienic surroundings and a good diet at a foundling home, babies received minimal social or physical stimulation and frequently died. Goldfarb's studies of children cared for in institutions and those removed to foster homes also showed abnormal development in the institutionalized children in areas of intelligence, motor co-ordination, behaviour, and language. Provence and Lipton (1966) found that institutionalized children showed impairment in a number of areas including reaction to peers and impulse control. More recently, studies of Romanian orphanages have shown that the majority of these children had suffered from extremes of privation and as a result were severely delayed in their development. They found that many of the older children preferred to take care of themselves and this created barriers to closeness with parents or other adults.

■ *Answer 1:* The studies quoted are accurate but each lacks sufficient detail. Possibly it would have been more effective to have covered less and added a little more detail on each. There is an occasional lack of clarity which probably also stops this answer from getting into the top mark band, but this would receive 4 of the 6 marks available.

■ *Answer 2:* This is clearly focused on the effects of privation. The earlier studies of Spitz and Goldfarb are reinforced with the more contemporary study of Romanian orphanages. There are enough studies to have a breadth of research findings, yet not too many that there is no detail in the answer. The occasional lack of a date or name is not important and does not stop the answer getting the full 6 marks.

(c) To what extent has day care been shown to have beneficial effects on children's cognitive and/or social development?

(18 marks)

Answer 1

Day care is where a child is cared for outside the home by someone who isn't a family member. Day care isn't the same as institutional care, such as in a residential nursery because this is 24-hour care. Examples of day care would include child-minding, and is available for children below school age. Cognitive development is defined as changes in mental abilities as a result of age (or experience). Social development is defined as changes in social behaviour (e.g. with peers) as a result of age or experience. Day care is thought to affect both cognitive and social development because it provides the right sort of experience for children to develop these skills.

There hasn't been a lot of research into the effects of day care on children's cognitive development, therefore it is difficult to draw any firm conclusions about whether it might be good or bad for the development of mental abilities. If day care is stimulating for the child however, then it stands to reason that it would be good for them and that it would cause beneficial effects for their cognitive development. Good child-minders spend lots of time stimulating the children they are looking after, and this has beneficial effects. However, different children react differently to this stimulation therefore what is beneficial for one child might not be beneficial for another.

There has been a lot more research on the effects of day care on children's social development, but the results are just as inconclusive. It makes sense that if children are allowed to play with others they learn how to get on with each other therefore their social skills improve. However, there is some evidence that day care can actually have harmful effects on children's social development. For example, in one study in America, the researchers found that children who had had a lot of day care when they were younger were more aggressive when they were older.

Answer 2

Although there is a lot of evidence to suggest that day care can have negative effects on children's social development, there is also evidence to suggest that it does have some positive effects. Clarke-Stewart et al. (1994) found that children who had attended day care coped better with social situations in their first year at school and got on better with their peers. Enrichment programmes such as the High/Scope Perry Preschool Project have also produced positive effects on social development over a much longer period. Schweinhart et al. (1993) found that children who had taken part in this day care programme had lower delinquency rates in adolescence and were less likely to have a criminal record when older compared to a control group who did not take part in this project.

The positive effects of day care on social development must be balanced against the possible negative effects of day care. Belsky (2003) claims that the more time that children spend in day care during their pre-school years, the more likely they are to display aggressive and disobedient behaviour as 4-8 year olds. He argues that children who experience poor-quality day care are more likely to experience these negative effects, as they fail to develop the secure sense of self that comes from the loving and attentive care needed for positive development. However, a study that evaluated the consequences of working mothers on the development of their children found that they suffered no permanent harm because of the mother's absence (Harvey 1999). Harvey concluded that whether or not day care had a positive (or negative) effect on children's social development depended on the quality of the parent–child relationship and the quality of the day care arrangement.

It is difficult to state conclusively that day care has either positive or negative effects on children's social development. This is because a lot depends on individual differences in the children themselves, and on the quality of the day care experience. Belsky suggests that some children are particularly vulnerable to the adverse effects of poor-quality day care. Research suggests that boys are more vulnerable than girls and so are more likely to show negative effects in their later social development. Pennebaker et al. (1981) found that shy children are more likely to find day care threatening and are less likely to benefit from the experience. It is also important to point out that some research fails to support the claim that 'high intensity' day care has inevitable negative effects on children's subsequent development (e.g. Clarke-Stewart et al. 1994). Therefore, any conclusions that we draw about the effects of day care on social development can only be tentative.

Answer 1: This answer does not actually say anything that is wrong, but a lot of it is either irrelevant or unsubstantiated. The definitions in the first paragraph are not required (they do not really address the specific question). The last sentence does make a statement about the effects of day care on development, and therefore would count as basic and lacking detail. The AO1 content would be worth just 1 mark. The AO2 content is a little better, but still contains a lot of speculation. However, there is an awareness of why day care might have positive effects, the importance of individual differences in children exposed to day care, and the existence of contradictory research evidence. The AO2 material would be worth 5 marks (basic with limited analysis). This would have been vastly improved if actual research evidence had been used to support the claims being made. That gives a total of just 6 marks.

Answer 2: This answer is far more focused and has sufficient material to address only the effects of day care on social development. The opening paragraph again contains all the AO1 material, but this time it is a clear, accurate and detailed description of appropriate research studies. This would receive the full 6 marks for AO1. The next two paragraphs are full of evidence and arguments that show good critical engagement with the topic. Much of this revolves around a counter argument that day care may, in some circumstances, have negative effects for a child's social development. This is fine, provided that it is used (as it is here) as part of a wider engagement with the requirements of the question set. This is informed and reasonably thorough, so would receive the full 12 marks for AO2. This gives a total of 18 marks for the question.

MODULE 2: PHYSIOLOGICAL PSYCHOLOGY & INDIVIDUAL DIFFERENCES

Physiological psychology: Stress

(a) Outline two ways in which the body responds to stress.　　　(3 marks + 3 marks)

Answer 1

The body reacts to stress by the General Adaptation Syndrome. This involves three stages, which are alarm, resistance and exhaustion. The body adjusts to stress, but if it is prolonged the body can no longer cope. This is the stage of exhaustion.

The second way is through the action of the autonomic nervous system. One part of this is the sympathetic nervous system, which is activated when the body encounters a stressor. This causes many different physiological changes that are associated with fight or flight.

Answer 2

When you are aroused, your pituitary gland releases adrenocorticotrophic hormone (ACTH) into the bloodstream. This travels to the adrenal cortex, which releases corticosteroids. These mobilize energy resources and maintain blood flow and heart rate to get oxygen to the muscles that may be needed in a 'fight or flight' response.

During arousal, the sympathetic division of the autonomic nervous system stimulates the adrenal medulla to release the hormones adrenaline and noradrenaline into the bloodstream. These hormones, in conjunction with corticosteroids, reinforce sympathetic arousal by stimulating heart rate and mobilizing further energy resources in the body. This enables the body to deal with the stressor by activating a 'fight or flight' response.

Comment

Answer 1: Both of these are accurate, but both lack sufficient detail to earn the full 3 marks. We might ask of the first "what goes on in these three stages?", and of the second, "what specific physiological changes are initiated by the sympathetic nervous system?" They would receive 2 marks each.

Answer 2: These outlines of two ways in which the body responds to stress are both accurate and detailed. Each is a very good précis of what is quite complicated biology – remember though, that this question might have asked for a description of one way rather than an outline of two. This would receive the full 6 marks.

(b) Outline the *procedures* and *findings* of one study of the relationship between stress and cardiovascular disorders.　　　(6 marks)

Answer 1

A study was done which divided over a thousand men into Type A or Type B. They were then watched for 8 years to see how many would have heart attacks. When they looked to see who had heart attacks, 70% were Type A. These are people who are rushed and pressured and this study shows that they are more likely to die of heart attacks.

Answer 2

Rosenman studied 3500 middle-aged men for eight years. First of all he interviewed them in order to classify them as either Type A (always rushing, competitive and time pressured) or Type B (the opposite of this), or Mixed Type A/Type B. Before the study began, he checked to see if any of the men had a history of heart disease. None had.

During the course of the study about 7% of the men had heart attacks. Of these, about 70% had previously been classified as Type A. The remaining 30% were those who had been classified as being mixed Type A/Type B, and none of the Type B men had a heart attack in the same period.

■ *Answer 1:* Although brief, this answer has a reasonable amount of information about the procedures and findings of this study. Detail and accuracy are not really as they should be, but there is just enough of each of these to move this beyond the bottom mark band and to achieve 3 marks out of 6.

■ *Answer 2:* Although there is a fair bit of 'rounding up'

and 'rounding down' when describing the figures in this study, we get the point nonetheless. Procedures are carefully described (3,500 middle-aged men, classified as Type A, followed for 8 years and so on) and in detail. The findings are also accurate and the extra detail (e.g. we are also told the outcomes for the Type B group) is appropriate elaboration. This is worth the full 6 marks.

> **[c]** Outline and evaluate attempts to explain the relationship between life changes and stress. (18 marks)

Answer 1

The Social Readjustment Rating Scale of Holmes and Rahe is an attempt to measure the number of life events that a person has experienced and the seriousness of those life events. This information can then be used to see if there is a relationship between stressful events and illness. The trouble with this is that it doesn't tell us much about the possible causal association between two things. For example, if a person has been divorced and they also have had depression, it is tempting to say that they are depressed because they are divorced. However, it is possible that it might work the other way, and that they became divorced because their partner got fed up with their depression!

Unfortunately the SRRS does not distinguish between a positive life event and a negative event. For example,

getting married and being fired at work have virtually the same score, yet one is surely positive and the other negative. The scale relies on people's retrospective reports of their life events in the previous two years. However, human memory is fallible! A study by Raphael et al. found that people tended to recall different life events when asked at different times. Some people may believe that there is a relationship between life events and illness, and therefore in their own mind they will have already made the connection, making a particular life event or events easier to recall. For others though, who believe that things like depression are just physical illnesses, the connection will not be made so easily. All of these criticisms mean that the SRRS is not a particularly valid way of relating life changes with stress.

Answer 2

The Social Readjustment Rating Scale (SRRS) was developed by Holmes and Rahe (1967). This scale uses a variety of life events rated on a 0–100 scale, with death of a spouse at 100 the most stressful of the events on the scale. The values of all the experienced events are then added together to give a total stress score. A number of studies have shown that people's illness rates increase following increases in stress scores. However, a number of the items on the scale are vague e.g. 'personal injury or illness' appears to suggest that someone could have the same score for flu and cancer. Second, there is a general failure to consider the impact of an event on the individual. Christmas is considered to be only mildly stressful, yet to many, Christmas is extremely stressful, perhaps because it emphasizes their loneliness. There is also a failure to distinguish between desirable and undesirable events. For example, pregnancy could be much desired if a couple are planning a family or viewed as a disaster to a single mother who is struggling to make ends meet. This is

critical, as research has shown that undesirable life events are correlated with illness, but desirable events are not.

There are other problems in the use of this scale. For example, there is a problem of inferring cause and effect, as the scale only suggests that the life events and illness are correlated. These major life events are also relatively rare and therefore cannot be a major cause of our day-to-day stress. According to Hopson (1981), there are different transitional routes for individuals coping with positive and negative life events. Each has the same potential for a later crisis because they are 'life stressors', but the likely adjustment outcomes are different. Hopson's model is important because, unlike the Holmes and Rahe model, it distinguishes between responses to positive and negative events, and focuses on transition and recovery rather than a static relationship between life event and stress reaction. It also acknowledges that positive life events such as marriage or the birth of a child have as much potential for psychological disruption as negative events.

Answer 1: This is a good response to the question, but more than one 'attempt' is asked for. This is what examiners refer to as a 'plurality requirement'. This answer only includes one 'attempt' (the SRRS), so unfortunately there is a maximum of 4 out of 6 for the AO1 component, and 8 out of 12 for AO2. In this answer, there is little in response to the 'outline' instruction, so just 2 out of 6 marks for AO1, but the AO2 is a lot better, so 7 out of 12 (8 maximum remember) giving a total of 9 marks out of 18.

Answer 2: This answer satisfies the plurality requirement of this question. The description of the SRRS has been kept suitably brief, and is followed by some excellent evaluative points. Hopson's transitional model is outlined accurately, and the positive evaluation of this model is effective AO2. This answer has fully addressed the requirement to outline and evaluate more than one 'attempt', which is where Answer 1 came unstuck.

Individual differences: Abnormality

> **(a)** Outline the clinical characteristics of bulimia nervosa. (6 marks)

Answer 1

There are two main eating disorders, anorexia and bulimia. They are becoming more common and sometimes affect famous people like Princess Diana. Anorexia means loss of appetite but this is not quite right because people with anorexia are often hungry although they do not eat enough. Bulimia is different because they eat a lot and then vomit. They don't die of starvation but they damage their bodies, e.g. their teeth go bad and they get puffy faces.

Answer 2

The main characteristics of bulimia nervosa are:
- Recurrent episodes of binge eating.
- Inappropriate compensatory behaviours to prevent weight gain, e.g. vomiting or the use of laxatives.
- Behaviours occurring on average at least twice a week for a period of three months or more.
- Self-evaluation being unduly influenced by body shape and weight.
- An awareness of hunger and of the disorder.
- More antisocial behaviour.
- Irregular menstruation.
- Often a perceived intense family conflict.

Answer 1: There is a fair amount of irrelevant information in this answer. The question is specifically related to bulimia nervosa and not eating disorders in general. There is no credit, therefore, for the material on anorexia nervosa. The outline of the characteristics of bulimia nervosa are basic and lacking detail, and would receive just 2 marks.

Answer 2: Eight points are made here. All are accurate and pertinent specifically to bulimia nervosa rather than eating disorders in general. For this type of question (i.e. a list of characteristics) it is acceptable to write in bullet points. At other times, answers should be in continuous prose. This answer receives 6 marks.

> **(b)** Outline assumptions made by the biological (medical) model in terms of the treatment of abnormality. (6 marks)

Answer 1

The biological model has a number of treatments of abnormality. The first of these is treatment through drugs. Drugs are used for the treatment of stress (e.g. beta blockers), and other disorders (such as schizophrenia). Beta-blockers reduce activity in the autonomic nervous system. Anti-schizophrenic drugs reduce the activity of the neurotransmitter dopamine. The second type of treatment is electro-convulsive therapy (ECT), which is used with severely depressed patients. The third type of treatment is psychosurgery. This is a last resort, but can be used to treat very violent patients or those with particular kinds of disorder that don't respond to other forms of treatment.

Answer 1: This is a common misunderstanding of this question. It does not ask for an outline of treatments, but an outline of the assumptions of the model regarding treatment. Under current AQA marking criteria, this answer would receive 4 marks and would need more explicit focus on the assumptions for the full 6 marks.

Answer 2

The main treatment associated with the biological model is drug therapy. This is based on the assumption that a chemical balance in the brain is the main cause of the problem. By administering drugs, it is possible to alter this chemical imbalance and so restore normal levels of brain functioning. A second form of treatment is ECT (electro-convulsive therapy), where an electrical current is passed through the brain for approximately half a second. This form of therapy works on the assumption that severe depression is caused by a depletion of certain neurotransmitters that are involved in the regulation of mood. Psychosurgery, although rarely used nowadays, might be appropriate if a particular mental disorder is thought to stem from dysfunction of particular areas of the brain. Removal or isolation of these areas may then be possible to restore normal behaviour.

■ *Answer 2:* This answer addresses the question in a much more direct way. It is the assumptions themselves that are the main focus of the answer (e.g. "...a particular mental disorder is thought to stem from dysfunction of particular areas of the brain"). This is accurate and detailed, and would receive the full 6 marks.

(c) "The main problem with abnormality as a concept is that we cannot agree exactly what constitutes abnormal behaviour."
Outline and evaluate two or more attempts to define abnormality. (18 marks)

Answer 1

There are approximately four definitions of abnormality, including deviation from ideal mental health, deviation from social norms and statistical infrequency. Deviation from social norms suggests that abnormality resides in the way that a person's behaviour and actions are different from the accepted norm of society. Different societies possess different values and opinions, so for example, in British society, we may see running around naked in public as abnormal behaviour, but some other societies may not. Also, different cultures have different views on abnormality, and these always differ from accepted behaviour in other cultures. This weakens the value of this definition of abnormality because it can't accommodate differences between cultures in what is considered acceptable behaviour.

Statistical infrequency offers the view that there is a distinct 'line' of normal behaviour and abnormal behaviour, and every person can be categorized somewhere on this line. What is considered 'normal' would be in the middle and

behaviours further away from the middle are less frequent, and therefore abnormal in this sense. However, one main criticism of this definition is that both genius and mental retardation are rare in society, but only mental retardation is considered to be abnormal. Another problem with this definition is that some disorders, such as depression, are not particularly infrequent in western societies, so would not be counted as abnormal under this definition.

Deviation from ideal mental health suggests that there is a lack of coping with the environment for the person. This could mean that they can't form emotional relationships with other people, or don't have a good perception of reality. A major problem with this definition is that many people would be excluded from what might be thought of as 'ideal' mental health because they have difficulties forming relationships or are neurotic in some way. It is difficult to know where to draw the line, and ideas about what is ideal mental health will always change over time.

■ *Answer 1:* The AO1 content of this answer is limited and generally accurate (e.g. the description of statistical infrequency is not particularly precise). It would be worth 4 marks. The AO2 material is also limited (being restricted to just a couple of critical points on each of the three definitions covered), but has been used in a reasonably effective manner. If these critical points had been developed a little more, to constitute a more thorough analysis of the definitions being offered, then the AO2 mark would have been a lot higher. However, this is still worth 8 marks, to give a total for this part of the question of 12 marks.

■ *Answer 2 (next page):* This is a very well structured answer. It does not try to do too much and restricts its focus to just two definitions. This is advantageous here because it gives the opportunity to add more detail in the outline and evaluation of the two 'definitions' that are chosen. The AO1 is no more than is required (and is accurate and detailed) and by keeping it all in the first paragraph you can 'manage' the whole answer much more effectively. The next two paragraphs are all AO2, neatly divided into evaluation of each definition in turn. The evaluation is clearly informed and effective and so deserves full marks. This would receive the full 18 marks for this part of the question.

Answer 2

The deviation from social norms definition of abnormality sees abnormality as departure from rules and standards considered normal within society. Some rules are explicit, but others are implicit in that they refer to expected standards of behaviour (such as not standing too close to someone in a social gathering). These rules become established within society and anyone who breaks them is considered deviant or 'abnormal'. The deviation from ideal mental health definition sees abnormality as deviation from six criteria that characterize a psychologically healthy person. These include having a positive self-concept, striving to fulfil our full potential (self-actualization) and showing resistance to stress. According to Jahoda (1958), anyone who does not show evidence of these criteria would be considered 'abnormal' and would be vulnerable to developing a mental disorder.

There are advantages to the deviation from social norms approach. It helps us to identify mental disorders because we know what to expect from people. Anyone whose behaviour departs drastically from social norms might have a mental disorder. Because many people with mental disorders are not motivated to help themselves by seeking help, others can more easily detect abnormal behaviour and act on their

behalf. However, some behaviour clearly departs from social norms but is considered 'eccentric' rather than 'abnormal', and so would not be thought to indicate an underlying mental disorder. This definition also fails to acknowledge that rules and standards of acceptable behaviour change over time. What is considered acceptable behaviour in one generation (e.g. homosexuality) may well have been considered abnormal in previous generations.

The main limitation of the 'deviation from ideal mental health' approach is that few people would be able to meet all six criteria suggested by Jahoda. For example, few people manage to reach their full potential in life. So, if self-actualization is a criterion for ideal mental health, few people would be regarded as mentally healthy. Showing resistance to stress also assumes that all stress is harmful. Briner (2003) argues against this assumption. He believes that many people actually work more efficiently when under conditions that are moderately stressful. This definition is also culturally biased in that it reflects a Western preoccupation with personal fulfilment. This is not necessarily the case in non-Western cultures where people are more concerned with collective interests than individual interests.

MODULE 3: SOCIAL PSYCHOLOGY & RESEARCH METHODS

Social psychology: Social influence

(a) Outline two differences between majority and minority influence. (3 + 3 marks)

Answer 1

Majority influence is conforming in public and minority influence is conforming in private. For example we might go along with others in public to save face but in private we don't have to worry about what others think and so we can change our mind without worrying about what others think.

Majority influence tends to happen straight away, but minority influence is only felt after a period of time, after the person has had time to think about the minority point of view.

Answer 2

Majority influence involves public compliance, where the person is more concerned with being accepted by others (normative social influence) than what is necessarily the right course of action. Minority influence, on the other hand, involves private acceptance of the minority position. The majority are more likely to examine the minority's arguments closely in private. Thus, they are more likely to be affected by informational social influence and so be converted to the minority position.

- *Answer 1:* The first difference is accurate and the example is quite appropriate as a way of fleshing out the answer sufficiently for a second mark. It would have been relatively simple to add a little more detail to earn the full 3 marks. The second answer is slightly better, but this is still lacking detail. This would get 2 marks for each answer, a total of 4 marks.

- *Answer 2:* This answer takes the same two differences but adds detail. It used the time allocated wisely and therefore ensures that all 3 marks for each difference are gained, for a total of 6 marks overall.

(b) Describe the findings and conclusions from one study of obedience. (6 marks)

Answer 1

Milgram in his classic study of obedience found some staggering results. All of the participants went to 300 volts and an amazing 65% went to the highest of 450 volts. In variations on this study, the findings were just as conclusive. He changed from a prestigious Yale University to a seedy office in town, and the obedience rate fell to 47.5%. When the teacher had to force the hand of the learner onto a metal plate to receive the shocks, the rate fell to 30%. When somebody else threw the switches at the instruction of the teacher, the rate rose to 92.5%. Milgram concluded that people will obey even sometimes against their better judgement or when they have said previously that they would not.

Answer 2

Milgram's study of obedience (Milgram 1963) found that all participants were willing to deliver at least 300 volts to the learner, and that 65% of these participants were willing to deliver the full 450 volts when told to do so by the experimenter. Milgram also found that the participants found the procedure very stressful, displaying signs of extreme anxiety. Although they dissented verbally, they tended to show obedient behaviour when 'prodded' by the experimenter to continue.

Milgram concluded that in some circumstances, particularly when in a subordinate role in a power hierarchy, people will obey orders even if they go against their conscience. Milgram believed that such 'blind obedience' could explain many of the atrocities carried out in wartime, with the pressure to obey superiors being greater than any feelings of empathy or compassion for the victim.

■ *Answer 1:* This is a good description of the percentage rates obtained by Milgram in (some of) the variations on his base rate study of obedience. Although these might technically be seen as coming from separate studies, they would be counted as part of one extended study of the same phenomenon. The conclusions (last sentence only) do not really add much, but do consolidate a mark of 4 for this question. Another sentence or two relating the findings to the overall aims of Milgram's study might well have secured the full 6 marks.

■ *Answer 2:* This answer is fairly evenly balanced across both findings and conclusions. It is an accurate representation of Milgram's base-line study of obedience. The description of how participants behaved (including their own anxiety during the procedure) is relevant as a research 'finding'. The conclusions take us beyond the studies findings and display a real understanding of what this study actually told us about obedience to authority.

(c) "The unacceptability of research into obedience is that it tells us very little about obedience in the real world."
To what extent have studies of obedience been shown to lack validity? (18 marks)

Answer 1

The key study to be examined for validity concerning obedience is Milgram. This study has been questioned both ethically and regarding validity. It initially consisted of the participant meeting a supposed other participant and then both being separated. The participant was informed and instructed to give the 'other participant' (really an accomplice) electric shocks beginning at 15 volts and going up to 450 volts, when they made incorrect answers. The participant was subjected to screams of the imposter participant (actually a recording) during the experiment. An alarmingly high result showed that all participants went up to 300 volts simply because they were instructed to do so.

However, many have criticized Milgram's work for lacking ecological validity, i.e. how true it is to real life situations. The question is, would this situation really occur in daily life? Critics have suggested that because the participants were paid, then they felt obliged to continue and so the research loses some validity here. Milgram replied by arguing that in everyday situations, people are continuously put upon by employers, colleagues etc., and so this factor increased the validity of the study. Further studies by Milgram, varying the conditions, e.g. in a seedy room instead of Yale University, allowing the participants support from others, support the claim for validity. The fact that participants were asked to continue when they showed signs of resistance has also been criticized, as interference from the researcher lacks experimental validity. His study was repeated many times, and so validity seems to be evident here.

Hofling's study of nurses obeying doctor's orders over the phone displays an extremely high rate of obedience. This was carried out in a real life setting, with unsuspecting nurses. However, although ecological validity is very high in this case, experimental validity has to be brought into question. Many ethical issues are also raised, e.g. informed consent, distress and humiliation when they realized what they had done. Both of these studies provide a good insight into the conditions needed for obedience and also act as a warning to people to question authority. However, as displayed above, if under good experimental conditions this can often produce good ecological validity.

Answer 2

There are two main issues of validity in obedience research. The first of these is experimental (or internal) validity. This is a measure of whether the procedures used in the study actually work. In the case of Milgram's study of obedience, Orne and Holland claimed that participants 'saw through' the deception and were merely playing out their role as naive participants. The second issue is that Milgram's study lacked ecological validity, in that the findings of the study could not be generalized beyond the context of the investigation. Other critics of Milgram's study have argued that Milgram's claim that he had discovered the processes by which people could have committed the atrocities of the Nazi death camps (i.e. they were simply obeying orders) was unfounded (Mandel 2003).

Milgram defended his original claim through evidence from debriefing sessions where participants admitted they had believed they were giving shocks, and through film evidence where participants appeared in considerable distress when delivering the shocks. If participants truly did not believe that they were giving shocks, then this does not explain why some participants (35%) refused to deliver the full range of shocks. However, the way in which Milgram's study was carried out may have been sufficient to allow some participants to recognize that they, rather than the victim, were the real subjects of the experiment. The fact that the experimenter appeared unconcerned about the learner's distress was one clue for the participants that this was not a 'real' situation.

Milgram's critics argued that being ordered to give electric shocks to poor learners did not involve the same psychological processes as those which affected German prison guards in concentration camps. Milgram did not accept this criticism. He argued that even though the circumstances were less severe superficially, the psychological processes were similar enough to allow us to draw inferences from the laboratory and apply them to real life. However, Mandel (2003) argues that Milgram's conclusions about obedience and the behaviour of Holocaust perpetrators were unjustified because the two situations were so dissimilar. In Milgram's study, when participants could choose what level of shock to give, they tended to choose less painful shock levels. In contrast, Holocaust perpetrators were often willing to torture their victims before killing them. This suggests that their motives went far beyond merely 'obeying orders'.

■ *Answer 1:* Too often students throw in everything they know about a topic without thinking whether it really is relevant to the question asked. This question requires a short description of aspects of obedience research that might (or might not) show questionable validity, followed by two-thirds of the answer engaging critically with these claims. This student has presented a limited outline of Milgram's study that doesn't really give us much to go on when assessing validity later on. There is some confusion about what constitutes 'ecological validity' and the claims made (e.g. "and so validity seems to be evident here") are not really substantiated. The treatment of Hofling's study is also rather vague, with the erroneous claim that this study has greater validity simply because it takes place in a real hospital with real nurses. The evaluation is not particularly effective. This would receive 3 marks for AO1 and 5 for AO2, a total of 8 marks.

■ *Answer 2:* This is a clearly structured answer. The AO1 material (in this case a statement of the arguments relating to the validity of obedience research) are clearly laid out in the first paragraph. These are arguments relating to internal validity and ecological validity. These are accurate and detailed, and would earn the full 6 marks for AO1. The next paragraph gives a balanced critical evaluation of the claims for lack of internal validity. Although it is not necessary to present both sides of the argument, that has been done effectively here. The third paragraph has been conducted in the same way, with good use of Mandel's supporting arguments concerning obedience and the Holocaust. This would receive the full 12 marks for AO2, for a total of 18 marks.

Total for this question 30 marks

Psychologists have recently become interested in the therapeutic effects of gardening among adults suffering from stress-related health problems. Earlier research had suggested that gardening, in conjunction with stress counselling, produced greater therapeutic gains in adults suffering from stress-related symptoms than counselling alone.

Two psychologists independently interviewed 20 young adults who attended weekly stress clinics. They then divided these adults into two matched groups based on age and severity of stress-related symptoms. Each participant was given a score based on the severity of their stress-related symptoms, with 1 being very low and 100 being very high. For the next ten weeks, the 10 adults in Group A received their weekly stress-counselling session with one of the psychologists, followed by an afternoon of light gardening work in the clinic garden. The 10 adults in Group B also received their weekly stress-counselling session with one of the psychologists but then simply returned home.

Table to show change in stress-related symptoms after 10 weeks

Group A (counselling plus gardening)		Group B (counselling alone)	
Score at Week 1	Score at Week 10	Score at Week 1	Score at Week 10
32	19	30	21
46	28	47	33
53	29	54	38
58	31	58	36
60	40	61	43
68	40	67	51
71	44	70	53
71	41	73	57
77	37	75	49
84	46	84	59

At the end of the 10-week experiment, each participant was again interviewed in order to establish the current severity of their stress-related symptoms. The results are shown in the table above.

(a) Give an appropriate experimental/alternative hypothesis for this study. **(2 marks)**

Answer 1

Adults who garden will feel better than those who don't.

Answer 2

Adults suffering from stress-related symptoms who receive counselling and gardening therapy for a ten-week period show greater improvement of these symptoms than adults who receive counselling alone.

■ *Answer 1:* With 2 marks available, it is wise to think how the examiner would discriminate between a 1-mark and a 2-mark answer. This is accurate but just lacks detail, so would receive 1 mark only.

■ *Answer 2:* In this answer, a full and technically accurate hypothesis is given that makes reference to both independent and dependent variables and a comparison between the two conditions. It would receive 2 marks.

(b) State whether the hypothesis given in response to part (a) is directional or non-directional and justify your choice. **(3 marks)**

Answer 1

It is directional because it states which way the results will go (that the gardening group will do better).

Answer 2

It is directional. A directional hypothesis is justified because previous research had found that gardening, in conjunction with stress counselling, produced greater therapeutic gains in adults suffering from stress-related symptoms than counselling alone.

■ *Answer 1:* The identification of direction is correct, but this is a definition of a directional hypothesis not a justification. Only 1 mark is given.

■ *Answer 2:* Both identification and justification are accurate and appropriately detailed, so all 3 marks are awarded.

(c) (i) What is meant by an 'independent variable'? (2 marks)
(ii) Identify the independent variable in this study. (1 mark)

Answer 1

(i) It is the change in a participant's behaviour as a result of the experimental manipulation.
(ii) The change in stress-related symptoms over the 10-week period.

Answer 2

(i) It is the something that an experimenter can vary in some way in order to see its effect on some aspect of behaviour – the dependent variable.
(ii) It is the gardening therapy.

■ *Answer 1:* (i) No, this is a *dependent variable*, so 0 marks. (ii) This is also a measurement of the dependent variable, so again 0 marks.

■ *Answer 2:* (i) An accurate and detailed definition that makes sure of both marks. (ii) Accurate – all that is needed for the 1 mark available.

(d) Suggest one advantage and one disadvantage of using a matched participants design in this study. (2 + 2 marks)

Answer 1

An advantage is that it overcomes participant variables (such as age) that might affect the outcome of the study.
A disadvantage is that it is difficult to do.

Answer 2

An advantage is that because participants are matched in important variables, any effect they might have on the dependent variable is the same for both conditions.
A disadvantage is that the researcher can never match in terms of all possible participant variables that might affect the dependent variable. Therefore it is only partially successful at controlling the influence of these variables.

■ *Answer 1:* The advantage is fine – it identifies an advantage and elaborates it for the full 2 marks. The disadvantage has a 'whiff of psychology' about it, so would just about be worth 1 mark.

■ *Answer 2:* This answer has enough detail to ensure both marks for the advantage and disadvantage, so 2 marks for each.

(e) Why was it necessary for both psychologists to interview participants before allocating them to Group A or Group B? (3 marks)

Answer 1

It was important so they knew how to match them into the two groups. For example, they would not want to put all the really stressed people in one group.

Answer 2

This was necessary so they could have some degree of inter-rater reliability when deciding the degree to which each of the adults showed stress-related symptoms (an important consideration when matching across conditions). This would help them to include only those participants for whom there was agreement concerning the severity of their stress-related symptoms.

■ *Answer 1:* This is one reason, but not the main reason. One psychologist working alone could have made decisions about matching, so only partially accurate for 1 mark.

■ *Answer 2:* An accurate and detailed answer that shows awareness of the need for inter-rater reliability in the assessment of the participants' stress-related symptoms. As the study is concerned with therapeutic outcomes, it is important to get agreement on the initial assessment.

(f) Identify one ethical issue that the researchers do not appear to have considered and explain how this ethical issue could have been dealt with. (3 marks)

Answer 1

The experimenters have deceived the participants by not telling them they were part of a study. They could have told them all about the study at the beginning and asked their permission.

Answer 2

An uncontrolled ethical issue is informed consent. It would be necessary for the researchers to give enough information (e.g. about the gardening therapy) at the beginning of the study for the participants to make an informed decision about whether they wanted to take part.

■ *Answer 1:* We can only assume that this was the case, but it seems reasonable here. The resolution of this issue is a little vague and needs clarification and development. This would receive 2 marks.

■ *Answer 2:* Again we can only guess at whether participants gave their informed consent but, as it wasn't stated in the stimulus material, it's okay to assume that they didn't. An appropriate and detailed account of how to deal with it brings a total of 3 marks.

(g) Explain two conclusions that might be drawn from the data in the table. (3 + 3 marks)

Answer 1

Both groups got better but Group A improved more than Group B.

At the end of the experiment, Group A (the gardening therapy group) showed less stress symptoms than Group B.

Answer 2

At the end of the 10-week period, Group A (gardening therapy plus counselling) show, on average, a greater improvement in terms of the severity of their stress-related symptoms than Group B (counselling alone).

The greatest improvement in participants who undertook the gardening therapy was in those who initially had the most severe stress-related symptoms. Those with less severe stress-related symptoms appeared to profit less from the gardening therapy.

■ *Answer 1:* The first conclusion is actually two conclusions, but could be counted as elaborated into one conclusion that is just about worth 2 marks. This second conclusion is actually an extended version of the second part of the previous one. Therefore if we ignore the second half of the first conclusion we can give 1 mark for that and 2 marks for the second conclusion (this is a case of the examiner working hard for the student!).

■ *Answer 2:* Both these conclusions are accurate and detailed, and the student has looked within the sets of data to work out that the gardening therapy has a differential effect dependent on the initial severity of the stress symptoms. Full marks again.

(h) Other than ethical issues, explain two ways in which the design of this study might have been improved. (3 + 3 marks)

Answer 1

It would be better if there were more participants. Twenty is not really enough for a study like this. It would be better if the psychologists had used 100 in each group. That way they would have got results that were more reliable and valid.

A second improvement would be if they had looked at the occupations the people did and matched them in terms of that as well as just age and stress symptoms.

■ *Answer 1:* There is a common belief that more is better in experimental research. This is not always true, and we are not told why having 100 participants would be a design improvement over having just 20. Words such as 'better' and 'more reliable and valid' are thrown around without really being appropriate in this context. This first 'improvement' would not get any marks. The second suggestion is better, as the student correctly identifies that some of the participants may have more stressful occupations (which would aggravate their stress symptoms) therefore they need to be matched in this variable as well. There is just enough here for 2 marks.

A design flaw in this study is that participants are rated at the end of the study by the same psychologists who gave them counselling during it. In order to avoid bias, it would be necessary for participants to be interviewed by an impartial psychologist who would not know whether they had been in Group A or Group B during the study.

Because the gardening therapy is the independent variable in this experiment, it would be important to test whether it really was the gardening that caused the improvement or simply the extra time spent 'in therapy'. Therefore Group B should be given extended counselling time so that each group spent the same time with a psychologist every time they attended the clinic.

■ *Answer 2:* There are two clear design flaws isolated in this answer. Both are explained first so that the resolution makes more sense. These are accurate and detailed, and it shows very efficient use of the time available to provide answers to this final part of the question. This would get the full 3 + 3 marks.

FINAL COMMENT

We have looked at how two hypothetical students have tackled a complete AS psychology paper. Answer 2 in each case is a full marker so that student would clearly get a Grade A. But what about the other 'student' (Answer 1 to each question)? It is difficult to be certain about what grade this level of performance would get as the grade boundaries change slightly year by year, but the table (right) gives you some idea of what you might expect with these marks for each of the unit papers. We will assume a mark of 2 for QoWC (Quality of Written Communication) for each paper, so the total mark per paper is 62.

Unit paper	Mark (out of 62)	Approx. grade
>> Cognitive and Developmental Psychology	27	D
>> Physiological Psychology and Individual Differences	36	B
>> Social Psychology and Research Methods	31	C

Topic 4 >> Doing well in psychology: 10 exam success tips

Top sportspeople such as Ellen MacArthur are renowned for their determination to succeed, but would be the first to admit that determination on its own is not enough. Sailing round the world single-handed takes a great deal of planning. Like many others before her, Ellen *wanted* to achieve, but knew that to do so, she would have to *prepare* for the task ahead in the most efficient way. The same is true for the AS examination:

Determination + Planning = Success

So, our focus throughout this unit is on *efficient* preparation and performance, not tears and toil. This final topic presents our 'Top 10' exam success tips.

Exam tip 1: Organization and planning

One of the best examples of *efficient* preparation concerns organization and planning. Good students break their work up into manageable chunks and set themselves goals to achieve. These goals may correspond to what your tutor will know as *learning outcomes*. Examples would be:

■ "By the end of my revision today I will be able to write an accurate and detailed description and evaluation of Bowlby's maternal deprivation hypothesis."

■ "By the end of my revision today I will be able to explain physiological approaches to stress management."

It helps to make a chart so that you know *exactly* what you need to demonstrate in the exam. We have included

revision summaries at the end of each topic so you can do this. For Developmental psychology, Topic 1, your revision summary (see p. 57) can be broken down and set out in a chart in the format shown on p. 266.

By breaking your topics into small and more tangible skills, you can keep a careful eye on your own progress. The three columns roughly equate to the division of marks, so a *basic* performance might get you 1 out of 3 marks or 2 out of 6 marks. A *reasonable* performance might get 2 out of 3 or 3/4 out of 6 marks, and a *good* performance would get 3 out of 3 or 5/6 out of 6. It may help motivate you to know that it *is* possible to get a Grade A on just two-thirds of the marks available, so don't get too dispirited if you don't get too many ticks in the third column. You must, however, aim for at least a tick in the second column for every item.

Setting yourself tangible targets will motivate you and will help you keep a check on how you are progressing, what you have achieved and what still remains for you to do. Two final points:

■ Don't set yourself huge, impossible goals, e.g. "Tonight I will learn everything about abnormality".

■ Remember to revisit what you have already learned. If skills and knowledge are not regularly re-addressed and reviewed, they can decay. This review often only takes a matter of a few minutes. Do this regularly for maximum impact.

Unit 8 // Preparing for the AS examination

	Tick if you could make only a basic attempt	Tick if you could make a reasonable attempt	Tick if you have complete mastery of this
Definition of attachment			
Definition of secure attachment			
Definition of insecure attachment			
Definition of cross-cultural variations			

Exam tip 2: Gain access to materials

The AQA examining board (at Stag Hill House, Guildford, Surrey GU2 5XJ) makes available a wide range of support material for the AS examination: specimen examination papers, marking schemes, suggestions for reading, and much, much more. Most of this is written for tutors but if you believe (as I think you should) that you should make sure that as much of your future is in your own hands as possible, then reading these will put you in the driving seat. The Chief Examiner writes a highly detailed report at the end of each exam series and by reading this you will be aware of the shortcomings of fellow students in the previous exam and so be able to avoid these yourself. Most important of all, get yourself a copy of the relevant specification for this exam. Know the specification and there will be no unpleasant surprises in the exam. You can download this free from www.aqa.org.uk (follow the links to AS Psychology, Specification A).

Exam tip 3: Use a wide variety of sources

Of course the writers of this book want to include everything possible that you will need in order to do well, but it is always good practice to cast your net wide. There are a number of magazines and periodicals written for psychologists and psychology students, and you should aim to make good, intelligent use of the Internet. As well as a lot of unmitigated junk, the Internet also contains a wealth of superb and bang-up-to-date material which cannot fail to impress your examiner, as well as increasing your interest and involvement with the topic. You may, of course, find some of the material held on these sites to be quite advanced (a good deal will be written for undergraduates and professionals) but there *will* be plenty to interest and help you.

Exam tip 4: Get plenty of exam practice

There is no substitute for practising the skills on which you will finally be assessed, in the actual situation in which they will be assessed. If you practise answering questions from mock papers under exam conditions – no books, with time limits, answering questions you have not seen before – every week during your revision, building up to the exam, the exam will hold no terrors for you.

As the exam approaches you should spend at least two hours a week doing 'mock exams' on your own. Your teacher will be able to supply you with typical exam questions and you should aim to work on these under exam conditions, two questions in one hour, with no books and so on. When you have finished, you should check your answers through – with your books this time – and seen how accurate and detailed your answers are. If you read the sample answers and examiner comments, you and your friends can assess each others' answers and talk about the merits and shortcomings of each one. It may be a bit embarrassing to start with, but it soon gives you mastery over the assessment side of the specification.

Exam tip 5: Know what will come up in the exam

We have already discussed the skills and content areas you will need to know about. But we can be even more specific. The detail of the specification shows *exactly* what you need to know. Put simply, if it's not in the specification, it can't be in a question.

If you have a copy of the specification, you can get inside the head of the Principal Examiner who sets the questions for each examination. He or she does not try to trip you up, but merely samples different areas of the specification for each examination. Remember that you cannot ignore *any* part of the specification because each subsection (e.g. stress as a bodily response, stress and illness, stress management) is sampled in every examination. However, because questions are set to the wording of the specification, you have a pretty good idea what a question in a particular area will look like.

ACTIVITY

Predicting examination questions

Use the information in Topic 1 in this unit to work out what questions could be asked for the following subsection of the specification, and compare your list with that of a friend.

Defining psychological abnormality

Attempts to define abnormality in terms of statistical infrequency, deviation from social norms, a failure to function adequately, and deviation from ideal mental health. Limitations associated with these attempts to define psychological abnormality (including cultural relativism).

Exam tip 6: Answer the question

This may sound obvious – even patronizing – but many candidates simply don't answer the questions set. Some candidates seem to think that the actual wording of a question doesn't really matter too much, as long as they write an answer 'in the general area'. Others seem to prepare too rigidly and go into the exam hall simply intent on reproducing 'prewritten' answers. For whatever reasons, the answers do not 'fit' the questions. You must go into the exam hall prepared to be flexible and deal with the specific demands of the paper in front of you.

To use two analogies, *don't* think of yourself as an actor in a play whose task it is to repeat the lines they have learned, word perfect. *Instead,* think of yourself as a doctor who has to deal with whatever comes your way in a particular surgery session.

Make sure you read the questions carefully, and don't start writing your answers until you have really thought about what you are being asked to do and planned your responses. Remember, it isn't just what you put into your answers; it's also to do with what you leave out. Almost certainly you will know a lot more psychology than you can write down in the exam. The trick is to make sure that you offer the examiner those parts of your psychological knowledge that are most relevant to the questions in front of you. Don't fall into the trap of writing what you want to; write what the examiner wants.

Exam tip 7: Plan your AO1 + AO2 response *carefully*

Choose carefully

The final part of each question carries the most marks, so it is wise to spend a bit of time at the beginning of the examination choosing which one you will answer. You will have a choice of one from two in Cognitive, one from two in Developmental, and so on. Don't be seduced by the relatively easy first part of each question; try to work out how well you could perform over all three parts, *particularly* how well you are likely to perform on the final part. The key then is to make the right choice *before* you begin writing.

The three paragraphs technique

This is probably the most straightforward way of responding to the AO1 + AO2 questions. You may remember that these questions are one-third AO1 and two-thirds AO2. By packing all your AO1 into the first paragraph and your AO2 into the two subsequent paragraphs, you can be confident that you have presented your material with the right balance (so making it more likely that you pick up more of the marks available for these two skills). Take the following question, for example:

> Outline and evaluate the physiological approach to stress management. (18 marks)

The three paragraphs could contain the following:

- *Paragraph 1:* An outline of the use of drugs and biofeedback in stress management.

- *Paragraph 2:* An evaluation (preferably the strengths and limitations) of drugs as a way of managing stress.

- *Paragraph 3:* An evaluation (preferably the strengths and limitations) of biofeedback as a way of managing stress.

The other advantage of using this approach is that you can impose neat time and space divisions on your work. If you allow 15 minutes of writing time for this part of the question, that's 5 minutes (100 to 120 words) for each paragraph. Having to write 100 words on one small area (e.g. evaluation of drugs as stress management) *appears* far less intimidating that having to write a mini-essay (of 300 to 360 words) on the physiological approach to stress management.

Working backwards from your conclusion

If you want to get somewhere, it is often a good idea to look on a map to find the place you're going, and then work backwards in an attempt to plan your route. Take a look at the question above – what do *you* think of the physiological approach to stress management? Is it good, bad, or are there good points and bad points? Think about this for a while, and then decide what arguments you will put together to justify that conclusion. There are three stages to this approach:

- What is my conclusion?

- What evidence would lead to that conclusion? This might be research evidence that supports your point of view or challenges others'. It might be the views of critics or supporters of this point of view.

- What arguments (or evidence) might I meet along the way, and how would I discount them?

The debate

As you develop your interest and involvement with psychology, you will become aware that not everybody agrees with a particular point of view. There are very few 'facts' in psychology, and psychologists spend a great deal of time arguing for their own views on a topic. You can represent that tension within a topic area by presenting your AO1 + AO2 response in the form of a debate. This works as follows:

- Begin by marshalling together everything you feel is relevant to a two-sided discussion. This includes 'facts', research evidence, points of view, alternative explanations, strengths, limitations, etc.

- Remember that when you describe something, this counts as AO1.

- If you comment on it, this counts as AO2.

Take the following question, for example:

> Consider the levels of processing model as an explanation of human memory. (18 marks)

Now look at the sample answer on the next page.

This was supported in research by Craik and Tulving (1975) who found that participants remembered most words from a list that had been processed for meaning and least from those that had simply been processed for their structure. This showed that deeper processing led to enhanced memory, a key assumption of the model.

However, many psychologists question the idea of 'depth'. To say that something is remembered if it is deeply processed and that deep processing leads to better memory is a circular definition.

This criticism may not be entirely fair as subsequent research extended what is meant by 'depth' to include organization, distinctiveness, elaboration and effort. Research by Eysenck and Eysenck (1980), for example, provided evidence for the importance of elaboration as an aspect of deeper processing.

This extract from an answer to this question shows how the argument moves from one side to the other, providing a critical overview of the agreements and disagreements within psychology concerning the value of levels of processing theory. Notice how the answer uses 'AO2 phrases' (such as 'this was supported in research', 'question the idea of ', 'this criticism was not entirely fair') to contextualize the material. In this way the answer *evaluates* levels of processing theory rather than simply providing more AO1 descriptive material.

Finally, and perhaps most importantly, is the effective use of material. This is what causes students most problems. Students frequently *describe* studies that are relevant and the examiner is aware that there is a link between the study and the point the candidate was trying to make, but the student *does not make that link*! In other words, they have the material but don't *use* it.

Exam tip 8: Good time-management

As we have seen, all the AS questions (excluding those on Research Methods) are set to a specific formula: the allocation of marks is always 18 for AO1 and 12 for AO2.

You must divide your answer to map that of the question. For your answers, you will have a little less than a minute per mark (30 marks available per question; 30 minutes allowed – but reading the questions, planning your answers and then checking them through at the end will, of course, use some of that time allowance, so let's say you have 25 minutes *writing* time). Alternatively, think of it another way: the average candidate is probably capable of writing around 500 words in 25 minutes.

What this means is that each 6-mark unit should be allocated approximately five minutes of writing time and should generate around 100 words.

Exam tip 9: Make your answers 'psychological'

The exam is in psychology, so, naturally enough, you will be judged on the quality of your psychology! Again, this may seem an obvious point, but senior examiners know from experience that a large number of candidates ignore this point.

You should try to avoid writing your answers in a chatty, anecdotal way, but should write in the third person ('it can be argued' rather than 'I reckon', for example). Try to write in an objective, logical manner and remember that you should always aim to give evidence to support what you

are saying. The bloke down the pub may be able to say "girls have eating problems these days because all the magazines are stuffed with photos of stick-like dolly birds," but you can't. You need to say, "Psychological research such as that carried out by XXX has shown that ..."

You may find this difficult to begin with, but it is a classic instance where practice can make perfect, as you will discover.

Exam tip 10: Performing well in Research Methods

This part of the exam is very different to the others. It focuses on how psychological research is carried out and is what we might call problem-driven.

There are two significant differences between how you need to write your Research Methods answers and how you answer other questions:

■ In Research Methods, you need not write in complete sentences/paragraphs. However, do note what we have just said about brief answers (getting 1 instead of 2, when 2 is available), so you should not aim to be too frugal with your words. The key point is that there is no point in merely putting in words for the sake of it.

■ In all other aspects of the exam, examiners use something known as 'positive marking'. What this means is that if you make a mistake, the examiner ignores it and doesn't take any marks away. The logic is that in writing something inaccurate, candidates penalize themselves because they have wasted precious time when they could have been writing something which would earn credit. 'Knocking marks off' would therefore be a double penalty. However, this logic isn't used in Research Methods.

For example, a question could ask you to identify a method used in a study; you could write 'survey, interview, experiment, correlation, observation'. Under the principles of positive marking, you would get the mark because you have given the right answer, albeit embedded in a list. However, the whole list would have taken you only seconds to write. This isn't allowed. The examiner is told to mark only the first answer you give in situations like this.

So there you have it. Now you know everything you need to know. All that is left is for you to put what you have learned in this unit into practice. *Good luck!*

Aim: the intended purpose of an investigation, i.e. what the research investigation is actually trying to discover.

Alternative hypothesis (may be referred to as the **experimental hypothesis** in an experiment): predicts that something other than chance alone has produced the results obtained; in a well-designed experiment this should be the effects of the independent variable.

Anorexia nervosa: an eating disorder characterized by the pursuit of extreme thinness and by an extreme loss of weight.

AO1: knowledge and understanding of specification content. Questions that require an AO1 response use terms such as 'outline', 'give a brief account of', 'describe', 'explain', 'give', 'what is meant by'. In general terms, this can be seen as equivalent to *description* of material.

AO2: analysis and evaluation of specification content. Questions that require an AO2 response use terms such as 'evaluate'. Some questions embed the AO2 requirement within more general instructions such as 'consider' and 'to what extent'. In general terms, this can be seen as equivalent to *commentary* on material. For material to count as AO2, you must be seen to be commenting on theories, studies etc., rather than simply describing them.

APFCC studies:
(a) *Aims* – What was the purpose of carrying out a particular study? What were the researchers trying to find out?
(b) *Procedures* – How did the researchers carry out the study? What did they do to whom?
(c) *Findings* – What did they discover? For example, saying that "Milgram discovered that 65% of participants delivered the full 450 volts" is a *finding*.
(d) *Conclusions* – What did researchers learn about the behaviour in question as a result of carrying out a study? A statement that "Milgram found that ordinary men and women will go against their conscience and blindly follow

instructions from an authority figure" is a *conclusion*.
(e) *Criticisms* – often seen as equivalent to listing what is bad about something, criticisms can also be *positive*, in that you can detail what is *good* about a theory, study or whatever.

Attachment: a strong emotional and reciprocal bond between two people, especially between an infant and its caregiver(s). Attachments serve to maintain proximity between infant and caregiver because each experiences distress when separated. The attachment relationship also serves as a basis for subsequent emotional development.

Bar chart: a series of vertical bars of equal width used to illustrate the frequencies of a non-continuous variable displayed on the x-axis. It is superficially similar to a histogram.

Behavioural model: a view that abnormal behaviours are maladaptive, learned responses in the environment which can be replaced by more adaptive behaviours.

Bulimia nervosa: an eating disorder characterized by secret binge eating followed by vomiting, misuse of laxatives, diuretics, excessive exercise, etc., in order to lose weight.

Capacity: the amount of information that can be stored in memory at any particular time.

Cardiovascular disorder: any disorder of the cardiovascular system, e.g. high blood pressure, coronary heart disease (heart attack) or stroke. (The cardiovascular system consists of the heart and the blood vessels. It is responsible for distributing oxygen and nutrients to the body's organs.)

Cognitive development: the changes that take place throughout one's life with respect to mental abilities, including memory, perception, language and intelligence. Attachment promotes cognitive development because it offers a secure base for exploration and increases opportunities for stimulation. Deprivation may therefore harm cognitive development.

Cognitive model: a view that stresses the role of cognitive problems (such as illogical or irrational thought processes) in abnormal functioning.

Commentary: a generic AO2 term used by examiners to describe any material used by a candidate to 'comment on' rather than 'describe' psychological material. Analysis and evaluation count as commentary, as does any other material that is *about* the material being described rather than a further description of it.

Conformity/majority influence: a form of social influence where people adopt the behaviours, attitudes and values of other members of a reference group.

Control (psychological): the sense that we can anticipate events that occur in our environment – a feeling that we can accomplish things and are not at the mercy of forces beyond our control.

Correlation: a term that refers to the degree of relatedness between sets of scores – that is, the extent to which different variables co-vary.

Correlation coefficient: a descriptive statistic with a numerical value on a scale between −1 and +1. It demonstrates the strength of any relationship that exists between two sets of data.

Cross-cultural variation: variations between people of different cultures. A culture is a set of beliefs and customs that bind a group of people together, such as child-rearing practices. These practices may influence the kind of attachments, so that people from different cultural groups have different kinds of attachments with their children. These differences tell us something about the effects of child-rearing practices on attachment.

Cultural relativism: the idea that judgements about definitions of human behaviour (e.g. abnormal behaviour) cannot be made in absolute terms but only within the context of a given culture.

Day care: a form of care for infants and children, offered by someone other than close family, taking place outside the home. Children spend part or all of the day in care, but return home at night. This is distinct from a residential nursery, where children are looked after for a short spell, such as a week, and sleep there as well. Day care also differs from institutional care, which refers to long-term, 24-hour care.

Decay: the memory trace fades away with time so that the memory is no longer available.

Deception: withholding information or misleading research participants. Deception may be trivial when only a few details of a hypothesis are withheld. On the other hand, deception is of more ethical concern when it involves deliberately providing false information that may influence a participant's willingness to take part.

Demand characteristics: occur when participants try to make sense of a research situation that they find themselves in and act accordingly.

Deprivation: to have something taken away, such as food or warmth, i.e. a loss. In the context of attachment, deprivation refers to the loss of emotional care that results in the breaking of emotional bonds. A child is denied emotional care for a period of time. Bowlby's maternal deprivation hypothesis proposes that emotional deprivation disrupts the attachment process, which may harm emotional and social development.

Deviation from ideal mental health: behaviour that does not meet the six criteria relating to mental health or optimal living first proposed by Jahoda (1958).

Deviation from social norms: behaviour that violates the implicit and explicit rules and moral standards of a given society.

Directional hypothesis: an alternative hypothesis which predicts the direction in which any differences (or any correlation in an investigation using correlational analysis) in the results of an investigation are expected to occur.

Displacement: items currently in STM are pushed out to make room for incoming new ones.

Duration: the length of time that information can be kept in memory.

Eating disorder: a condition where there is serious disruption of healthy eating habits or appetite.

Ecological validity: the degree to which the findings from a study can be generalized beyond the context of the investigation. Problems with ecological validity tend to emerge only when other researchers try to rerun the study in different situations.

Encoding: changing sensory input into a form or code to be processed by the memory system.

Ethical guidelines: prescriptive guidance given by professional associations (e.g. the British Psychological Society) on how psychologists should practise or carry out their research.

Ethical issue: an ethical issue will arise in research where there is a conflict between the rights and dignity of participants and the goals and outcomes of research. For example, there may be conflict between the rights of participants to give fully informed consent and the importance of studying behaviour in as natural a setting as possible.

Ethics: in psychology these are fundamental principles that respect the rights and feelings of those taking part in research.

Evaluate: a requirement to make an informed judgement about the *value* of something, e.g. by arguing that it is supported by research studies (or not, if your evaluation is negative), or that it has important applications. Evaluation should always be aimed at whatever it is you are evaluating, rather than simply *describing* an alternative point of view.

Experiment: an investigative technique involving changes to one variable (the independent variable) in order to see its effect on another variable (the dependent variable), and to establish cause-and-effect relationships.

Experimental (internal) validity: a measure of whether the experimental procedures actually worked and the effects observed were genuine (i.e. caused by the experimental manipulation). The conclusions of a study are justified when there is a high level of experimental validity.

Extent: see *To what extent*

External validity: is concerned with the extent to which results can be generalized to other settings beyond that of the study concerned. A distinction can be drawn here between *population validity* (the extent to which results from research can be generalized to other groups of people) and *ecological validity* (the extent to which research findings can be generalized to situations outside the research setting).

Eyewitness testimony: an area of memory research that investigates the accuracy of memory following an accident, crime or other significant event, and the types of errors that are commonly made in such situations.

Failure to function adequately: an assessment of an individual whose disability prevents them from pursuing normal activities and goals (e.g. alcohol addiction preventing normal performance at work or interfering with social activities).

Field experiment: an experiment carried out in a real-world setting (such as a classroom) rather than the more artificial setting of the laboratory.

Flashbulb memory: a vivid, long-lasting memory of a highly significant event accompanied by recollection of details such as where we heard the news and what we were doing at the time.

Forgetting: the loss of the ability to recall or recognize something previously learned.

Frequency polygon: a form of graphical representation used to present data on interval or ratio levels of measurement. It consists of a line linking points that represent the frequencies of the variable placed on the x-axis.

General Adaptation Syndrome (GAS): a model, described by Hans Selye, of how the body reacts during stressful situations. There are three stages:
(a) *alarm stage* when an arousal response is activated
(b) *resistance stage* when the body is apparently coping with the stressor
(c) *exhaustion stage* – if stress continues for too long, it can lead to physical symptoms such as a stomach ulcer or heart attack.

Histogram: a form of graphical representation used to present data on interval or ratio levels of measurement. It consist of a series of vertical bars of equal width, which represent the frequencies of the variable placed on the x-axis.

Hypothesis: a testable statement. A research hypothesis is a general prediction made at the beginning of an investigation about what the researcher expects to happen.

Immune system: the system that protects the body against infection; a network of cells and chemicals that seek out and destroy invading particles.

Independent groups design: an experimental design which involves using different participants in each condition of the experiment.

Informed consent: an ethical requirement that participants should have sufficient information about a research study to enable them to make an informed judgement as to whether or not to take part.

Insecure attachment: a less optimal form of attachment, at least in Western culture. Insecurely attached children show disturbed behaviour during separation and reunion. One type of insecure attachment is called resistance-insecure. Children who are resistant-insecure are distressed on separation and resist reunion with their caregiver. A second type, avoidant-insecure, are indifferent at separation and avoid contact on reunion. Insecurely attached children tend to have less successful relationships with peers, lovers and their own children later in life.

Interference: memory traces are disrupted or obscured by other information.

Internal validity: is concerned with the extent to which we can be sure that research findings are due to the mechanisms suggested, such as manipulation of the independent variable in an experiment, and not to the action of some other unwanted variable, such as individual differences or the effects of practice.

Interview: any face-to-face situation where one person (the interviewer) asks a series of questions of another person (the respondent). These questions may be structured, semi-structured or unstructured.

Investigation using correlational analysis: an investigation using a type of analysis to measure the extent of the relationship between variables that are thought likely to co-vary (e.g. height and weight).

Investigator effects: result from the effects of a researcher's behaviour and characteristics on an investigation. They include expectation effects and the effects that the presence of a researcher can have on the behaviour of participants, resulting in their behaving in ways different from those that would normally be displayed.

Laboratory experiment: an experiment carried out in a laboratory, allowing the researcher to exert a high level of control over the independent variable, and to eliminate or control for confounding variables.

Levels of processing: a theory of memory put forward by Craik and Lockhart, that the amount of information retained in LTM depends on how deeply it is processed during learning.

Life changes: major life events, such as marriage, divorce, moving house and having a baby, that are scored according to their psychological impact within the *Social Readjustment Rating Scale (SRRS)* and used to investigate the relationship between life changes and stress-related health breakdown.

Long-term memory (LTM): an unlimited capacity system for storing information for long periods.

Matched participants design: an experimental design which involves matching each participant in one of the experimental conditions as closely as possible with another participant in the second condition on variables considered to be relevant to the experiment in question.

Mean: the arithmetic average of a set of scores, calculated by adding all the scores together and dividing by the number of scores.

Measure of central tendency: a descriptive statistic that provides a single value which is representative of a set of numbers by indicating the most typical (average) value. The mode, median and mean are measures of central tendency.

Measures of dispersion: descriptive statistics that enable us to examine the variability within sets of data; they help us to understand whether scores in a given set of data are similar to, or very different from, each other. The range and standard deviation are measures of dispersion.

Median: the middle value of a set of scores arranged in ascending or descending order.

Medical model (or biological model): a view of abnormality that sees mental disorders as being caused by abnormal physiological processes such as genetic and biochemical factors. Abnormality according to this model is seen as an illness or disease.

Memory: the mental processes involved in registering, storing and retrieving information.

Minority influence: a form of social influence where a persuasive minority exerts pressure to change the attitudes, beliefs or behaviours of the majority. Minorities are most influential when they appear consistent and principled.

Mode: the most frequently occurring value in a data sequence.

Model: a term that is used synonymously with theory. In psychopathology, it refers to an explanation of the causes of psychological disorders.

Multi-store model of memory: an explanation of memory as a flow of information through a series of stages in a fixed sequence. The best-known model of this type was proposed by Atkinson and Shiffrin.

Natural experiment: a type of quasi-experiment where the allocation of participants to the different experimental conditions is outside the control of the researcher, but rather reflects naturally occurring differences in the independent variable (e.g. two schools using different methods to teach reading).

Naturalistic observation: an observational technique where behaviour is observed in its natural context without intrusion by the person who is doing the observing.

Negative correlation: a measurement of the extent to which high values on one variable are associated with low values on another. A negative correlation is indicated by a correlation coefficient between zero and −1.

Non-directional hypothesis: an alternative hypothesis which does not predict the direction in which any differences (or any correlation in an investigation using correlational analysis) in the results of an investigation are expected to occur.

Null hypothesis: predicts no differences between the results from the different conditions of an experiment (it predicts no correlation in an investigation using correlational analysis). Under the null hypothesis, any difference (or correlation) found is due to chance alone.

Obedience to authority: an outcome of social influence where an individual acts according to the orders of some authority figure. It is assumed that without such an order the person would not have acted in this way.

Operationalization: the process of achieving precise descriptions of particular key terms in research – for example, what researchers understand by key variables such as the independent variable and the dependent variable. Operationalizing these variables usually results in a narrowing down of the research focus.

Opportunity sample: a type of sample where the researcher selects anyone who is available to take part from a given population.

Outline: a description of something that is pared down to the bare essentials. It is a less detailed account of a theory, explanation, factor, etc. Outline responses should be written in continuous prose rather than in note form.

Physiological approaches to stress management: the use of drugs and biofeedback to target directly the stress-response systems themselves.

Pilot study: a small-scale prototype of a research investigation. It is carried out on a small number of participants in order to find out whether there are any problems with the design, the instructions for participants, the measuring instruments used or any other aspect of the proposed study.

Positive correlation: a measurement of the extent to which high values on one variable are associated with high values on another. A positive correlation is indicated by a correlation coefficient between zero and +1.

Privation: a lack of the necessities of life. In the context of attachment, privation refers to a complete lack of emotional care, especially during the first few years of life. Such a lack of emotional care results in no attachments being formed. It has been proposed that this lack of early attachment results in permanent harm to emotional and social development.

Protection of participants from psychological harm: an ethical requirement that research participants should be protected from undue risk during an investigation. Risks they should be protected from include humiliation, embarrassment and loss of dignity or self-esteem.

Psychodynamic model: a view that abnormal behaviour is caused by underlying psychological forces of which the individual is probably unaware.

Psychological abnormality: behaviours and psychological functioning that are considered different from normal behaviour within a given society.

Psychological approaches to stress management: these include: (a) general psychological approaches such as the use of techniques of relaxation and meditation to reduce bodily arousal associated with stress (b) specific psychological approaches, such as cognitive and behavioural training, to help people control specific stressors in their lives.

Qualitative data: information collected in the course of a research study that is in non-numerical, narrative form, such as the transcript of what was said during a series of interviews.

Quantitative data: information collected in the course of a research study that is in a quantified (numerical) form (e.g. speed of response in milliseconds).

Questionnaire survey: a technique, using a structured set of questions, for asking a large sample of people about their views and behaviours, etc. Questionnaire surveys may be conducted in person, by telephone, by post, via the Internet, etc.

Random sample: a subset of a target population in which every person or item stands an equal chance of being selected for inclusion. This requires the researcher to be able to identify every person or item in the target population before selection of a sample takes place. The selection process therefore takes place in a completely unbiased way.

Range: the difference between the highest and lowest scores in a given set of data.

Reconstructive memory: a term usually associated with Bartlett which refers to a memory distorted by the individual's prior knowledge and expectations.

Reliability: a term that means dependability or consistency. If the findings are replicated consistently, then the outcome can be said to be reliable.

Repeated measures design: an experimental design which involves exposing every participant to each of the experimental conditions, so, in effect, participants are used as their own controls.

Repression: an unconscious process in which a distressing memory or impulse is excluded from conscious awareness.

Retrieval failure: items stored in LTM cannot be accessed because no suitable retrieval cues are available.

Sample: a subset of a target population which shares the characteristics of the population despite its smaller size.

Scattergraph (or scattergram): a graphical technique used to illustrate sets of data that are being correlated with each other. Data from one of the variables being correlated are presented on the x-axis, and data from the same individual for the second variable on the y-axis.

Secure attachment: the optimal form of attachment, associated with healthy emotional and social development. Securely attached infants feel content to explore a strange environment using their caregiver as a safe base. They show some distress when left by their caregiver, but are relatively easily comforted and show joy at reunion. Securely attached children are more likely to show stranger anxiety than insecurely attached children.

Separation: to be physically set apart from something – in the context of attachment, to be physically apart from one's caregiver, especially one's mother figure. Separation does not inevitably result in deprivation. Substitute emotional care can be provided to avoid the disruption of emotional bonds.

Short-term memory (STM): a limited capacity system for storing information for short periods.

Social development: the changes that take place throughout one's life with respect to social behaviour, such as relationships with friends and family, popularity, ability to negotiate with peers, friendliness and aggressiveness. Attachment promotes social development because it provides an internal working model for conducting relationships. Separation may therefore harm social development.

Social influence: the process by which a person's attitudes, beliefs or behaviours are modified by the presence or actions of others. There are two types of social influence that lead people to conform: *normative social influence* (based on our desire to be liked) and *informational social influence* (based on our desire to be right).

Standard deviation: used to measure the variability (i.e. the typical deviation) of a given sample of scores from its mean; the most powerful of the measures of dispersion available to the researcher.

Statistical infrequency: in psychopathology, this term is used for behaviour that occurs rarely within the general population.

Stress management: methods of managing the negative effects of stress. These include: (a) the use of drugs and biofeedback (b) the use of relaxation and meditation (c) cognitive and behavioural training (d) the use of exercise and social support networks.

Stress: can be defined in three ways: (a) as a response or reaction to something in the environment (b) as a stimulus or stressor, i.e. a feature of the environment that produces a stress-response (c) as a lack of fit between the perceived demands of the environment and the perceived ability to cope with those demands; this transactional model of stress is the most popular among psychologists.

Stressor: any stimulus in the environment that produces the stress-response, as described by Selye – for example, life events (such as dealing with death and bereavement or the breakdown of a long-term relationship) or events associated with the workplace (such as workload, conflict between home and work, keeping up with changes or lack of career prospects).

Target population: a group of people that share a given set of characteristics, about which a researcher wishes to draw conclusions.

To what extent: an instruction to consider arguments surrounding a particular point of view (e.g. "To what extent can anorexia nervosa be explained from a biological perspective?"). It is not necessary to reach a conclusion based on this information, although by balancing different points of view against each other, this should be possible.

Validity: a concept concerned with the extent to which a research instrument measures what it sets out to measure. A distinction may be drawn between different types of validity, including *internal validity, external validity* and *ecological validity.*

Working memory: a model of memory formulated by Baddeley and Hitch to replace the concept of short-term memory. It proposes a multi-component, flexible system concerned with active processing and storage of short-term information.

Workplace stressor: any stimulus in the workplace environment that produces the stress-response, such as work overload or role ambiguity.

Ainsworth, M.D.S. (1967) *Infancy in Uganda: Child Care and the Growth of Love*, Baltimore: John Hopkins University Press.

Ainsworth, M.D.S. and Bell, S.M. (1970) 'Attachment, exploration, and separation: illustrated by the behavior of one-year-olds in a Strange Situation', *Child Development*, 41, pp.49–65.

Ainsworth, M.D.S., Bell, S.M. and Stayton, D.J. (1974) 'Infant/mother attachment and social development as a product of reciprocal responsiveness to signals', in M.P.M. Richards (ed.) *The Integration of the Child into a Social World*, Cambridge: Cambridge Univ. Press.

American Psychiatric Association (1994) *Diagnostic and Statistical Manual of Mental Disorders* (4th edn), Washington, DC: American Psychiatric Association.

Andersson, B.-E. (1992) 'Effects of daycare on cognitive and socio-emotional competence of 13-year-old Swedish schoolchildren', *Child Development*, 63, pp.20–36.

Andersson, M. (1982) 'Female choice for extreme tail length in widow bird', *Nature*, 299, pp.818–19.

Angst, J. (1992) 'Epidemiology of depression', *Psychopharmacol*, 102, pp.71–74.

Arendt, H. (1963) 'Eichmann in Jerusalem: a report on the banality of evil', New York: Viking Press, cited in A.G. Miller (1986) *The Obedience Experiments*, New York: Praeger Publishers.

Aronson, E. (1999) *The Social Animal* (7th edn), New York: W.H. Freeman.

Asch, S.E. (1951) 'Effects of group pressure upon the modification and distortion of judgements', in H. Guetzkow (ed.) *Groups, Leadership and Men*, Pittsburg: Carnegie Press.

Atkinson, R.C. and Shiffrin, R.M. (1968) 'Human memory: a proposed system and its control processes', in K.W. Spence and J.T. Spence (eds) *The Psychology of Learning and Motivation*, Vol. 2, London: Academic Press.

Attanasio, V., Andrasik, F., Burke, E.J., Blake, D.D., Kabela, E. and McCarran, M.S. (1985) 'Clinical issues in utilising biofeedback with children', *Clinical Biofeedback and Health*, 8, pp.134–41.

Baddeley, A.D. (1966) 'Short-term memory for word sequences as a function of acoustic, semantic and formal similarity', *Quarterly Journal of Experimental Psychology*, 18, pp.362–5.

Baddeley, A.D. (1986) *Working Memory*, Oxford: Clarendon Press.

Baddeley, A.D. (1988) 'But what the hell is it for?', in M.M. Gruneberg, P.E. Morris and R.N. Sykes (eds) *Practical Aspects of Memory: Current Research and Issues*, Vol. 1, Chichester: John Wiley & Sons.

Baddeley, A.D. (1997) *Human Memory: Theory and Practice* (revised edition), Hove: Psychology Press.

Baddeley, A.D. (1999) *Essentials of Human Memory*, Hove: Psychology Press.

Baddeley, A.D. and Hitch, G. (1974) 'Working memory', in G.H. Bower (ed.) *The Psychology of Learning and Motivation*, Vol. 8, London: Academic Press.

Baddeley, A.D. and Hitch, G.J. (1977) 'Recency re-examined', in S. Dornic (ed.) *Attention and Performance*, New Jersey: Erlbaum.

Baddeley, A.D., Grant, S., Wight, E. and Thomson, N. (1973) 'Imagery and visual working', in P.M.A. Rabbitt and S. Dornic (eds) *Attention and Performance V*, London: Academic Press.

Baddeley, A.D., Thomson, N. and Buchanan, M. (1975) 'Word length and the structure of short-term memory', *Journal of Verbal Learning and Verbal Behaviour*, 14, pp.575–89.

Bahrick, H.P. (1984) 'Memory for people', in J.E. Harris and P.E. Morris (eds) *Everyday Memory, Actions and Absentmindedness*, London: Academic Press.

Bahrick, H.P. and Hall, L.K. (1991) 'Lifetime maintenance of high school mathematics content', *Journal of Experimental Psychology: General*, 120, pp.20–33.

Bahrick, H.P. and Phelps, E. (1987) 'Retention of Spanish vocabulary over eight years', *Journal of Experimental Psychology: Learning, Memory and Cognition*, 13, pp.344–9.

Bahrick, H.P., Bahrick, P.O. and Wittlinger R.P. (1975) 'Fifty years of memory for names and faces: a cross sectional approach', *Journal of Experimental Psychology: General*, 104, pp.54–75.

Bales, R.F. (1970) *Personality and Social Behaviour*, New York: Holt, Rinehart & Winston.

Bandura, A. (1973) *Aggression: A Social Learning Analysis*, London: Prentice Hall.

Banister, P., Burman, E., Parker, I., Taylor M. and Tindall, C. (1994) *Qualitative Methods in Psychology: A Research Guide*, Buckingham: Open University Press.

Bartlett, F.C. (1932) *Remembering*, Cambridge: Cambridge University Press.

Baumrind, D. (1964) 'Some thoughts on ethics of research after reading Milgram's "Behavioural study of obedience"', *American Psychologist*, 19, pp.421–3.

Beck, A.T. (1963) 'Thinking and depression', *Archives of General Psychiatry*, 9, pp.324–33.

Beck, A.T. (1991) 'Cognitive therapy: a 30-year retrospective', *American Psychologist*, 46, pp.382–9.

Bee, H. (1999) *The Developing Child* (9th edn), Boston: Allyn & Bacon.

Bekerian, D.A. and Bowers, J.M. (1983) 'Eye-witness testimony: were we misled?', *Journal of Experimental Psychology: Learning, Memory and Cognition*, 9, pp.139–45.

Bekerian, D.A. and Dennett, J.L. (1993) 'The cognitive interview: reviving the issues', *Applied Cognitive Psychology*, 7, pp.275–97.

Belsky, J. and Rovine, M.J. (1987) 'Temperament and attachment security in the Strange Situation: A rapprochement', *Child Development*, 58, pp.787–95.

Belsky, J. and Rovine, M.J. (1988) 'Non-maternal care in the first year of life and the security of parent–infant attachment', *Child Development*, 59, pp.157–167.

Bemis-Vitousek, K. and Orimoto, L. (1993) 'Cognitive-behavioural models of anorexia nervosa, bulimia nervosa and obesity', in K.S. Dobson and P.C. Kendall (eds) *Psychopathology and Cognition*, San Diego: Academic Press.

Bennett, M. (1995) 'Why don't men come to counselling? Some speculative theories', *Counselling*, 6(4), pp.310–13.

Berkowitz, L. (1970) 'The contagion of violence: an S-R meditational analysis of observed aggression' in W.J. Arnold and M.M. Page (eds) *Nebraska Symposium on Motivation*, 18, Lincoln: Univ. of Nebraska Press.

Bickman, L. (1974) 'The social power of a uniform', *Journal of Applied Social Psychology*, 4, pp.47–61.

Bower, G.H. and Winzenz, D. (1969) 'Groups structure, coding and memory for digit series', *Journal of Experimental Psychology*, Monograph 80 (No. 2, Pt 2), pp.1–17.

Bowlby, J. (1944) 'Forty-four juvenile thieves: their characters and home lives', *International Journal of Psychoanalysis*, 25, pp.107–27.

Bowlby, J. (1953; 2nd edn 1965) *Child Care and the Growth of Love*, Harmondsworth: Penguin.

Bowlby, J. (1969) *Attachment and Loss*, Vol. 1, *Attachment*, London: Hogarth Press.

Bowlby, J. (1981) 'Psychoanalysis as a natural science', *International Review of Psychoanalysis*, 8(3), pp.243–56.

Bowlby, J., Ainsworth, M., Boston, M. and Rosenbluth, D. (1956) 'The effects of mother–child separation: a follow-up study', *British Journal of Medical Psychology*, 29, pp.211–47.

Bradley, B.P. and Baddeley, A.D. (1990) 'Emotional factors in forgetting', *Psychological Medicine*, 20, pp.351–5.

Brady, J.V., Porter, R.W., Conrad, D.G. and Mason, J.W. (1958) 'Avoidance behavior and the development of gastroduodenal ulcers', *Journal of the Experimental Analysis of Behavior*, 1, pp.69–72.

Brandimonte, M.A., Hitch, G.J. and Bishop, D.V.M. (1992) 'Influence of short-term memory codes on visual image processing: evidence from image transformation tasks', *Journal of Experimental Psychology: Learning, Memory and Cognition*, 18, pp.157–65.

Bransford, J.D. and Johnson, M.K. (1972) 'Contextual prerequisites for understanding; some investigations of comprehension and recall', *Journal of Verbal Learning and Verbal Behaviour*, 11, pp.717–26.

Brewer, W.F. and Treyens, J.C. (1981) 'Role of schemata in memory for places', *Cognitive Psychology*, 13, pp.207–30.

British Psychological Society (2000) *Code of Conduct, Ethical Principles and Guidelines*, Leicester: BPS.

Brown, A.S. (1991) 'A review of the tip-of-the-tongue experience', *Psychological Bulletin*, 109, pp.204–33.

Brown, G.W. and Harris, T.O. (1978) *The Social Origins of Depression*, London: Tavistock.

Brown, R. and Kulik, J. (1977) 'Flashbulb memories', *Cognition*, 5, pp.73–99.

Bruch, H. (1979) *The Golden Cage*, New York: Vintage Books.

Bryant, B., Harris, M. and Newton, D. (1980) *Children and Minders*, London: Grant McIntyre.

Bushnell, I.W.R., Sai, F. and Mullin, J.Y. (1989) 'Neonatal recognition of the mother's face', *British Journal of Developmental Psychology*, 7, pp.3–15.

Button, E.J., Sonuga-Barke, E.J.S., Davies, J. and Thompson, M. (1996) 'A prospective study of self-esteem in the prediction of eating problems in adolescent schoolgirls: Questionnaire findings', *British Journal of Clinical Psychology*, 35, pp.193–203.

Campbell, F.A., Pungello, E.P., Miller-Johnson, S., Burchinal, M. and Ramey, C.T. (2001) 'The development of cognitive and academic abilities: Growth curves from an early childhood experiment', *Developmental Psychology*, 37(2).

Camras, L.A., Malatesta, C. and Izard, C. (1991) 'The development of facial expression in infancy', in R. Feldman and B. Rime (eds) *Fundamentals of Non-verbal Behavior*, Cambridge: Cambridge University Press.

Cannon, W. (1914) 'The interrelations of emotions as suggested by recent physiological researches', *American Journal of Psychology*, 25, pp.256–63.

Cardwell, M.C. (2000) *The Complete A–Z of Psychology Handbook* (2nd edn), London: Hodder & Stoughton.

Carlat, D.J., Carlos, M.D., Camargo Jr, A. and Herzog, D.B. (1997) 'Eating disorders in males: a report on 135 patients', *American Journal of Psychiatry*, 154, pp.1127–32.

Christianson, S.A. and Hubinette, B. (1993) 'Hands up! A study of witnesses' emotional reactions and memories associated with bank robberies', *Applied Cognitive Psychology*, 7, pp.365–79.

Christie, D.F. and Ellis, H.D. (1981) 'Photofit constructions versus verbal descriptions of faces', *Journal of Applied Psychology*, 66, pp.358–63.

Clark, D.M. and Teasdale, J.D. (1982) 'Diurnal variatons in clinical depression and accessibility of memories of positive and negative experiences', *Journal of Abnormal Psychology*, 91, pp.87–95.

Clark, R.D. III. (1994) 'A few parallels between group polarization and minority influence', in S. Moscovici, A. Mucchi-Faina and A. Maass (eds) *Minority Influence*, Chicago: Nelson Hall.

Clarke, A.D.B. and Clarke, A.M. (1979) 'Early experience: Its limited effect upon later development', in D. Shaffer and J. Dunn (eds) *The First Year of Life*, Chichester: John Wiley.

Clarke-Stewart, K.A., Gruber, C.P. and Fitzgerald, L.M. (1994) *Children at Home and in Day Care*, Hillsdale, NJ: Erlbaum.

Clutton-Brock, T.H. and Albon, S.D. (1979) 'The roaring of red deer and the evolution of honest advertisement', *Behaviour*, 69, pp.145–70.

Cochrane, R. (1977) 'Mental illness in immigrants to England and Wales: an analysis of mental hospital admissions, 1971', *Social Psychiatry*, 12, pp.25–35.

Cochrane, R. (1983) *The Social Creation of Mental Illness*, London: Longman.

Cochrane, R. (1995a) 'Mental illness and the built environment', *Psychology Review*, 1(4), pp.12–15.

Cochrane, R. (1995b) 'Women and depression', *Psychology Review*, 2(1), pp.20–4.

Cochrane, R. and Sashidharan, S.P. (1995) 'Mental health and ethnic minorities: a review of the literature and implications for services', Paper presented to the Birmingham and Northern Birmingham Health Trust.

Cochrane, R. and Stopes-Roe, M. (1980) 'Factors affecting the distribution of psychological symptoms in urban areas of England', *Acta Psychiatrica Scandinavica*, 61, pp.445–60.

Cohen, D. (1988) *Forgotten Millions: The Treatment of the Mentally Ill – A Global Perspective*, London: Paladin.

Cohen, G. (1993) 'Everyday memory', in G. Cohen, G. Kiss and M. LeVoi, *Memory: Current Issues* (2nd edn) Buckingham: Open University Press.

Cohen, G. (1996) *Memory in the Real World* (2nd edn), Hove: Psychology Press.

Cohen, S., Tyrrell, D.A.J. and Smith, A.P. (1993) 'Negative life events, perceived stress, negative affect, and susceptibility to the common cold', *Journal of Personality and Social Psychology*, 64, pp.131–40.

Comer, R.J. (2000) *Abnormal Psychology*, New York: W.H. Freeman.

Condor, S. (1991) 'Sexism in psychological research: A brief note', in *Feminism and Psychology*, 1, pp.430–4.

Connell, C.M. and Gibson, G.D. (1997) 'Racial, ethnic, and cultural differences in dementia caregiving: Review and analysis', *Gerontologist*, 37, pp.355–64.

Conrad, R. (1964) 'Acoustic confusions in immediate memory', *British Journal of Psychology*, 55, pp.75–84.

Constable, J.F. and Russell, D.W. (1986) 'The effect of social support and the work environment upon burnout among nurses,' *Journal of Human Stress*, 12, pp.20–6.

Conway, M.A. (1995) *Flashbulb Memories*, Hove: Erlbaum.

Conway, M.A., Anderson, S.J., Larsen, S.F., Donnelly, C.M., McDaniel, M.A., McClelland, A.G.R. and Rawles, R.E. (1994) 'The formation of flashbulb memories', *Memory and Cognition*, 22, pp.326–43.

Coolican, H. (1999) *Research Methods and Statistics in Psychology*, London: Hodder and Stoughton.

Craik, F.I.M. and Lockhart, R.S. (1972) 'Levels of processing: a framework for memory research', *Journal of Verbal Learning and Verbal Behaviour*, 11, pp.671–84.

Craik, F.I.M. and Lockhart, R.S. (1986) 'CHARM is not enough: comments on Eich's model of cued recall', *Psychological Review*, 93, pp.360–4.

Crutchfield, R.S. (1955) 'Conformity and character', *American Psychologist*, 10, pp.191–8.

Curtiss, S. (1977) *Genie: A Psycholinguistic Study of a Modern-day 'Wild Child'*, London: Academic Press.

Darley, J.M. (1992) 'Social organization for the production of evil', *Psychological Inquiry*, 3(2), pp.199–218.

De Boer, M.F., Ryckman, R.M., Pruyn, J.F.A. and Van den Borne, H.W. (1999) 'Psychosocial correlates of cancer relapse and survival: a literature review', *Patient Education and Counseling*, 37, pp.215–30.

DeLongis, A., Coyne, J.C., Dakof, G., Folkman, S. and Lazarus, R.S. (1982) 'Relationship of daily hassles, uplifts, and major life events to health status', *Health Psychology*, 1, pp.119–36.

Deutsch, M. and Gerard, H.B. (1955) 'A study of normative and informational influence upon individual judgement', *Journal of Abnormal and Social Psychology*, 51, pp.629–36.

Dewe, P.J. (1992) 'Applying the concept of appraisal to work stressors: some exploratory analysis', *Human Relations*, 45, pp.143–64.

Dollard, J. and Miller, N.E. (1950) *Personality and Psychotherapy: An Analysis in terms of Learning, Thinking and Culture*, New York: McGraw-Hill.

Dyer, C. (1995) *Beginning Research in Psychology: A Practical Guide to Research Methods and Statistics*, Oxford: Blackwell.

Egeland, B. and Hiester, M. (1995) 'The long-term consequences of infant day-care and mother–infant attachment', *Child Development*, 66, pp.474–85.

Eich, J.E. (1980) 'The cue-dependent nature of state-dependent retrieval', *Memory and Cognition*, 8, pp.157–73.

Ellis, A. (1962) *Reason and Emotion in Psychotherapy*, New Jersey: Citadel.

Evans, G., Bullinger, M. and Hygger, S. (1998) 'The effects of chronic exposure to aircraft noise', *Psychological Science*, 9, pp.75–7.

Evans, P.D. (1990) 'Type A behaviour and coronary heart disease: when will the jury return?', *British Journal of Psychology*, 81, pp.147–57.

Eysenck, H.J. (1967) *The Biological Basis of Personality*, Springfield, IL: Charles C. Thomas.

Fairburn, C.G., Cooper, Z., Doll, H.A. and Welch, S.L. (1999) 'Risk factors for anorexia nervosa', *Archives of General Psychiatry*, 56, pp.468–76.

Fisher, R.P., Geiselman, R.E. and Amador, M. (1989) 'Field test of the cognitive interview: enhancing the recollection of actual victims and witnesses of crime', *Journal of Applied Psychology*, 74, pp.722–7.

Flanagan, C. (1996) *Applying Psychology to Early Child Development*, London: Hodder & Stoughton.

Foster, J.J. and Parker, I. (1995) *Carrying out Investigations in Psychology: Methods and Statistics*, Leicester: BPS Books.

Foster, R.A., Libkuman, T.M., Schooler, J.W. and Loftus, E.F. (1994) 'Consequentiality and eyewitness person identification', *Applied Cognitive Psychology*, 8, pp.107–21.

Fox, N. (1977) 'Attachment of Kibbutz infants to mother and metapelet', *Child Development*, 48, pp.1228–39.

Frankenhaeuser, M., Dunne, E. and Lundberg, U. (1976) 'Sex differences in sympathetic adrenal medullary reactions induced by different stressors,' *Psychopharmacology*, 47, pp.1–5.

Freud, A. (1936) *The Ego and the Mechanisms of Defence*, London: Chatto and Windus.

Freud, S. (1915–1918) *Introductory Lectures on Psychoanalysis*, London: Hogarth Press.

Friedman, M. and Rosenman, R.H. (1974) *Type A Behavior and Your Heart*, New York: Knopf.

Furman, C.E. and Duke, R.A. (1988) 'Effect of majority consensus on preferences for recorded orchestral and popular music', *Journal of Research in Music Education*, 36(4), pp.220–31.

Gale, A. (1995) 'Ethical issues in psychological research', in A.M. Colman (ed.), *Psychological Research Methods and Statistics*, London: Longman Essential Psychology.

Gallo, P.S., Smith, S. and Mumford, S. (1973) 'Effects of deceiving subjects upon experimental results', *Journal of Social Psychology*, 89, pp.99–107.

Gamson, W.B., Fireman, B. and Rytina, S. (1982) *Encounters with Unjust Authority*, Homewood, IL: Dorsey Press.

Garner, D.M., Garfinkel, P.E., Rockert, W. and Olmsted, M.P. (1987) 'A prospective study of eating disturbances in the ballet', *Psychotherapy and Psychosomatics*, 48, pp.170–5.

Gauld, A. and Stephenson, G.M. (1967) 'Some experiments relating to Bartlett's theory of remembering', *British Journal of Psychology*, 58, pp.39–50.

Geiselman, R. (1988) 'Improving eyewitness testimony through mental reinstatement of context', in G.M. Davies and D.M. Thomson (eds) *Memory in Context: Context in Memory*, Chichester: Wiley.

Geiselman, R.E., Fisher, R., Mackinnon, D. and Holland, H.L. (1985) 'Enhancement of eyewitness testimony with the cognitive interview', *American Journal of Psychology*, 99, pp.385–401.

Gelder, M., Gath, D., Mayou, R. and Cowen, P. (1998) *Oxford Textbook of Psychiatry* (3rd edn), Oxford: Oxford Medical Publications/Oxford University Press.

Glanzer, M. and Cunitz, A.R. (1966) 'Two storage mechanisms in free recall', *Journal of Verbal Learning and Verbal Behaviour*, 5, pp.351–60.

Glass, D. and Singer, J. (1972) *Urban Stress: Experiments on Noise and Social Stressors*, New York: Academic Press.

Godden, D. and Baddeley, A. (1975) 'Context-dependent memory in two natural environments: on land and under water', *British Journal of Psychology*, 66, pp.325–31.

Goodwin, D.W., Powell, B., Bremer, D., Hoine, H. and Stern, J. (1969) 'Alcohol and recall: state dependent effects in man', *Science*, 163, p.1358.

Greenough, W.T., Black, J.E., and Wallace, C.S. (1987) 'Experience and brain development', *Child Development*, 58, pp.539–59.

Grossmann, K.E. and Grossmann, K. (1991) 'Attachment quality as an organizer of emotional and behavioural responses in a longitudinal perspective', in C.M. Parkes, J. Stevenson-Hinde and P. Marris (eds), *Attachment across the Life Cycle*, London: Tavistock/Routledge.

Guarnaccia, P.J., Good, B.J. and Kleinman, A. (1990) 'A critical review of epidemiological studies of Puerto Rican mental health', *American Journal of Psychiatry*, 147, pp.1449–56.

Gull, W.W. (1874) 'Anorexia nervosa', *Transactions of the Clinical Society of London*, 7, pp.22–8.

Gustafson, R. (1992) 'The relationship between perceived parents' child-rearing practices, own later rationality, and own later depression', *Journal of Rational-Emotive and Cognitive Behaviour Therapy*, 10(4), pp.253–8.

Halpern, D. (1995) *More Bricks and Mortar? Mental Health and the Built Environment*, London: Taylor and Francis.

Harlow, H.F. and Harlow, M.K. (1962) 'Social deprivation in monkeys', *Scientific American*, 207(5), pp.136–146.

Harlow, H.F. and Zimmerman, R.R. (1959) 'Affectional responses in the infant monkey', *Science*, 130, pp.421–32.

Harvey, E. (1999) 'Short-term and long-term effects of early parental employment on children of the National Longitudinal Survey of Youth', *Developmental Psychology*, 35(2), pp.445–59.

Hazan, C. and Shaver, P.R. (1987) 'Romantic love conceptualised as an attachment process', *Journal of Personality and Social Psychology*, 52, pp.511–24.

Hazen, N.L. and Durrett, M.E. (1982) 'Relationship of security of attachment to exploration and cognitive mapping abilities in 2-year-olds', *Developmental Psychology*, 18, pp.751–9.

Hebb, D.O. (1949) *Organisation of Behaviour*, New York: Wiley.

Hiroto, D.S. and Seligman, M.E.P. (1975) 'Generality of learnt helplessness in man', *Journal of Personality and Social Psychology*, 31, pp.311–27.

Hodges, J. and Tizard, B. (1989) 'Social and family relationships of ex-institutional adolescents', *Journal of Child Psychology and Psychiatry*, 30(1), pp.77–97.

Hofling, C.K., Brotzman, E., Dalrymple, S., Graves, N. and Pierce, C.M. (1966) 'An experimental study in nurse-physician relationships', *Journal of Nervous and Mental Disease*, 143, pp.171–80.

Hogg, M.A. and Vaughan, G.M. (1998) *Social Psychology: An Introduction*, Hemel Hempstead: Prentice Hall/Harvester Wheatsheaf.

Holland, A.J., Hall, D.J., Murrey, R., Russell, G.F.M. and Crisp, A.H. (1984) 'Anorexia Nervosa: A study of 34 twin pairs and one set of triplets', *British Journal of Psychiatry*, 145, pp.414–18.

Holmes, D.S. (1990) 'The evidence for repression: an examination of sixty years of research', in J. Singer (ed.) *Repression and Dissociation: Implications for Personality Theory, Psychopathology and Health*, Chicago: University of Chicago Press.

Holmes, D.S. (1993) 'Aerobic fitness and the response to psychological stress' in P. Seraganian (ed.) *Exercise Psychology: The Influence of Physical Exercise on Psychological Processes*, New York: Wiley.

Holmes, J. (1993) *John Bowlby and Attachment Theory*, London: Routledge.

Holmes, T.H. and Rahe, R.H. (1967) 'The social readjustment rating scale', *Journal of Psychosomatic Research*, 11, pp.213–18.

Howell, E. (1981) 'The influence of gender on diagnosis and psychopathology', in E. Howell and M. Bayes (eds) *Women and Mental Health*, New York: Basic Books.

Howes, C., Galinsky, E. and Kontos, S. (1998) 'Caregiver sensitivity and attachment', *Social Development*, 7(1), pp.25–36.

Hsu, I.K.G. (1990) *Eating Disorders*, New York: Guildford Press.

Hunt, R.R. and Elliott, J.M. (1980) 'The role of non-semantic information in memory: orthographic distinctiveness on retention', *Journal of Experimental Psychology: General*, 109, pp.49–74.

Hunter, M., Philips, C. and Rachman, S. (1979) 'Memory for pain', *Pain*, 6, pp.35–46.

Hyde, T.S. and Jenkins, J.J. (1973) 'Recall for words as a function of semantic, graphic and syntactic orienting tasks', *Journal of Verbal Learning and Verbal Behaviour*, 12, pp.471–80.

Insko, C.A., Drenan, S., Soloman, M.R., Smith, R. and Wade, T.J. (1983) 'Conformity as a function of the consistency of positive self-evaluation and being liked and being right', *Journal of Experimental Social Psychology*, 19, pp.341–58.

Isabella, R.A., Belsky, J. and Von Eye, A. (1989) 'Origins of infant–mother attachment: an examination of interactional synchrony during the infant's first year', *Developmental Psychology*, 25, pp.12–21.

Jahoda, M. (1958) *Current Concepts of Positive Mental Health*, New York: Basic Books Inc.

Jennings, G., Nelson, L., Nestel, P., Esler, M., Korner, P., Burton, D. and Bazelmans, J. (1986) 'The effects of changes in physical activity on major cardiovascular risk factors, hemodynamics, sympathetic function, and glucose utilization in man: a controlled study of four levels of activity', *Circulation*, 73, pp.30–40.

Jimerson, D.C., Wolfe, B.E., Metzger, E.D., Finkelstein, D.M., Cooper, T.B. and Levine, J.M. (1997) 'Decreased seratonin function in bulimia nervosa', *Archives of General Psychiatry*, 54. pp.529–33.

Johansson, G., Aronsson, G. and Linstrom, B.O. (1978) 'Social psychological and neuroendocrine stress reactions in highly mechanised work', *Ergonomics*, 21, pp.583–99.

Johnstone, L. (1989) *Users and Abusers of Psychiatry: A Critical Look at Traditional Psychiatric Practice*, London: Routledge.

Joiner, T.E. Jr, Heatherton, T.F. and Keel, P.K. (1997) 'Ten-year stability and predictive validity of five bulimia-related indicators', *American Journal of Psychiatry*, 154, pp.1133–8.

Jones, D.N., Pickett, J., Oates, M.R. and Barbor, P. (1987) *Understanding Child Abuse* (2nd edn), London: Macmillan.

Kagan, J. (1982) *Psychology Research on the Human Infant: An Evaluative Summary*, New York: W.T. Grant Foundation.

Kalven, H. Jr, and Zeisel, H. (1966) *The American Jury*, Chicago: University of Chicago Press.

Kamarck, T.W., Peterman, A.H. and Raynor, D.A. (1998) 'The effects of the social environment on stress-related cardiovascular activation: current findings, prospects, and implications', *Annals of Behavioral Medicine*, 20, pp.247–56.

Kamen, L.P. and Seligman, M.E.P. (1989) 'Explanatory style and health', in M. Johnston and T. Martineau (eds) *Applications in Health Psychology*, New Brunswick: Transaction.

Kanner, A.D., Coyne, J.C., Schaefer, C. and Lazarus, R.S. (1981) 'Comparison of two modes of stress measurement: daily hassles and uplifts versus major life events', *Journal of Behavioural Measurement*, 4, pp.1–39.

Keesey, R.E. and Corbett, S.W. (1983) 'Metabolic defence of the body weight set-point', in A.J. Stunkard and E. Stellar (eds) *Eating and Its Disorders*, New York: Raven Press.

Kelly-Radford, L. (1999) 'Diversity', Paper presented at the National Institute for Occupational Safety and Health/American Psychological Association Conference on Work Stress and Health, March 1999.

Kelman, H.C. (1958) 'Compliance, identification and internalisation: three processes of attitude change', *Journal of Conflict Resolution*, 2, pp.51–60.

Kendler, K.S., McLean, C., Neale, M., Kessler, R., Heath, A. and Eaves, L. (1991) 'The genetic epidemiology of bulimia nervosa', *American Journal of Psychiatry*, 148, pp.1627–37.

Kessler, R.C., McGonagle, K.A., Zhao, S., Nelson, C.B., Highes, M., Eshleman, S., Wittchen, H.U. and Kendler, K.S. (1994) 'Lifetime and 12-month prevalence of DSM-III-R psychiatric disorders in the United States', *Archives of General Psychiatry*, 51, pp.8–19.

Kiecolt-Glaser, J.K., Dura, J.R., Speicher, C.E., Trask, O.J. and Glaser, R. (1991) 'Spousal caregivers of dementia victims: longitudinal changes in immunity and health', *Psychosomatic Medicine*, 53, pp.345–62.

Kiecolt-Glaser, J.K., Fisher, L.D., Ogrocki, P., Stout, J.C., Speicher, C.E. and Glaser, R. (1987) 'Marital quality, marital disruption, and immune function', *Psychosomatic Medicine*, 49, pp.13–34.

Kiecolt-Glaser, J.K., Garner, W., Speicher, C., Penn, G.M., Holliday, J. and Glaser, R. (1984) 'Psychosocial modifiers of immunocompetence in medical students', *Psychosomatic Medicine*, 46, pp.7–14.

Kiecolt-Glaser, J.K., Glaser, R., Cacioppo, J.T. and Malarkey, W.B. (1998) 'Marital stress: immunologic, neuroendocrine, and autonomic correlates', *Annals of the New York Academy of Sciences*, 840, pp.656–63.

Kim, H.K. and McKenry, P.C. (1998) 'Social networks and support: A comparison of African Americans, Asian Americans, Caucasians, and Hispanics', *Journal of Comparative Family Studies*, 29, pp.313–36.

Klaus, M.H. and Kennell, J.H. (1976) *Parent–Infant Bonding*, St Louis: Mosby.

Kline, P. (1988) *Psychology Exposed, or, The Emperor's New Clothes*, London: Routledge.

Knight, R. and Knight, M. (1959) *A Modern Introduction to Psychology*, London: University Tutorial Press.

Kobasa, S.C. and Maddi, S.R. (1977) 'Existential personality theory', in R. Corsini (ed.) *Current Personality Theories*, Itasca: Peacock.

Kobasa, S.C., Maddi, S.R., Puccetti, M.C. and Zola, M.A. (1985) 'Effectiveness of hardiness, exercise and social support as resources against illness', *Journal of Psychosomatic Research*, 29, pp.525–33.

Kohlberg, L. (1969) 'Stage and sequence: the cognitive-developmental approach to socialization', in D.A. Goslin (ed.), *Handbook of Socialization Theory and Research*, Chicago: Rand McNally.

Kohlberg, L. (1973) 'Continuities in childhood and adult moral development revisited', in P.B. Baltes and K.E. Schaie, *Lifespan Development Psychology* (2nd edn), New York: Academic Press.

Koluchová, J. (1976) 'A report on the further development of twins after severe and prolonged deprivation', in A.M. Clarke and A.D.B. Clarke (eds) *Early Experience Myth and Evidence*, London: Open Books.

Koriat, A. and Goldsmith, M. (1996) 'Memory metaphors and the real life/laboratory controversy: correspondence versus storehouse conceptions of memory', *Behavioural and Brain Sciences*, 19, pp.167–228.

Kulik, J.A. and Mahler, H.I.M. (1989) 'Social support and recovery from surgery', *Health Psychology*, 8, pp.221–38.

Lamb, M.E. (1977) 'The development of mother–infant and father–infant attachments in the second year of life', *Developmental Psychology*, 13, pp.637–48.

Lambe, E.K., Katzman, D.K., Mikulis, D.J., Kennedy, S.H. and Zipursky, R.B. (1997) 'Cerebral gray matter volume deficits after weight recovery from anorexia nervosa', *Archives of General Psychiatry*, 54, pp.537–42.

Langer, E.J. and Rodin, J. (1976) 'The effects of choice and enhanced personal responsibility for the aged', *Journal of Personality and Social Psychology*, 34, pp.191–8.

LeBon, G. (1947, first published 1895) *The Crowd: A Study of the Popular Mind*, London: Ernest Benn.

Levinger, G. and Clark, J. (1961) 'Emotional factors in the forgetting of word associations', *Journal of Abnormal and Social Psychology*, 62, pp.99–105.

Lichstein, K.L. (1988) *Clinical Relaxation Strategies*, New York: Wiley.

Lifton, R.J. (1986) *The Nazi Doctors: Medical Killing and the Psychology of Genocide*, New York: Basic.

List, J.A. (1986) 'Age and schematic differences in reliability of eyewitness testimony', *Developmental Psychology*, 22, pp.50–57.

Lock, A.J. (1980) *The Guided Reinvention Of Language*, London: Academic Press.

Loftus, E.F. (1975) 'Leading questions and the eyewitness report', *Cognitive Psychology*, 7, pp.560–72.

Loftus, E.F. (1979) 'Reactions to blatantly contradictory information', *Memory and Cognition*, 7, pp.368–74.

Loftus, E.F. (1997) 'Creating false memories', *Scientific American*, September, pp.50–5.

Loftus, E.F. and Ketcham, K. (1991) *Witness for the Defence*, New York: St Martin's Press.

Loftus, E.F. and Loftus, G.R. (1980) 'On the permanence of stored information in the human brain', *American Psychologist*, 35, pp.409–20.

Loftus, E.F. and Palmer, J.C. (1974) 'Reconstruction of automobile destruction: an example of the interaction between language and memory', *Journal of Verbal Learning and Verbal Behaviour*, 13, pp.585–9.

Loftus, E.F., Miller, D.G. and Burns, H.J. (1978) 'Semantic integration of verbal information into a visual memory', *Journal of Experimental Psychology: Human Learning and Memory*, 4, pp.19–31.

Lorenz, K.Z. (1937) 'The companion in the bird's world', *Auk*, 54, pp.245–73.

Lorenz, K.Z. (1952) *King Solomon's Ring: New light on animal ways*, London: Methuen & Co.

Lynch, K. (1960) *The Image of the City*, Cambridge, MA: MIT Press.

McCarthy, G. (1999) 'Attachment style and adult love relationships and friendships: A study of a group of women at risk of experiencing relationship difficulties', *British Journal of Medical Psychology*, 72, pp.305–21.

McCloskey, M., Wible, C.G. and Cohen, N.J. (1988) 'Is there a special flashbulb memory mechanism?', *Journal of Experimental Psychology: General*, 117, pp.171–81.

Maccoby, E.E. (1980) *Social Development: Psychological Growth and the Parent–child Relationship*, San Diego: Harcourt Brace Jovanovich.

McDermott, M. (1993) 'On cruelty, ethics and experimentation: profile of Philip G. Zimbardo', *The Psychologist*, 6(10), pp.456–9.

McGeoch, J.A. and MacDonald, W.T. (1931) 'Meaningful relation and retroactive inhibition', *American Journal of Psychology*, 43, pp.579–88.

McKenna, S.P. and Glendon, A.I. (1985) 'Occupational first aid training: decay in cardiopulmonary resuscitation (CPR) skills', *Journal of Occupational Psychology*, 58, pp.109–17.

McLelland, L., Mynors-Wallis, L. and Treasure, J. (1991) 'Sexual abuse, disordered personality and eating', *British Journal of Psychiatry*, 158, pp.63–8.

Main, M. and Cassidy, J. (1988) 'Categories of response to reunion with the parent at age six: predicted from infant attachment classifications and stable over a one-month period', *Developmental Psychology*, 24, pp.415–26.

Mandel, D.R. (1998) 'The obedience alibi: Milgram's account of the Holocaust reconsidered', *Analyse und Kritik: Zeitschrift für Sozialwissenschaften*, 20, pp.74–94.

Mantell, D.M. (1971) 'The potential for violence in Germany', *Journal of Social Issues*, 27, pp.101–12.

Marmot, M.G., Smith, G.M., Stansfield, S., Patel, C., North, F., Head, J., White, I., Brunner, E. and Feeney, A. (1991) 'Health inequalities among British Civil Servants: the Whitehall II study', *The Lancet*, 337, pp.1387–93.

Maslow, A.H. (1968) *Towards a Psychology of Being* (2nd edn), Princeton, NJ: Van Nostrand Reinhold.

Masters, J.C., Burish, T.G., Hollon, S.D. and Rimm, D.C. (1987) *Behavior Therapy: Techniques and Empirical Findings* (3rd edn), San Diego: Harcourt Brace Jovanovich.

Matthews, K. and Haynes, S. (1986) 'Type A behavior pattern and coronary disease risk', *American Journal of Epidemiology*, 123, pp.923–7.

Maurer, D. and Maurer, C. (1989) *The World of the Newborn*, London: Viking.

Meichenbaum, D.H. and Cameron, R. (1983) 'Stress inoculation training: toward a general paradigm for training coping skills', in D. Meichenbaum and M.E. Jarenko (eds) *Stress Reduction and Prevention*, New York: Plenum.

Meichenbaum, D.H. and Turk, D. (1982) 'Stress, coping, and disease: a cognitive-behavioral perspective', in R.W.J. Neufield (ed.) *Psychological Stress and Psychopathology*, New York: McGraw-Hill.

Melhuish, E.C. (1993) 'Behaviour measures: a measure of love? An overview of the assessment of attachment', *ACPP Review and Newsletter*, 15 (6), pp.269–75.

Miale, F.R. and Selzer, M. (1975) *The Nuremberg Mind: The Psychology of the Nazi Leaders*, New York: Quadrangle.

Milgram, S. (1963) 'Behavioural study of obedience', *Journal of Abnormal and Social Psychology*, 67, pp.371–8.

Milgram, S. (1964) 'Issues in the study of obedience: a reply to Baumrind', *American Psychologist*, 19, pp.848–52.

Milgram, S. (1974) *Obedience to Authority*, London: Tavistock.

Miller, G.A. (1956) 'The magical number seven, plus or minus two: some limits on our capacity for processing information', *Psychological Review*, 63, pp.81–97.

Millward, L. (1998) 'Social Psychology', in M. Eysenck (ed.) *Psychology: An Integrated Approach*, Harlow: Longman.

Milner, B. (1966) 'Amnesia following operation on the temporal lobes', in C.W.M. Whitty and O.L. Zangwill (eds) *Amnesia*, London: Butterworth.

Mineka, S., Davidson, M., Cook, M. and Keir, R. (1984) 'Observational conditioning of snake fear in rhesus monkeys', *Journal of Abnormal Psychology*, 93, pp.355–72.

Minuchin, S., Rosman, B.L. and Baker, L. (1978) *Psychosomatic Families: Anorexia Nervosa in Context*, Cambridge, MA: Harvard Univ. Press.

Mixon, D. (1972) 'Instead of deception', *Journal of the Theory of Social Behaviour*, 2, pp.139–77.

Moos, R.H. and Swindle, R.W. Jr (1990) 'Stressful life circumstances: concepts and measures', *Stress Medicine*, 6, pp.171–8.

Moscovici, S. (1980) 'Towards a theory of conversion behaviour', in L. Berkowitz (ed.) *Advances in Experimental Social Psychology*, London: Academic Press.

Moscovici, S. (1985) 'Social influence and conformity', in G. Lindzey and E. Aronson (eds) *Handbook of Social Psychology* (3rd edn), New York: Random House.

Moscovici, S., Lage, E. and Naffrechoux, M. (1969) 'Influence of a consistent minority on the responses of a majority in a colour perception task', *Sociometry*, 32, pp.365–80.

Mugny, G. and Perez, J. (1991) *The Social Psychology of Minority Influence*, Cambridge: Cambridge University Press.

Mumford, D.B., Whitehouse, A.M. and Plattes, M. (1991) 'Sociocultural correlates of eating disorders among Asian schoolgirls in Bradford', *British Journal of Psychiatry*, 158, pp.222–8.

Murdock, B.B. (1961) 'The retention of individual items', *Journal of Experimental Psychology*, 62, pp.618–25.

Murstein, B.I. (1972) 'Physical attractiveness and marital choice', *Journal of Personality and Social Psychology*, 22, pp.8–12.

Myers, D.G. (1999) *Social Psychology* (6th edn), Boston: McGraw-Hill College.

Nasser, M. (1986) 'Comparative study of the prevalence of abnormal eating attitudes among Arab female students of both London and Cairo universities', *Psychological Medicine*, 16, pp.621–7.

Naveh-Benjamin, M. and Ayres, T.J. (1986) 'Digit span, reading rate, and linguistic relativity', *Quarterly Journal of Experimental Psychology*, 38, pp.739–51.

Neisser, U. (1978) 'Memory: what are the important questions?', in M.M. Gruneberg, P.E. Morris and R.N. Sykes (eds) *Practical Aspects of Memory*, London: Academic Press.

Neisser, U. (1982) *Memory Observed*, San Francisco: W.H. Freeman.

Nemeth, C. (1986) 'The differential contributions of majority and minority influence', *Psychological Review*, 93, pp.23–32.

NICHD Early Child Care Research Network (1997) 'The effects of infant child care on infant–mother attachment security: Results of the NICHD study of early child care', *Child Development*, 68(5), pp.860–79.

NICHD Early Child Care Research Network (2001) 'Further explorations of the detected effects of quantity of early child care on socio-emotional development', Paper presented at the Biennial Meeting of the Society for Research in Child Development, Minneapolis, MN.

Nicholson, N., Cole, S.G. and Rocklin, T. (1985) 'Conformity in the Asch situation: a comparison between contemporary British and US university students', *British Journal of Social Psychology*, 24, pp.59–63.

Orne, M.T. (1962) 'On the social psychology of the psychology experiment with particular reference to demand characteristics and their implications', *American Psychologist*, 16, pp.776–83.

Orne, M.T. and Holland, C.C. (1968) 'On the ecological validity of laboratory deceptions', *International Journal of Psychiatry*, 6(4), pp.282–93.

Parke, R.D. (1981) *Fathers*, Cambridge, MA: Harvard University Press.

Parker, K.C. and Forrest, D. (1993) 'Attachment disorder: An emerging concern for school counselors', *Elementary School Guidance and Counseling*, 27(3), pp.209–15.

Pavlov, I.P. (1927) *Conditioned Reflexes*, Oxford: Oxford University Press.

Pennebaker, J.W., Hendler, C.S., Durett, M.E. and Richards, P. (1981) 'Social factors influencing absenteeism due to illness in nursery school children', *Child Development*, 52, pp.692–700.

Perrin, S. and Spencer, C. (1980) 'The Asch effect – a child of its time', *Bulletin of the British Psychological Society*, 33, pp.405–6.

Perrin, S. and Spencer, C. (1981) 'Independence or conformity in the Asch experiment as a reflection of cultural and situational factors', *British Journal of Social Psychology*, 20, pp.205–9.

Peterson, L.R. and Peterson, M. (1959) 'Short-term retention of individual verbal items', *Journal of Experimental Psychology*, 58, pp.193–8.

Piaget, J. (1954) *The Construction of Reality in the Child*, New York: Basic Books.

Pike, K.M. and Rodin, J. (1991) 'Mothers, daughters and disordered eating', *Journal of Abnormal Psychology*, 100(2), pp.198–204.

Quinton, D., Rutter, M. and Liddle, C. (1985) 'Institutional rearing, parenting difficulties, and marital support', *Annual Progress in Child Psychiatry and Child Development*, pp.173–206.

Rack, P. (1982) *Race, Culture and Mental Disorder*, London: Routledge.

Rahe, R.H., Mahan, J. and Arthur, R. (1970) 'Prediction of near-future health-change from subjects' preceding life changes', *Journal of Psychosomatic Research*, 14, pp.401–6.

Rank, S.G. and Jacobson, C.K. (1977) 'Hospital nurses' compliance with medication overdose orders: a failure to replicate', *Journal of Health and Social Behaviour*, 18, pp.188–93.

Raphael, K.G., Cloitre, M. and Dohrenwend, B.P. (1991) 'Problems of recall and misclassification with checklist methods of measuring stressful life events', *Health Psychology*, 10, pp.62–74.

Ratcliffe-Crain, J. and Baum, A. (1990) 'Individual differences and health: Gender, coping, and stress', in H.S. Friedman (ed.) *Personality and Disease*, New York: Wiley.

Rattner, A. (1988) 'Convicted but innocent: wrongful conviction and the criminal justice system', *Law and Human Behaviour*, 2, pp.283–93.

Reicher, S.D. (1984) 'The St Paul's riot: an explanation of the limits of crowd action in terms of a social identity model', *European Journal of Social Psychology*, 14, pp.1–21.

Reicher, S.D. and Potter, J. (1985) 'Psychological theory as intergroup perspective: a comparative analysis of "scientific" and "lay" accounts of crowd events', *Human Relations*, 38, pp.167–89.

Reitman, J.S. (1974) 'Without surreptitious rehearsal, information in short-term memory decays', *Journal of Verbal Learning and Verbal Behaviour*, 13, pp.365–77.

Richardson, J.T.E. (1984) 'Developing the theory of working memory', *Memory and Cognition*, 12, pp.71–83.

Robertson, J. and Robertson, J. (1971) 'Young child in brief separation', *Psychoanalytic Study of the Child*, 26, pp.264–315.

Robinson, J.O., Rosen, M., Revill, S.L., David, H. and Rus, G.A.D. (1980) 'Self-administered intravenous and intramuscular pethidine', *Anaesthesia*, 35, pp.763–70.

Rosenhan, D.L. (1973) 'On being sane in insane places', *Science*, 179, pp.250–8.

Rosenhan, D.L. and Seligman, M.E.P. (1984) *Abnormal Psychology*, New York: W.W. Norton

Rotter, J.B. (1966) 'Generalised expectancies for internal versus external control of reinforcement', *Psychological Monographs*, 80, pp.1–28.

Ruhm, C.J. (2000) *Parental Employment and Child Cognitive Development*, National Bureau of Economic Research, NBER Working Paper No. 7666.

Russell, C.M. (1999) 'A meta-analysis of published research on the effects of non-maternal care on child development', *Dissertations Abstracts International, A (Humanities and Social Sciences)*, 59(9-A), p.3362.

Rutter, M. (1976) 'Parent–child separation: psychological effects on the child', in A.M. Clarke and A.D.B. Clarke (eds) *Early Experience: Myth and Evidence*, London: Open Books.

Rutter, M. (1981) *Maternal Deprivation Reassessed* (2nd edn), Harmondsworth: Penguin.

Rutter, M., Anderson-Wood, L., Beckett, C., Bredenkamp, D., Castle, J., Dunn, J., Ehrich, K., Groothues, C., Harborne, A., Hay, D., Jewett, J., Keaveney, L., Kreppner, J., Messer, J., O'Connor, T., Quinton, D. and White, A. (1998) 'Developmental catch-up and deficit, following adoption after severe global early privation', *Journal of Child Psychology and Psychiatry*, 39, pp.465–76.

Rymer, R. (1993) *Genie: Escape from a Silent Childhood*, London: Michael Joseph.

Sapolsky, R.M. (1994) *Why Zebras Don't Get Ulcers*, New York: Freeman.

Sarason, I.G., Johnson, J.H. and Siegel, J.M. (1978) 'Assessing the impact of life changes: development of the Life Experiences Survey', *Journal of Consulting and Clinical Psychology*, 46, pp.932–46.

Savin, H.B. (1973) 'Professors and psychological researchers: conflicting values in conflicting roles', *Cognition*, 2(1), pp.147–9.

Schaffer, H.R. (1998) *Making Decisions about Children*, Oxford: Blackwell.

Schaffer, H.R. and Emerson, P.E. (1964) *The Development of Social Attachments in Infancy*, Monographs of the Society for Research in Child Development, 29(3), Serial No. 94.

Schweickert, R. and Boruff, B. (1986) 'Short-term memory capacity: magic number or magic spell?', *Journal of Experimental Psychology: Learning, Memory and Cognition*, 12, pp.419–45.

Schweinhart, L.J., Barnes, H.V. and Weikart, D.P. (1993) 'Significant Benefits: The High/Scope Perry Preschool Study through Age 27', *Monographs of the High/Scope Educational Research Foundation*, 10, Ypsilanti, MI: High/Scope Press.

Sebrechts, M.M., Marsh, R.L. and Seamon, J.G. (1989) 'Secondary memory and very rapid forgetting', *Memory and Cognition*, 17, pp.693–700.

Seligman, M.E.P. (1975) *Helplessness: On Depression, Development and Death*, London: W.H. Freeman.

Selye, H. (1956) *The Stress of Life*, New York: McGraw-Hill.

Shallice, T. (1967) Paper presented at NATO symposium on short-term memory, Cambridge, England.

Shanab, M.E. and Yahya, K.A. (1977) 'A behavioural study of obedience in children', *Journal of Personality and Social Psychology*, 35, pp.530–6.

Shekelle, R.B., Hulley, S.B., Neaton, J.D., Billings, J.H., Borhani, N.O., Gerace, T.A., Jacobs, D.R., Lasser, N.L., Mittelmark, M.B. and Stamler, J. (1985) 'The MRFIT Behavior Pattern Study: II. Type A behavior and incidence of coronary heart disease', *American Journal of Epidemiology*, 122, pp.559–70.

Skeels, H. (1966) 'Adult status of children with contrasting early life experiences: A follow-up study', *Monographs of Society for Research of Child Development*, 31(3), whole issue.

Skeels, H. and Dye, H.B. (1939) 'A study of the effects of differential stimulation on mentally retarded children', *Proceedings and Addresses of the American Association on Mental Deficiency*, 44, 114–36.

Skinner, B.F. (1974) *About Behaviourism*, New York: Knopf.

Skodak, M. and Skeels, H. (1949) 'A final follow-up study of 100 adopted children', *Journal of Genetic Psychology*, 75, pp.85–125.

Smith, P.B. and Bond, M.H. (1998) *Social Psychology across Cultures: Analysis and Perspectives*, Massachusetts: Allyn and Bacon.

Smith, S.M. (1979) 'Remembering in and out of context', *Journal of Experimental Psychology: Human Learning and Memory*, 5, pp.460–71.

Snedecor, G.W. (1956) *Statistical Methods*, Iowa State University Press.

Spitz, R.A. and Wolf, K.M. (1946) 'Anaclitic depression', *Psychoanalytic Study of the Child*, 2, pp.313–42.

Srole, L., Langner, T.S., Michael, S.T. and Opler, M.K. (1961) *Mental Health in the Metropolis*, New York: McGraw-Hill.

Sroufe, L.A., Carlson, E.A., Levy, A.K., and Egeland, B. (1999) 'Implications of attachment theory for developmental psychopathology', *Development and Psychopathology*, 11, pp.1–13.

Stoney, C.M., Mathews, K.A., McDonald, R.H. and Johnson, C.A. (1990) 'Sex differences in acute stress response: lipid, lipoprotein, cardiovascular and neuroendocrine adjustments', *Psychophysiology*, 12, pp.52–61.

Stroebe, W., Stroebe, M.S. and Abakoumkin, G. (1999) 'Does differential social support cause sex differences in bereavement outcome?', *Journal of Community and Applied Social Psychology*, 9, pp.1–12.

Stroop, J.R. (1935) 'Studies of interference in serial verbal reactions', *Journal of Experimental Psychology*, 18, pp.643–62.

Szasz, T. (1972) *The Manufacture of Madness*, London: Routledge and Kegan Paul.

Takahashi, K. (1990) 'Are the key assumptions of the 'strange situation' universal?' *Human Development*, 33, pp.23–30.

Tanford, S. and Penrod, S. (1986) 'Jury deliberations: Discussion content and influence processes in jury decision making', *Journal of Applied Social Psychology*, 16, pp.322–47.

Taylor, S.E., Klein, L.C., Lewis, B.P., Grunewald, T.L., Gurung, R.A.R. and Updegraff, J.A. (2000) 'Biobehavioural responses in stress in females: tend-and-befriend, not fight-or-flight', *Psychological Review*, 107, p.3.

Thomas, L.K. (1998) 'Multicultural aspects of attachment', http://www.bereavement.demon.co.uk/lbn/attachment/lennox.html. *See also* Thomas, L.K. (1995) 'Psychotherapy in the context of race and culture', in S. Fernando (ed.) *Mental Health in a Multi-ethnic Society*, London: Routledge.

Tizard, B. (1979) 'Language at home and at school', in C.B. Cazden and D. Harvey (eds), *Language in Early Childhood Education*, Washington, DC: National Association for the Education of Young Children.

Triseliotis, J. (1984) 'Identity and security in adoption and long-term fostering', *Early Child Development & Care*, 15(2-3), pp.149–70.

Tronick, E.Z., Morelli, G.A. and Ivey, P.K. (1992) 'The Efe forager infant and toddler's pattern of social relationships: Multiple and simultaneous', *Developmental Psychology*, 28, pp.568–77.

Tulving, E. (1966) 'Subjective organisation and effects of repetition in multi-trial free-recall learning', *Journal of Verbal Learning and Verbal Behaviour*, 5, pp.193–7.

Tulving, E. (1983) *Elements of Episodic Memory*, Oxford: OUP.

Tulving, E. and Osler, S. (1968) 'Effectiveness of retrieval cues in memory for words', *Journal of Verbal Learning and Verbal Behaviour*, 5, pp.381–91.

Turner, J. (1991) *Social Influence*, Milton Keynes: Open University Press.

Tyler, S.W., Hertel, P.T., McCallum, M.C. and Ellis, H.C. (1979) 'Cognitive effort and memory', *Journal of Experimental Psychology: Human Learning and Memory*, 5(6), pp.607–17.

Ucros, C.G. (1989) 'Mood-state dependent memory: a meta-analysis', *Cognition and Emotion*, 3, pp.139–67.

Underwood, B.J. (1957) 'Interference and forgetting', *Psychological Review*, 64, pp.49–60.

Van Avermaet, E. (1996) 'Social influence in small groups', in M. Hewstone, W. Stroebe, G.M. Stevenson (eds), *Introduction to Social Psychology*, Oxford: Blackwell.

Van der Doef, M. and Maes, S. (1998) 'The job demand-control (-support) model and physical outcomes: a review of the strain and buffer hypotheses', *Psychology and Health*, 13, pp.909–36.

Van IJzendoorn, M.H. and Kroonenberg, P.M. (1988) 'Cross-cultural patterns of attachment: A meta-analysis of the Strange Situation', *Child Development*, 59, pp.147–56.

Van IJzendoorn, M.H., Sagi, A. and Lambermon, M.W.E. (1992) 'The multiple caretaker paradox: Data from Holland and Israel', in R.C. Pianta (ed.) *Beyond the Parent: The Role of Other Adults in Children's Lives*, San Francisco, CA: Jossey-Bass Publishers.

Vogele, C., Jarvis, A. and Cheeseman, K. (1997) 'Anger suppression, reactivity, and hypertension risk: Gender makes a difference', *Annals of Behavioral Medicine*, 19, pp.61–9.

Wade, T., Martin, N.G. and Tiggemann, M. (1998) 'Genetic and environmental risk factors for the weight and shape concerns characteristic of bulimia nervosa', *Psychological Medicine*, 28, pp.761–72.

Wartner, U.G., Grossman, K., Fremner-Bombik, I. and Guess, G.L. (1994) 'Attachment patterns in south Germany', *Child Development*, 65, pp.1014–27.

Watson, J.B. and Rayner, R. (1920) 'Conditioned emotional reactions', *Journal of Experimental Psychology*, 3, pp.1–14.

Watson, S.L., Shively, C.A., Kaplan, J.R. and Line, S.W. (1998) 'Effects of chronic social separation on cardiovascular disease risk factors in female cynomolgus monkeys', *Atherosclerosis*, 137, pp.259–66.

Waugh, N.C. and Norman, D.A. (1965) 'Primary memory', *Psychological Review*, 72, pp.89–104.

Weaver, C.A. (1993) 'Do you need a "flash" to form a flashbulb memory?', *Journal of Experimental Psychology: General*, 122(1), pp.39–46.

Weg, R.B. (1983) 'Changing physiology of aging', in D.S. Woodruff and J.E. Birren (eds), *Ageing: Scientific Perspectives and Social Issues*, (2nd edn), Monterey: Brooks/Cole.

Weinstein, B.A. (2002) 'Gender differences in the moderating effects of social support on college student stress: a prospective study', *Dissertation Abstracts International: Section B:- The Sciences and Engineering*, 62, pp.543–5.

Wickens, D.D. (1970) 'Encoding categories of words: an empirical approach to meaning', *Psychological Review*, 77, pp.1–15.

Williams, L.M. (1992) 'Adult memories of childhood abuse: preliminary findings from a longitudinal study', *The Advisor*, 5, pp.19–20.

Willis, L., Thomas, P., Garry, P.J. and Goodwin, J.S. (1987) 'A prospective study of response to stressful life events in initially healthy elders', *Journal of Gerontology*, 42, pp.627–30.

Wonderlich, S.A., Crosby, R.D., Mitchell, J.E., Roberts, J.A., Haseltine, B., DeMuth, G. and Thompson, K.M. (2000) 'Relationship of childhood sexual abuse and eating disorders in children', *Journal of the Academy of Child and Adolescent Psychiatry*, 39, pp.1277–83.

Wonderlich, S.A., Wilsnach, R.W., Wilsnach, S.C. and Harris, T.R. (1996) 'Childhood sexual abuse and bulimic behaviour in a nationally representative sample', *American Journal of Public Health*, 86, pp.1082–6.

Young, J.E. (1994) *Cognitive Therapy for Personality Disorders: A Schema Based Approach* (2nd edn), Sarasota, FL: Professional Resource Press.

Zimbardo, P.G., Banks, P.G., Haney, C. and Jaffe, D. (1973) 'Pirandellian prison: the mind is a formidable jailor', *New York Times Magazine*, 8 April, pp.38–60.

Zimbardo, P.G., McDermot, M., Jansz, J. and Metaal, N. (1995) *Psychology: A European Text*, London: Harper Collins.

AS Psychology